American Automobile Advertising,
1930–1980

ALSO BY HEON STEVENSON

British Car Advertising of the 1960s
(McFarland, 2005; paperback 2016)

American Automobile Advertising, 1930–1980

An Illustrated History

HEON STEVENSON

McFarland & Company, Inc., Publishers
Jefferson, North Carolina

The present work is a reprint of the illustrated case bound edition of American Automobile Advertising, 1930–1980: An Illustrated History, *first published in 2008 by McFarland.*

Dates of advertisement illustrations

In this book, the dates given in picture captions are the cover dates of the magazines in which the advertisements appeared. In some cases, a magazine may have been published a few weeks before the beginning of the month of its cover date. Where the month of publication of an advertisement is not known, the model year of the campaign is given instead.

American Automobile Advertising, 1930–1980: An Illustrated History is an extensively revised and expanded edition of *Selling the Dream: Advertising the American Automobile 1930–1980* which was first published by Academy Books in England in 1995.

LIBRARY OF CONGRESS CATALOGUING-IN-PUBLICATION DATA

Stevenson, Heon, 1966–
American automobile advertising, 1930–1980 : an illustrated history / Heon Stevenson.
    p.   cm.
Includes bibliographical references and index.
ISBN-13: 978-1-4766-9347-7
softcover

1. Advertising—Automobiles—United States—History—20th century.   2. Automobile industry and trade—United States—History—20th century.   I. Title.
HF6161.A9S749   2023
659.19'629222097309045—dc22   2008023063

BRITISH LIBRARY CATALOGUING DATA ARE AVAILABLE

© 2008 Heon Stevenson. All rights reserved

No part of this book may be reproduced or transmitted in any form or by any means, electronic or mechanical, including photocopying or recording, or by any information storage and retrieval system, without permission in writing from the publisher.

Cover photograph © 2023 Shutterstock.

McFarland & Company, Inc., Publishers
Box 611, Jefferson, North Carolina 28640
www.mcfarlandpub.com

To my late father,
Stuart D. Stevenson, BSc., C. Eng., A.M.I.E.E.

Acknowledgments

This book would have been difficult, if not impossible, to write without the help of many people in England. I would like to thank the librarians at the British Library in London, at Cambridge University Library, at the Sutton Libraries and Heritage in Croydon and Wallington, Surrey, and at York City Library, for making available much rare research material from the pre-war and early postwar periods.

Sincere thanks are also due to Lynda Springate of the National Motor Museum at Beaulieu, Hampshire, for the chance to study dozens of rare catalogs and period documents and for providing copies of advertisers' originals of early Ford, Mercury, and Lincoln advertisements; to Tony Freeman for much useful advice and encouragement in the book's early stages; to Margaret Rose, general manager, and Chloe Veale, curator, of the History of Advertising Trust (HAT) Archive at Raveningham, Norfolk, for information on British advertising for Chrysler, Ford, and General Motors Vauxhall cars; to Taylor Vinson, editor of the Society of Automotive Historians' *Automotive History Review*, for a selection of postwar American MG advertisements; to Bernie Weis of the Pierce-Arrow Society for information about the 1935 Pierce-Arrow advertisement seen on page C2 of the color plates; to Paul Veysey for the 1927 Dodge and 1938 Hudson advertisements on page 61, and for the 1935 Ford V-8 on page C3 of the color plates; and to Mrs. Joan Coombs for a number of the earliest advertisements illustrated in this book. I am also grateful to Pamela Blore for a social historian's view of the portrayal of women in early advertising.

The generous support and encouragement of all of the American automobile manufacturers is appreciated, particularly from Ed Lechtzin, Public Relations Director at Pontiac Division of General Motors; and Public Relations Co-ordinator Alan E. Miller of Chrysler Plymouth, for comprehensive information on their respective companies' products of the early 1990s.

Finally, may I thank my old friend Jeremy Kendall for hospitality and entertainment in Bury St. Edmunds, Suffolk during the preparation of the manuscript; and my good friends and fellow-students Clare McCourt, Matthew Shiels, David Higgs, and Jasper Denning for their support and encouragement, even when their house was temporarily overtaken by a sea of automotive literature, and for helping to choose many of the advertisements illustrated in this book.

Contents

Acknowledgments vii
Preface 1

Part One: Fueling a Fantasy 3

1. Igniting Desire 3
2. Fantasy by Design 29
3. "There's Added Joy in Added Cylinders" 58
4. Pushbuttons and Plastic Tops 74

Part Two: Beyond Mechanism 81

5. "Wouldn't it be nice to have an Escape Machine?" 81
6. A Neurosis Unleashed 90
7. "Plymouth — The Car That Likes to be Compared" 105

Between pages 118 and 119 are 16 color plates with 21 images

8. The Objectivity Factor 119
9. "Remember How You Hungered for It?" 129
10. "There's a Ford in Your Future" 136
11. "Lady, Relax!" 145

Part Three: Reality Supervenes 161

12. Justifying the Indulgence 161
13. The Sybarite's Progress 172
14. "Get More 'GO' From Every Gallon!" 182
15. Padding and Prejudice 189
16. From Utility to Suburban Chic 199

17. Back to Basics	214
18. Fantasy Under Siege	222

Overview and Conclusion 240
Collector's Note 247
Notes 251
Bibliography 255
Index 259

Preface

> Somewhere west of Laramie there's a broncho-busting, steer-roping girl who knows what I'm talking about. She can tell what a sassy pony, that's a cross between greased lightning and the place where it hits, can do with eleven hundred pounds of steel and action when he's going high, wide and handsome. The truth is—the Playboy was built for her. Built for the lass whose face is brown with the sun when the day is done of revel and romp and race. She loves the cross of the wild and the tame. There's a savor of links about that car—of laughter and lilt and light—a hint of old loves—and saddle and squirt. It's a brawny thing—yet a graceful thing for the sweep o' the Avenue. Step into the Playboy when the hour grows dull with things gone dead and stale. Then start for the land of real living with the spirit of the lass who rides, lean and rangy, into the red horizon of a Wyoming twilight.
> —Jordan advertisement from the *Saturday Evening Post*, June 23, 1923

The aspirations of an era are captured vividly in its advertising, which is the focus of a multitude of human concerns and ambitions. At its best, advertising displays the finest fruits of engineering and the graphic arts. By their nature ephemeral, advertisements are compelling freeze-frames of the times that give them meaning.

The automobile, for its part, as a provider of freedom and symbol of affluence, and as a projection of its owner's world-view, has enjoyed a uniquely wide-ranging influence on American life. This is particularly apparent in the advertising of the "modern" period in the history of the American automobile, beginning with the entrenchment of the "Big Three" in the early 1930s, and concluding with the fuel crises of the 1970s and the establishment of the Japanese automobile in America.

Individual automobile advertisements are interesting in their own right, and for what they reveal about the products that they attempted to sell. Particular campaigns stand out from the contemporary norm, and are memorable for their imagination and impact — such as J. Stirling Getchell's "Look At All Three" series for Plymouth in the 1930s, and J. Walter Thompson's "Ford in Your Future" campaign of 1945–47. David Ogilvy's advertisements for Rolls-Royce (1958–62) and Doyle Dane Bernbach's long-running, iconoclastic assault upon conventional automotive values with the Volkswagen (beginning in 1959) have become famous, and are well documented.

Among conventional advertisements of this period, Studebaker's photographic series of 1946–50, De Soto's dramatic portraits of the finned Forward Look (1957), and Ford's atmospheric Thunderbird campaigns of the early 1960s are well remembered today. A few advertisements were controversial, such as Ford's "Lifeguard" promotion during the early part of the 1956 model year, which, with its emphasis on the passive safety of the product, anticipated later trends by more than a decade.

Some advertisements appear retrogressive to modern eyes— one thinks of much Studebaker copy of the early 1960s which, echoing the functionalism of the earliest automobile advertising, insisted that the product combined the best of all possible (prestigious and economical) worlds, which it did not. There were a few instances of *déjà vu*, the more amusing for not having been apparent to the advertisers themselves. Car buyers, meanwhile, usually proved cannier than one might believe from some of the modern period's more lurid copy.

Most of the themes and techniques evident in copy by 1980 were already apparent, if only in embryo form, at the beginning of the 1930s. Generalizations according to decade can therefore be misleading. It can be argued that the 1930s were years of functionalism; the 1940s (wartime prestige advertising apart) of escapism; the 1950s of fantasy; the 1960s of realism; and that the 1970s brought a fragmentation of approaches along "class" and size-category lines. There are, however, so many exceptions to this glib summary that it has only limited use as a temporary scaffold around which to build a more complete picture of the subject.

This book therefore follows a thematic rather than strictly chronological structure, tracing the development of the principal elements in American automobile advertising over fifty years. Advances in advertising layouts and graphics are discussed in Part One, together with the ways in which automobile styling, mechanical improvements, and convenience features were portrayed and highlighted in copy over the years. Part Two explores the advertising themes which were concerned less with the attributes of the cars themselves, but rather with the ways in which advertisers hoped that consumers would perceive and identify with their products. The practical aspects of automobile ownership are addressed in Part Three, which concludes with an account of the advance of imported cars into America after World War II. The Overview and Conclusion includes a discussion of advertising themes revisited and developed since 1980. Snapshots are taken of representative campaigns from the recessionary year of 1993, and from 2005-2006.

Choosing illustrations for this book has been an enjoyable but difficult task. As it is not possible to illustrate every campaign launched over fifty years, the advertisements selected have been chosen to be representative of their types, and to illustrate the themes of the text. The majority of the advertisements in this book have been taken from the unusually wide selection published in the *National Geographic*, whose clear print showed them at their best, and whose high-quality paper has preserved them in good condition. Most also appeared in several other magazines at the same time, with the layout of each advertisement, and sometimes the length of its copy, being adjusted as necessary to the size and shape of a particular publication's pages. European advertisements for American cars are included where relevant, as is American advertising for imported cars.

Many parallels can be drawn between press advertisements and contemporary catalogs, particularly where pictures, slogans, and layouts were carried from one medium to the other as part of a coordinated marketing strategy. But the advertisement is not an abridged catalog, and the two have distinct, if sometimes overlapping, functions. This account is confined to the advertising published in the general media, which was not aimed primarily at car enthusiasts or at those who had already shown an interest in a particular product. This emphasis has also meant that a wide variety of advertisements can be shown here, an advantage given that many are often less easily found than brochures or catalogs which, in proportion to the numbers originally produced, have in many cases been more widely preserved.

I hope that this overview of fifty years of American automobile advertising will interest automobile enthusiasts, students of advertising and, not least, those who saw the advertisement, bought the car, and thereby sustained that powerful synthesis of illusion and aspiration which is the American dream.

Heon Stevenson
Cambridge, England, fall 2008

Part One : Fueling a Fantasy

Chapter 1

Igniting Desire

The beginning of a new model year was always exciting for Americans. In Europe, cars trickled onto the market when they were ready, and motor shows boosted enthusiasm for motoring as much as for particular cars. By contrast, the American automobile market was rejuvenated annually. After 1923, a year's new model was rarely exactly the same as what had gone before, and the new car buyer's first point of contact with the new model was usually an advertisement.

An advertisement is, and has always been, evangelical. It must cajole, bully, and entice its reader to spend on the strength of its promise, to partake of the enchanted life that the product will bring. Only after the potential buyer has been at least partly convinced does he fill in the coupon or enter the sanctuary of the showroom for a brochure. The brochure may confirm a consumer's desire for a car, but it is the advertisement which must ignite it. A brochure can run to several pages if necessary; the advertisement must do its job on one page, within seconds. It must make the reader stop and look, then read, then dream, and then become convinced, so that ownership of the automobile is integrated into his idealized self-image.

An advertisement therefore either succeeds or fails within a few seconds, after which its job is done, and it is thrown away and forgotten. Throughout the modern period in American automobile advertising it was an advertisement's appearance that had to make a reader stop; the car, as illustrated, had to persuade him to look; and the copy and backdrop against which the car was set invited him to read and, perhaps, to dream. Against this background, automobile advertisers' manipulation of layout and illustration reached new heights of subtlety and, sometimes, of elaboration.

There was a myth, widely perpetuated, that early advertisements were unrealistic, even dishonest, and that later copy was realistic, presenting the product in its true colors; that "accurate" photography superseded "impressionistic" artwork. In the beginning, it was argued, the consumer was duped by advertisers' fanciful rendering of their products, but later rose up against the artists who were the cause of his confusion, and demanded realism instead.

This analysis appears superficially convincing. Its advocates need only produce an impressionistic rendering of a Chrysler or Lincoln, *circa* 1930, juxtapose it with a resolutely realistic portrait of a Chrysler or Lincoln, *circa* 1970, and point triumphantly to this supposedly irrefutable evidence of progress. This myth sustains a belief in progress itself, and may be attractive to the tastes of professional nostalgists, but it is not the whole story, not least because no advertisement can be wholly realistic about its subject, and no portrait is impartial. The strictest impartiality might be said to consist not in the identification of a single, "true" perspective to the disdain of all others, but in the practical and perhaps conceptual absurdity of an unmediated presentation of all possible perspectives simultaneously.

It has been claimed that the inception of color photography in automobile advertising from around 1932 removed the interpretative artistic middleman who had hitherto stood between the reader and the product; but, in reality, the artist, including the "deceitful" elongator, continued to work alongside the photographer until after 1970. And the imaginative photography that captured the "high, wide and heavenly" view enjoyed by Ford Thunderbird buyers in 1969, for example, was vastly more sophisticated than the simple, faux-color photograph which had been considered adequate for British buyers of the Model A in 1931. Moreover, the impressionism which was once the preserve of the illustrator was increasingly achieved not only by the artist and photographer, but by the copywriter as well.

Photographers and artists sometimes worked simultaneously on separate campaigns, and in several cases they worked together. In 1939, for instance, Oldsmobile used paintings in advertisements which highlighted styling features and the novelty of the year's range, while black and white photographs appeared in advertisements for low-priced variants which were promoted on their "realistic," down-to-earth merits of low cost and economical running. Plymouth used both media in the same year. The marque's black and white photographs were unequivocally dull, but paintings, in which about five inches were removed from the height of the car, made it look adequately attractive without exaggerating its length. In the 1950s, photographs and illustrations were sometimes combined in individual advertisements, as in 1955 when a painted Studebaker President sedan, elongated at the front and resplendent in pink and black, was surrounded by photographs of similar cars in scenic settings to show off the design's useful features.

The artistic elongator, who portrayed an automobile realistically in its details, but not in its proportions, was particularly popular among aspiring middle-market advertisers from 1933 onwards. The exaggerated illustrations deployed by Nash during 1934 recalled the proportions of earlier Cords and Duesenbergs, while adding embryonic suggestions of streamlining—suggestions that were taken up more fervently by Hudson, Studebaker and, notably, Hupmobile, who had a genuinely streamlined car to work with in 1934's Aerodynamic sedan.

The advance of the elongator represented a natural synthesis of two existing schools in automobile advertising. On the one hand, Nash's socially optimized architectural backdrops recalled the static, neo-classical tableaux favored by Lincoln, Packard, Cadillac, and Marmon in the late 1920s. On the other hand, the modern elongator's preoccupation with the horizontal elements in car design, together with an emphasis on speed and power, recalled the dynamic impressionism imported from Europe, initially by Chrysler through its distinctive Bauhaus-pastiche idiom, at the same time.[1] Though innovative and influential, this idiom rarely strayed beyond Chrysler Imperial advertising in the automotive field in America, and was by no means universal in publicity even for that marque. Dynamic impressionism in general was more frequently encountered in Europe, notably in Fiat's home-market advertising for its larger models from 1927 to 1936, and with copy for the streamlined 1937 Panhard Dynamic in France.

The aim of both neo-classicist and dynamic impressionist was to convey the totality of the automotive experience by visual means rather than to show the product realistically in a technical sense. In 1954, G.H. Saxon ("Bingy") Mills, copywriter for W.S. Crawford Ltd., Chrysler's British and continental European advertising agent from 1925 until the early 1930s, recalled:

Mild impressionism from Chrysler in 1926. More extreme forms would follow (December 1926).

The elongator versus artist-as-realist. Backgrounds in both cases were realistic, but Oldsmobile's fun-oriented illustration was more typical of its period than Plymouth's sober practicality (November 1938 and March 1939).

Ashley [Havinden, the agency's advertising artist and, from 1929, art director] argued that an ordinary half-tone photograph in black and white would scarcely make the [Chrysler] look different from any other make. In other words, it was impossible to convey glamour by reproduction methods. Therefore he devised impressionistic drawings of a car being driven at high speed, plus a free "dynamic" layout, plus exciting and exclamatory headlines. So striking were these advertisements that ... people in England were shortly [afterwards] talking about "Rolls Royces, Chryslers and Bentleys".... [T]his advertising style was ... to prove additionally valuable in the difficult circumstances of European reproduction.... [T]he few black and white lines embodied in the drawings survived even the abominable paper and printing characteristics of most of the foreign newspapers. [And] the arresting and almost childishly-simple presentation was equally effective in countries ranging from the Baltic to the Balkans.... It sold *exhilaration* associated with the name of Chrysler — internationally.[2]

The artistic elongator sought the best of both worlds, reinstating accurate detail, but retaining the necessary dynamism through modified proportion. Only rarely could an adequate emotional and sensual content be combined with dimensional realism before the advent of atmospheric color photography in the 1960s.

By 1939-40, Nashes were shown in paintings by the Connecticut artist Steven Dohanos in bright yellows, greens and reds, longer, lower and much wider than in life; a vertical grille, vaguely reminiscent of an earlier LaSalle, acquired a rakish, forward-leaning appearance which had no basis in fact. The car looked most attractive in front three-quarter view, taken at ground level, and this angle was consistently chosen. Little was made of the car's trunk, which was concealed on fastback "torpedo" shapes, but which appeared apologetically as an indeterminate hump on trunkback sedans. It actually looked more attractive on the real car, to whose dumpier proportions it was better suited.

So entrenched was the elongator by the late 1930s that Ford, announcing the new Mercury marque in 1938, felt it necessary to reassure buyers that "The size of the Mercury is not an illusion. This is a big, wide car, exceptionally roomy, with a large luggage compartment." The car's shape was familiar to Ford buyers, and there was a real danger that devotees of the parent marque would mistake the Mercury 8 for an optimistically drawn Tudor sedan. British monochrome illustrations of the smaller Ford V-8 suggested that it was as long as a Lincoln-Zephyr, which was far from the case.

In America, realism was achieved more often with monochrome photography than with the color illustrations suitable for "glamour" pieces. Buick published many such "realistic" advertisements in the late 1930s, displaying more flair and imagination, within the constraints of the chosen medium, than Plymouth. The views chosen were not always those that would be natural to the car buyer. A particular favorite was the ground-level shot, taken with a wide-angle lens, with buildings receding dramatically into the background. The effect was of dominance, length, and mastery of the modern world which was the Buick's natural environment. It was anything but realistic, yet conviction was achieved by the accurate rendition of detail which was possible with the camera. By colluding with the copywriter, both artist and photographer co-operated in the creation of an automotive fantasy for the moment, igniting the consumer's desire for a product laden with personal and social potentialities.

It was argued by many that the adoption of photography as an illustrative medium had banished fantasism forever. Harold Costain, a British commentator, wrote in 1935:

> We have become "purists" in that the subject is photographed faithfully with the idea of appealing to the intelligence of the buyer rather than to his imagination or emotions, whether his need is for apples, shoes or automobiles.[3]

This was true of a great many British advertisers in the 1930s, but it was not always true on the other side of the Atlantic, and the American practitioner was more than once mistakenly cast in the role of benevolent ingénu:

> American advertisers no longer tolerate photographs which require photo retouching or indeed any alteration before use.

This was not always the case, as a cursory look at 1939's artwork for the Oldsmobile 60, among others, confirms. Costain continued:

> [The Americans] appreciate the fact that the great buying public is intelligent and will recognize and appreciate dependable representations in advertising. They are generally proud of their merchandise and proud to show it as it is, and even though it is photographed in a dramatic manner in order to arrest the reader's attention and create interest in the descriptive text ... no attempt is made to mislead the public.[4]

Except, of course, when unsightly aspects of the product were carefully concealed by the angle and composition of the photograph. Costain's view was, at best, simplistic. What was evident was increasing subtlety and a careful integration of copy and artwork to create a compelling overall impression.

Chrysler's dynamic impressionism entered its mature phase in the middle of the Depression. Copy styles and typefaces were suitably "artistic"— or pretentious (1931 campaign).

Nash's "angled block" layout was a masterpiece of ingenuity. No other manufacturer combined a multitude of illustrations with more than a dozen typefaces to such elegant effect (June 1939).

Contrast of styles. Mercury combined realistic illustration with factual copy in 1939, while Ford's British advertising for the 1937 V-8 "30" was sometimes cluttered. The "angled block" headline derived from an earlier, more exuberant idiom, and perhaps sat uneasily with the style of the copy and humdrum, if elongated, picture (April 1937 and March 1939).

A theory of new-found public wisdom presupposed an earlier stupidity, and on neither count was this early form of the progressivist myth wholly supported by the reality.

Nevertheless, as motoring became ever more popular and widely accessible, advertisers had to cater to a wider audience: wider in outlook, in aspiration, in geographical extent. The Depression, and the popularization of the automobile, signaled an end to Bauhaus-pastiche and other instances of what has been called

> ...an epidemic of freak advertising, masquerading under the banner of the progressively modern movement, which has brought no commensurate results to any but its perpetrators.[5]

In fairness to advocates of the "freakish," such copy had almost invariably been confined to upmarket automobiles. When Chrysler in America adopted dramatic angles, stylized speedlines, and vivid tonal contrasts in the late 1920s, this copy was addressed to an upper-class elite in such magazines as *House and Garden*. It was assumed that readers would be familiar with Bauhaus and, latterly, Cubist and Art Deco–inspired visual motifs, and the strategy was simply a visually dramatic manifestation of the snobbery that had often pervaded upmarket automobile advertising. Most car advertisements of the period were simple and functional, like the cars that they depicted. Copy for the Model T Ford was consistently down-to-earth, and even deliberately stylized renderings of the Model A, Model B, and V-8 which followed in the 1930s were comparatively innocuous.

Esoteric artistic motifs were criticized as much for their implicit elitism — on the basis that the majority of the public did not "understand" and therefore would supposedly not like them — as for any failure to sell upmarket cars. Their advocates, commercially rather than socially motivated, wondered whether it mattered that those who would not buy Chrysler Imperials disliked or were mystified by copy for such cars. Did the critical, self-appointed, guardians of public taste within the advertising industry forget that it was as patronizing to try to "protect" the public from artistic excess as to inflict pretension on it in the first place? And were those critics secretly dismayed to see art purloined by avowedly commercial interests, notwithstanding that the Bauhaus was a school of the machine age, which sought to integrate art and three-dimensional design?

Advertisers delightedly foisted asymmetrical layouts and

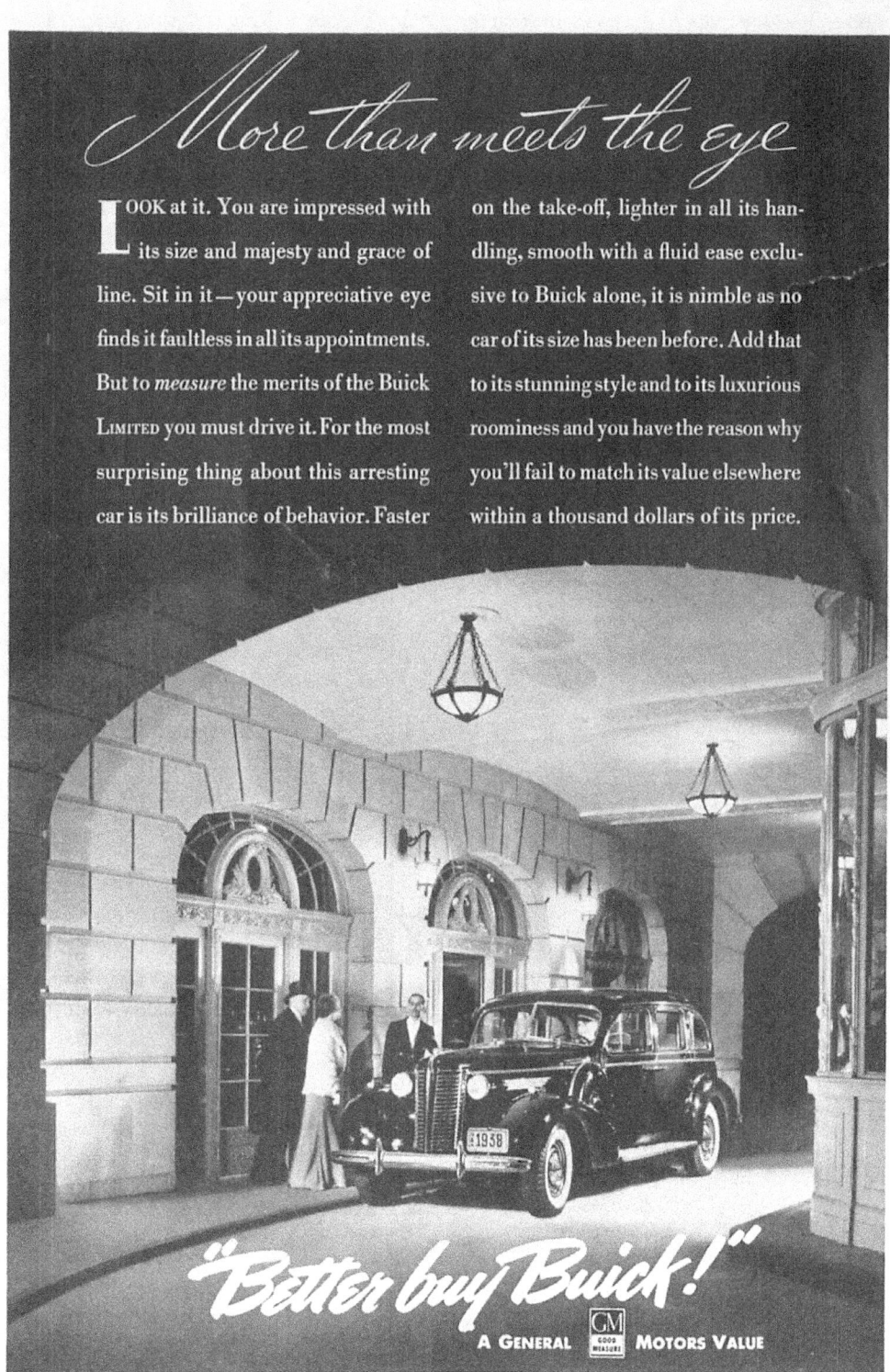

Realistic photography was not confined to utilitarians. In 1938, Buick evoked an earlier neo-classical style, long favored by upmarket advertisers (March 1938).

minimalist representation on automobiles which had been designed with scant regard for the ideals that sired those distinctive Bauhaus signatures. It was perhaps understandable that the purists should shudder; less so that they expected their purism to alight upon the aesthetic consciences of the advertisers and paralyze them into disregard of a potent and sales-catching innovation. Asymmetry caught the eye easily in a medium where symmetry was the norm; strong tonal contrasts could be reproduced faithfully in color or monochrome, the latter being particularly effective in newsprint of indifferent quality.

The artistic debate was never resolved, and in any event was rapidly subsumed within a general need to create new, flexible advertising styles for successive model years in order to bring the products of an expanding industry as close as possible to the viewpoints and aspirations of a widening consumer base. Not all upmarket manufacturers had succumbed to the transient allure of the Bauhaus fetish. In its advertising, as in its automobiles, Marmon in particular exhibited a flair and restraint which were closer in spirit to the Bauhaus ideal than Chrysler's graphic exuberance.

Any academic debate, as such, was peripheral to the business of selling cars, and a new realism came to the fore after the onset of Depression in 1929. Such fanciful renderings as did recur in the late 1930s were rarely as bizarre as the Bauhaus pastiches of ten years earlier. Optimism and national confidence had brought extremes of style, while cautious retrenchment was apparent in later, less whimsical copy.

If there was a discernible movement towards increased visual realism in the 1930s, it did not always entail unappealing and dogmatic authenticity. There were pedantic exceptions, but even they should perhaps be evaluated according to their effectiveness in selling automobiles, and not scorned simply because they are aesthetically unpalatable. The elongator — whether armed with palette, airbrush, or wide-angle lens — had an important role to play in enhancing the automobile itself, but the backdrops against which the cars were highlighted were predominantly realistic, rather than self-consciously surreal or abstractly atmospheric. Stylization — in detail, perspective, and coloring — was inevitable, but it was an optimized reality rather than contrived fantasy that prevailed by 1935.

Visual effects were carefully aligned with accompanying copy, with the result that specific codes for upmarket, popular, and middle-class automobiles could be detected without reference to the substance of the copy itself, or even to the marque depicted. These graphic codes were inherited from an earlier period, even if the mechanics of advertisers' visual language had changed radically since the 1920s. Low-priced automobiles were usually shown in small-town provincial and rural settings, while upmarket models could be encountered at recognizably "sophisticated" venues.

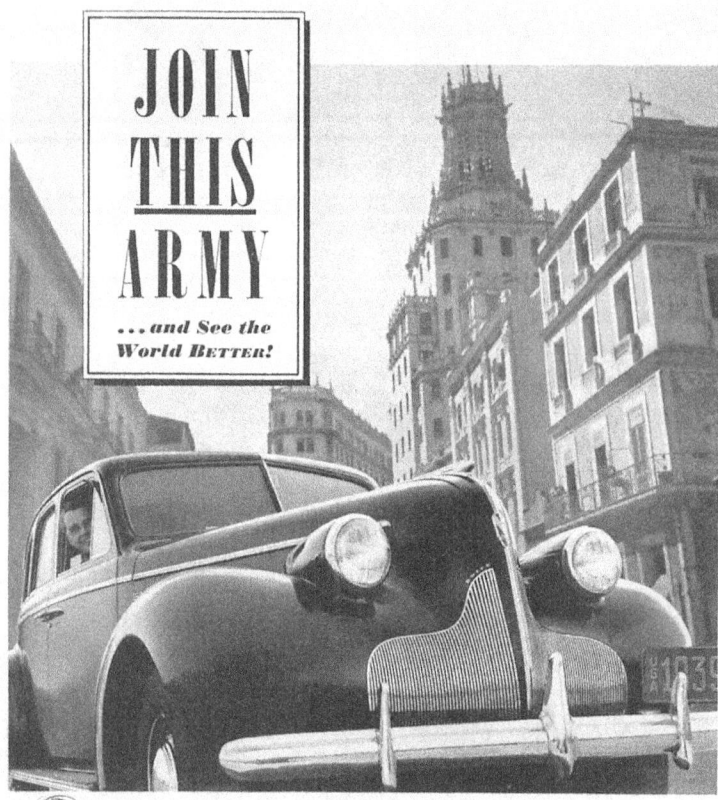

Photographic anti-realism from Buick. The wide-angle, ground level shot was a favorite with advertisers at all levels of the market (March 1939).

A "distanced" backdrop for the stylish Lincoln-Zephyr coupe. Care was taken not to submerge this middle-class car within a socially constricted visual environment (March 1937).

This Plymouth advertisement was typical of the catalogs in miniature that enjoyed a brief vogue among low and lower-middle priced marques in the 1930s (November 1937).

In both cases, the automobile itself was often shown at rest, creating a freeze-frame of the desired social image. The greatest variety was reserved for the traditionally unstable middle ground: the territory of Nash, Hudson, the smaller Buicks, and Lincoln-Zephyr. Dynamism and power were dominant visual themes; ostensibly indicating mechanical potency, they also vivified the social and cultural pretensions of the targeted consumer.

Compared with those of the upper and lower price sectors, these cars were anchored less solidly into a static physical and social environment. It was this fluid middle ground which provided the most fertile soil for the neutral backdrop, against which the lines of the automobile in question could be displayed without distraction. In 1938, a green Lincoln-Zephyr sedan was shown in front of a blue-grey background which faintly suggested sky and earth; in the same year, a blue Zephyr coupe could be seen against almost total darkness, which brought out its smooth, avant-garde lines convincingly, while allowing the reader to create his or her own preferred environment around the car.

Such layouts also suited the Lincoln-Zephyr's consciously rationalist copy.[6] The middle-class buyer might be inspired by the styling of the car and all the connotations, mechanical and social, of its V-12 engine, but he needed to justify his choice, to be reassured that what he desired was attainable. This selective rationality was perceived to be the hallmark of middle-class values and was thus reflected in illustration. Within the constraints of this rationale, Lincoln also used stylized landscapes (occasionally similar to Adler's in Germany) and, in 1939, more obviously quasi-naturalistic studio poses. In one advertisement, the car was posed on a grass-green floor with a lilac panel behind. Rural serenity — and its psychological parallel, peace of mind — were suggested by cherry blossom hanging over the roof of the car.

Apart from neutral and stylized-naturalistic portraits, there were also "distanced" backdrops, as in 1937 when an authentically proportioned Lincoln-Zephyr coupe was superimposed upon a monochrome aerial view of New York, patron city of the newly affluent. Yet in all of these advertisements the copy was never submerged within a constricting visual environment, and a deliberate, underlying open-endedness remained.

Throughout the 1936–41 period, a time of sometimes fragile but increasing prosperity, established "fine cars"—the big Lincolns, Chrysler Imperials, Packards, and Cadillacs—stayed aloof from the turbulent middle market. But the middle ground was expanding, with Oldsmobile, Dodge, De Soto, Nash, and (from October, 1938) Mercury leading the way out of low-priced simplicity, while new "small" Packards and Chryslers invaded the upper strata of the sector from above.

Even in the sub-$800 range, where common-sense virtue and value for money were most persuasive, advertisers sometimes looked balefully upward, with occasionally unfortunate

Pre-war minimalism was revived in copy for the most expensive cars, such as this $5,000 Buick Skylark, in the early postwar years. This illustration was one of the first for General Motors by Arthur Fitzpatrick (1953 campaign).

Modest and realistic photography, used in much Studebaker advertising since the mid–1930s, continued into the late 1940s, reflecting the clean-lined modernity of the car itself. This is a top-line Commander Land Cruiser (September 1948).

consequences for layout and illustration. The exigencies of depression led manufacturers to put as much information as possible in every advertisement, and the catalog in miniature enjoyed a brief vogue.

The best-known exponents of this genre were the low- and middle-priced marques in the Chrysler Corporation line-up, with Plymouth leading the way. A typical advertisement for the 1938 models used six typefaces and five captioned photographs, while in 1939's copy ten typefaces, augmented by a large photograph and one or two auxiliary pseudo-technical diagrams illustrating gearshifts and suspension assemblies, were the norm. Plymouth's backdrops were visually realistic, but unadventurous in content, showing unglamorous but comfortable vignettes of small-town American life in both photographs and paintings. In several 1939 advertisements the car was shown in sober, dark colors and, for added realism, even the car's chromium was dull, suggesting a hard-used car which had not been washed for weeks.

Thus not only were the cars themselves shown authentically; they were seen in plausible surroundings and as worthy accessories to real life, rather than life-as-aspired-to. This visual style complemented the themes explored in copy, which centered around durability, value for money, and testimonials from contented users. The Plymouth was portrayed as a good, working car rather than as an expression of a desirable lifestyle, and, in this marketing context, the layouts chosen were sensible, rather than inept. It was questionable, however, whether the use of similar visual themes with more exciting, aspirational copy in Dodge and De Soto advertising was equally effective, as, whatever the advantages of continuity within the Corporation's range in reassuring buyers who could afford to trade up from Plymouth, mere mechanical competence was not enough for middle-market aspirants.

Small diagrams were not confined to the Chrysler Corporation, however, and they worked effectively in large-format advertisements published in Sunday newspapers. In January, 1938, Ford showed a DeLuxe coupe in one such piece, surrounding the main illustration with eighteen drawings of features "included in the Ford price" of $689. These ranged from a lockable glove compartment to an "attractive, dependable clock." An appearance of clutter was avoided by the sheer size of the advertisement — 24 inches by 16 inches — and Ford wisely eschewed the diagram idiom in smaller magazine advertisements.

Mercury also favored miniature auxiliary diagrams. A late 1938 advertisement for 1939's two-door sedan used one to show the trunk capacity of the car, while another in the same series depicted the stylish dashboard and steering wheel of the convertible. It was recognized that one extra illustration was enough, even when color was used, in cases where only a small magazine page was available. The Ford Motor Company's agency, N.W. Ayer & Son, did not usually attempt to cram visually complex copy or illustrations into media ill-designed to accommodate them. In Britain, N.W. Ayer's color advertising for both V-8 and Lincoln-Zephyr was unusually clear and elegant.

Perhaps the best and worst examples of a generally uninspired school were placed by two of the "independents," Hudson and Nash, in 1939.[7] Any monochrome advertisement covering a mere 60 square inches which included a painting and a diagram of an entire car, together with seventeen blocks of print in thirteen typefaces, was bound to be less than elegant, and by cramming so much into a small magazine page, Hudson did not show the year's Six Touring Sedan in the best possible light. Nash, however, with a color painting, three auxiliary diagrams, and only seven blocks of print in a similar number of typefaces, conveyed a sense of style and escapism by artfully using diagonal columns of print which moved from top-right to bottom-left to complement the car's forward-leaning grille. The blocks survived into the postwar "Airflyte" era.

Nash copy and illustration acquired a distinctive style during 1939-40. Each piece showed a car (usually a sedan) in the center of the page, with smaller stylized renderings, in different colors, positioned around the main illustration. These smaller pictures showed cars in various escapist settings: speeding along highways, parked beside lakes or illuminated by the moon as their occupants slept within. In each case, copy, layout, and illustration were carefully integrated into a euphoric whole. As a car, the Nash did not have a strong identity; grilles and body styles changed every two or three years, but continuity and consequently a measure of marque identity were achieved by a consistent copy style and visual harmony within each advertisement, together with heavy emphasis on particular features such as, from 1938, the famous "Weather Eye" ventilation system.

From 1946, new methods of presentation gained ground, with every feature reinterpreted as fantasy potentially fulfilled. Unlike earlier Bauhaus-pastiche, the new fantasy was not concentrated in any particular niche of the market. For a few short years, some advertisements for the finest cars, particularly for Lincolns during 1946–48 and for Continental, as a discrete marque with the Mark II in 1956-57, returned to a neo-minimalism which had its roots in the 1920s and which was consciously retrospective, promising at least a pale re-enactment of diminished certainties. The Lincoln Continental, born of the old Zephyr and retaining much of that car's mechanism, was shown in side profile against a white background with yellow, green, or gold borders, evoking an earlier elegance. Buick preferred to set the 1953 Skylark against a jet-black background; the car itself was bright yellow, and the script below pompously laconic, offering to reveal the price "on request." Copy for the lesser Buicks was more conventional, reinforcing the Skylark's status as a car apart. A similar strategy was adopted for the Cadillac Eldorado.

The shambolic excesses of the 1930s had departed, but

Above and opposite: Evolution of a genre. Cadillac advertising retained a distinctive flavor throughout the 1950s, reinforcing its marque identity (1952 campaign, April 1955, May 1958, and 1959 campaign).

rows of auxiliary diagrams, ever more frequently in color, persisted. Studebaker's announcement copy of the late 1940s was modest and well laid out, but when the new "Loewy" range had become established, miniature photographs of seat cushions, brakes, and other mundanities appeared, together with sentimental portraits of Studebaker's father-and-son production line teams to suggest quality control, the personal touch, and a humane (and therefore enterprisingly American at its best) working environment in one go. The latter contrasted starkly with the increasingly public turmoil at Ford, and with industrial relations problems throughout the industry.[8] In another contrast, impressionistic and colorful watercolor illustrations appeared in Frazer's distinctive, upmarket advertising for 1949.

In the 1950s, advertising followed style. When a car looked dowdy, it was promoted as a provider of fun and economical transportation; it was the means to a desirable end. If an automobile was stylish and avant-garde, copy and illustration highlighted design features. Cadillac, in particular, consolidated its marque identity not only with a visible evolution in design, but with illustrations and layouts which, though

developing steadily from year to year, nevertheless retained elements of what had gone before. In 1952, Sixty Specials and Coupe de Villes were shown at country clubs and ski resorts, or in neutral settings that suggested affluence. The Cadillac "V" and crest were prominently displayed, and decorated with exotic jewelry. The upmarket visual impression was complemented by the copy, which was never written in obtrusive typefaces, or allowed to distract from the impact of an illustration.

In its continuity and restraint, Cadillac's advertising was essentially conservative, but in 1955 the latest models were illustrated in paintings which, unlike 1952's touched-up photographs, exaggerated the cars' already considerable length. The main illustration in each advertisement showed a social scene such as a family at home, a board meeting, or a dinner party. Below the main illustration, which took up half a page or more, would be shown the Cadillac with a few paragraphs of copy. A year later, both car and social scene were combined in many pieces, enabling the Cadillac (often a convertible) to be admired by the sophisticates assembled at a private swim-

ming-pool or exclusive club. Roman columns and elaborate porticos were particular architectural favorites which had a long history in upmarket automobile advertising. The social scenes were photographed, while the cars were illustrated in their entirety in separate paintings.

In 1957, a single illustration sufficed for most pieces, each of which might either be a social scene or an artistic impression; among the most dramatic was an elongated pink Sixty Special, set against a deep blue background, with the Cadillac "V" in "jewels by Harry Winston" shown at the top of the page. Another advertisement showed a metallic green car against a gold cloth background. For 1958, social settings similar to 1957's continued, albeit with temporary desertion of the jewelry.

For the 1959 model year, Cadillac ran a series of advertisements which in many ways resembled the copy of three years earlier. In each piece, a grille or taillight would be shown, with an elegant model or venue in the background. Beside the photograph there would be a column of copy, and below both was a slogan with an elongated illustration of the car — and an elongated 1959 Cadillac was very long indeed. The 1959 car represented a greater stylistic break with the past than any previous model since 1948, but continuity was retained with a now-familiar advertising style and unmistakably "Cadillac" detailing on the car itself.

A preoccupation with stylistic details characterized much Cadillac advertising of the late 1950s. One 1957 Cadillac advertisement, for instance, showed not only the regular Sixty Special sedan, but also the unique and instantly recognizable tail fin of an Eldorado parked nearby. Stylistic details, and tail fins in particular, were also highlighted by Lincoln in 1955, Chevrolet during 1957–59, and several Chrysler divisions between 1955 and 1960. Once power features had become commonplace across all sectors of the market, the shape of a new car's tail fin was one of its principal distinguishing characteristics, whether that car was cheap or prestigious. "Can you identify them?" asked Diamond Chemicals in 1957 about nine different fin-mounted taillight clusters, photographed close-up, whose bases were chrome-plated with the help of an additive developed by the company.

It was a game which Cadillac had started in 1948 and, by the early 1950s, Chevrolet owners could buy accessory Cadillac-style fin and taillight assemblies to fit onto 1949–52 models. In 1956-57, a Detroit millionaire, Reuben Allender, offered the El Morocco, a new Chevrolet which was carefully customized to resemble an opulent Cadillac Eldorado Brougham. It sold

Above and opposite: Chevrolet's layouts reflected its advertising themes, ranging from practical virtue in 1952 through performance in 1955 to styling in 1959 (September 1952, 1955 campaign, and December 1958).

in minuscule numbers, and hoped-for support from General Motors did not materialize, but the project vividly illuminated the automotive climate of the time, and explained what might otherwise have appeared to have been a peculiar narcissism among advertisers.

Advertising for General Motors' low-priced marque offered an interesting contrast to that deployed by Cadillac. Chevrolet's styling did not evolve with Cadillac's measured pace, and neither did its advertising. Continuity was expressed more in an overall philosophy — to provide the most car for the least money — than in a consistent style of illustration. The only visual link between 1950 and 1959 was a continued emphasis on fun, sociability, and a modern, though not exclusive, lifestyle.

Chevrolet's last year for miniature diagrams, whether arranged around a single painting of the car or in a line underneath the body copy, was 1952. In many 1952 Chevrolet advertisements, paintings of the car in realistic settings were shown, together with three or four postage-stamp sized auxiliary pictures which emphasized a model's versatility by placing it in a variety of settings, or which demonstrated the wide variety of body styles available. There were exceptions to this trend, but the ten pseudo-technical illustrations which appeared in an announcement advertisement for the Bel Air Sport Coupe were unusual.

Sunshine and happy faces predominated in 1953. New Bel Airs and Two-Tens were shown on beaches and at rodeos, historic monuments, and cities. There was also the occasional studio-style pose, although paintings rather than photographs were used, all of which made the new model look longer, lower, and wider than it really was. The same applied in 1954, when the majority of the settings chosen were realistic, and the future was only lightly hinted at in one piece, which showed an orange and ivory sedan at a city airport with jets flying overhead. There was also at least one very dull advertisement, which used a painting of a sky-blue sedan set against a plain orange background. For no obvious reason a smaller picture of the car's rear was added, and the accompanying copy, in seven typefaces, was uninspired and old-fashioned. The piece would have looked much better in a catalog, and was not representative of its year.

A change of image in 1955 led to more dynamic and confident advertising for Chevrolet. The new car, with a V-8 engine, was shown on freeways and at fashionable resorts. While 1953's Bel Air convertible had been illustrated on a beach, driven by two mature ladies, the 1955 convertible was shown at a sports-car club meeting, admired by enthusiasts thirty years younger. If a 1954 sedan looked good at an airport, the 1955 model looked even better with a fighter plane. For 1956, layouts were similar, as were preferred pictorial settings, which reinforced Chevrolet's newly vigorous image. Paintings continued to be used except for a photographic series placed in female-oriented publications. A year later, the message was the same, albeit with plenty of new features in the car itself.

Chevrolet's second major change of the decade came in 1958, when a decision by all manufacturers to de-emphasize performance in advertising resulted in greater stress being placed on effortless cruising and comfort. The steep hills and fast freeways of 1957 gave way to flat country roads, and admiring neighbors replaced envious fighter pilots. Many illustrations showed only the car itself, perhaps with a few admirers scattered about, in preference to a complete tableau.

The 1959 Chevrolet was much larger and plusher than the 1955–57 models, and was instantly recognizable by its dramatic "bat-wing" fins. The artistic elongator's skill was employed to the full, particularly with the Impala Sport Coupe. Later in the model year photographers took over and sedans, sports sedans, and station wagons were shown in larger illustrations than had been adequate in the early 1950s. During 1959 and 1960 there were more photographs than paintings (the reverse having been true in 1958), and although paintings featured in range advertising for full-size models and Corvairs in 1961, those range pieces were modest and sober. The overall effect was of greater realism, bringing the product closer to the consumer. To some extent, the role of the fantasist was adopted as much by the copywriter as by the illustrator, and this development represented a natural progression from the increasingly integrated presentations of 1955–57. Settings were traditional Chevrolet leisure venues: lakes, country parks, rural stores, and suburban homes.

The progress of Cadillac and Chevrolet advertising typified the principal developments in layout and illustration during the 1950s, and other marques followed similar paths. Mercury made extensive use of color photography in 1954; it was particularly effective with metallic paint, and added clarity to the myriad smaller illustrations which demonstrated the car's new handling and power features. It was not unusual for a single advertisement to use five or six photographs including, inevitably, poses alongside modern aircraft. Surprisingly, not all of the aircraft were jets.

Oldsmobile was the best-known exponent of aeronautical imagery, showing stylized rockets in abundance in the early 1950s. Nash preferred rural panoramas for its main illustrations during 1953, but their impact was diminished by an insistent retention of 1939-style diagrams, albeit without 1939's "angled block" effect. The photographer took over in 1954, and achieved eye-catching results with 1956's three-tone color schemes.

Chrysler tried a watered-down version of Cadillac's approach in 1954, showing couples in evening dress to suggest sophistication. In one piece, a metallic red and white New Yorker was seen from above on what might have been brick-red gravel outside a house, but which looked like a pink carpet surrounded by indoor plants. The car's owner seemed much more interested in his partner than in the car, and even the unusual angle of the photograph could do little for an outmoded shape. In 1955, the male owner disappeared, and his partner became a fashionable model while the car itself, modern and more dynamic than its predecessors, was shown in studio poses which suggested romantic summer evenings. Chrysler suffered from the lack of a stable image nurtured carefully over the long term and, in this respect, Cadillac reigned supreme. Lincoln, whose photographic illustrations were well composed but who had no overall theme for 1955, suffered similarly.

Dullest of all in 1955 was Pontiac, whose lack of direction, not to mention dynamism, was painfully obvious. While many middle-market advertisers had adopted photography

Multiple illustrations were popular until the mid–1950s. Photographers were beginning to take over from artists by 1954 (April 1954).

Look at the car—and you know the man likes action

Nowadays, you can tell the man by the *car* he keeps.

Obviously, the car you see here belongs to a person who likes to go places. And he likes to get there with a minimum of effort and a maximum of pleasure.

We had such a man in mind when the design of this 1955 Lincoln began. And we gave our designers and engineers a goal that we believe has been achieved.

The aim was this: to build a fine car with *action* to surpass any other car—with beauty to match the tastes of Americans on the move who demand the finest.

Lincoln achieves matchless action with its new *Turbo-Drive* and new high torque V-8 engine. These two combine to set a new standard for fine-car performance.

Here is a new combination of utter smoothness with ultra quick acceleration. No jerk, no lag—just one unbroken sweep of power from zero to superhighway speed limits.

If you want a car with performance far ahead of its time—a car with beauty that speaks for itself and says so much about your own good taste—the new 1955 Lincoln is for you.

Prove it to yourself with a visit to your Lincoln dealer, to look at a new Lincoln Capri —*and to drive one.*

LINCOLN DIVISION . FORD MOTOR COMPANY

LINCOLN
for modern living
for magnificent driving

Lincoln's 1955 advertising was confident and eye-catching, but otherwise avoided a consistent theme beyond "modern living." This layout, with photograph, headline, and body copy clearly segregated, would become more common in the 1960s (May 1955).

The car with a "Built-in Future" was advertised in a style of twenty years past. This layout and style of illustration were carried through a series of similar pieces, which arguably lacked impact and conviction when compared with the 1955 norm (May 1955).

Ford used distinctive, atmospheric photography to promote the Thunderbird from 1959 onwards (May 1959 and January 1964).

in the early 1950s (lending instant novelty), Pontiac continued with uninteresting paintings. Where Chevrolet's painted settings were exciting and evocative, Pontiac's were unadventurous. Rarely was a car even seen in motion. A yellow and black Series 870 hardtop was shown in a forest; yet this was not a romantic, moody forest on a summer's evening, but a half-cleared commercial timber forest with children playing nearby who took no notice of the car. "When you buy a Pontiac you make a solid investment in the future," promised the copy, which reinforced the dullness of the illustration.

The overall layout of the piece was unimaginative, too, with a few paragraphs of prose and a superfluous painting of an engine which, even if it was "the most modern, most advanced engine you can buy" (and others could reasonably dispute this self-bestowed accolade), did not look like it. Consistency within the year's copy was achieved with a whole series of similar pieces, although not all used complete scenes. It was advertising of a kind that would have been more than adequate in 1935, but which was far from suitable for the market of twenty years later. At least one of 1956's pieces used a photograph, and a few others depicted cars in motion. One even showed a hardtop on a test track, but, taken as a whole, the year's effort appeared half-hearted. A new car and a new, more dynamic advertising style eventually arrived for 1957.

The 1960s were marked by an increase in the use of photography and "atmospheric" depictions, of which the most elaborate were Ford's tableaux for the Thunderbird from 1964 onwards. Each Thunderbird piece was color-toned into its background, suggesting an aura around the car and giving a new perspective to otherwise realistic surroundings. All divisions of General Motors used paintings as well as photographs during the decade, both often appearing in a marque's advertising for any one model year.

To a large extent, Cadillac's copy became less instantly recognizable. In 1960, a single illustration sufficed, with copy below and a jeweled crest and "V" above. This layout was used for both regular sedans and the more exclusive Eldorado convertible, finished, in one piece, in bright metallic emerald green. The jeweled crest, naturally, was executed in emeralds, while "diamonds and platinum by Cartier" had to suffice for a Sixty Special. In 1961, copy was reduced to a single, if pretentious, sentence. "A new Cadillac car is one of the few ma-

THE CADILLAC "V" AND CREST interpreted in Emeralds and Diamonds BY VAN CLEEF & ARPELS

Unique acclaim—even for a Cadillac!

Rarely has a motor car—even a Cadillac—received the high degree of public acclaim that has attended the introduction of the 1960 "car of cars". This praise has, indeed, been heart-warming. But it has also, we feel, been entirely logical. Certainly, no one could question the fact of its great beauty and luxury—so inspiring that it has already established a new era of automotive elegance. And surely, no one could deny the brilliance of its new performance—smooth, quiet, silken and eager beyond any previous Cadillac standard. Have you seen and driven the 1960 Cadillac for yourself? If not, you should do so at your earliest opportunity. We feel certain that you will give it your unqualified endorsement.

CADILLAC MOTOR CAR DIVISION • GENERAL MOTORS CORPORATION

Opposite and above: Typical Cadillac advertisements of the early 1960s. For 1963, the marque adopted the kind of photographic realism that predominated elsewhere (February 1960, May 1961, and November 1962).

terial possessions for which there is no completely acceptable substitute" described the 1961 Coupe de Ville.

Illustrations, which were sometimes photographic and sometimes painted, grew larger and more garish, as jeweled crests were mounted on color-matched, embroidered cloth, with the car standing in the foreground. Gold, pink, and turquoise were typically favored colors. In 1962, Cadillac's layouts remained similar, as did the style of the car itself, but embroidery gave way to vignettes of affluent life, and to more modest jewelry. Wrought-iron gates and stone columns echoed the aristocratic visual references which had been popular among upmarket advertisers in the 1920s.

In 1963, realism suddenly took over, as dream settings in turn gave way to modest depictions of the new models that actually looked like conventional photographs. Evening dresses were replaced by less formal clothes, and the copy began to describe technical features which had been largely unmentioned since the early 1950s; pre-eminence had to be fought for and demonstrated, and could no longer simply be asserted by portentous language and improbable surroundings.

This new, more relaxed, and less overtly snobbish style was continued for 1964. Cadillac advertising consequently lost much of its individuality as it was brought into line with the styles of rival marques. With the demise of the tail fin (which disappeared entirely from Cadillacs in 1965), luxury cars increasingly resembled medium-priced automobiles while full-size low and medium-priced models grew larger and more luxurious. Indeed, earlier price and size categories were no longer reliable indicators of status. Compact and subcompacts took the lower ground while Chevrolet Impalas and Ford Galaxies infiltrated the medium-priced arena, almost by default.

In the early 1960s, increasing convergence was apparent between advertisements for different luxury cars, as Lincoln developed a stable image and Cadillac shed the formalized settings and social scenes of the 1950s. Moreover, downmarket marques began consciously to imitate the advertising motifs hitherto reserved for their fine-car siblings. The seeds of this trend had been sown in 1958, when copy for low-priced cars began to emphasize comfort and size rather than perform-

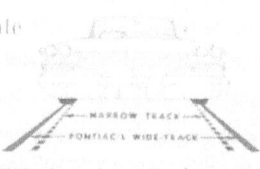

Pontiac's 1960 campaign combined upmarket elegance with Thunderbird atmosphere. The car's width, rather than its length, was exaggerated (February 1960).

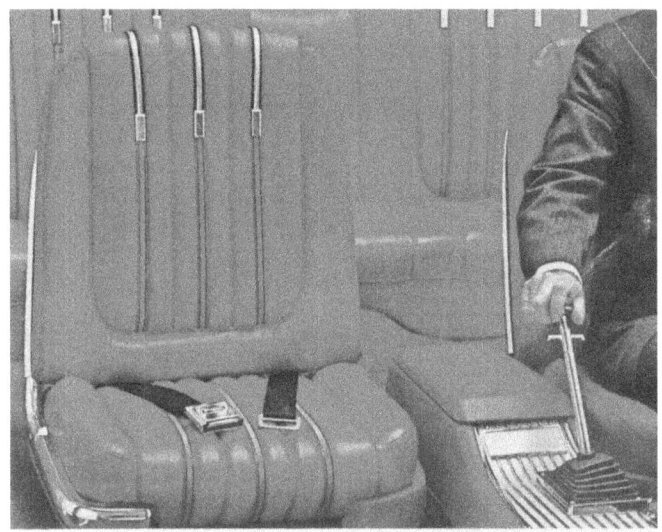

Ford's quality control promotions of 1962–64, spanning all of the company's products, used photography at its most detailed and realistic (May 1963).

ance. When Chevrolet deliberately imitated Cadillac's layouts in 1966-67, the convergence resulted in a uniformity within the full-size field which would have been inconceivable ten years earlier.

For the first time, it seemed that a standard layout for family car copy had emerged. This archetype comprised a photograph of the car against a realistic—if socially optimized—background, a slogan, and a few paragraphs of copy at the foot of the page. Technical and status differentiation were increasingly established within the copy itself, rather than by illustration. This process was highlighted by the use of cleanlined body styles at all levels, which were not easily distinguished by the layman, and which lacked the design gimmicks that artists and photographers had latched onto in earlier years. No one had ever mistaken a Lincoln tail fin for that of a De Soto, even if both cars, in engineering terms, were technically similar. But, by 1964, anonymity threatened.

It couldn't last. Pontiac reacted by deserting 1957's photographs and reverting, in selected advertisements, to paintings. Whereas earlier artists had confined their license to a car's proportions, rather than to its detailing or to the background scenery, Pontiac's illustrators frequently employed stylized illustrations that made no claim to technical realism.

The advent of "Wide Track" styling in 1959 allowed width, rather than length alone, to be exaggerated. Photographs were more often used for smaller Tempest models, and for scenes where motion and dynamic power were highlighted over the static elegance which was claimed for full-size Bonneville sedans and convertibles. Chevrolet also reverted to paintings in 1963, but the majority of Chevrolet advertisements in the 1960s used the photography which had predominated since 1959-60. In the late 1960s, Pontiac countered Ford's photographic "Thunderbird atmosphere" with similarly anti-realist paintings of the GTO and Firebird.

The underlying innovation of the final years of the decade was a new flexibility. Undoubtedly, the photographer had the upper hand, as the camera could be stoutly realistic about interior and other details in quality control promotions such as Ford's campaign of 1962–64, yet dreamy and almost surreal

Buick's art nouveau series of 1967 recalled upmarket advertising of fifty years earlier (October 1966).

Dark backgrounds were popular in sporty-car advertising during the 1970s. This piece combines the prevailing idiom with upmarket neo-minimalism from an earlier period (January 1976).

in its depiction of a personal-luxury coupe. Paintings could never be wholly realistic, and improvements in printing techniques meant that photographs in magazines could be much more detailed and lifelike than the static portraits of the 1930s, or even of the 1950s. Color definition, particularly for romantic twilight scenes, grew ever more precise and, therefore, evocative. Boulevard Photographic's 1963 Ford Thunderbird, seen at sunset on its own miniature island in a deep blue ocean, became a minor classic.[9] As Bill Rauhauser, retired professor of photography at Detroit's Center for Creative Studies, recalled in 1996:

The highly innovative work of Detroit photographers during the 1950s and '60s ... advanced the ability to capture the desired effects on film and allowed photography to supplant illustration in automotive advertising. Such shooting techniques as tent lighting; cove construction to eliminate the line where wall meets floor; motion mechanisms; liquid light; the use of various lenses, particularly anamorphic and wide-angle; and most importantly the ability to reproduce the stretch effect on film made a new look in automotive photography possible.[10]

Other techniques were developed during the late 1960s and early 1970s. For example, the photographer Warren O. Winstanley "would often accentuate the vehicle through the use of large black mesh screens placed between the car to be photographed and the background scene.... This diffused and reduced the light intensity of the background and placed the main emphasis on the car."[11]

Yet until the early 1970s, paintings had their place, and were used in deliberate contrast to photography, particularly in campaigns such as Pontiac's, which sought to differentiate the images of mid-size and compact models, on the one hand, from the traditional full-size "Wide-Tracks" on the other. Pontiac's 1959–71 series of illustrations by Arthur Fitzpatrick against aspirational, often European, backgrounds by Van Kaufman, became famous.[12]

During 1968–70, advertisers of high-performance muscle cars reverted occasionally to paintings of cars being driven hard on winding roads, while humorous, distorted color drawings, particularly from Plymouth and Dodge, and in milder forms from Ford and Chevrolet, appealed to teenaged and twenty-something readers of high-selling specialist magazines such as *Motor Trend*, *Car Life*, *Car and Driver*, and *Hot Rod*. And similar, if simpler, color drawings also appeared in turn-of-the-decade advertising for the new Chevrolet Vega.[13]

This new flexibility of outlook and medium allowed illustration to be tailored ever more closely to copy, the combination defining the market niche to be targeted. All this took place in the context of a new car arena which had changed radically since the advent of the modern compacts in 1959. The American automotive market had become subdivided into prioritized, and often mutually exclusive, segments. After a brief flirtation with near-uniformity in 1963–67, advertising styles once again diverged, now visibly consolidating along size-category and niche rather than traditional, but now obsolete, marque boundaries.

Chapter 2

Fantasy by Design

"You turned your Head." Of course you did when you first saw one of these beautifully, scientifically stream-lined Chrysler Airflows. For this is real beauty — the beauty of true functional design.

Let's speak of value <u>beneath</u> the style. Asked to name the one car responsible for today's handsome designs, most people would say Lincoln-Zephyr.... The influence of this car has been great.... From the beginning, the Lincoln-Zephyr has pioneered. The first forward-looking feature that set the car apart was the unit-body-and-frame.... The results are efficient, economical operation.... Why not enjoy a car modern in *all* its ways?

The first of these cars was a Chrysler Airflow, as promoted to British motorists in advertising with an American flavor in 1935; the second was a 1939 Lincoln-Zephyr. The Airflow was a sales disaster with only around 29,500 Chrysler and 25,700 De Soto Airflows sold over four seasons, but the Zephyr, though inherently a more specialized car, was a successful product whose styling was widely copied. Both were sold on the strength of streamlined design; the difference lay in the marketing approaches used. The Airflow was designed to be streamlined, and declared to be attractive simply because it was aerodynamically more efficient than the opposition. The Zephyr was intended to be both streamlined and attractive. Although it proved to be even more efficient aerodynamically than the Airflow, its designer, Eugene Gregorie, developing earlier and more radical ideas by John Tjaarda, realized that any scientific advance had to be made palatable to the consumer.

The need for compromise was widely realized by industrial designers of the period. In 1934, Herbert Read put the point concisely:

> One false theory [of design] assumes that if [an] object ... performs its function in the most efficient way possible, it will *ipso facto* possess the necessary aesthetic qualities. To this argument we must reply that an object which functions perfectly may, and probably will, possess aesthetic qualities, but that the connection is not a necessary one.[14]

In an automotive context, the compromise was not between any fixed idea of "aesthetic quality" and an immutable notion of function. Streamlining was ostensibly adopted to reduce wind resistance in the name of efficiency, but it also gave a new design a dramatically modern look that allowed the consumer to feel that he was participating in progress. Automobile design reflected a broader trend. As one later critic remarked:

> The curvilinear forms or "streamlining" that came to the fore in the 1930s had European roots, but in America were extended in application to all manner of design....[15]

Even pencil sharpeners and refrigerators, which remained immobile all their lives, adopted "streamlined" forms. This general movement was seen, and promoted, as the outward sign of technological and, by extension, social advancement. Perhaps more than any other artifact of its time, the streamlined automobile vitalized and nurtured the consumer's sense of the wider progress by being the object with which he engaged most closely. The automobile was meaningless without motion, direction, without intimate involvement with the consumer. In this, it was unique.

Against such a background, it was not surprising that successful individual examples of streamlined design were not always aerodynamically efficient. Provided that a design was symbolically efficient to the consumer, it did not need to be empirically efficient. Whatever the legitimate preoccupations of Chrysler's aerodynamicists, an automobile had to conform

Chrysler hoped that the reader's heart would follow his head, while Lincoln assured him that his head could safely follow where his heart already wanted to go. The Lincoln was more attractive, shrewdly advertised — and successful (May 1934, and 1939 campaign).

to the consumer's visual expectations, which may have been determined not by any scientific criteria, but simply by what he had come to expect in car design. And the consumer's eye was largely trained by the appearance of earlier cars whose proportions had not been determined by aerodynamics at all.

For Chrysler, the adoption of empirically efficient streamlining involved such a radical departure from the automotive norm that the new car buyer could not be relied upon to integrate the Airflow's design into his expectations. *MoToR* realized this in January, 1934:

> At first glance, these cars will look strange to most people, but ... after you have looked at them for two or three days you become accustomed to them, and sooner or later you begin to admire them. Finally, you ... come round to the viewpoint that these cars look right and that conventional cars look strange.

Most car buyers, however, were not prepared to pay for this aesthetic reorientation, and advertisers' enthusiasm for "scientifically streamlined" design was not enough to persuade them. This was realized at the outset by those who promoted the Lincoln-Zephyr two years later.

Advertisers also realized that when the consumer bought a car for its appearance he needed to rationalize his decision, and to be convinced that he was not sacrificing practicality and functional transportation-value. Throughout the late 1930s, Lincoln-Zephyr advertising always mentioned the practical advantages, as well as the styling, of the various body types available. Chrysler, on the other hand, having designed a robust and advanced type of body frame, did not always mention it in advertisements. Nor was attention always drawn to the advantages of rigidity, weight distribution, and interior space that accrued from the car's novel proportions. The consumer was often left with the mistaken impression that he was being sold a strange design for which much else had been sacrificed. *The Times* in England wrote in 1935:

> There is much that is logical in the advanced design of the Airflow ... chassis and body, and it results in sports performance with standard saloon comfort.[16]

experts describe as "the most highly refined expression of the modern motif."

It became clear that motorists would accept progressive innovation, and that consumers were eager to endorse futuristic design ideals, but that popular taste required gradual, rather than sudden, conditioning.

Harley Earl of General Motors is considered by many to be the father of styling in its modern sense, and while he neither invented the concept, nor was alone in realizing its importance, he was uniquely responsible for developing a pragmatic philosophy of automobile design that was able to accommodate all the variable factors involved within a continuing corporate new model program. Body design and advertising were integrated under Earl's regime as never before.

As early as 1921, General Motors' product policy program acknowledged "the very great importance of style in selling"[17] at a time when styling, as a facet of a product's initial conception, was widely disregarded. In 1920, design was decided largely by engineers, and the overall form of an automobile was determined by its immediate function as mechanism. By 1925, it was apparent that car buyers were no longer content with simple, unadorned transportation; the market was dividing into many price sectors, and every purchaser wanted a product with a measure of individuality commensurate with its owner's status, and which was conspicuously more modern than its predecessors.

The annual model change had been *de facto* policy within General Motors' divisions since 1923 but, two years later, it was explicitly endorsed and made a permanent feature of the Corporation's product planning strategy. The need for a competitive edge against Ford and the newly emergent Chrysler Corporation reinforced the importance of styling, and in July, 1926 the president of General Motors, Alfred Sloan, wrote to Buick's general manager:

> I am sure we all realize ... how much appearance has to do with sales ... and in a product such as ours where the individual appeal is so great, it means a tremendous influence on our future prosperity....[18]

"I cannot say that this form of streamlining is attractive to me in appearance," said the motoring correspondent of *The Times* in England in 1935. But he admitted that "the stability and smooth travel of the [eight-cylinder] saloon are out of the ordinary in their excellence" (1935 campaign).

But in Britain, as in America, few car buyers felt inclined to investigate.

Hupmobile was much more cautious in 1934, and British advertising for that marque's Aerodynamic sedan carefully reconciled the futurism of Raymond Loewy's design to more conventional ideas of automotive excellence:

> To this Hupmobile belongs a new interpretation of motoring.... Yet if the spirit of the car is of the sky ... its lines are sanely down to earth — air-moulded without freakishness or exaggeration.

Home market copy pursued a similar theme in a *Saturday Evening Post* advertisement of November 9, 1935:

> The car that was some day to come — is here!... The moment you see the new Hupmobile, you will know that it's the car you have wanted and waited for. You will see its smoothly-moulded, stream-line beauty. Here is nothing bizarre or "freakish." Instead, a harmony, symmetry and grace which

Cadillac's general manager, Lawrence P. Fisher, visited a number of dealers and distributors in order to gain a general appraisal of the current design trends which would soon percolate down to the mass-market. He also visited Cadillac's west coast distributor, which in 1919 had purchased the Earl Automobile Works, at which Harley Earl, son of the owner, continued to design custom bodies for wealthy clients. During the spring of 1926, as a consultant to General Motors, Earl produced a low and attractive body design for the upper middle-class LaSalle of 1927, and it sold so well that Fisher soon afterwards brought Earl to Detroit to head GM's new Art &

Colour section (which he rechristened the Styling Section in 1937). Earl had studied European design but concluded that, owing to the different conditions under which American and European cars operated, European ideas had only very limited application within the mainstream American market.

The LaSalle was followed by a modest restyling of the contemporary Buick for the 1929 model year, but that car, which looked modern and elegant in the form outlined by Earl's studios, became a laughing-stock when it was introduced, as the exigencies of mass-production had destroyed its original proportions, while retaining a characteristic bulge below the waistline. Earl recalled the resulting fiasco in 1954:

> The Styling Section then had not been as well integrated into other company operations as it is now, and I was unaware of what had happened until I saw the completed cars. Of course, I roared like a Ventura sea lion, but it was too late to keep buyers from having a lot of fun naming the poor *enceinte* Buick.[19]

Following the failure of the "pregnant Buick," Earl was careful to ensure that production engineers did not alter the proportions of his designs without the necessary consultation; moreover, such a public repudiation of self-consciously "modern" design meant that designers throughout the industry were cautious—a skepticism which was reinforced by the Airflow débâcle five years later.

There appeared to be no obvious solution to the problem. How was innovation to be made palatable? Consumers liked a car to be in some way "scientific" and demonstrably modern, but appeared to object when scientific principles were applied to its design. Car buyers also liked the idea of a streamlined automobile, provided that it remained visibly related to earlier, familiar forms which themselves owed little to aerodynamics; many had been more efficient traveling backwards than forwards.

General Motors' solution to the complexities of consumer taste in the 1930s was elegantly simple. The "one-piece solid steel 'Turret Top' Body by Fisher," new for 1935 and heavily advertised throughout the rest of the decade, looked modern, yet largely retained familiar proportions. Streamlining was suggested by the use of rounded contours, smoothly integrated grilles and strategically placed chromium trim.

Fisher Body advertising not only emphasized the functional aspects of streamlining, but also promoted the practicality of the design and pointed to the genuinely scientific construction of the Turret Top body structure. The new car buyer was offered a product which was attractive, yet also demonstrably in the forefront of technological progress. Moreover, the availability of the Turret Top on all of GM's six passenger car marques underlined the parent company's corporate identity and image, while marque differentiation was left to the marque advertisements. Copy for Fisher Body concentrated on the beauty and safety offered by the Turret Top, and each advertisement was illustrated with a suitable car, from Chevrolet to Cadillac, with any number of Buicks, Oldsmobiles, Pontiacs, and LaSalles in between.

Fisher Body advertisements were invariably eye-catching, and close-up color photographs were frequently employed from 1934 onwards. In March, 1937, a bright yellow Pontiac Eight sedan was shown on a vast, part-completed iron bridge, its owner admiring the architectural colossus that was taking shape above him. The body frame of "the most beautiful thing on wheels" was illustrated in a small diagram at the foot of the page, its complex construction of steel panels and girders visibly reminiscent of the bridge. "Security gets a lift!" said the headline, "It's nice to know that you're riding surrounded by steel...." Like other Fisher Body advertisements in the series, the piece combined emotive and stylish photography with a functional, yet dynamic, theme.

The Lincoln-Zephyr was specifically intended and acknowledged as one of the most futuristically styled cars on the road at the time of its launch in November, 1935, and copy for the car was more overtly futuristic than Fisher's, particular during the Zephyr's early years. In May, 1937, a blue two-door sedan was shown under a concrete bridge, with the famous Burlington Zephyr streamlined train speeding over the track above. The car and train were described as:

> ... the newest things on wheels.... One is a streamlined train, rolling up new records on the rails. One is a motor car ... rolling up new records on the roads. Common to both is a break with the past ... a new point-of-view towards travel.

The accompanying artwork was tastefully stylized, exhibiting the car's Art Deco design features to maximum effect. When an improved 1939 model was announced, the bridge analogy was reworked to reinforce the connection between styling, body engineering, and the wider parallels in contemporary industrial technology which characterized much automobile advertising of the period.

A newspaper advertisement for the 1939 Lincoln-Zephyr built upon a reputation consolidated since 1936:

> Style alone does not make a motor-car.... For beneath this outward beauty ... is a framework of steel trusses—the famous "arch-bridge" construction. You have stood on such a bridge, spanning some wide valley, and marveled that so light a structure could support great weight. Here is the same principle—body and frame a rigid unit combining lightness and strength.

The copy appealed to the reader's personal experience and thus cemented the product into his imagination. A small, but highly detailed, diagram of the body frame was included to reinforce the consumer's appreciation of the car's important features. It was noticeable that, throughout a long-running campaign, a few points were stressed again and again, driving home a consistent message. Lincoln's copywriters appreciated that an appeal to personal experience, together with the reiteration of facts recalled from past advertisements and imagery

Above and right: Three interpretations of the popular "bridge" analogy which allied automobile styling to general technological developments of the post–Depression era (April and May 1937 and 1939 campaign).

derived from areas not directly connected to the automobile, if suitably blended, would add up to a potent sales message.

During the 1940s, and particularly after World War II, the technical connection between a car's styling and its structural integrity, and the wider association between the automobile and other accessible products of the technological revolution, became ever more tenuous. The elements of that idealistic triumvirate of aesthetic, technical, and social growth, whose potency had been strikingly evident at the New York World's Fair in 1939, lost much of their earlier cumulative impact upon the public mind. In the 1940s, the symbolic element of automobile body design was increasingly separated from any theoretical connection it once had with genuine scientific developments in other spheres.

This divergence of technologies, and of symbol from empirical science, was partly an unavoidable result of technical progress and functional specialization within diverse industrial and design fields, but it was accelerated by the need for perpetual innovation in automobile design. By 1948, the social idealism which had underpinned the earlier movement towards a futuristic homogeneity in industrial design no longer existed in its original form.

The postwar consumer wanted to sustain his own fantasy with symbols that evoked, but did not necessarily contribute to, the industrial and socio-technological advances of the new era. If the 1950s are traditionally viewed as the years in which the "American dream" matured, the elements of that all-enveloping dream (or the "autocracy of progress" as some skeptics called it) had begun to dissipate some years previously. The consumerist dream which took its place was the inevitable product of a broader national aspiration, but its focus was narrowed, before an arguably fatal implosion among self-enclosing, personal fantasies in the 1960s and beyond.

There were, however, significant developments that impinged more visibly on automobile advertising. The rapid development of jet and rocket propulsion, and the possibilities of space travel that came with them, gave rise to a new kind of symbol. The visual characteristics of space-rockets and jet aircraft were appropriated by automobile stylists, even though they had no directly scientific application to any aspect of a production automobile's function. Designers and the advertisers who collaborated with them were careful to maintain a visible, sensual link between car design and the aeronautical revolution. This was particularly necessary after American self-confidence was undermined by the successful launch of Sputnik by the Russians on October 4, 1957. The consumer who drove his (optionally air-suspended) "Air Born B-58 Buick" to town every day participated vicariously in the greater progress; his was a personal, individualized fantasy, but it was defined by the conscious anticipation of a better America. This microcosm of a larger expectation was revitalized for the consumer every time he got into his car.

The continuing potency of such an apparently fanciful approach to design was demonstrated by the failure of Ford's Edsel Division in 1958. Advertising for the Edsel was carefully planned, and began long before the car's launch in late 1957. Foote, Cone & Belding's pre-launch press advertisements stressed the novelty of the Edsel concept — a glamorous car that would cover the middle price range — and promised special features. A "Teletouch" pushbutton transmission was unusual in that the operating buttons were fitted in the steering wheel hub, but self-adjusting brakes, heavily promoted, had been offered by Studebaker ten years earlier.

Once revealed, the Edsel was sold mainly on its styling, which was claimed to be predictive — "Edsel styling leads the way." It was not, however, "here to stay," whatever the copywriters might have wished. Pseudo-classical grille apart, the Edsel itself was not inherently innovative; it was far less radically conceived than, say, the Lincoln-Zephyr. More importantly, it lacked those stylistic flourishes that gave a design its all-important symbolic content. It had no fins; its taillights

Conventional advertising for a generally conventional car. A cynical marketing exercise, the Edsel failed to sell, and consumers had the last laugh (1958 campaign).

evoked nothing, while nevertheless being self-consciously stylized. The radiator grille, lacking elegance, also lacked aeronautical connotations.

Measured against functional parameters, the Edsel was no more peculiar than many of its contemporaries, but, unlike them, it stated no allegiance to a wider American aspiration. By aping the anti-functional form of contemporary automobile design, while visibly remaining removed from what the consumer saw as its underlying raison d'être, it was a parody, and as such was rejected by car buyers. In one *New Yorker* cartoon, a woman looked up from her newspaper and remarked happily to a less than cheerful-looking husband: "My, it's a big week for everybody! The Russians have the Intercontinental Ballistic Missile, and we have the Edsel." The psychological point was sharply made. Only 110,847 Edsels were sold between September, 1957 and November, 1959, and the car reputedly lost its makers $250 million.

An elaborate, noisy, and protracted sales and advertising effort did little for the car's fortunes, and was toned down when it became apparent that sales would not pick up. Most surprising of all, however, was that the car, hyped up in the summer of 1957 in a series of "taster ads" and heavily promoted after launch, was not advertised at first as a 1958 model. As all involved licked their wounds, other advertisers watched the affair with close interest, and were content to fuel the established fantasy. Within that context, "new styling features were introduced that were far removed from utility, yet they seemed demonstrably effective in capturing public taste."[20] The Edsel affair proved effective in demonstrating that no amount of ingenuity on the part of copywriters could rescue an unpopular design. It was a lesson that would not readily be forgotten.

A few cars of the early postwar period appealed to the public while also retaining a substantial element of "European" functionalism. One of these was the 1947 Studebaker, introduced in the spring of 1946. Early advertisements were triumphant: "First by far with a post war car!" ran the introductory slogan. "Your dream car is here — and in production!" continued the copy in July 1946. The full-width styling of the Commander Regal De Luxe 5-Passenger Coupe was simple and clean, and was illustrated with an "actual color photograph" to dispel any doubts that might have lingered if paintings had been used.

In August of the same year, a Champion Regal De Luxe four-door sedan was hailed as:

> Sweet and low ... a melody in metal.... That picture of it you see above is a color photograph of the real thing — the new 1947 Studebaker "in person".... Here's more than a car out ahead in point of time — it's unmistakably far ahead in distinctive post-war styling — completely new from every view.

The color photograph of a pastel green car had been lightly airbrushed to give added sleekness, but the Champion's compact yet elegant proportions were accurately depicted. In October, 1946, a blue Commander Regal De Luxe sedan was shown in a similar piece, "styled to step up your spirits." The makers rammed their point home:

> You may be an unpretentious person about most other things. But you're sure to like the envious attention your car receives everywhere you go in a stunningly styled new 1947 Studebaker.

By September, 1947, the Big Three had still not caught up with Studebaker's lead, and in a piece for the top-line Regal De Luxe Land Cruiser the copywriter unashamedly gloated:

> Most people know that there's just one showpiece among today's cars.... This is the fresh, new kind of style that people hoped to see in all automobiles by now.... [The Land Cruiser] is a photogenic dream car that proudly leads a Studebaker fashion show of equally distinctive Champions and Commanders.

Studebaker did not need to lend glamour to the product by employing the elongator with his airbrush aerodynamics, even if a little tinkering was considered helpful alongside, one suspected, a sandbag or two in the trunk and under the hood to make the car look lower and sleeker on its springs. If there was no mention of a "European look" as such, it was perhaps because in 1946 the Studebaker looked more modern than any mainstream European production car, the more so for displaying an almost European compactness and restraint in decoration. America, and Studebaker in particular, still held the international stylistic lead in 1948, although others would catch up by 1950. The car was still in production, virtually unmodified, in 1948:

> Vision produced this car of vision!... Studebaker engineers and stylists knew you wanted a better view in back as well as in front when you're driving. So they envisioned a car with panoramic windows all round — spent years in designing and redesigning it — came up with this dreamlined new Starlight Coupe!... First in style ... first in vision ... first by far with a postwar car.

The copywriter's claims were hardly modest, but they were valid. Until the introduction of the 1949 Fords in June, 1948, the Studebaker was stylistically America's most advanced automobile, and it had a lasting impact. The 1947 Kaisers and Frazers, even with flush sides, looked leaden by comparison, an effect compounded by their design's high, domed hood, bulbous trunk and relatively small window area. Unadorned straight-through sides were notoriously difficult to get right, and even Howard "Dutch" Darrin, who had largely conceived the shape, dissociated himself from its eventual production form, which lacked the "Darrin dip" in the rear fender line with which he had originally solved the problem.

The 1947 Studebaker was designed by Robert Bourke and Virgil Exner of Raymond Loewy Associates, Bourke having worked for Studebaker before Loewy hired him formally to work with Exner on the 1947 proposals. Although the version

Advertising for the first generation of postwar "Loewy" Studebakers capitalized on the car's role as an international style leader (July 1946 and February 1948).

finally announced in 1946 was prepared independently of Loewy's studios, and was chosen over Loewy's official proposal, it was advertised as the "New 1947 Studebaker with Raymond Loewy body designing," and became known as the "Loewy Studebaker." It was widely advertised as a revolutionary concept in automobile body design. A 1949 advertisement showed a red Starlight coupe on a beach and outlined the design's rationale:

> Studebaker's the stand-out in savings that count and style that sings.... You start cutting your car operating costs right away, thanks to Studebaker's trim, sleek dream lines.

The copy, and the design, were unusual for achieving an apparently successful synthesis of conflicting design priorities. Only rarely in America was attractive styling, which gained general approval amongst new car buyers, combined with good fuel consumption. Loewy was aware of the iconoclastic nature of such a concept for 1947. In a paper presented at the beginning of World War II to the Society of Automotive Engineers, he declared:

> Weight is the enemy. The average automobile weighs thirty-five hundred pounds. Thirty-five hundred pounds of materials to transport one or two people just does not make sense. Statistics show that ninety-two per cent of the cars on the highways travel with empty rear seats. The weight trend in the past years, I believe, has been decidedly retrogressive. This must change.[21]

In 1979, Loewy recalled:

> I had felt for the last forty years that the American automobile was too bulky and heavy.... I lectured about it, wrote articles about it, said it on the radio, and achieved only one thing: Detroit's resentment and hostility.... Finally, when gasoline shortages developed [in the 1970s] ... Detroit was forced to accept the fact that weight *is* the enemy.[22]

Yet although in later years Loewy was proved right, a successful design studio does not achieve renown in its own time by designing what "ought" to be made if the public does not want it. Whatever rationale might, with hindsight, be imputed to the design, it was the car's appearance which gathered sales of over 160,000 in the extended 1947 model year, at least 184,000 in 1948 and approximately 129,000 in 1949. Studebaker's copywriters were well aware of the effect that even a cursory glimpse of the new model had on automobile enthusiasts. In 1990, Bruno Sacco, Director of Design for passenger cars at Mercedes-Benz, recalled seeing a 1950 Regal De Luxe Starlight Coupe in Italy:

> It was the year 1951, late spring in Tarvisio, in the Italian Alps. I was cycling along the main street of the town.... Suddenly I became aware of a car coming the other way. I think it was electric blue — it was certainly something out of the ordinary. I realized in that moment of encounter that I had seen something that put everything else in the shade. I stopped, looked back, and got another surprise: the rear view of this vehicle was also different from anything I had seen before....[23]

The design was a unique amalgam of "European" functionalism and that quintessentially American obsession with the technically superfluous, but visually dramatic, design feature. It was not necessary, for adequate visibility, to use such a dramatic rear window, yet it was this feature above all others that captured the public imagination. Like Harley Earl's Cadillac tail fin of 1948, it was an aesthetic reinterpretation of utilitarian aircraft design — in this case, a canopy. The genuine functionalism of lightweight body design was combined with the quasi-functionalism of the aeronautical motif, while at the same time a lack of added decoration gave the car an international feel, with an element of "Eurochic" on which copywriters, explicitly or implicitly, could capitalize.

Studebaker was among the few automobile manufacturers of the late 1940s that tried to break away from the herd by claiming leadership in design, or by endeavoring to rise above the need for annual restyling by questioning the presuppositions that lay behind it. Not all who attempted the break were successful but, armed with a genuinely novel product with practical and aesthetic advantages over the opposition, a copywriter could self-consciously jump off the bandwagon without being forced to rely on functionalist rhetoric alone, whose limited effectiveness in mainstream automotive advertising had been proven.

Unable to retool for substantial annual styling changes, Studebaker was able to make a virtue out of necessity in the late 1940s. A February, 1948 advertisement was clever:

> All over America the word for style is Studebaker.... Time flies faster than most of us realize. It's just a little more than eighteen months since you first read the thrilling Studebaker announcement, "Your postwar dream car is here and in production." Now the 1948 version of that dream car has arrived.... They're more than fresh 1948 interpretations of the "new look" in cars that's a Studebaker style mark. They're the dramatic encore....

In fact, the 1948 models were almost exactly the same as before, and were not even "fresh interpretations." The car remained advanced, however, and the bold, disingenuous approach — an approach that would not save many of the "independents" once the postwar sellers' market had subsided — worked for Studebaker in this instance, even if it would not always do so in the future.

The car was updated in 1950. "All eyes are on this 'next look' in cars," crowed one advertisement for the Land Cruiser sedan. "You get thrift plus luxury in this new Studebaker!" said another headline, the thrift "because there's no bulging excess bulk to over-burden a Land Cruiser's trim, sleek structure." Claims that it was "dynamically new in form and substance" were untrue, but with restyled rear fenders and a new spinner-nosed front, it was undoubtedly different.

By the time that the 1950 model was conceived, Robert Bourke was working for Loewy, and his version was chosen by Studebaker's management over an independent proposal from Virgil Exner, who subsequently left Studebaker to work for Chrysler. In 1981, Bourke recalled:

> We were impressed with fighter aircraft and wanted to impart some of that flavor to the Studebaker. It was basically the old 1947 body, but the new nose really set Studebaker apart.[24]

By 1950, aeronautical design motifs had appeared on Ford and General Motors cars as well, and it was clear that such features, regardless of whatever else a car offered, were important to consumers. They contributed to the motorist's fantasy that he was not only driving his car, but participating in the aeronautical revolution: He could pretend he was controlling something created in the spirit of a fighter aircraft, rather than chugging along the highway behind a 102–h.p. L–head six. An optional spinning propeller could be fitted into the Studebaker's nose to complete the illusion.

The 1950 recipe was a success, and the 1947 original was outsold more than two to one. The American car buyer's desire for innovation had robbed the car of its earlier, semi–European appearance, but 1953 marked a return to simplicity with a new pair of coupes, called the Starlight and Starliner — the latter a pillarless hardtop. "The new American car with the European look" aimed to bring buyers "the continental charm of Europe's most distinguished cars" according to one advertisement. Independent critics agreed. In November, *The Autocar* commented that:

> One of the lowest and certainly one of the best-balanced and beautifully styled cars ... in the United States, this [car] reflects the Italian styling influence that is becoming increasingly popular in that country as well as in Europe.

The car proved to be something of a false dawn for Studebaker's fortunes, and it did not herald a significant adoption of European styling in America; rather, American stylists occasionally appended European-seeming design features to an indigenous idiom. Even the 1952–54 Nash, "styled in the continental manner by Pinin Farina" according to a 1953 advertisement, remained, as eventually produced, essentially a Nash design which incorporated some exterior and interior touches from a Pinin Farina proposal. Yet the Italian designer's name made it more saleable. "Nash presents for 1954 New Continental Dream Cars by Pinin Farina" announced the

Aeronautical design motifs were commonplace by 1950, but Studebaker's spinner nose was not followed elsewhere (November 1949).

marque in a double-spread in which four paintings of different models appeared alongside a small black and white photograph of the designer himself. "The genius of Pinin Farina sparkles in every line of the new Nash Ambassador 'Country Club,'" added the copy. No one familiar with Farina's designs for European chassis believed a word of it.

Unlike its 1950 sedans, Studebaker's new coupe did look genuinely "European," even to Europeans. In Italy the American advertising slogan was repeated: "La nuova vettura Americana nella Linea Europa .... Ecco la machina all'avanguardia della produzione automobilistica del mondo," announced a Milanese distributor in 1953.

Both "Loewy" designs gave rise to cross-fertilization with European manufacturers. The 1947's style was easily discernible in the 1949 Rover 75, and an early Rover development chassis was fitted with a Studebaker body and inevitably called the "Roverbaker." It was not surprising to find elements of the same design in the Rootes Group's 1948 Hillman Minx and Humber Hawk, which were styled by Loewy's London studios. The 1953 Starliner was reinterpreted in 1955 for the Group's Sunbeam Rapier of that year, and, when the Studebaker sprouted fins for 1957, so did the Sunbeam in 1958. The copywriter's enthusiastic prose was not just cynical marketing. It was amusing, however, to see the 1948-shape Minx marketed in 1954 in its home country, in Californian hardtop form, on the strength of a fashionable Detroit-and-soda style.

By 1958, Loewy's original coupe had been so heavily modified that to European eyes it was indistinguishable from the American norm. "Rarely ever, such glamour in an automobile" began one advertisement for that year's Starlight, now sedan-based and heavily chromed while retaining the earlier name:

> Here is a star of the first magnitude in the constellation of Studebaker-Packard automobiles ... an entirely new hardtop of perfect proportions crafted to high standards of workmanship and styled to standards of high fashion.

All pretense of European sophistication had been given up, and only a few thousand buyers were persuaded to try the new version. The advertisement, in monochrome, was now more distinctive than the car.

It was significant that each "Loewy" design was progressively Americanized during successive years of production, suggesting that, in the climate of the 1950s, European function-

Widely regarded as the best of postwar American designs, the 1953 Studebaker coupe was sold on its European look — even in Europe (1953 campaign).

alism could never be truly accommodated to the American consumer's desire for constant change. Walter Dorwin Teague was among those who changed the face of American industrial design during the 1930s, but he felt ill at ease with the constant and apparently directionless innovation that preoccupied Detroit. In 1963, he wrote:

> If you *must* do something different, you are apt to do something bad, something bizarre. That is why car design has grown so extreme in this country.[25]

Harley Earl, who continued to head the Styling Section at General Motors until his retirement in December, 1958, called the process "dynamic obsolescence." Critics, with varying degrees of disparagement, referred to it as "planned" or "built-in" obsolescence.[26] The latter term was misleading.

By 1958, the restraint of Loewy's 1953 original had been deserted. This sedan-based Starlight, like the year's Hawk coupes, was heavily decorated (March 1958).

Early critics of the strategy, whose sympathies in many cases lay with the supposedly European design virtues of simplicity and resistance to change once an ideal solution to a design problem had been found, believed that dynamic obsolescence consisted in designing a product that would break down after a period of use predetermined by its manufacturer, so that the consumer would be forced to buy a replacement. Not only was such a policy dishonest, argued the critics; it was also wasteful and, by extension, inimical to those ethical (if not always economic) bedfellows, stability and progress.

Such an analysis was oversimplistic and naive. The American automobile was intrinsically robust and, as Packard found to its cost in 1956, consumers were quick to desert manufacturers whose quality control standards lapsed. Dynamic obsolescence was necessary precisely because the average American automobile worked well and, in order to keep the economic machinery in motion, the consumer had to be encouraged to buy a replacement long before his existing car wore out.

In the 1930s, the strategy had a rationale beyond the need simply to fuel demand for new products for their own sake: By buying new cars the public actively contributed to the regeneration of the American economy after the Depression of 1929–34, and the residual goodwill generated by this wider purpose operated in the minds of consumers until the 1950s. Only in the late 1950s, when constant revision of design threatened actually to undermine the functional capability of the automobile, rather than simply exist independently of it, was the value of the whole process brought seriously into question.

Dynamic obsolescence did not disappear at this point; rather, it was modified by the segmentation of the new car market, which allowed demands for overtly functional cars to be satisfied. If the ingress of functionalist ideas encouraged replacement of anti-functional cars, the underlying economic machinery was maintained. It did not matter *why* cars were replaced, provided that they *were* replaced. Thus the marketing, advertising, and design strategies nurtured by Harley Earl remained in place, and Detroit continued to support the buying habits that ensured frequent replacement of mechanically healthy automobiles.

It became apparent that advertisers' role was not simply to promote products which had been designed from afar. Their primary task was to fuel the consumer's fantasy and constantly to regenerate his desire for novelty, regardless of whether or not his existing car worked well. Thus "new" and "different" became synonymous with "better." Against this background (which was fundamentally alien to the European doctrine whereby the best design was that which most nearly fulfilled a range of functional priorities), Loewy's "European look" was simply a reinterpretation of an American theme. It incorporated only the superficial appearance of a European car, and not the design precepts that oriented genuine European design. The apparent move towards European ideas which characterized a variety of automobiles in 1953 was in fact a chimera. Dynamic obsolescence, or "embarrassing people into buying,"[27] would only be widely questioned after 1970.

The process of styling and restyling was carefully structured around the annual model year, and the creation, over several decades, of corporate and marque identities. The prevailing design philosophy in Detroit required that millions of essentially similar automobiles should be sold every year, but there remained recognizable Ford, General Motors, and Chrysler styles and, within each corporate structure, marque — and latterly model — identities.

Each existed within an overall corporate idiom, which was dictated in part by the need to retain the consumer's loyalty to a manufacturer when he moved upmarket from, say, Chevrolet to Oldsmobile. It was also encouraged by a desire to reduce costs by spreading design facilities and actual components across a manufacturer's overall product range. The individual styling feature was a way of distinguishing one year's model from the next, and it also defined a car's status in the corporate hierarchy. By stimulating the consumer's curiosity and desire, advertisers kept this multi-faceted juggernaut intact and in motion. "[I]t is not too much to say," said Alfred Sloan in 1963, "that the 'laws' of the Paris dressmakers have come to be a factor in the automobile industry — and woe to the company which ignores them."[28] But many of the smaller manufacturers could not afford to obey those laws, to their ultimate cost.

The major car producers divided their advertising into three layers. Underpinning the whole marketing apparatus were the corporate images, reinforced and developed by corporate advertising, which often referred to diesel engines and Frigidaire refrigerators (GM), aircraft (Ford) and other products not directly related to automobiles. In the automotive sphere, marque advertising predominated, promoting the products of one marque by year. Announcement copy sometimes concentrated on a single, prestigious model, but the bulk of such advertisements promoted a whole marque range while illustrating and describing one or two models of special interest. Modern specialty advertising arrived in the 1950s with the 1953 Chevrolet Corvette, 1954 Kaiser-Darrin 161, and 1955 Ford Thunderbird, and it became an important component of every manufacturer's strategy when the new car market fragmented into size and specialty sectors in the 1960s. By 1965, as many advertisements were published for individual models as for a year's model range as a whole.

Styling was important at all levels. In 1952–53, Chrysler ran a series of corporate advertisements by N.W. Ayer & Son that concentrated on various features and design priorities that were common to all of the Corporation's products, from the lowliest Plymouth to the prestige Chrysler Imperial. Uniquely among the Big Three, Chrysler's corporate advertising of the early 1950s promoted style as a facet of functional engineering. In this case, the designs that resulted were conservative rather than radical in appearance, but the strategy, at odds with consumer preoccupations of the time, suggested that Chrysler had failed to understand the wider lessons of the Airflow's failure. It did not matter whether the product was radically streamlined or, as in this case, unusually conservative. Once again empirical functionalism, albeit with a different emphasis, was allowed to detract from the cars' public acceptability.

"What's the beauty secret of Chrysler-built cars?" asked one unassuming monochrome advertisement in 1952. "A car need not be four wheels, a body and an engine lumped into any shape that designers please. It can be a graceful mechanism, the form of which is chiefly determined by function." The essay continued:

> A plain example is the beautiful flowing lines of the roof on a Chrysler-built car. Chrysler engineers and designers consider the passengers' needs— the space for sitting, the depth of seats, the clearance between head and roof [a preoccupation of the Corporation's president, K.T. Keller]. All this is function. The graceful outer form then follows. This approach to design produces cars which are rightly proportioned, handsome, and eminently suited to your purposes.

Unfortunately for Chrysler sales, it was the new car buyer rather than its designer who decided what was "suitable" and what was not, and the recondite intellectual satisfaction of knowing that a form expressed its own underlying function could not compete with the immediate thrill of stylistic novelty.

A December, 1952 corporate advertisement showed three recent "dream cars." Of the three, the Phaeton, which prefigured 1955's "100-Million-Dollar Look," was arguably the most impressive, if the least exotic. More interesting were the K-310 coupe and C-200 convertible which had been designed by Virgil Exner at Chrysler and "handcrafted by Ghia of Turin, Italy" during 1951 and 1952.

The K-310 was intended to dispel Chrysler's growing reputation for uninspired design. Exposed, fender-mounted taillights and a simulated, decklid-mounted spare wheel cover were obvious references to earlier European practice, attractively reinterpreted. Both ideas appeared on later Chrysler products. The car's chrome wire wheels and fully cut-out rear wheel openings were echoed on the 1953 Buick Skylark and Packard Caribbean. The C-200 convertible, built in 1952, was based around a similar styling theme. It survived being dropped accidentally by New York dockers when it arrived from Italy, and was impressive in two-tone pale green and black, with a matching leather interior. According to the advertisement, "The handsome chrome-plated 17" wire wheels combine lively sports car styling with practical brake-cooling design."

By 1952, however, American car buyers did not respond well to such understatement, and the decision to portray the Corporation's glamorous trio of concept cars so modestly would not have been made by General Motors, whose advertisements featuring dream cars were colorful and dramatic. Chrysler's copy was almost willfully anti-climactic:

> These ... are "idea cars"— expressions in line and in form of the imagination always at work at Chrysler Corporation.... [T]hey reflect continuing Chrysler principles— that beauty, in an automobile, follows function, and that car designs can best be created by designers *and* engineers, working together.

The emphatic "*and*" hinted at past battles. Until 1955, Chrysler's copywriters had to make the most of outdated production designs. The 1949 New Yorker, for example, was billed as "The Beautiful Chrysler Silver Anniversary Model ... created with common sense and imagination in engineering." But even in advertisements, it was not easily distinguished from an artistically elongated Plymouth, especially as both were shown in the same dark blue. A year later, "beautiful new things were

BEAUTY AND FUNCTION. The Plymouth, like all Chrysler Corporation cars, is styled not by body designers alone, but by engineers, production men and designers working together. From the finely-appointed interior to gleaming finish, it is designed and engineered to give superlative transportation.

BEAUTY AND SPACE. Wide seats, and ample head room in this De Soto. Extra space inside, no extra bulk outside.

WHAT'S THE BEAUTY SECRET OF CHRYSLER-BUILT CARS?

A car need not be four wheels, a body and an engine lumped into any shape that designers please. It can be a graceful mechanism, the form of which is chiefly determined by function.

This is the practical principle that underlies the building of every Plymouth, Dodge, De Soto and Chrysler.

A plain example is the beautiful flowing lines of the roof on a Chrysler-built car. Chrysler engineers and designers consider the passengers' needs—the space for sitting, the depth of seats, the clearance between head and roof. All this is function. The graceful outer form then follows.

This approach to design produces cars which are rightly proportioned, handsome, and eminently suited to your purposes.

BEAUTY AND VISIBILITY. Note how much glass area this Chrysler has all around. Visibility blends with beauty, too.

CHRYSLER CORPORATION engineers and builds
PLYMOUTH, DODGE, DE SOTO, CHRYSLER CARS & DODGE TRUCKS
Chrysler Marine & Industrial Engines • Oilite Powdered Metal Products • Mopar Parts & Accessories
Airtemp Heating, Air Conditioning, Refrigeration • Cycleweld Cement Products

BEAUTY AND COMFORT. Seats in this Dodge, as in all Chrysler-built cars, are chair height. And the whole interior is harmoniously and fashionably designed.

Above and opposite: Sober, intellectual copy from N.W. Ayer & Son promoted Chrysler's corporate priorities in 1952-53. Several advertisements in this series appeared in the *Scientific American*, which did not normally carry automobile advertising in the early 1950s (September and December 1952).

2. Fantasy by Design

THE NEW PHAETON is a Chrysler-built custom automobile. Powering it is the Chrysler FirePower Engine. It has a wheelbase of 147½" and is distinguished by full-time Power Steering, Oriflow Shock Absorbers, Fluid-Torque Drive and other Chrysler engineering exclusives. Tonneau top is concealed.

STYLING THAT INFLUENCES YOUR CHRYSLER-BUILT CAR

From the dramatic cars on this page — each an example of creative styling and engineering — come advances that appear in every Chrysler Corporation car.

Chrysler designers and engineers developed the K-310, the C-200 and the new Chrysler Phaeton to express certain ideas of construction and styling—to put to the test of steel and fabric their newest, most promising automotive developments. A superior motor car evolves; it does not suddenly come into being: these graceful, pleasing designs, and the lessons learned perfecting them, are reflected in the creation of your Plymouth, Dodge, DeSoto or Chrysler.

These, therefore, are "idea cars" — expressions in line and in form of the imagination always at work at Chrysler Corporation. Exciting outside and inside, they reflect continuing Chrysler principles—that beauty, in an automobile, follows function, and that car designs can best be created by designers *and* engineers, working together.

CHRYSLER CORPORATION engineers and builds PLYMOUTH, DODGE, DE SOTO, CHRYSLER CARS & DODGE TRUCKS

Chrysler Marine & Industrial Engines • **Oilite** Metal Powder Products • **Mopar** Parts & Accessories
Airtemp Heating, Air Conditioning, Refrigeration • **Cycleweld** Cement Products

THE K-310, designed and engineered by Chrysler and handcrafted by Ghia of Turin, Italy. Only 59" high, with a wheelbase of 125½", it is designed to use the Chrysler FirePower V8 Engine and full-time Power Steering. This "idea car" represents an entirely new American theme in motor car functional styling.

The C-200, designed by Chrysler and handcrafted, like the K-310, by Ghia of Turin, Italy. It is powered by the Chrysler FirePower Engine and its brakes are the new, exclusive Chrysler self-energizing disc type. The handsome chrome-plated 17" wire wheels combine lively sports car styling with practical brake-cooling design.

The proportions, if not the styling details, of the 1949 Chrysler were old-fashioned even when the car was announced, and little apart from the rear fenders changed in 1950, although the artists did their best (June 1949 and March 1950).

done to these 1950 Chryslers," but the modified sedans did not have a "New Low Look," a "New Long Look," let alone a "New Lovely Look," whatever the copywriter, with help from an accommodating artist and lengthened rear fenders, tried to claim.

The Autocar found that the 1953 New Yorker had "clean, flowing lines and a smooth exterior contour," but in American terms it was dowdy, if well built. A 1954 Chrysler looked much the same. According to a tenacious copywriter, "The power and look of leadership" were "yours in a Beautiful Chrysler," yet the car lacked Cadillac's glamour and Lincoln's modern, square-lined style.

Suddenly, Chrysler woke up with a new style and colorful advertising in 1955. "Announcing America's most smartly different car" in December, 1954, Chrysler offered:

> The new 100-Million-Dollar Look.... Everything about this dazzling Chrysler is completely new and dramatically different. It brings you a totally *new* fashion in modern motor car design. The new Chrysler is inches lower in its sweeping silhouette ... washed free of clutter ... purposeful as an arrow shot from a bow.

One hundred million dollars was the new line's development cost and, this time, buyers were convinced. A July, 1955 advertisement noted, "As proof of this year's growing preference — *motorists are switching to Chrysler in record numbers!*" The year's sales figures, at over 150,000 compared with 1954's model year total of about 105,000, backed up this contention.

Chrysler's copywriters had tried hard in the early 1950s, but it was the dream-car look, rather than the functionalist ideal expressed in 1952's corporate advertising, that inspired buyers. 1956's "18 gleaming feet of power, eager to call you master" consolidated Chrysler's integration of futuristic styling and dynamic engineering into a car with which buyers could sustain their fantasies, and 1956's "year-ahead car" was followed in 1957 by a new interpretation of the "Forward Look."

This revived image was carried through into De Soto, Dodge, and Plymouth copy. The "Aerodynamic Plymouth '56" featured "tomorrow's styling today" while the following year's De Soto offered "New Flight Sweep styling!.... The new shape of motion — upswept tail fins, low lines...." One advertisement for the car capitalized on De Soto's new image as a fast, agile

250 HP Chrysler New Yorker Deluxe St. Regis in Navajo Orange and Desert Sand

ANNOUNCING America's most smartly different car

CHRYSLER FOR 1955
WITH THE NEW 100-MILLION-DOLLAR LOOK

Everything about this dazzling Chrysler is completely new and dramatically different. It brings you a totally *new* fashion in modern motor car design.

The new Chrysler is inches lower in its sweeping silhouette . . . washed free of clutter . . . purposeful as an arrow shot from a bow. Its sleek new 100-Million-Dollar Look will make you feel like a hundred million dollars the *instant* you step inside!

And in performance this magnificent new Chrysler stands above all others. *All Chryslers are now V-8 powered* with engines up to 250 HP . . . with Power-Flite, the only *fully-automatic* no-clutch drive that works without jerking or "time lag" . . . with the added safety of Power Brakes and the feather-light control of Chrysler *Full-time* coaxial Power Steering.

No other car on the road can offer you such an exciting sense of personal *power* and personal *pride.* Visit your Chrysler dealer today and see why now, more than ever before, *the power of leadership is yours in a Chrysler.*

Colorful advertising reflected a change in Chrysler's priorities for 1955, and sales improved (December 1954).

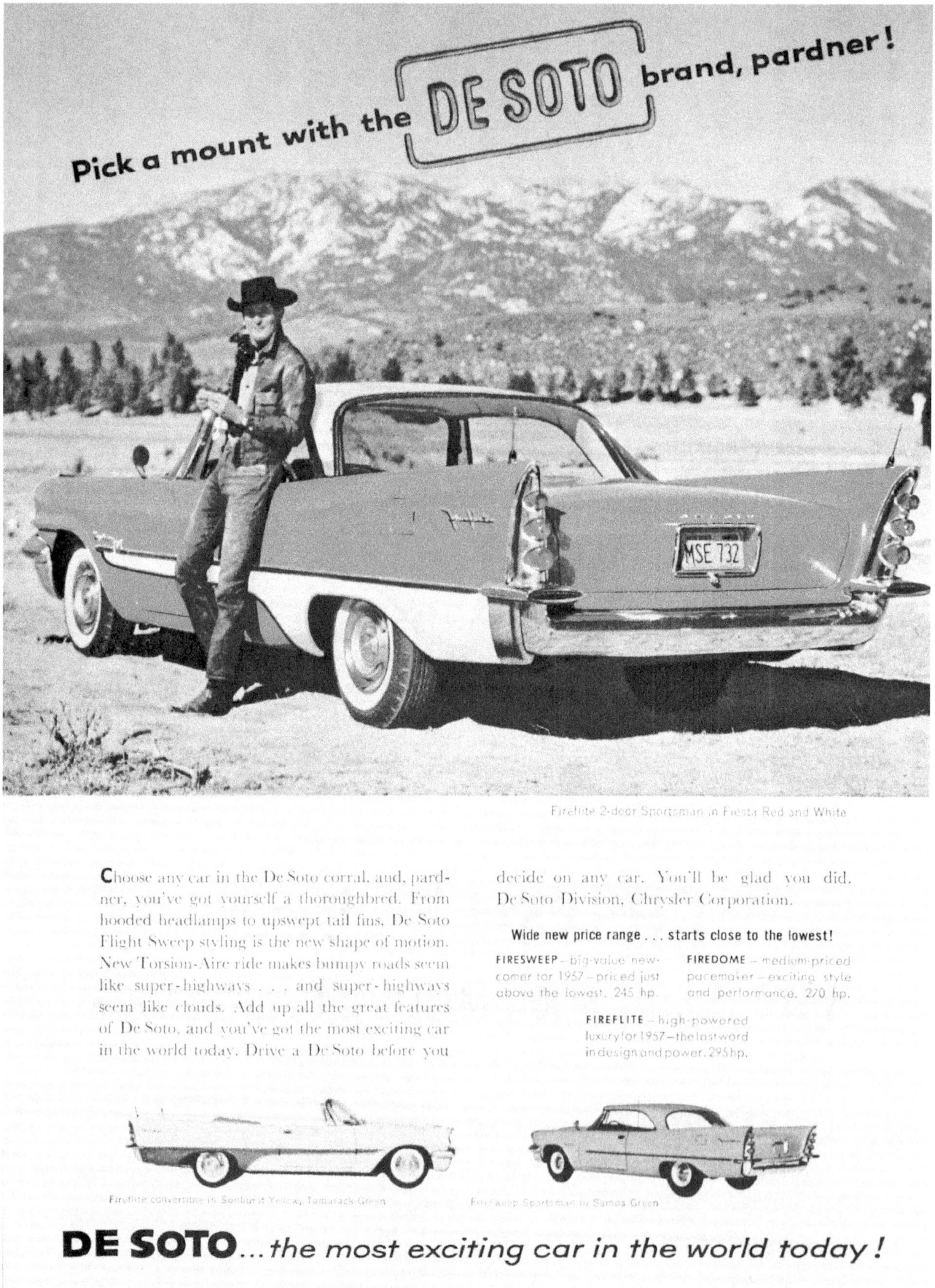

In 1957, the Chrysler Corporation took the stylistic lead, and De Soto had one of the best interpretations of the new idiom (May 1957).

car by suggesting that it was the modern equivalent of a good horse:

> Choose any car in the De Soto corral, and, pardner, you've got yourself a thoroughbred. From hooded headlamps to upswept tail fins, De Soto Flight Sweep styling is the new shape of motion.

"Suddenly, it's 1960," crowed Plymouth in its 1957 slogan, and even Chrysler's corporate copy became more exciting. One magazine spread explained "Why new 1959 cars of the Forward Look can do what they look like they can do." The excitement was explicitly given by "The Look that started the trend," rather than by function, and in gadgets, not headroom and the assurance, offered in 1952, that the driver could wear "his proudest hat without ducking." A remnant of the old functionalism remained in the claim of "true aerodynamic styling that helps keep the car steady on the road." But if the fins had any benign aerodynamic effect at all, no one imagined that this had actually influenced their design.

At General Motors, Harley Earl's approach was different. Production engineers had to accommodate stylists as early as the 1930s, often with difficulty. But GM realized the sales potential not only of attractive design, but also of inexpensive styling gimmicks appended to otherwise ordinary cars—the realization that accompanied Loewy's success at Studebaker and elsewhere. The 1936 Pontiac typified this technique. It was promoted in one advertisement as "The most beautiful thing on wheels and America's most distinctive car." The illustration, like the car, was unexciting, but the copy graphically defined not only a Pontiac, but GM's wider strategy for success:

> Count up the different makes of cars and you will find no less than thirty. But count up the number that are uniquely styled and you will find very few indeed. And of those few, only Pontiac's design is an entirely new departure. Pontiac alone is both different and new!... The Silver Streak is the answer — the reason why America calls Pontiac the natural choice of the fastidious few.

All for a few chromium strips on the radiator grille and hood. The theme lasted, along with a "Chief" hood ornament, until after World War II. The 1950 Pontiac was the "only car in the world with Silver Streak styling" as well as almost the only car in the world that was still promoted on the strength of a prewar styling gimmick. It gave rise to a postwar British imitator (the Austin A90 Atlantic) and the streaks continued to appear on Pontiac hoods as late as 1956, when, according to one advertisement for a pink and grey 860 series hardtop, "A glance at the fresh, new beauty of its twin-streak styling tells you *this* is easily the most distinctive car on the road."

But it was not distinctive by 1956, and a measure of real individuality would return only for 1959, with the advent of the "Wide-Track Wheels" which distinguished large Pontiacs throughout the 1960s.

During the 1950s, advertisers' language became far more elaborate and was often wildly optimistic. The independents, in particular, were frequently more creative on paper than in metal. Studebaker's near-hysterical copy for the 1958 Starlight was typical, as was Hudson's description of the 1952 version of its "Step-down" body, which had first appeared in 1948. "Year's most beautiful cars powered to out-perform them all!" began one advertisement, but stock car race wins could do little for an outmoded shape. "See Hudson-Aire Hardtop Styling ... in the fabulous Hudson Hornet and its new, lower-priced running-mate, the spectacular Hudson Wasp," it continued. The latter was described in full as the "Hudson Wasp two-door Brougham" but in reality it was a regular sedan with two-tone paint.

Desperation was evident in overstatement remarkable even for the period. "One glance tells you Hudson has the glamor" [sic] appealed dangerously to the reader's own observation, which told him otherwise. "Inspired new ... Hardtop styling—the newest look in motor cars" was all but

"One glance tells you..." that Hudson's Step-down style of 1948 was still alive and well in 1952 (1952 campaign).

mendacious, yet the copy went on to point out that the car had brought hardtop glamour to motorists at "standard sedan and coupe prices." No one was fooled; the illustration showed a Hornet in bright yellow with a brown roof, 1948's thick door and window pillars intact.

Chevrolet, "The Only Fine Car Priced So Low," was spared Hudson's traumatic decline. The 1952 Bel Air hardtop was modestly described as "Smarter looking ... smoother-running ... softer riding ...." and it, rather than Hudson, pointed the way forward. The 1953 version lacked the earlier car's elegance, however, even if it was a little more modern-looking than its predecessor. One painting of the almost identical 1954 Chevrolet made "The Brilliant New 'Two-Ten' 4-Door Sedan" look boxy and crude compared with earlier incarnations, and did not do its subject justice.

Chevrolet's advertising of 1953–54 emphasized power increases and value for money, but styling was mentioned from time to time. "Why Chevrolet's eye-catching good looks wear so well and last so long" sounded in 1953 like an earnest prelude to a long and tedious recitative on the advantages of modern paint finishes, but Chevrolet's priorities were different:

> Look at the smooth, gracefully rounded lines ... the clean, uncluttered design ... the slim and sweeping panel on the rear fender — an individual styling touch of the Chevrolet Bel Air models that you'll see on no other car.

In the face of competition from a Ford restyled in 1952, if not effectively from Plymouth, Chevrolet was clutching at stylistic straws, but respite would come, as for Chrysler, in 1955.

If 1953's Bel Air was distinguished by little more than a color-flash on each rear fender, the 1955 model was widely admired. One advertisement claimed that it was the "Blue-ribbon beauty that's stealing the thunder from the high-priced cars!" which, if wishful thinking, could never have been said about the 1954 model. The car's new grille, in particular, was unusual for its simplicity; inspired by a Ferrari, it was nevertheless replaced in 1956 after buyers expressed a preference for a more conventional, elaborate style. Ford countered in

Longer, lower, and wider: Harley Earl's priorities were vividly demonstrated by the change in Chevrolet's styling in 1955 (1953 campaign and May 1955).

1955 with "Thunderbird styling" which was visibly related, particularly on the Fairlane Sunliner convertible, to that of Ford's prestige roadster. Several Ford advertisements showed the two cars together, as in the *Saturday Evening Post* of July 16, 1955: "Rarin' to go.... There's a touch of Thunderbird in every Ford ... you can *see* it.... You can *feel* it! Not only does Ford look like the Thunderbird, it behaves like it, too, with Trigger-Torque performance!" Chevrolet, with a Corvette that bore no resemblance to the regular line, was unable to use any similar trick so convincingly.

In December 1956, Chevrolet could claim "Chevy goes 'em all one better for '57 with a daring new departure in design ... from its daring new grille and stylish lower bonnet to the saucy new slant of its High-Fashion rear fenders." In other words, fins and an integrated grille and bumper assembly had arrived, and, as a facelift of the 1955–56 body, it worked well. For 1958 there was "just something about Chevy's low, straining-at-the-bit beauty that makes people sit up and take notice." 1959's "fresh and fashionable" new styling included horizontal fins that looked especially dramatic on the otherwise unadorned Biscayne two-door sedan. Even GM's most popular marque suffered the occasional year of uninspired styling, but Chevrolet's advertising always managed to highlight at least one or two novelties every year.

Altogether more acute was the position of the independents, such as Frazer. Forced to rely on a body shape that had been around since the 1947 model year, Frazer could only offer a clever facelift in 1951. Promoted as a "new handcrafted" 1951 model, the revised design was not handcrafted in any sense, even if it looked new when viewed from the front or rear. But Kaiser-Frazer's copywriters were not as literal-minded as Chrysler's, and gave competing fantasists a run for their money:

> The Frazer ... expresses completely all that the word "custom" implies. It is without doubt the newest, most satisfying form of *individual* transportation for you who enjoy the luxury of the unusual....

The car sold better than expected, so that although 55,000 orders were taken, fewer than a fifth could be fulfilled by the time that the marque was discontinued before the end of the 1951 model year. New front and rear fenders and associated trim had rejuvenated 1947's shape, but Kaiser-Frazer lacked the resources to design the new body and engine which the marque would soon have needed, and developed the more promising, and fully restyled, 1951 Kaiser. The original shape had been a success by independents' standards, but it was not an effective competitor against the Big Three, whose stiff price competition rendered other marques comparatively more expensive than their own.

Individuality nevertheless thrived within the prevailing idiom. Frazer's expensive but widely publicized four-door convertible and Manhattan hardtop sedan anticipated later

Idiosyncratic artwork promoted the last of the Frazers, announced early for 1951. The craftsman's hands echoed a prewar British advertisement for the 136 cu. in. Ford V-8 "22" (May 1950).

trends. Throughout the 1950s, individual styling features sold cars. The 1948 Cadillac tail fin, inspired by the twin tail booms of a Lockheed P-38 Lightning aircraft, evolved gradually, reaching flamboyant proportions in the late 1950s before disappearing entirely for 1965.

Lincoln's development was more typical. 1952's design was modern, but conservatively styled and, if anything, slightly smaller than expected for a luxury car. The 1955 Capri was advertised as "stunning ... in sweep of line, dynamic use of color, tasteful use of chrome," all of which were highlighted by a close-up view of an embryonic tail fin, its blazing red rear light set in a chrome base, the whole surrounded by salmon-pink bodywork. The 1956 Lincoln Premiere sedan was even more impressive, with a "fresh clean sweep of steel" achieved by adding several inches of rear overhang. The essence of the "Lincoln Beauty" of the Premiere convertible was the "clean line ... the uncluttered sweep of its breathtaking length." Even the British gained a mild version of the car's

Above and opposite: The art of the facelift, as practiced by Lincoln. The 1957 style was inspired by the Futura dream car, subsequently better known as the Batmobile (April 1956 and March 1957).

Lincoln Premiere Two-Door Hardtop

There's just no end to the distinctive newness of this long, low, lovely Lincoln

First you see dramatic new beauty, from Quadra-Lite Grille to canted rear blades. Then, every mile you drive brings a new revelation of handling ease that's uniquely Lincoln's. The newness never ends, and that's why more and more fine car owners are changing to this finest Lincoln ever.

From the first moment you relax behind the wheel, you find how magnificently Lincoln's crisp, new styling fulfills itself —in action.

No other fine car is so effortless to drive. The most complete array of power luxuries in any car brings a new, easy mastery to every driving situation.

The new Turbo-Drive transmission puts this most powerful Lincoln of all time instantly and smoothly at your command . . . and Lincoln's exclusive new Hydro-Cushion suspension system relaxes you along your way as no other car can.

See all this exciting newness at your Lincoln dealer's—drive it where you will. Then and only then will you know why the trend among discerning fine car buyers is unmistakably to Lincoln.

LINCOLN DIVISION, FORD MOTOR COMPANY

LINCOLN

Unmistakably . . . the finest in the fine car field

rear styling in their new Ford Zodiac Mk II of 1956. In 1957, Lincoln could boast of "dramatic new styling everywhere ... from the unmistakable newness of Quadra-Lite grille to the sweep of canted rear blades...." As in Lincoln copy with "sweep," particular words and phrases often reappeared in successive advertisements for a given marque.

The 1957 Lincoln was not really the "totally new *concept* of styling" claimed in advertising, and it did not "shape fine car design for years to come" or even for 1958, but its paired head and fog lights were novel, and the "canted rear blades" were visibly inspired by the 1955 Lincoln Futura dream car which was later made into the Batmobile.

In the early 1960s, Lincoln was among those who could claim individuality beyond mere marque identity. The overall style of the 1961 Lincoln Continental was unusually clean and attractive: "Now America has a new kind of fine car" began a typical advertisement, "one that combines even greater luxury with 14 inches *less* length." It was imitated by Chrysler Corporation in 1964 with a new Imperial, and the imitation was carried out by Elwood Engel, who had designed the Lincoln original. The four-door Lincoln Continental convertible was a novel variant, and was vigorously promoted on its individuality: "Count the doors ..." began a typical 1962 advertisement, which compared the car with an ordinary, inconvenient two-door convertible: "Four doors mean you <u>walk</u> into the rear seat compartment of a Lincoln Continental convertible instead of climbing around the front seat."

Several advertisers who could not claim leadership or novelty within one of the regular size categories tentatively pursued a policy of anti-obsolescence in relation to particular models. The strategy often served as a warning of a make, marque, or model's imminent demise, and car buyers, mindful of projected resale values, usually took heed.

Ironically, it was Studebaker whose copy typified this approach in the early 1960s, and 1948's confident iconoclasm was thus transmuted into a flaccid defense of outmoded design. The 1953 Loewy coupes had come and gone, surviving, much-modified by Brooks Stevens, as the Gran Turismo Hawk; and the sporting Avanti (Loewy's final design for the company) was proving difficult to produce and could capture only a limited specialty market at best. Enter in 1963 the "Car of Quiet Substance — The Cruiser." It tried to be all things to all buyers:

> If you want a car built to the maker's highest standard of quality and appointments, yet at a price that fits the family budget, consider the Cruiser.... [Y]ou'll find it sensibly

The 1961 Lincoln Continental was a genuinely distinctive car, with styling that changed only in detail between 1961 and 1965 (March 1961).

sized, outside, with no overhang.... You'll like, too, its quiet beauty. Distinctive, dignified, smart.... reflecting the substance and good judgment of its owner.

By 1965, Studebaker had adopted a more radical — and desperate — stance:

> Save the Cost of Changing Automobile Body Styles Every Year.... Studebaker's beautiful modern style doesn't need yearly styling changes.... Because Studebaker styling won't become obsolete, your car will look new year after year.

Until it rusted, of course, as late Studebakers tended to. Neither car nor marque survived beyond 1966.

Imperial attempted a similar tactic in 1960, with snobbish overtones. "Styled for an era just beginning" was an unfortunate headline for a marque whose finned hardtop sedans had been designed in the style of an era just ended, but the copywriter's task, with Imperial as with Hudson, was to deflect the reader's attention from what was obvious:

> The *look* of an Imperial will very likely change from time to time ... but its *style* is purposefully timeless. Style, as any good fashion designer will tell you, is more than a matter of looks.

It was a pleasing inversion of Alfred Sloan's dress-maker analogy, and the copywriter elaborated the theme, attempting to disentangle himself from unconvincing sophistry by stressing build quality, which had the advantage of being measurable, more or less: "The things that give a fashion design its style are the magnificent detail of its cutting and construction...." Readers were not supposed to be reminded of magnificently constructed Airflow Custom Imperials. The approach was forced, its premise doubtful, and the car itself, with enormous fins and taillights that still harked back to the K-310 coupe of almost ten years earlier, was irredeemably out-of-date. Chrysler's forays into

Conceptually the modest 1963 Studebaker had much in common with the early postwar cars. The market, however, had changed (March 1963).

design philosophy had a habit of backfiring with embarrassing resonance, and more would follow in the late 1960s.

Lincoln was on firmer ground in 1965, with a style that had just been imitated, rather than deserted: "Lincoln Continental is the luxury motorcar that stands apart from all other cars.... It is unique in its classic look." And so it was —

Styled for an era just beginning

The *look* of an Imperial will very likely change from time to time . . . but its *style* is purposefully timeless.

Style, as any good fashion designer will tell you, is more than a matter of looks. The things that give a fashion design its style are the magnificent detail of its cutting and construction . . . the knowing how to make it drape well and fit and move and feel exciting to wear.

This is Imperial's style, too. The patient attention to the fit and action of a door . . . the slow hand-cutting and fitting of interior leathers . . . the persistence of inspectors who check the production of every car more than six hundred times before it's finished.

This is style that has nothing to do with time, model years, or even miles. It has everything to do with how this remarkable automobile drives and handles, and with the pride you can have in owning it.

Caught on the hop. Fins, chrome, and bulbous sides were on their way out by 1960, but Imperial was stuck with them for another year (April 1960).

Intended to recall the distinguished 1956 Continental Mark II, this 1968 model was less "decisively individual" than its forebear, although the faux-classical grille set a trend (October 1968).

Styling did not usually attract humorous copywriting unless the car was a Volkswagen, but in 1966 Chevrolet worked with a popular theme (May 1966).

Imperial's imitation of the previous year was only approximate, and it was heavier-looking. By 1968, the elegant Lincoln Continental Mark III, so-called in pointed disregard of the unsuccessful and confusingly designated Continental Mark III of 1958 and Lincoln Continentals Mark IV and Mark V of 1959–60, could be described in a single copy line, with some credibility, as "The most authoritatively styled, decisively individual motorcar of this generation."

The most convincing domestic case for rejecting the values of dynamic obsolescence was made by Chevrolet in 1971, for a new subcompact that was overtly functionalist in conception from the outset. It was billed, echoing Volkswagen, as "Chevy's new little car: if you like the 1971, you'll like the 1975." The advertisement was long and explanatory and featured a humorous drawing of a kind seen in muscle-car advertising aimed at younger drivers during 1968–70. The Vega survived by specifically targeting a market that did not set great store by "dignity" and "substance" or even style, provided that the car was not gratuitously odd. It was a market which Chevrolet wanted to claw back from the importers, both European and Japanese, who were gaining ground. But in 1971, only a small (if rapidly growing) proportion of the car-buying public subscribed to Vega values. The Caprice was still available, large as life, for those who wanted (or, with large families, needed) a car that, in the words of a 1971 headline, "looks and rides like twice the price."

For genuine non-conformists there remained the Checker Marathon, best known as a Yellow Cab but also available in civilian trim. In *The Waste Makers* (1960), Vance Packard praised the Model A Ford and France's Citroën 2CV for their designed-in durability, and added:

> One of the happiest motorcar owners I know is a sales representative who must often travel fifty thousand miles a year and has long felt bedeviled by the high maintenance cost of his cars.... Every time he went to New York, he made a point of riding in Checker cabs and pumped the drivers on performance. He relates, "They always gave it high praise for durability, and seemed unanimous that it goes one hundred thousand miles without a valve or ring job."... Several months ago this man bought a Checker Superba and has become very fond of it.[29]

A 1963 advertisement set Checker's agenda, prefiguring the Vega's theme: "This is our 1963 model; it looks like our

Anti-obsolescence writ large: The 1958-style Checker Marathon survived for a generation, chiefly as the "Yellow Cab" (1963 campaign).

1962. Most Checker owners plan to keep their cars 5 years or longer and appreciate our policy of making improvements without obsoleting the car."

Even the most resourceful of copywriters found that those who lived by the annual model change could also die by it; perhaps they also believed, like the majority of those for whom a car was more than mere transportation, that those who lived with a Checker Marathon for five years had never lived at all.

Chapter 3

"There's Added Joy in Added Cylinders"

America's automotive fantasy was fueled not only by dramatic styling, but also by equally dramatic power. In the 1930s, power was intrinsically exciting and attractive for the effortless driving it allowed. By 1940, most American cars offered the 80–100bhp needed to make motoring adequately painless and rapid. By 1946, dynamic fantasy, structured around styling and performance, began to take over from the escapism and pastoral idylls which had been popular during 1939–42.

In 1938, Lincoln's copywriters allied the excitement and utility of the Zephyr's V-12 engine with that essential ingredient, status. A simple photograph of a Zephyr sedan was shown against a neutral backdrop; the copy elaborated: "There's added joy in added cylinders.... People who have never driven a twelve-cylinder car may think of it, primarily, as capable of high speed. The Lincoln-Zephyr is that, most certainly, but the joy of driving it comes in many other ways. Always it has power in reserve. In traffic, or on the open road, it goes gently."

The Zephyr was the only V-12 in the middle price field and was exciting enough for that reason, as well as for its conspicuously modern styling. The buyer was carefully persuaded that his choice was not only agreeable, but rational: "New owners discover that familiar trips are made more quickly — but, that they drive less fast than before. Having picked up an even pace, they maintain it, without pressure, without fatigue."

By playing down the obvious attractions of a stylish and powerful automobile, Lincoln's strategy anticipated Chrysler's understated copy of the early 1950s, but, unlike Chrysler's, Lincoln copy was appropriate for the automotive climate of its time. American copy for the Zephyr was written almost in the language of the independent, if favorable, road tester, and it contrasted amusingly with the sometimes effusive praise of actual independent testers who were used to less powerful cars. In England, *The Autocar* considered the Lincoln-Zephyr's performance "... terrific ... [T]here is so much power, even in top gear, that it is necessary to apply it with some care on a wet surface if sliding is to be avoided."

The magazine recorded a top speed of nearly 90mph and a 0–60 acceleration time of sixteen seconds, which was adequately fast for Americans and more than enough for most Britons. A number of Zephyrs were bought by British motorists, and the importers produced a brochure, *Testimony to a Fine Car*, in which owners' letters were printed, praising various aspects of the new model. Unusually for the period, British copy for the Zephyr was much more fanciful than the American equivalent. An elegant color advertisement of May 1937 showed a light grey car at a quayside, and was euphoric in a style that mimicked middle-class manners:

> [C]osting so little [£480], either to buy or run, it appeals to anybody and everybody able to appreciate the super-performance of a really fine motor car, built like a presentation watch, lively as an antelope in the getaway, and *Oh*, so unbelievably smooth and sweet when, occasionally, you put your foot down, and let it revel in its inexhaustible stream of power, translated into speed without apprehension — because it is always and ever under complete control....

American advertising copy, particularly that deployed for middle and upper market automobiles, did not always quote figures. "Once you drive a Hudson, nothing else will do" was a copy line typical of its period (1939) and marque. New owners of the sleek and bulbous Hudson Six Touring Sedan were reported to be "amazed at the superior smoothness of Hudson's eager power." They were not mentioned by name, and it was not clear whether they were established devotees or trading up from other marques.

In much pre-war copy, promises of speed were implied in discussion of effortless power, comfort, and easy manipulation of controls. In December, 1937, Buick anticipated postwar copy styles in advertising for its 1938 models which made much of a special piston design that swirled the fuel mixture as it entered each cylinder:

> It's literal fact that you ride the whirlwind when your foot is on the treadle that bosses the new Buick DYNAFLASH engine.... It is not mere high-compression — it's *cyclompression*.

The copy exemplified the increasingly prevalent use of the word "literal" to add weight to hyperbolic jargon, which was a subtle portent of verbal hysteria to come. In 1939, Buick combined the "satin-smooth power of its almighty Dynaflash straight-eight engine" with the "level-flying comfort of its BuiCoil Springing."

In the middle price field, horsepower figures sometimes infiltrated the euphoria. "You'll find in Olds' 90 H.P. Econo-Master Engine power for top-flight pep and pace...." said Oldsmobile about its low-priced 60 sedan, seen as a two-door ($838) in light town traffic. But the marque was not beyond mild lyricism, as another advertisement in the same 1939 series demonstrated, in copy beneath a four-door sedan on the highway:

> Step into an Olds Sixty and step out for a wonderful drive! The way its 90 H.P. Econo-Master Engine whisks you away from stop lights, whizzes up the steepest hills and hums down the straightaway will make you mighty proud of its performance.

Performance in its widest sense was stressed in advertising for the Lincoln-Zephyr which, despite its twelve cylinders, was not unusually fast (March 1938).

Gear-changing was a perennial preoccupation, and the steering-column gearshift was almost universal as a standard fitting or option by 1939. Hudson promised "Easier shifting with new mechanical Handy Shift at the steering wheel" to complement its "eager power." Oldsmobile also offered a "Handi-Shift Gear Control" which, like Hudson's, was simply a column-mounted lever. Plymouth's version of the device was billed as "Perfected Remote Control Shifting with new All-Silent Auto-Mesh Transmission," in what was probably the year's most indigestible copy line devoted to the theme. Nash promised that "never, in all your car-owning experience, have you felt such performance!" while inviting car buyers to pay a "slight extra charge" in order to "Marvel at gear-shifting from your wheel."

Not all performance-oriented copy was inspired. Plymouth was frequently pedantic in advertisements and catalogs, as in 1939: "*Every* Plymouth model has the same, big, 82–horsepower 'L-Head' engine — giving full power...." No one ever accused Plymouth of hyperbole. Following Lincoln-Zephyr's success in the middle-class market, Ford introduced the Mercury marque in October, 1938 for the 1939 model year, to compete with Oldsmobile, Pontiac, and Dodge in the lower-middle price field. Less pedantically than Plymouth, Mercury offered a "brilliant, economical new 95-horsepower V-type

In 1939, Hudson capitalized on a reputation for performance established in the early years of the decade (1939 campaign).

Buick anticipated the hyperbole and fanciful copy of later years in 1938 (December 1937).

8-cylinder engine" in a typical advertisement showing a black Eight convertible.

American cars were popular in Britain during the late 1920s and 1930s, particularly with high-mileage business users who valued them for their durability, speed, and silence when compared with much of the domestic opposition. British importers consistently stressed the performance-per-pound-sterling-cost of their products in advertising. Hudson, in particular (with Essex, Terraplane, and Railton derivatives), was notably successful in the 1930s, as was Chrysler, which operated assembly plants at Kew, west of London in England, and at Antwerp in Belgium.

In 1925, Chrysler's English agent approached the well-known advertising agency, W.S. Crawford Ltd. of High Holborn in London, to devise and handle its British publicity campaign, and the resulting copy became famous, establishing Chrysler's reputation in Britain, and, by extension, promoting the cause of the American car in general. The principal elements of an innovative campaign were recalled in detail by the agency's artist, Ashley Havinden, in 1969:

In early 1925 the English agent for Chrysler cars decided to come to Crawfords for his advertising.... We all had trial runs in the Chrysler. We were astonished at its terrific acceleration and flexibility in top gear. These were entirely new qualities in American cars which had hitherto the reputation in England of being big, cumbersome and rather sluggish.... We decided to put the whole emphasis on *speed and performance* and to create advertisements which expressed this as dramatically as possible. We proposed to use bold headlines ... set at angles to the horizontal.... Our aim was to produce a new kind of dynamic effect which, with the major elements in the advertisement placed *at angles*, would *stand out* in the press by reason of bold "contrast in weight" (i.e. degree of blackness) and, especially, by contrast to the normal appearance of the vertical columns, with horizontal text and headlines, in the rest of the pages, whether in newspapers or magazines.... There can be no question ... that at the time this new, bold and asymmetric approach to the designing of motor-car advertisements (echoing the original *Bauhaus* "Moholy-Nagy" influence of 1923) was a landmark in British advertising.... [T]he basic aim of the advertising was not so much to "sell" the appearance of the car, as to "sell" its performance.[30]

In 1927, Havinden brought the American-born poster and advertising designer Edward McKnight Kauffer to the agency, and Kauffer's work for Chrysler between 1927 and 1929 included publicity material which was remarkably sophisticated for its time. In a 1928 brochure, for example:

> A bronze-coloured ink was used for the cover, with lettering in terracotta and a symbol in dark blue. Each page opening [was] a variation of squares and circles printed in aluminium and royal blue, with text and diagrams in chocolate brown. The trick of using positive and negative lettering, which Kauffer first tried out in 1925 [in the symbol of the Film Society in London, of which Kauffer was a co-founder and which was a "principal channel through which England became aware of modern experimental film"], became a favourite device. This habit of reversing lettering into light and dark as a word "crosses over" broad rectangles of colour was a hallmark of Russian experimental graphics in the early twenties....[31]

Thus was born the Bauhaus-pastiche typography that remained popular among upmarket automobile advertisers in Europe and America for several years, and of which Chrysler, at home and abroad, were particularly avid exponents. The campaign also established the ground on which British promoters of American cars advertised their products until the outbreak of war in Europe in 1939. Performance remained the dominant motif long after what Havinden's detractors called the "set it crooked" school of advertising design, in both Bauhaus-pastiche and later dynamic impressionist phases, had run its natural course.

Claims of performance, particularly in British advertising for American automobiles, were often accompanied by an insistent drone of specifications and prices that diluted the impact of otherwise powerful copy which, if written in a style familiar to British readers, was more ponderous than the American equivalent.

But there were beacons of inspiration within a generally uninspired genre. Chevrolet deployed a distinctive slogan in 1935: "Speed-boat acceleration — and silence unbelievable," which, combined with highly stylized renderings of the car that would have been too pretentious for its home market, made for arresting copy.

Studebaker quoted an unusually eloquent testimonial in

What a difference a decade makes! Static photographs and tableaux were commonplace in British advertising for American cars in the 1920s. By the late 1930s, however, new models offered good performance at modest cost, and were advertised accordingly (December 1927 and March 1938).

April, 1935. Written by a satisfied owner, it was also a succinct expression of copywriters' priorities:

> Never in the course of my 250,000 miles of motoring have I experienced so unexpected a thrill as when I took the wheel of the latest 8-cyl Studebaker saloon. I had been looking for a car which would be suitable for a Continental tour ... a car in which one might maintain high speeds with comfort and without fatigue, whatever the road surfaces might be. I had tried out almost every suitable car under £800 and over £500, when it occurred to me that I might at least try the Studebaker in spite of what one might fear from its comparatively low price. I had not driven more than a few yards before I was surprised, nor a few miles before I was amazed at its performance. For acceleration, for road-holding and even for high speed, I had met nothing to better it.... [O]nce on the open road, there is the over-top gear brought into action merely by momentary deceleration. At once the engine seems to disappear; one seems to be coasting, yet still the car has remarkable hill-climbing and accelerating ability. One could hardly wish for a better car.

Nor could Studebaker's London distributors have wished for a better testimonial, whose theme was continued in a lavish six-page advertisement placed in *The Autocar* in March, 1936:

> The success of the new Studebakers is remarkable ... yet not at all surprising when you consider what these magnificent cars offer. Automatic Overdrive plus 50 other brilliant new features! Overdrive alone will bring new thrills to your motoring. Just imagine driving at, say, 45mph and then finding that the speed can be increased at the same time as the engine revolutions are decreased.... Individually the points are important; together they make this Studebaker a car of cars ... almost a phenomenon.[32]

After World War II, Britons could not usually buy new American cars because imports were restricted. In 1954, for example, only 211 cars were officially imported from the United States alongside 21 from Canada, with a combined 671 following in 1955.[33] When American cars did become more readily available they were much more expensive, compared with the native product, than their pre-war counterparts. But in their domestic market American manufacturers increasingly paced each other, marque for marque. Copywriters promised ever greater horsepower, and Buick set the pace in December, 1945:

> Yes, its Engine is still out Front.... Certainly, it is no surprise to old-time Buick followers that the long, reaching bonnet of this car houses a power plant that is still out in front in its field.... Put foot to treadle, and in the leaping response of weight-thrifty Fliteweight pistons you find still more lift and life than in the last Buicks to come your way.

The unusual use of "bonnet" for the car's hood suggested an appeal to servicemen returning from Europe who had spent time under the "bonnets" of local military and civilian vehicles, and the headline amusingly reassured those who

Numerous aids to gear-changing were created and advertised before Hydra-Matic arrived as an option on 1940 Oldsmobiles. This reliable but rarely-specified four-speed predecessor of mid–1937 to 1939 required a clutch pedal only for starting and stopping (and engaging reverse). If started with the lever in "L" (low), it shifted to second automatically. Then, after the lever was moved clutchlessly to "H" (high), it shifted immediately to third and, as necessary, to fourth. Started in "H," it ran through first and third to fourth, omitting second. Flooring the accelerator in fourth reengaged third for maximum acceleration. Would explaining all this in magazine advertising have increased its sales, or was the $100 it cost in 1938 just too much? (1938 campaign).

The postwar horsepower race began for Buick in late 1945, and received a boost with the adoption of a modern V-8 in 1953 (December 1945 and September 1953).

had heard all about the Wolfsburg Volkswagen plant, which at the end of 1945 was still a marginal operation, under British control.

By 1953, "treadles" had vanished from copy, and the competition had finally forced Buick to jettison its old straight-eight. "Make way for power with a new thrill!" began one advertisement for the Roadmaster convertible. "The world's newest and most advanced V8" was not unusually advanced by international standards, but it was well engineered and powerful, offering 188bhp compared to 1946's 144bhp, and it was combined with "Twin Turbine Dynaflow" transmission to give it a competitive edge against Lincoln's new-for-1952 "overhead valve, high compression V-8 engine." This was "monitored by the smooth magic of dual-range Hydra-Matic Transmission" bought, in the absence of a Ford-built alternative, from General Motors until Ford's own "Turbo-Drive ... one unbroken sweep of smooth, silent power through every speed range," could take over in 1955.

In its home market in the early 1950s, Hydra-Matic led a varied life, appearing in Frazer advertising in 1951 ("Hydra-Matic drive optional at extra cost") and on some Hudsons to replace a semi-automatic Drive-Master (or, with overdrive, Super-Matic) in the same year. It became available on various Nashes during 1950–53. Given Hydra-Matic's origins, it was not surprising that General Motors gave it far more prominence in advertising than did its other users, none of whom volunteered to humiliate themselves by declaring that, in order to remain competitive, they needed to buy transmissions from the competition.[34]

Oldsmobile, which had pioneered the use of fully automatic gears by offering Hydra-Matic from the 1940 model year, had no such reservations, and integrated it enthusiastically into its advertising. Several 1940 and 1941 advertisements were devoted to it. According to one piece, Hydra-Matic made the 1940 Oldsmobile "the most modern car in the world." An advertisement for the 1941 models, while concentrating on low prices and economy, nevertheless devoted a block of copy to Hydra-Matic, inviting the reader to "learn for yourself how it simplifies driving — steps up performance — saves on gasoline...." A very different piece showed a letter written by "Sue" to her husband on the headed notepaper of "The Greenbrier" in West Virginia:

> Hello darling: Here I am, bags unpacked and still two hours till dinner. Now don't be worried, dear — I wasn't driving fast! It's simply that an Olds Hydra-Matic cuts down driving time. No clutch to press and no gears to shift saves delays in going through cities. And the special pick-up gear makes it easy and safe to gain time on mountain roads.... It's the greatest thing that ever happened to make driving safe and easy for a woman.

Sue's husband must have wondered whether his wife might be collaborating rather too closely with an Oldsmobile dealer. The theme would be revived with a lighter touch in the early 1960s when General Motors' British subsidiary, Vauxhall, offered Hydra-Matic on its six-cylinder models.

Hydra-Matic was integrated enthusiastically into Oldsmobile's postwar "Rocket" theme. "Make a Date with a 'Rocket 8'" was a typical headline, used with a bright green "88" convertible in a characteristically exuberant advertisement in 1950. "Oh, the go-ing's great in the '88,' It's a dri-ver's dream come true!" trilled another headline, with the first bar of the jingle's musical score appearing in faint grey above a bright red sedan, as an excited young couple shot into the stratosphere astride a silver-grey rocket. With "Thrilling 'Rocket' Engine action! Smart Futuramic styling! Ultra-smooth Hydra-Matic Drive*!" (starred as being "at reduced prices, now optional on all models"), the car with the "Rocket 8" was promoted as the "most talked about car in America" which, if probably untrue, was a reflection of Oldsmobile's confidence in a reputation for power and roadability which flowed from offering 135bhp in relatively light bodywork.

Copy for the larger "98" sedan continued the theme: "*Discover* the dramatic new experience of 'Rocket' Engine teamwork with Whirlaway Hydra-Matic ... soon. *Drive* the 'Rocket' and Whirlaway — in a new Futuramic OLDSMOBILE." In 1951, a "great new Oldsmobile!... a *magnificent* new Oldsmobile" was "launched at Oldsmobile dealers' showrooms everywhere!" In a strange combination of the nautical and the aeronautical, car buyers were invited to "Meet the new flagship of the 'Rocket' fleet — Oldsmobile '98' for 1951!" Copy for the parallel "Super '88'" was similar; a bright yellow sedan was shown against a deep blue background as a rocket, trailing fire and vapor, sped overhead.

By 1951, rockets and space travel had become a national fascination. In 1952, Wernher von Braun, one of wartime Germany's leaders in the field, now working for the American rocket research program, wrote:

> Within the next 10 or 15 years, the earth can have a new companion in the skies, a man-made satellite which will be man's first foothold in space. Inhabited by human beings, it will sweep round the earth at an incredible rate ... completing a trip round the globe every 2 hours [at] ... 15,840 miles per hour....[35]

With such predictions from experts in space technology, coupled with optimistic articles in magazines such as *Scientific American*, American scientists, and the public who followed their experiments, were optimistic, too. Oldsmobile's copywriters, with consumers' eager collusion, luxuriated in quasi-phallic rocket-oriented imagery for over a decade.

The horsepower race soon acquired its own momentum. "The surging might of Miracle H-Power" offered on the 1952 Hudson Hornet, with a name that reminded readers of the recently invented hydrogen bomb, was no longer enough.

Chrysler, with an established reputation for

Oldsmobile summed up the priorities of an era in its 1950 campaign, and the theme was carried through the decade (July 1950).

excellent engineering, was in the technical lead by 1953. 1949's copy had been uninspired, offering "smoother, faster acceleration from our high compression Spitfire engine," together with the "greatest driving advance of all — Prestomatic Fluid Drive Transmission," the latter a development within a family of transmissions with fluid couplings which had become progressively available on Chryslers, Dodges, and De Sotos during 1939–41. It was almost immediately rendered old-fashioned by the introduction of GM's Hydra-Matic. But Chrysler's 135bhp, which had been adequate, if not startling, in 1949–50, grew to 180bhp in 1951's "hemi" V-8.

By 1954, the exclamation marks were out in force: "It's Number One for sheer driving leadership! Giving you new wonders in power and control ... is America's highest-rated drive power: 235HP FirePower V-8 engine. Proved *Number One* in official performance tests from Indianapolis to Daytona Beach!" A modern automatic had arrived in mid–1953, in the form of PowerFlite, "the most modern no-clutch drive of all." The name was familiar to Nash buyers as an engine type (spelled "Powerflyte" after Nash's "Airflyte" bodies) but, as the two marques were not in effective competition by 1954, no litigation resulted.

PowerFlite and 235bhp were not enough to halt the decline in Chrysler's sales, which finally improved in 1955 when even more power was combined with new styling to give "*Extra* performance for style-conscious motorists!" as one headline put it. "Up to 250 hp" was offered in regular models, and 300bhp could be had in the Chrysler C-300, which looked like a regular Chrysler Windsor with an Imperial grille. In late 1955, the "new Power-Style Chrysler" was announced for 1956 with "Pushbutton PowerFlite — world's most automatic transmission. Operated by pushbutton on dashboard."

In 1954, Chrysler's main advantage was power rather than styling (August 1954).

The Automobile Manufacturers' Association agreed to de-emphasize performance in advertising from 1958 and, although 1959's "Lion-Hearted Chrysler" was available with engines ranging from 305 to 380bhp, pre-war vagueness returned, with assurances of "the economy of Golden Lion engines" together with a modest encouragement to "Go for the open road."

Performance featured prominently in advertising for other Chrysler Corporation marques in the mid–1950s. In 1953, De Soto offered "the mighty 160 h.p. Fire Dome V-8" which was called, disingenuously, "The world's most powerful, most *efficient* engine design" even though it was not the most powerful of engines in this Fire Dome form. By adding the word "design" to the copy, De Soto stopped just short of mendacity, and "efficient" could, of course, mean different things in different usages. This copywriting tactic was not confined to De Soto.

In 1957, horsepower-based advertising reached its apogee, and De Soto's campaign was imaginative. "This baby can flick its tail at anything on the road!" cried an early 1957 headline, above a wide-angle photograph of the 1957 De Soto's tail fin in "seatone blue and white." The "baby" was available with "up to 295 hp." In 1958, the emphasis changed, and a new

A classic of its kind, this well-known advertisement from De Soto marked the high point of copywriters' performance race of the late 1950s, which was toned down in 1958 (March 1957).

"Turboflash V8" engine, more powerful than 1957's, was nevertheless billed as "smoother, quieter" to give "all the power you need for safe, effortless driving." This was worthy, but it made for dull copy.

Lincoln's advertising followed a similar pattern. "Performance proof" was offered in 1955: "For the *third year in a row* Lincolns swept the first two places in the large stock car division of the grueling Mexican Pan-American road race." The advertisement did not mention who was in the other divisions, let alone any overall results.

In the low-price field, Chevrolet boasted a year later that: "This is the car, you know, that broke the Pikes Peak record. The car that proved its fired-up performance, cat-sure cornering ability and nailed-down stability on the rugged, twisting Pikes Peak road."

Other Chevrolet advertisements for 1956 showed a speeding sedan being led by a police escort ("Of course, you don't have to have an urgent errand and a motorcycle escort to make use of Chevrolet's quick and nimble ways"), and as the favorite choice of firemen, although it was not stated how many fire services actually used Two-Ten four-door sedans with flashing red lamps like the one shown in the illustration. "Horsepower that ranges clear up to 225 explodes into action to zoom you out ahead with extra seconds of safety" said the copy, perhaps with an eye on Ford's aggressive safety campaign of that year, although "this tigerish power" was also "as tame to your touch as a purring kitten." "The Hot One's Even Hotter" said the slogan, unambiguously.

Such copy marked a decisive turnaround from the "famous valve-in-head engine centered, poised and cushioned in rubber by new high-side mountings" of 1952. What was popularly known as the "stovebolt six" had continued through 1953 ("The mighty 115–h.p. 'Blue-Flame' engine teamed with Powerglide automatic transmission") and 1954 ("the 'Blue-Flame 125' in Powerglide models and the 'Blue-Flame 115' in gearshift models"), eventually to give way in 1955's advertising to a 162bhp "new 'Turbo-Fire V8'... strictly in charge when the light flashes green" with an 8:1 compression ratio. A "Special to adventure lovers: 180 h.p. '*Super* Turbo-Fire V8'" was an option, and Blue-Flame sixes of 136bhp with Powerglide and 123bhp without were mentioned regularly, if at times just in passing. In 1956, Chevrolet's performance image had only just been established, and copywriters fought hard against Ford's V-8 tradition (updated, ahead of Chevrolet, with a new overhead-valve "130–h.p. Y-block V-8" in 1954) and a rejuvenated "Aerodynamic Plymouth '56" with new fins, described as "the jet-age Plymouth" with "sensational higher-horsepower Hy-Fire V-8 and PowerFlow 6 engines ... [giving] 90–90 Turbo-Torque getaway for Top Thrust at Take-Off...."

Chevrolet returned for 1957 with a colorful series of advertisements which showed the car overtaking coaches, climbing hills, and speeding along highways: "Lively performance is part and parcel of Chevy's light touch personality. That's why V8 options go all the way up to 245 h.p.*" The starred small print added: "270–h.p. high-performance V8 engine also available at extra cost. Also Ramjet fuel injection with engines up to 283–h.p."

The last feature, in particular, was a first in the low-price field and unusual by any standard. Combined with a number of favorable NASCAR and Daytona Speed Week placings, it helped Chevrolet to gain a reputation as the best-performing low-priced car of the year. Chevrolet's 1957 copy also emphasized the nimble handling and roadability which came from a car that was smaller than rival Plymouths and Fords. For Chevrolet in 1957, handling was as much to do with roadholding and quick maneuvering than with the "easy handling" more often referred to by American copywriters, which was concerned as much with the effort needed to move a car's controls as with any idea of agility and responsiveness in the European sense.

Chevrolet's 1957 advertising was a long way removed from the rural panoramas of 1952. Is the broken down hot rod a Ford? (June 1957).

During 1959–60, Ford promised sporty escapism in a lavish series of double-page spreads for the Thunderbird (June 1960).

By 1960, the themes of performance and comfort were regularly combined, as they had been in 1939. This was true even of copy for sporty cars like the Ford Thunderbird, which had become a four-seater "personal car" in 1958. A 1960 advertisement was typical:

> A Thunderbird is action ... sweet, swift, spirited action — an adventure in flowing, controlled motion.... Power and performance are two solid reasons [al]most everyone longs to own a Thunderbird.... Turn the ignition ... listen to the husky, soft-and-easy hum of its barrel-chested engine. This is the sound of the Thunderbird — 300 horses, 350 horses, take your pick.

The excitement and semantic inventiveness of the 1950s were receding, and were replaced by low-key, if escapist, assurances of potency. The 1960 Thunderbird was photographed beside a steeple-chase course, with a horse flying over a fence and past the car. There was no explicit rocket imagery, except in the Thunderbird's spear-shaped door panel moldings, and in jet-exhaust taillights which, in most advertising illustrations, were hidden from view.

For 1961, the personal-car character of the Thunderbird was brought out more strongly, and the "new high-performance Thunderbird 390 Special V-8" engine was modestly promoted as one element in a "precision team for a new high in automatic driving." Other contributions to the "new high" were a "Swing-Away Steering Wheel ... Power Brakes ... Power Steering" (the last two to be expected by 1961, even on lowlier Fords, if only as options) and "Cruise-O-Matic Drive" transmission. By 1961, however, elaborate names and capital letters for conventional power features were becoming old-fashioned, and they soon disappeared for good.

After several years promoting comfort and gadgets, advertisers began to return to performance in the early 1960s, and did not confine themselves to copy for large cars. Chevrolet promoted 1959's compact débutante for 1960, the air-cooled, rear-engined Corvair as "The Sporty Car in Chevrolet's New World of Worth" in 1962. Even if the Corvair was not a high-performance automobile by absolute standards, it was more exciting than a regular Ford Falcon.

Ford counter-attacked with the Falcon Futura, and enjoyed the advantage over Chevrolet that engines from larger Fords could be "shoe-horned" into Falcons, whereas the air-

Left and above: A new phase in performance-based advertising began in 1963 and continued with the Mustang in 1964 (March 1963 and May 1964).

cooled Corvair, a mechanical law unto itself, could not be fitted with conventional GM V-8 engines. The air-cooled motor was nevertheless developed enthusiastically, and the Corvair became quite potent, particularly in Monza coupe form. Before long, the horsepower race had resumed in more than one size category as performance options began to fill pages of print in dealers' catalogs. Power outputs of between 300 and 400 bhp were commonplace in full-size cars by 1966.

Ford enjoyed competition success with its full-size Galaxies, and in 1963 advertised a "Report from Monaco" presenting "the Liveliest of the Lively Ones— new Command Performance Cars for 1963½." Big-engined Fairlanes, Falcons, and a full-size "Super Torque Ford Sports Hardtop," with a "fastback" roofline less formal and more aerodynamic than that of the regular hardtop, typified Ford's new approach to the performance car market, identified and targeted as such with a range of models. In April, 1964, the Mustang was introduced in hardtop and convertible forms and advertised heavily. Some versions, with unexciting six-cylinder engines, were little more than sporty-looking Falcon-based shopping cars, but those who wanted to "try Total Performance for a change!" could "add the big 289-cu. in. V-8 engine (the same basic V-8 that powers the famous Cobra!) ... [plus] 4-speed stick shift (synchro on all forward speeds) and Rally Pac (tachometer and clock)" to make the Mustang a genuinely sporting car. Younger enthusiasts were invited to send $1.00 to the makers for an "exciting, authentic scale model" of the new car.

In Britain, Lincoln Cars Ltd., who were established American Ford dealers in Brentford, Middlesex, offered in May, 1966 to "build up your own custombuilt Mustang from a host of options," while also advertising the "Galaxie 500 convertible, built for total performance — proved in competition."[36]

General Motors offered a number of sporting cars, of varying degrees of specialization and performance. A sports model was often shown in advertising for a complete model range, as it lent glamour to the more mundane representatives of its marque. A 1964 Buick advertisement was headed, "Everybody out of the rut ... the '64 Buicks are here!" Above the headline, a Wildcat hardtop was shown on a deserted beach, an escapist setting which became popular with advertisers on both sides of the Atlantic.

Buick's personal-luxury Riviera moved into the sports sector in 1965, in "Gran Sport" guise, available with a "360–hp Wildcat V-8" and a variety of performance options, including a "limited slip differential ... heavy-duty springs, shocks and stabilizer bar." "You need not be a professional driver to qualify" added the copywriter, to the lasting regret of America's insurance companies.

Oldsmobile offered the full-size Starfire in 1964: "High adventure starts right here!" began one piece, which showed the new coupe roaring up a mountain road. "From its bold grille to its exclusive dual-chambered exhausts, this beauty's new action silhouette says '64 belongs to Starfire. Sample the response of the 345–h.p. Starfire V-8...." By later standards this was tame copy, but "action" had emerged as the buzzword of the moment and it often reappeared, sometimes with wit and sometimes as an inevitable cliché, in the copywriters' repertoire of "sporty" words. The Starfire's image was consolidated in 1965:

> Every line says "let yourself go" ... where the action is!... You see it standing there, poised and eager, every sleek line tingling with anticipation. And it seems to whisper, "Let's go. Let's *fly!*"... Then a turn of the key ... a flick of the console-mounted T-stick Turbo Hydra-Matic or 4-on-the-floor — and 370 high flying horses put wings to your wheels!

Buick's Riviera was the first of a new breed of sporty personal-luxury cars (May 1965).

Dramatic scenery, photographs of sportsmen, snappy slogans: these were the main ingredients of most performance-car advertisements of the early 1960s (January 1964).

Ned Jordan would have been proud. Not only was Oldsmobile's winged chariot powerful; the "Rocket Action Car" had lost the chromium excesses of the 1950s, and was shown against a simple, deep-red backdrop with not a missile in sight.

Of General Motors' performance cars, the Pontiac GTO ("The Great One") enjoyed the highest profile. It grew out of the attractive but anonymous Pontiac Tempest in 1964, and until 1966 was not strictly a model in its own right, but a package of options which could be personalized from a list of further extras. With a distinctive twin-grille at the front, it rapidly acquired its own identity, assisted by tailored advertising which contrasted vividly with copy for the regular Tempest, including that for the Tempest Le Mans on which it was based. "We spoil you a bit in the '65 Tempest with interiors restyled in cloth and Morrokide.... And tempt you with 12 handsome models, including a new Custom Hardtop Coupe" declared a typical Tempest advertisement with an eye to the housewives who made up a large part of Pontiac's regular market.

GTO copy was much more energetic: "Two seconds behind the wheel of a Pontiac and you know ... you're in tiger country.... There's a six or one of two rambunctious V-8s available in the Le Mans. And a snarling 335–hp GTO or its 360–hp cousin. So go drive a tiger!" To prove the point, a tiger was shown clambering over the windshield of a yellow GTO convertible as it rested on the inevitable deserted beach. Another advertisement showed the car against a black background, facing the reader with a tiger skin on the hood, head snarling: "There's a live one under the hood.... Purrs if you're nice. Snarls when you prod it. Trophy V-8, standard in Pontiac GTO. 389 cubic inches. 335 horsepower. 431 lb–ft of torque.... Want something wilder? Got it: 360 hp. Want something tamer? Got that, too— Pontiac Le Mans." In 1966 Ford showed the front of its rival high-performance Fairlane GTA, with a toy tiger-tail clamped between hood and grille above the headline: "How to cook a tiger."

Sportiness, carefully diluted, extended to Pontiac's six-cylinder cars which were aimed, at least in part, towards the more adventurous elements within Pontiac's established clientèle. While the GTO was shown with tigers and seductive models, a 1967 Sprint appeared with a woman at the wheel who clearly owned the car, and did not just pose in it. "With an OHC six like this who needs an 8?" asked the headline, while the copy described the car's "special suspension" and

How to tell a tiger from a regular Tempest? Give it a special grille, wheels, and options and its own advertising campaign. Niche marketing flourished in the 1960s (May 1965).

"all-synchro 3-speed floor shift." Three speeds were perhaps more sporting than automatic gears, but they did not suggest a dedication to raw performance. Nor was the Sprint a "high–rpm driving machine ... with the agility and grace of a European sports car," whatever the copy said. Given that most potential buyers had never driven a European sports car, it hardly mattered.

By 1967, the GTO's reputation was established, and copywriters could caption atmospheric artwork with the laconic slogan, "The Great One. GTO Hardtop. Need we say more?" Inevitably, some elaboration was irresistible, if only to describe the special equipment available, such as "a spirited

Horsepower and safety equipment went side by side in Pontiac copy of the late 1960s, as with this Firebird (November 1967).

250–hp regular gas V-8 or its 285–hp premium gas cousin," along with such sporting gadgets as a "Hood-mounted tach." The regular Pontiac slogan, "Ride the Wide-Track winning streak" was shortened to a more dynamic "Wide-Track Pontiac/67."

In 1968, the sports and "Wide-Track" themes were combined in copy for the GTO and a new Mustang competitor, the Firebird convertible. "The Great One" was made 1968's Car of the Year by *Motor Trend* magazine, which commended it for "a revolutionary bumper so new you have to kick it to believe it ... it won't chip, fade or corrode." It was an understandable tactic in view of increasing concern about automobile safety, and it also looked modern, sleek, and muscular, a look that was enhanced by concealed headlamps. In case anyone thought that the marque was going soft, reassurance was given with a "400-cubic-inch, 4-barrel V-8" or an optional "Ram Air engine with deep-breathing scoops." Options on the Firebird included "mag-style wheels" and "stereo tape," the latter an answer to Ford's heavy promotion of a similar device some years earlier.

Like Ford's Mustang, the Firebird was advertised with a wide variety of engines, from a "175 hp Firebird" to a "330–hp Firebird 400." A Firebird 400 was as fast as many earlier, larger sports cars with higher quoted power outputs, even if Pontiac's "400" referred to cubic inches and not optimistically rated horsepower. Significantly, advertising for the Firebird mentioned safety features, such as "padded armrests, front and rear side marker lights."

In the 1970s, performance cars were progressively detuned to comply with exhaust emissions legislation, and muscle cars kept a lower profile until the 1980s. In 1976, even a marque advertisement for the whole Pontiac range promoted the Formula Firebird on its gas mileage, but, contrary to some predictions of the time, technology eventually overcame many apparent restrictions and put "action" back on the car buyer's agenda by the late 1980s.

Chapter 4

Pushbuttons and Plastic Tops

Some American cars were stylish — others were not. There were powerful, charismatic automobiles, and there were ordinary sedans with so few outstanding virtues that no one felt much inclined to investigate their vices. There were also a few products that represented comprehensive "improvement opportunities" for their makers. Car buyers, however, were rarely unanimous in deciding which car belonged to what category. An automobile with an anemic engine and dowdy styling could be promoted as "frugal" and "practical" if its promoter was unusually honest, or as a stalwart in the face of transitory fads if he was an optimist. Occasionally, gratuitous obsolescence was elevated into practical virtue — which was plausible if the maker's name was Checker or Rambler; less so if it was Hudson or Kaiser. But whatever their individual difficulties, copywriters were united in their quest for The Gadget.

The Gadget could be anything from a self-adjusting brake mechanism to a transparent roof. It could be useful, like power steering, or superfluous if it involved holding a switch for as long as it would take to move an equivalent handle for, say, a vent window. In the absence of a suitable gadget, ordinary features could be described in extraordinary English, with the addition of Capital-Letters-And-Hyphens, to create a sense of importance that might be conspicuously lacking in the product itself. If the car could conceivably move under its own power without The Gadget, a special name for it had to be invented. Occasional coincidence was inevitable, as with the Oldsmobile Handi-Shift/Hudson Handy Shift gear shifts and the Chrysler PowerFlite/Nash Powerflyte, which was logically Nash's inheritance, since Airflyte bodies had been around since 1948.

Buick's mixture of the useful and the banal was typical for 1946. A Canadian advertisement listed, *inter alia*, "Permi-firm" steering, "Panthergait" springs, and a "StepOn" parking brake which was not, by 1946, a novelty. In 1949, Chrysler's semantics ranged from the gently imaginative "Cyclebonded Brake Linings" to a "Waterproof Ignition System," the latter an example of a description masquerading as an original name for a feature. Plymouth promoted "Ignition Key Starting" in the same year, along with an "Automatic Electric Choke" and other assurances of mechanical worthiness. Studebaker's equivalent copy represented an oasis of common sense. "Your brakes adjust themselves," in 1949, was modest and sensible. Chevrolet, on the other hand, was uncharacteristically fanciful in a 1952 advertisement which drew attention to "Royal-Tone Styling," "Color-Matched Two-Tone Interiors," "Center-Point Steering," and the inimitably euphonious "Jumbo-Drum Brakes."

By 1953–54, power features, once confined to prestige cars, were becoming more widespread, particularly on medium- and lower-priced cars. In the medium sector, De Soto offered "Full Power Steering," which was claimed to reduce steering effort by 80 percent, in 1953. The system was intended to eliminate the woken-from-slumber sensation given by some early power steering systems which were prompted into action only after the steering wheel had been turned a little. In the same year, De Soto also offered soberly titled "Power Brakes," which reduced pedal effort by some 50 percent.

In 1954, power gadgets continued to move downmarket. Chevrolet claimed to be "First in its field with all these power features for you," which included Powerglide transmission (optional since 1950); a power-brake option with Powerglide cars; and power steering, windows, and seats as stand-alone extras, the steering being carried over from 1953. Not to be

4. Pushbuttons and Plastic Tops

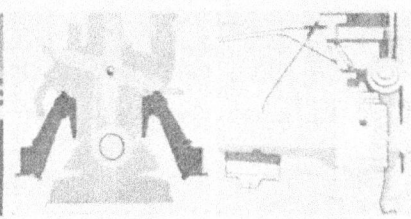

Royal-Tone Styling features smooth and colorful new beauty of lines.

26 Exterior Colors and two-tone color combinations to choose from.

Color-Matched Two-Tone Interiors bring new beauty to De Luxe models.

New Centerpoise Power is smoother — "screens out" engine vibration.

Improved Carburetion with Automatic Choke in Powerglide models.

Brilliantly NEW *for '52!*

The Beautiful New Chevrolet Bel Air

SMARTER looking... smoother running... softer riding ... this brilliant new 1952 Chevrolet is the finest ever built. And it's the lowest-priced line in the low-price field! See your Chevrolet dealer and see all the reasons why it's true year after year: More people buy Chevrolets than any other car.... Chevrolet Division of General Motors, Detroit 2, Michigan. *(Continuation of standard equipment and trim illustrated is dependent on availability of material.)*

CHEVROLET
The Only Fine Cars **PRICED SO LOW!**

New Softer, Smoother Ride with new and improved shock absorber action.

Powerglide Automatic Transmission De Luxe model option at extra cost.

Trend-Setting Valve-in-Head Engine performance and all-round economy.

Center-Point Steering gives smoother feel to the wheel, easier steering control.

Jumbo-Drum Brakes with Dubl-Life rivetless linings for long, safe service.

Capital-Letters-And-Hyphens, together with elaborate names for mundane features, were widespread in early postwar copy (1952 campaign).

Power features trickled down from the fine car field to the middle- and low-priced sectors during 1953-54 (May 1953 and March 1954).

out-gadgeted, Ford promoted five similar power options that were claimed to "take the 'drive' out of driving in the '54 Ford." Ford's power steering reduced driver effort by 75 percent and the brakes offered normal standards of stopping power with "up to a third less push." "Power Lift Windows," a "*4-Way* Power Seat," and "Fordomatic Drive" completed the list. With a body design dating from 1952, Ford fought back against Chevrolet not only with its "new 130–h.p. Y-block V-8 and 115–h.p. I-block Six" but also by virtue of those "Power-Lift Windows," being unique in the low-price field in having "push-button control of all four side windows," and its power seat being "the only power seat in Ford's field that goes *up and down* as well as forward and back."

Mercury offered a similar selection of devices in 1954, and devoted several advertisements to handling features, particularly "the ball that makes the new Mercury far easier to handle!" when ball-joints replaced conventional kingpins in the front suspension. One advertisement explained the advantages of this feature with several colored diagrams, for the benefit of those who did not want to crawl under a Monterey,

let alone dismantle it, to find out. British Ford Consul and Zephyr buyers had enjoyed the advantages of ball-joints, albeit with MacPherson struts rather than conventional A-arms or wishbones, since 1951.

Ford's main novelty of the year was a transparent plastic roof section of "tinted Plexiglas," fitted to Ford Crestline (Skyliner) and Mercury Monterey (Sun Valley) hardtops. "See the scenery through the roof" said a typical Mercury advertisement, "see traffic lights easily — yet tinted transparent top protects against heat, wind, glare.... [Y]ou have a wonderful sensation of driving with no top at all — but with the wind and weather protection of a sedan."

It worked best in cool weather, and although the Sun Valley was "America's first transparent top car to be put into regular production," the idea remained a Ford specialty outside the realm of the dream car, where such ideas were commonplace. At $2,582, the Sun Valley cost $130 more than a comparable steel-topped coupe and, whatever the copywriter claimed, the plastic top caused the car's interior to overheat uncomfortably in hot weather. Fewer than 10,000 were sold in

Mercury's plastic top was a dream car feature that proved unpopular with buyers, but it drew attention to the regular Mercury range, which was partly its purpose (March 1954).

1954, and, following sales of 1,787 in 1955, the idea was dropped. The car nevertheless featured prominently in Mercury advertising as a range-topping glamour model, as well as in copy exclusive to the car.

As automobile interiors grew more elaborate and stylized in the mid–1950s, the gadgets multiplied. The 1955 Chevrolet Bel Air had "a lot to offer in the power-feature department.... Braking, steering, gear shifting — even seat and window adjustments on Bel Air and 'Two-Ten' models." If none of these were novel by 1955, increasing numbers of buyers ordered them, and they were promoted more excitably than in 1954. "All these little motoring pluses" could be "done the 'pushbutton' way in the Motoramic Chevrolet through extra-cost options."

In the same year, Chrysler offered similar devices alongside its standard "famous new *sweptback* Super-Scenic Windshield," "Twin-Tower tail lights that say 'STOP' with great authority," and other styling innovations. By 1957, when the novelty value of power windows and seats had worn off, copywriters centered on engines and transmissions, as the lists of features which had predominated in the early 1950s gave way to "integrated" advertising in which style, power, and gadgets were united in every area of the market into a fantasist whole.

A year or two later, with performance de-emphasized, Chrysler's copywriters reverted to an earlier idiom, punctuating copy with such disparate enticements as "Total-Contact Brakes," "Swivel Seats," and "Torsion-Aire Ride." Many of these features were available across the Corporation's range, and corporate advertising described them all. Some, like the "compound windshield" which curved up into the roof of the car as well as to the sides, were styling touches of doubtful practical advantage, but others, including "Mirror-Matic Electronic Mirror" and an "Automatic Beam Changer" similar in concept to General Motors' "Autronic Eye," were genuinely useful when properly adjusted.

Every manufacturer offered a host of minor options, from chrome-plated splash-guards to lavish interior trim fabrics, all of which were carefully illustrated and promoted in sales literature, even if they could not be described in detail in press advertising. In a few cases, a marque's model and option ranges were so extensive that they merited a hardback catalog, as offered to Mercury buyers in 1957.

In the 1960s, hyperbole and capital letters gave way to more subtle forms of inducement. Equipment, *per se*, was described soberly. 1964's Buick LeSabre, for instance, offered "15-inch wheels, finned aluminum front brakes, extra cushioning for middle-seat travelers and separate heat ducts and controls for the rear seat." Excitement did not disappear, but its focus shifted from the car itself to the sensual experience of driving it. Copywriters increasingly sought to identify with the consumer's latent expectations, to seduce the car buyer rather than bludgeon him with endless— and pointless— electrical devices.

The consumer who changed (albeit improbably) from a 1947 Ford Tudor to its 1957 equivalent underwent considerable re-orientation, from a high, boxy shape to a low and sleek one; from simple manual controls to automatic gears and power-assistance; from a top speed between 80 and 90mph to one of 100–110mph with a V-8 engine option; from 0–60 acceleration in the 21-second range to around half of that. Changing again in 1967 to a new model, the consumer's re-orientation would not have been nearly as fundamental — the proportions of the 1957 and 1967 models were broadly similar, with a few inches

Three-tone paint, an optional "high-fidelity long-playing record player"— and pushbutton gears. Chrysler had come a long way since the "cycle-bonded brake linings" of 1949 (1956 campaign).

gained in the hood and lost from the trunk, and the power features were similar, too, even if fins and chromium had given way to a sleek, uncluttered, "Coke-bottle" look.

Stabilization brought diversity, just as it had in the 1920s, though the differences between marques and sizes were now determined as much by function as by status. If one believed the copywriters, 1957's new car buyers were all excited by essentially the same themes, which were reinforced by the automobile's wider association with America's technological consciousness. By 1967, the common aspirations that had sustained 1957's automotive fantasy were in retreat as increasing concern over fuel availability, pollution, and safety encouraged the dispersal of earlier, uncomplicated expectations.

Effortless driving nevertheless remained a priority; and air conditioning, almost universal as an option, was now more widely fitted in practice. In 1969 the Ford Thunderbird could be ordered with the push-button sliding steel roof that, manually operated, had been promoted as an option in 1960, so that personal-car buyers could continue to "see the moon and the stars." But the fantasy was fragmenting, and it gave way to a widespread, individualized desire for personal lifestyle-enhancement in a climate in which one person's lifestyle might not have much in common with another's.

The disparity of fortune and, more importantly, of ambition, which had always existed under the surface glitz of American consumer culture, was now reappearing on copywriters' agenda. By 1970, the prospect of affluent cultural homogeneity, which had inspired industrial designers in the 1930s, had almost entirely dissipated.

Copywriters varied their tone accordingly. The lush prose appropriate for a Chevrolet Monte Carlo ("Standard is an instrument panel with the rare look of hand-rubbed burled elm") was inappropriate for a Vega; elaborate gadgets which the Thunderbird buyer sought in his "personal car" were

Gadgetitis was in retreat by 1964, when a Buick convertible could be shown with the top up, and "finned aluminum front brakes" and "big 15-inch wheels" could be mentioned in copy. The automotive fantasy took an escapist, rather than technological turn in the 1960s (May 1964).

The "sliding sun roof Thunderbird" was promoted as a model in its own right in 1960, and this optional feature, electrically operated, dominated the marque's escapist 1969 advertising (February 1969).

consciously scorned by the suburban professional whose transport was a compact station wagon. And when prestigious European luxury car makers challenged the fundamentals of American car design with advertising copy that mocked the domestic product's lack of dynamism and technical sophistication, the fantasy became self-conscious, aware of its partiality, and was thereby rendered largely impotent. Where motorists continued to look for old-style automotive values, they did so self-consciously, aware that they did not participate in a dream that was universal, or even necessarily popular.

From the mid–1960s, advertisers increasingly identified with particular sectors of the new-car market. In each case, the copywriter tuned in to the imagined point of view of the target sector, addressing the priorities and life-perspective of a particular type of buyer. No longer was it possible to appeal, even in passing, to a common automotive fantasy. A view of the world which was attractive to traditional luxury car buyers was not only unappealing, but actually repellent, to the champions of functionalist imports.

In 1955, Cadillac could write: "At a conservative estimate, fifty percent of all the motorists in America would rather own a Cadillac than any other automobile," confident that, of the other fifty percent, the great majority would like a Cadillac (or one of its direct rivals) if it were offered to them. By 1975, not only had the percentage of Cadillac aspirants, particularly among young people and college graduates, declined, but many new car buyers would have refused a Cadillac even if it were offered at the cost of the lowliest import. To environmentalists, the large Cadillac was a symbol of a decadent and intransigent adherence not only to a past view of the world, but an irresponsible one. The vast majority of young car buyers were simply indifferent to it, and to others of its kind, however good it might have been of its type.

With such a diversity of perspectives, it was inevitable that the copy styles which had included so much color and invention in the 1950s would be superseded by something more subtle, more sophisticated and, perhaps, less memorable.

PART TWO : BEYOND MECHANISM

Chapter 5

"Wouldn't it be nice to have an Escape Machine?"

The question was asked by Oldsmobile in a series of advertisements in 1970, but it had been formulated in a thousand different forms by the time that the Oldsmobile Cutlass Supreme was posed in a restaurant scene by its makers to encourage the new car buyer to "escape from the ordinary."

Escapist advertising invited the motorist to give up a dull existence led without the car for an exciting and fulfilled life with it. In the early days of motoring, the choice was between owning a new car and owning none at all. Until the 1930s, mass-market advertisers usually relied on their products' mechanical merits while the attendant euphoria was allowed to take care of itself. This approach was understandable but it made for uninspired copy. There were a few exceptions to this trend, of which the most famous is Edward S. Jordan's "Somewhere West of Laramie" advertisement, published in two forms in the *Saturday Evening Post* in 1923.[1]

By the 1950s, most cars were bought as repeat purchases by established motorists for whom motoring was no longer a novelty. It was difficult to persuade the consumer to become as excited about a replacement car as he had once been about motoring in general, and the "excitement factor" had to be induced artificially with promises of fun and escape from monotonous routine. As Harley Earl once remarked, "You can design a car so that every time you get in it, it's a relief — you have a little vacation for a while."[2]

Styling and engineering features incorporated into the automobile had to represent fun, escape, and adventure. This orientation of the consumer's perspective — in which he willingly colluded — had little to do with the car as transportation, and everything to do with the fantasies and aspirations evoked by its particular characteristics.

The escapist promise took many forms, and the process was avowedly psychological. Advertisers promised adventure and travel opportunities, fun, and an improvement in lifestyle. A combination of snobbery with escapism promised new social, as well as geographical, horizons. Copywriters offered the consumer a chance to construct a self-image that was more appealing than the reality. When this artificial persona became convincing, the consumer was hooked. When it became vital to his sense of ease and well-being in his family, community, and social relations; when not buying the new car could indicate apparent failure to the outside world and make the consumer feel himself that he had failed, that new car became a necessary component of an enjoyable life. In it, motoring would take on a new meaning, even if one drove along the same highways as before.

Such promises of escape and adventure became inextricably intertwined with the threat of a return to mundane anonymity, with an added, corrosive sense of missing out, of being passed over, of not participating any more in the social process. Beneath the promise of fun was a subtle, covert initiation into social paranoia, and, however they might have expressed it, copywriters knew its potency.

Among the early escapists, Nash's copywriters were in a class of their own. Armed with a distinctive, if boxy, sedan, a thermostatic heater and overdrive, they set to work in 1939:

You're going to take a journey.... It's written in the stars — this month you're in tune with a disturbing vibration. Be doubly careful, if your orbit crosses a Nash showroom. For then — a dark car will come into your life.... In ghost-like silence, you flick past other cars seemingly chained to the ground.... It's uncanny ... exhilarating ... this feeling of floating. Only when you touch the brake and feel the tires dig in, do you realize than this is what people call "an automobile"!...

One of an unusual series of advertisements from Oldsmobile, who showed cars in indoor environments that their owners wanted to escape from, rather than at actual outdoor escape venues (October 1969).

Another advertisement continued the theme:

> Don't Let Others Spoil Your Fun! If someone tries to tell you about the new Nash — stop him. And if you meet a silver bullet of a car flashing up the street — look the other way. For that's not the way to learn about a Nash.... You've got to get inside — and drive it ... yourself — on an open road....

The copy was imaginative and unusually humorous, even for its type. Seasonal advertising (also used by Lincoln-Zephyr) was employed in the spring of 1939, and escapist motifs were adapted accordingly:

> The Hounds of Spring Are At Your Heels.... Here's a car that knows ... why colts kick their heels in the spring ... why little boys run away from home ... why trout rods are being revarnished.... As you ripple across space, don't regret the coming end of the day. Spring *can* last forever!... Yes, a Nash is as catching as measles, and twice as hard to quarantine. Get into the driver's seat *once*, and you can never get yourself out of it.

The message here was innocent enough, and typical of the whimsical style that characterized Nash advertising of the

Appeals to consumers' emotions were not new in 1923, but Jordan was a pioneer in combining copy and artwork into a euphoric whole. The technique was condemned as "absurd" by David Ogilvy forty years later, but is still in use today (June 1923).

period. "You've Had that Longing Long Enough.... Does Spring do funny things to you?" asked a similar piece a year later. In February, 1940, a bright pink four-door sedan was shown among skaters:

> A shrieking gale has smothered the sun and swept the lake bare of skaters.... Suddenly — a flash of light, and laughing faces ... a whisper of tires on the snow. Someone's brought a new Nash! You slip into the broad, welcoming front seat — someone twirls a mysterious little dial, and instantly it's June!

If one believed the copy, the car was not only comfortable, but a panacea: "It's priced so low, with resale value so high ... that it will pay to trade away your troubles to your Nash dealer today — and start having year 'round fun!" The car itself was fast and refined, particularly in eight-cylinder form. According to a British tester of the 1939 model:

> It becomes increasingly wonderful what the Americans can do in providing value for money. This big Nash is 17 ft. long, is a really roomy six-seater, has air conditioning [Weather Eye thermostatic heating], overdrive, a maximum speed of ... 85m.p.h. in real silence and comfort.... Altogether, for the money required [£465] this car is a very remarkable product.[3]

Stylish, fun-oriented escapism from Nash in 1939 and 1953. The seats of both cars reclined to form double beds, to the delight of wags and teenagers, and the consternation of parents and sexual moralists of all ages (1939 and 1953 campaigns).

In England, it was far from cheap at nearly £200 more than the £280 asked for an American-designed Ford V-8 "30," but in its homeland a six-cylinder variant was not expensive at $985.

Nash continued to offer fun and escape in "the 'Travelingest Car' Ever Built" in 1953: "You'll find a whole new world of travel fun in the 1953 Nash Airflytes. Cars built to make long trips easier, more enjoyable!" The theme was pursued in a series of advertisements, many of which showed the most glamorous car in the Nash range, the Ambassador Country Club hardtop. According to another piece: "[A]s the road unreels and new enchantments greet your eye you'll know why we even built sleeping beds in a Nash." This was bold copy, given that parents were already banning their teenage children from borrowing the cars whose front seats were advertised to "become Twin Beds in seconds."

The car rental companies in particular emphasized the recreational potential of the automobile, and convertibles dominated their advertising. "See more ... do more ... have more fun the Hertz Rent-A-Car Way!" said Hertz in 1954, in a headline above a bright red Chevrolet convertible in the lush North Carolina countryside. In another advertisement in the same series, a yellow Ford Sunliner convertible was photographed at "the famous Kona Kai Club on Shelter Island in the Bay of San Diego, California, where even the name has a musical sound of romance."

Ford decided to eliminate the middle-man in 1957, in an advertisement for the "Ford Dealers of New England" which promoted the region as a vacation resort and, of course, the Fairlane convertible as the ideal vacation car. The Sunliner was "the heaviest, longest, loveliest car the money can buy" according to Ford, who even in such delightful surroundings needed to keep an eye on the competition from Plymouth's new incarnation of the Forward Look, as well as Chevrolet's attractively facelifted (and new-looking) Bel Air convertible. In 1960, Avis showed a Ford Galaxie convertible in a similar setting. "Have more fun, get more done with Avis minute-saver service" said the headline, which echoed Hertz's strategy more closely than 1957's "600 mile business trip in 24 hours—without strain!"

Ford promoted the New England countryside for its 1956 and 1957 models. This is a Fairlane 500 Sunliner convertible (April 1957).

In the late 1940s, copywriters began to integrate escapism into the promotion of the technical and "design" features of their products, and escapism was bound up more closely with what the particular automobile offered. This was to be expected, given the prevailing climate. Buick had set the standard for such pieces as early as 1936. In a piece headed "Thrill for sale!" the mechanical pill was sugared as much as possible:

> You'll think the driver's seat of that new Buick was tailored to your measure, so comfortably will you settle into place.... [T]his phenomenal performer seems to settle closer and steadier on the road as you press the treadle, and the lightest tip-toe pressure on those big hydraulics slows you to a safe swerveless stop....[4]

The car itself was not even shown in this advertisement.

Oldsmobile's advertising of the early 1950s set a number of precedents, not least in its colorful descriptions of mechanical features, but the "Rocket" engines and automatic gears were placed in an escapist context in 1950:

> Rocket ahead with Oldsmobile!... *Drive* the car that makes distance an exciting adventure. *Drive* an Oldsmobile — the *only* car with the smoothest "power package" ever built — the "Rocket" Engine and new Whirlaway Hydra-Matic Drive!

Escape, excitement, fantasy — Oldsmobile combined these elements so that they were not easily distinguished. Nor were they meant to be separated, for their potency lay in coalition.

The names given to automatic features were carefully devised to conjure up the required associations of smoothness, power, and escape from more mundane motoring. "Nothing without wings climbs like a '56 Chevrolet!" began a 1956 advertisement which went on to describe the excitement that came from owning the year's 205hp V-8. No longer was it necessary for the consumer actually to travel anywhere to find the desired stimulation. Even ordinary driving could be adventurous with the "Exciting Escape" offered by Chrysler in 1959. The Chrysler Windsor hardtop was itself a "lion-hearted call to the open road" with "pushbutton TorqueFlite transmission," "Torsion-Aire Ride," and "Golden Lion" engines.

The promise of escape was resolutely tied to the characteristics of the car, rather than to any transcending of geographical or social boundaries. This move towards self-containment of the escapist promise reached its logical conclusion in the introverted, recuperative escapism that was advertised as the main appeal of "personal cars" in the early 1960s. No

Indirect escapism from Oldsmobile with a "98" sedan in 1950. It fitted easily with the marque's performance image (March 1950).

longer was the motorist explicitly participating in American technological expansion; his fantasies were largely divorced from any social or realistic context. The automobile itself, through what it evoked for its owner, provided the whole escape experience.

Ford's Thunderbird was the archetypal personal car, which came into its own in the climate of the early 1960s. The 1960 convertible may have offered "action ... sweet, soft, spirited action — an adventure in flowing, controlled motion," but from 1961 the emphasis was more openly on luxury. According to the copywriters, it was "so uniquely new that it stands alone in the fine-car field." The very similar 1962 model was accompanied by what amounted to its own aura, within

The ordinary made extraordinary: the 1959 Chrysler was not an obvious choice for the committed escapist, and was targeted at the 40–50 age group (June 1959).

A contemplative, introverted escapism characterized Ford Thunderbird copy during 1962-63 (June 1962 and May 1963).

which the world outside had no place: "Thunderbird Hour ... is the shimmering part of any day, the moments when this subtly sculptured motor car moves at your lightest hint ... gliding as silently as sea mist ... soaring to the imperative of Thunderbird power." In another piece, "Thunderbird Spell" was the "lasting enchantment that makes the green-gold of trees seem brighter, the sun more ardent ... and adventure closer." Even Nash's copy had been literalist by comparison.

In each advertisement, the Thunderbird was shown in an isolated country setting, driven by a young(ish) couple, with never any children or admiring passers-by in sight. The message was consolidated with the 1963 model, which included "refinements that make Thunderbird yours, *personally*, as no other car can be." A hardtop version was the way to "get away from them all.... Suddenly you're in Thunderbird Country, where velvet silence and silken smoothness reflect years of engineering refinement." It was something of a comedown to be reminded of engineering in any form amid the "velvet silence," but such interpolations did not disrupt the pastiche romance of "Thunderbird Hour" for long.

Within the personal-car theme, individual Thunderbirds were allowed a measure of separate identity. Copy for the Sports Roadster (a regular convertible with wire wheels and a rigid, body-colored tonneau covering the rear seats) subtly anticipated muscle-car copy of later years: "How to catch a Thunderbird.... Find one that's standing still. In full flight this is a most elusive species— with a rare talent for disappearing from the view of lesser cars."

But the buyer who wondered whether the Sports Roadster was really like other versions was reassured: "Although it may remind you of a sports car, particularly in the Sports Roadster version shown here, it still ranks among the world's foremost luxury cars." There was also a Limited Edition Landau, the obligatory "sophisticated" model in the Thunderbird range, which was shown at that archetypal upmarket venue, the opera house — at Monte Carlo in this case.

In 1964, a new body style arrived, and luxury was augmented by an emphasis on styling for its own sake, together with a host of "novelty" features. "Thunderbird for 1964 — So different, so beautifully different!" gushed an announcement advertisement. "New styling sets the Thunderbird mood. Inside, it is maintained by advances that make even Thunderbird veterans sigh.... New contoured 'shell' front seats cradle you in luxurious Thunderbird comfort. Instruments are positioned and lighted for flight deck clarity." Illustrations, of a deep maroon hardtop in a newly harvested field at sunset, combined with the copy to set an escapist mood, and 1965's slogan, "The Private World of Thunderbird" reinforced the car's image.

As the personal-car market subdivided into "sports" and "luxury" sectors in the mid–1960s, the Thunderbird's position was more closely defined in advertisements. Copy for 1965's limited edition underlined the luxury theme, describing it as the "Special Landau ... unique among the unique." Advertising stressed the exclusivity of the car: "Only a limited number will be built. The owner's name will be engraved on a personalized limited edition numbered name plate. Landau's body finish is of Special Ember-Glo, repeated on special wheel covers and inside the flight deck in thick, cut-pile carpeting...."

Four and a half thousand copies of this Special Landau were eventually made, and for the 1967 model year a four-door Thunderbird Landau sedan, "inspired by Lincoln Continental," distanced the car still further from the sporting ancestry highlighted in a 1963 advertisement which had compared that year's model with its two-seat ancestors, declaring that the concept had "stood the test of time."

Others followed Ford's lead. The Buick Riviera had the advantage of a prestigious marque name, and enjoyed a slightly more sophisticated image. The underlying message in 1965, however, was familiar: "Drive a Riviera home tonight. Who cares if people think you're younger, richer and more romantic than you really are?" You were what you drove.

Mercury's Cougar of 1967 was another stylish two-door coupe that sold as a personal car in its milder versions, bridging the gap between the Mustang and the Thunderbird. It could also, like the Riviera Gran Sport, become a muscle car when ordered in XR-7 form. The regular Cougar, which accounted for nearly 80 percent of the model's sales in 1967, was promoted on its looks as much as its power:

> Untamed elegance! That's Cougar.... With a European flair to its styling.... Above all, Cougar is a lithe, contemporary car, with the kind of excitement that runs through the entire '67

The 1972 Thunderbird.

Attempting to be all personal cars to all people, the Cougar combined Mustang and Thunderbird virtues — as did Mercury's copy (October 1966).

Thunderbirds of the 1970s were more luxurious than sporting, and features rather than euphoria dominated copy (March 1972).

Mercury line…. We believe Cougar is the best equipped luxury sports car you can buy for the money.

The car's promoters had to balance precariously across several stools, but the car remained an individualist, of sorts. Unfortunately, it was more luxurious than sporting. According to a British tester, "[The Cougar] handled like a row of books sliding off a shelf … and generally acted very much like the boulevarde [sic] cruiser that it is. The Mustang is a vastly better motorcar."[5] But American and British sports-car enthusiasts rarely spoke the same language.

By 1972, the confidence of earlier years was receding. The Thunderbird of that year, now corpulent and visibly similar to the related Lincoln Continental, was "A magnificent new personal automobile…. Personal in its luxurious appointments as well…. It's personal, too, in its options. For example, an electronic anti-skid brake system and the split bench seat, the vinyl roof, the whitewalls and the deluxe wheel covers pictured above."

Here, as in much advertising for full-size cars in the early 1970s, there was an aroma of desperation, as the language of romantic fiction combined with that of the service manual to produce copy that was both tense and mundane. Yet the new model sold better than its predecessors of 1969–71, and in 1976 "The Private World of Thunderbird" remained for a very similar-looking car which was shown beside a lake as the sun went down. It was still owned by the romantic couple who had defined the car's image in near-identical surroundings in 1959. No longer was there any explicit suggestion of power; the emphasis was on gadgets and features, and the headline, "Could it be the best luxury car buy in the world?" defined the Thunderbird's priorities.

In the 1970s, personal-car values were increasingly taken up by makers of two-door sedans with no particular history of exclusivity. Chevrolet Monte Carlos and Cadillac Eldorado hardtops blurred any distinction that might once have existed between the personal car, the sports car, and the luxury coupe. The 1970s were years in which old-style large cars of all varieties found themselves huddled together in one category, espousing similar automotive values. They were also years of a certain homogeneity in large-car design as sportiness and individualism were increasingly left to compacts, sub-compacts, and European imports which, in a decade of restrictions and power-sapping emissions equipment, offered more fun and excitement per cubic inch than a Ford Thunderbird.

Chapter 6

A Neurosis Unleashed

"But Darling" said the girl to her husband, "they're staring at our new '52 Dodge."

"Start packing—we're moving out" said the man to his wife. "Moving, dear?" she replied, "It's four in the morning." Her husband sat down wearily and explained. Everyone else in the neighborhood could afford a new Dodge. "I'm so ashamed. Grab the other end of the davenport, dear."

The first declaration was the headline of a press advertisement; the second, part of a 1962 radio commercial. In both cases, the message was the same: You would be admired and envied if you drove the new car, and would be ridiculed and considered a social failure if you did not. The point was sometimes put lightheartedly, but even if an individual advertisement were dismissed with a smile, it would still fuel that social neurosis whose maintenance was so essential to the doctrine of dynamic obsolescence that supported the American automobile industry.

The whirling mélange of emotional impulses by which advertisers hoped the motorist's choice of car would be governed was carefully nurtured in a wide variety of copy styles, tailored in each case to the prejudices and aspirations of the target market. The car buyer was encouraged to be aware of what others would think of his car and, by extension, how they would assess its owner. However excellent as mechanism, however reliable, however attractive, an automobile had to be socially acceptable; it needed to excite the admiration of those whose esteem its owner prized most highly.

By 1930, mere ownership of an automobile *per se* conferred little social prestige; indeed, it was assumed that prosperous families would own two cars—and replace them regularly. Increasing reliability and a growing consensus as to what constituted an acceptable automotive aesthetic led advertisers to distinguish their products by referring to nuances of styling—particularly those by which a mass-produced body resembled a custom-built equivalent.

The technique was popular with Chrysler Corporation's marques in the 1930s. In late 1935, for instance, a double-spread in the *Saturday Evening Post* announced that there was a "New Who's Who" among owners of the 1936 De Soto:

> De Soto presents the smart car of 1936, a custom-styled car in the low-price field.... "Why didn't someone think of this before?"... Imagine ... a car as exquisitely finished, as brilliantly appointed, as the most expensive cars built today....

In the copy that followed, the reader's attention was drawn to a "beautifully rounded radiator" with "hood louvres deftly fashioned in wing-like sections," the "[m]ost beautiful instrument panel in the world ... finished in golden beige, with Circasian walnut grain moldings" to complement the "French pleated and artistically tufted seat cushions and door panels"—and so on, for five hundred words or so, with the obligatory miniature photographs. The "Airflow De Soto," meanwhile, whose sales were trailing far behind those of the regular "Custom" models, was relegated to a tiny photograph in the bottom corner of the right-hand page. In its Chrysler incarnation, the Airflow was similarly underplayed in an equivalent spread for the Corporation's top-line marque which, less hysterically than De Soto, offered "Custom car luxury at a practical price."

Snobbery was an important part of the copywriters' repertoire, and it took many forms. The consumer who wished to appear glamorous needed only to buy a car that had been endorsed by a film star; to be proven a person of sophisticated taste (that is, a taste which suggested familiarity with affluence, rather than merely its recent achievement), he bought the make of car preferred by those to whose status he aspired. To be proven as a person of sound judgment, the buyer was encouraged to take the word of those who had owned several examples of the marque in the past — with the suggestion that one was joining an established elite whose values were both immutable and recognized as superior by society as a whole.

In the aspirational copy which pervaded the middle market during the mid–1930s, prosperous arrivistes were explicitly encouraged to incite the envy of their peers: By emulating what they thought were upmarket tastes and aesthetic mores, they would achieve the status that eluded those unable to buy the new car. Nash's "Eyes Right, Eyes Left — All Turned on Nash!" in 1934 was typical of the "look at me" school of headline which gained currency during the insecure mid–1930s. In the same year, with the worst of the Depression receding, a Buick was portrayed as the natural accoutrement to a modern, affluent lifestyle:

> Men and women are living splendidly once more ... seeking the tasteful and the beautiful in all things ... and, naturally, this new era of gracious living suggests the ownership of a gracious motor car.

In the realm of the genuinely upmarket car, a delicate balance had to be achieved between a successful appeal to current owners of the marque in question, or of equivalent products, and an appeal to the aspirations of those who were contemplating the purchase of an upper-class car for the first time. It was also essential to demonstrate that the marque's status was not merely a matter of snobbery, but of the product's proven mechanical worth, and it needed to be remembered throughout that advertisements would be read by those who might never buy the car in question, but whose admiration ensured that the car remained a socially worthwhile purchase for those who did buy it.

Then there was the matter of a marque's tong-term reputation: The reader who could not afford the product in 1935 might remember the impression made on him by successive advertisements, and consider buying it in 1940. Present owners, meanwhile, needed to be assured by the advertisements published after their ownership had begun that their choice of car had been a wise one, and that just as they had previously looked up to past owners, non-owners currently admired — or envied — them. Thus, in the automotive sphere,

Watch out, there's a social climber about. Snobbish copy from Nash and Buick in 1934 (both ads: March 1934).

as elsewhere, status-conscious advertising had a wider purpose than merely to persuade the car buyer to choose a particular product in the short term. An advertisement was therefore not only a private entreaty ("...the car you have always desired..."), but a public statement which invited permanent allegiance to a set of values which the car and the marque exemplified.

With emphasis that varied from marque to marque, and more generally from decade to decade, upmarket advertisers fulfilled this wide and subtle brief by employing five main themes within the genre.

First, the product was presented as intrinsically excellent, so that its possession could satisfy the modern dream of a superlative automobile, identified as such by its appearance and competence as mechanism. Secondly, by buying the product, the reader's personal dream of being envied would be realized (or, if he had bought previous examples, maintained). Thirdly, aspirants who were moving upmarket were assured that they could afford the automobile in question — although expensive, it was of such very high quality that it provided excellent value for money by rational, long-term criteria.

Fourthly, the aspirant was invited to consider the marque's established clientèle. Packard's long-standing slogan, "Ask the Man Who Owns One," fortified this appeal with an implied testimonial: The man who owned one would be a man of sound judgment, and he would be able to describe the particular, functional merits of the product in question. Whether or not the reader actually bounded out of his armchair and accosted a succession of Packard owners was, of course, beside the point; he needed only to be persuaded that they existed. In Cadillac copy the point was often made with a social emphasis. As one 1957 advertisement put it, the people who bought Cadillacs would be "probably the kind of people you would enjoy knowing."

Finally, the reader was invited to enjoy the fruits of his good judgment; the merits of the product were described, and it was assumed that the "intelligent" reader would appreciate them. Possession of the select automobile on offer merely confirmed its owner's subscription to rational values, and allowed him to distinguish his judgment from the impulses of those who were easily swayed by tawdry ephemera. His was a higher instinct, reflected in the choice of a better product.

Of course, the supposedly rational buyer of an upmarket car was lured into consideration of the product by the same means that engaged his "lowlier" compatriot. There was, in fact, little qualitative difference between the motivation of the man who wished to show off by buying an expensive car and that of his fellow–American who felt the need to declare to the world that he was beyond such things; the "will to declare" was common to both. But if the upmarket buyer could be persuaded that his choice was rational, he might also be persuaded to buy the product. And if, on closer acquaintance, the automobile in question proved to be of intrinsically good quality, its virtues would soon become obvious, and would ensure its owner's continued loyalty. Snob-appeal might persuade the buyer to choose one car; alone, it could not ensure a repeat purchase.

In many advertisements, particularly those in which aspirational copy was aimed at buyers who sought the prestige of an upmarket marque through purchase of its lowest-priced model, the appeal was by implication made negatively. Unless the reader bought the product on offer, his dreams would not be realized; he would be unable to conform to the habits of the group his ambition impelled him to join; he would not be envied and would be scorned; he would appear unable to afford anything as good as the advertised product; he would ally himself with the "sort of people" whose values he did not wish to emulate; he would appear to lack sound judgment, and so on. And, as advertisers' illustrations of happy couples quietly hinted, even if he did not mind these things, his wife would.

Advertisements for upmarket automobiles therefore displayed a number of discrete yet mutually supportive elements, and the ways in which those elements were articulated and adjusted to the demands of the particular product defined a marque's public image. The best advertisements conveyed an overall *sense* of the product which coincided with the reader's latent sense of what was desirable. For copy to be potent and effective, it was not necessary for the copywriter's calculations to be tangible. On the other hand, there was little to be gained from being over-subtle, and, with the benefit of hindsight, the modern reader sees the copywriter goading his readers and, perhaps, mocking them as he does so.

Within these constraints, individual manufacturers developed distinctive and recognizable advertising styles — a trend revealed by comparing advertisements from the dominant upmarket marques of Packard, Lincoln, and Cadillac. All reveal a gradual move away from functionalism with a social undercurrent towards a more overt display of status. The product did not merely confer status because of its intrinsic excellence; rather, the value of that excellence lay in its social potency. The seeds of this development were sown at the beginning of American automobile advertising, but the transition was most marked during the late 1920s and early 1930s. It was a development intimately bound up with the establishment of the annual model year from around 1923, and the entrenchment of dynamic obsolescence within the ranks of upmarket manufacturers as well as the mainstream producers.

Packard's copy of the mid–1920s was measured and rational, stressing the quality of the product as mechanism, from which social status could be extrapolated. It was implied that the "man who owned one" bought it because it was good, and not merely because it displayed his wealth. A December, 1925 advertisement, showing a $4,750 Packard Eight Sedan, was typical:

> The new series Packard Eight brings a new zest for motoring to those who long ago ceased to drive for pleasure. Smooth, quiet, truly beautiful in performance, it is pleasing to sense

your mastery of its eighty horse-power.... Behind the wheel of a Packard Eight you may learn the true meaning of luxury, comfort and distinction in travel.

In December 1926, the emphasis was placed more heavily on the Packard as a possession. It reflected not only its owner's appreciation of quality, but his sense of taste and aesthetic balance. In its implication that one taste was more refined and of a higher quality than another, the copy was overtly snobbish:

> Pride of possession.... There are those who understand the subtle pleasure, the inner satisfaction, gained from ownership of things which the whole world approves and acknowledges to be fine and genuine. A gown by Poiret; an etching by Whistler; an authentic Chippendale; a blooded hunter ... such possessions mean far more to those of taste and discrimination than the sums they cost. Is it strange that such people turn instinctively to Packard for their motor cars— that they count their Packards among their most prized possessions?

Packard, for a generation, has built its cars for such a clientèle.

Inherent in this advertisement was the assumption of quality rather than the demonstration of it; the reader was asked to take the judgment of the kind of man who owned one on trust, and to trust also in Packard's consistent reputation. Nowhere were the characteristics and features of the car, as mechanism, mentioned. The realistic background of 1925 had vanished, and was replaced by a portrait of a fashionable woman in an obviously grand house admiring her other possessions. The car, set against a predictably "classical" backdrop, was juxtaposed with the painting.

This advertisement also revealed a set of tensions which would haunt upmarket advertising for many years. How could a car whose appearance changed every few years reflect the aesthetic integrity which was supposedly the hallmark of the rare objects with which the copywriter liked the reader to compare it? Could the principle of dynamic obsolescence be

Claims of intrinsic excellence gave way to social pretension in much Packard copy for 1926-27. In this context, "good taste" was a stick with which to beat social inferiors rather than an absolute standard of aesthetic integrity (December 1925 and December 1926).

reconciled to the belief that the highest aesthetic standards were exalted precisely because experience had shown them to be immutable? Compared with the "things which the whole world approves and acknowledges to be fine and genuine," would not the car — any car — inevitably appear of transient worth? And if successive models were claimed to be characterized by obedience to the highest aesthetic principles (which no copywriter could ever define), how could so many different cars demonstrate individual, let alone collective, allegiance to those principles?

The answer, inevitably, was that no such adherence could be demonstrated; it was merely stated to be obvious, and when American automobiles carried spurious decoration which changed from year to year, the assertion would seem idiotic. It was no surprise to discover that advertisers, unable to reconcile conflicting mores, gradually ceased, by and large, to describe *why* a car reflected the discrimination of its owner and instead appealed directly to his emotional desire to be admired and envied.

To this extent, Packard's advertising began to underplay or ignore the substantial basis of the marque's reputation, and merely traded on the fact of public renown. While the car itself remained excellent, it was a safe strategy; in later years, the marque's reputation, temporarily bolstered by public awareness of the functional excellence of earlier products, would deteriorate rapidly. A fine reputation, and concomitant social standing, could only give its maker, at best, a few years' grace if the product itself were inadequate.

In the mid–1930s, Packard moved downmarket to the upper-middle sector with the 120 and Six. A Packard was at last within the reach of the aspirant middle classes whose social antennae were traditionally the most sensitive, and a 1938 advertisement appealed overtly to the potential buyer's awareness of the fragility of his new-found status. A young couple recalled the ambitions they had held when they were first married. The wife of "James," proud owner of a new Packard, spoke for them both, and recalled what she had said to him before they decided to buy the car: "We're tired of leading a second-best life .... whatever happened to all our dreams, and hopes, and ambitions?... Where are all the fine things we were going to have? Can it be true that we've become content with second-best?... Looking at our car, we were reminded of what we had said when we were married: 'And some day, we'll own a Packard.' This was a good, serviceable take you there and bring you back car. But it was no Packard."

The following day, the couple "marched down ... to see the new Packard Six." Assured that it was "a real Packard," they bought it. A small illustration showed the couple with their new car, their social life rejuvenated. "We like to be seen in it" said James's wife, "and because driving is a thrill again, we're out more enlarging our world and our horizons, having fun again. Yes, we have *our* Packard ... *our* dream has come true."

James, meanwhile, remained mute throughout the story, as well he might; substitute "I" for "we" throughout his wife's account, incorporate the expectations that pre-war society placed on a man to provide for his family, and the lethal character of the copywriter's message becomes apparent. It was a superb piece of copy by Young & Rubicam, and the campaign received an honorable mention in the year's Annual Advertising Awards for "a series of advertisements most distinguished by excellence of copy."[6]

A similar theme was pursued, albeit less elaborately, in a 1941 advertisement for the $4,685 Packard Custom Super 8 One-Eighty Convertible Victoria. It was "naturally, a Packard ... so smart, so sophisticated, so patrician.... Owners tell us that whenever this distinguished Custom Packard parks or pauses, traffic is well nigh disrupted by admirers." The copy went on to describe the car's features, among them Electromatic Drive, electric windows and "at extra cost ... a sensational Packard 'first'—*real, refrigerated* Air Conditioning!" This was a genuine, pioneering advance. Yet it was noticeable that, whereas 1925's sedan had been described as superlative because its mechanism was superior to that of other cars, the 1941 Convertible Victoria was sold for its features. Moreover, no attempt was made to compare the car with the finest fruits of the decorative arts; the car was distinctive, gadget-laden, and excited admiration — and that was enough.

By 1958, Packard's earlier cachet had been diluted beyond recognition, but even in this, the marque's final season, copywriters attempted to recapture a lost distinction. "Wherever You Go, People Know Packard" began a stylish monochrome advertisement for the latest batch of modified Studebakers. It was no longer wise to ask the man who owned one, as such people were increasingly rare, and not always complimentary about the latest cars. The rest of the copy was ominously ambiguous: "Go where you will in a 1958 Packard and you will note the car is always a standout." The same could have been said of an Edsel. Overstatement set in: "In any setting, elegance is immediately apparent in every line of the Packard's carefully crafted exterior." Apart from a unique, and bizarre, frontal aspect, which looked much better in the advertising illustration than on the car itself, any remaining elegance was inherited from the parent Studebaker. The copywriter worked hard:

> [T]he most striking feature of the new Packard styling is its *originality*. A long, forward sloping hood sweeps down to a simple, tastefully proportioned grille that is unmistakably identifiable on the highway.

The claim was true (as was Edsel's equivalent: "... you can recognize the classic Edsel lines much faster, much farther away, than you can any other car in America!"), but the copywriter's parting shot, "Flatter yourself...with this distinction" was not enough to ensure Packard's survival into 1959.

Lincoln developed a distinctive copy style during the late 1920s and 1930s which emphasized the car's intrinsic quality,

Wherever you go, park it out of sight. Eccentric styling did little for Packard's diminishing prestige in the marque's last year (1958 campaign).

the good taste that ownership of a Lincoln indicated in its owner and, more insistently than Packard, the extent to which possession of a Lincoln indicated adherence to the best of the past combined with a ready appreciation of what was modern.

A 1926 advertisement indicated the direction that Lincoln copy would take:

> Faultless precision gives that matchless reliability which makes the Lincoln car master of every travel demand — with incomparable smoothness and high speed, indefinitely sustained.

Compared with copy for lowlier cars, Lincoln's style was measured, flowing, almost languid; the essence of the car's functional appeal was described in long sentences, rather than in the short phrases and pointed injunctions which were considered necessary to capture the reader's attention in downmarket copy. Styling was referred to, in a subtle reminder of its social role, as "appearance":

> Lincoln appearance is conservative yet commanding — every detail of appointment conforming to the edicts of good taste.

Best of all — the Lincoln you drive today is the car of your pride next year and far into the future.

Good taste, though not defined, was implied to be immune from depredation by time; a Lincoln would not, the reader inferred, become outmoded quickly. The point was made forcefully in January, 1927, in copy that perhaps revealed too much nervousness about developments in the new car market driven by General Motors:

> There are no yearly or periodic Lincoln models; the Lincoln has reached such a state of development that drastic changes are neither necessary nor desirable. Whenever it is possible to achieve an improvement in the Lincoln it is made interchangeable with previous design. Thus the Lincoln owner is permanently protected against the artificial depreciation that invariably results from an announcement of new models.

Written at any time after 1928, such copy would have seemed desperate, naive, or breathtakingly cynical, and this advertisement was more specifically of its period than most. By 1930 the car itself was old-fashioned and it was replaced in 1931.

Above and opposite: **From the classical *via* the minimalist to the starkly modern, Lincoln's backdrops changed radically over a quarter-century, but the consumer's desire to impress his fellow Americans did not (December 1926, March 1934, July 1947, and 1952 campaign).**

In the same year, in the middle of Depression, Lincoln attempted to achieve a sense of stability, of progress undeflected. As in earlier copy, the quality of the present product grew out of the application to it of timeless standards of excellence:

> There is something in the clear bright beauty of a fine mechanism that is peculiarly symbolic of our age. For today we live in pursuit of an ideal, in search of perfection of function and line and form. To this ideal, the Lincoln Motor Company is dedicated.

Unlike Packard, Lincoln did not believe that perfection had yet been found — which, a few years after its protest of 1927, gave endless scope for tinkering, year by year. It was the ideal which was implied to be constant, and adherence to it indicated confluence with the best of human aspirations. Build quality was also emphasized:

> The new Lincoln is long, wide and low for added safety and comfort. It is built slowly, painstakingly ... and it will serve you as any fine thing will serve you — with lasting satisfaction year after year — born of the moment, built for the years.

Not only was the car of good quality; if one believed the copywriter, it represented an oasis of consistency amid the economic turbulence of the period.

Much Lincoln copy of the early 1930s was modest and functional; if it was written in a style intended to appeal to affluent buyers, and therefore impliedly excluded the car from universal consideration, it was not viciously snobbish. The product, after all, was merely targeted towards the appropriate sector of the new car market. A sense of measured rationality was achieved not only in copy, but also in illustration and layout. In 1934, a Lincoln Two-Window Town Sedan was shown in the obligatory ancient-classical setting, but that setting was uncluttered. It was combined with a simple headline ("The Lincoln"), and clear copy in an unadorned typeface, lending a sense of space, elegance, and harmony to the advertisement as a whole. In 1935, the emphasis subtly changed:

> The Lincoln appeals first to the sophisticated motorist. Those who know most about motor-cars, who need not compromise about price, are its loyal adherents.... modern beauty has been achieved without the sacrifice of the dignity traditional with Lincoln.

The implied assumption of continuity with the elegant trappings of an earlier era was made explicit in 1938:

> This brilliant vehicle, the Lincoln, meets every demand of town driving as graciously as did superb custom carriages of

another era. On famous avenue and suburban lane, it proceeds with poise and aristocratic assurance. Its bearing bespeaks an owner who will have the best....

Above the copy was shown "The Two-Window Berline by Judkins at the Rittenhouse Square Flower Mart." In another 1938 advertisement, depicting "The Brougham by Brunn," the copywriter declared: "Ownership of a Lincoln is one of life's pleasant and rewarding experiences. Wherever the car may be driven, it announces quietly: 'My people recognize the best.'" The "quietly" was simply a copywriter's ruse, of course: That the car announced its owner's supposed status was the significant point, as a chauffeur-driven Brougham was far from unobtrusive. The marque's exclusivity was underlined by the list of models available: "Twenty-one body types include custom models by Brunn, Judkins, Le Baron, Willoughby. Lincoln Motor Company, builders of Lincoln and Lincoln-Zephyr." The Zephyr, though mentioned in regular Lincoln copy, was usually advertised separately and in copy of a very different style.

Yet for all the assurances of prestige inherent in Lincoln copy, the large Model K V-12 was all but discontinued in 1939. A Ford Motor Company corporate advertisement appeared in industry and dealer publications in October, 1939, with the headline: "The Lincoln V-12 — the Lincoln-Zephyr V-12 — New Size — New Power — New Beauty." A 1940 Lincoln-Zephyr was shown beside what was implied to be a 1940 Model K, but this traditional model petered out during the model year once remaining 1939 chassis had been used up. The main body of the copy in October's advertisement was devoted to the Zephyr. The large Lincoln had become altogether too exclusive to remain viable, and several of the coachbuilders who had clothed it closed down during 1939–40.

When the large Lincoln disappeared in 1939–40, the "dignified" prose which had been the hallmark of Lincoln advertising largely disappeared with it, but snobbery, as an advertising theme, was by no means abandoned. The Lincoln Continental, though based on the Zephyr, was considered to be a prestige model in its own right, and for the 1947 model year a minimalist approach was adopted in Continental advertising, which showed the car in simple side views. Coupe and convertible versions were depicted in a distinctive series of advertisements, each captioned "Nothing could be finer," which, even allowing for the car's pre-war Zephyr ancestry, was largely true.

But the Continental was discontinued in 1948 to make way for the 1949 Lincoln Cosmopolitan, which was an upmarket extension of the new, regular model range rather than a direct successor to the Continental. The Cosmopolitan lacked the earlier car's distinction and was advertised both separately and alongside the regular Lincoln line. 1947's restraint would return for Continental as a separate marque in 1956, when a black Mark II was shown in side, front, and rear views against a plain white background with the headline, "Now, in America, a refreshing new concept in fine motor cars." Brief copy appealed to "those who admire the beauty of honest, simple lines" and "who most appreciate a car which has been conscientiously crafted."

In 1952, new Lincolns were promoted in a memorable campaign which renounced traditionalism, and portrayed the new car as a natural accoutrement to a fashionable, affluent, and above all modern lifestyle:

In Lincoln, modern living reaches new heights.... Like the modern apartment, Lincoln makes practical use of every inch of space, achieving an air of openness and freedom.... The modern living approach has come to town in the distinctive, modern Lincoln.... [W]hether you are living in town or country — or both [sic] — see the new Lincoln Cosmopolitan and Capri at your dealer's showroom.

Another 1952 advertisement drew an analogy with "the livable comfort of a new-day playroom." As with the playroom, so with the car:

Fabrics and fittings are breathtakingly beautiful — eminently sturdy. Seats cradle you in a relaxing combination of springs and foam rubber. Great windows provide superb views. Lincoln matches modern living in every way.

Both cars — respectively a Capri hardtop and a Cosmopolitan sedan — were shown in a distinctive deep maroon, with contrasting roofs in cream for the hardtop and in black for the sedan. In a third advertisement, a Cosmopolitan hardtop in sober blue and black was compared with a modern office, and shown with a picture of "the glass-walled Lever House, New York's newest sky-scraper":

Executive-office luxury.... The office with the roll-top desk is as dated as a cupid's statue on the lawn. For modern living reaches out everywhere ... from the casual magnificence of the glass-walled home ... to the spacious simplicity of the glass-walled office. And now, there is the distinctive new Lincoln to fit in with the modern American scene.

That scene showed the businessman soberly at work rather than at home, and Lincoln's early invocation of the workplace as the seat of aspiration would be followed by Buick in 1963. Home-based domestic and social scenes would soon be confined more closely to inexpensive family car and station-wagon advertising.

Although these advertisements employed themes that echoed Lincoln's 1935's campaign, "the car that lets you take modern living with you" could not, by 1952, be promoted with the confidence that characterized Cadillac copy. Among traditional luxury car buyers, Cadillac was the preferred choice. It was no accident that, in 1952, Lincoln targeted the more "progressive" sector of the luxury car market, for whom the marque's modern styling (which lacked Cadillac's ostentation and dignity but which nevertheless made the Cadillac appear dated) was a point in its favor.

By the mid–1960s, Lincoln's copy had become overtly

elitist, and also more brutal in its message. Each piece in a 1967 series chose an upmarket leisure activity which typified a desirable lifestyle, and aimed to show that only with a Continental could such a lifestyle be lived to the full. The copywriters were helped by the car's styling which, though little changed since 1961, was clean and tasteful. "What does the Continental life say about you?" asked an advertisement for the Continental hardtop. "It says that you enjoy today's good life and live it with zest." In another piece, the sedan version of "America's most distinguished motorcar" was shown at a riding stables. The invitation to "come live the Continental life" was selectively, if clumsily, targeted:

> The Continental life may include riding lessons for your daughter. Certainly it includes the luxury motorcar driven by the kind of person whose discernment matches his means.

Among upmarket automobile makers, Cadillac's advertising was probably the most consistently and brazenly snobbish, and copywriters concentrated on appealing to a desire for social acceptability and public recognition. It was not enough simply to have arrived; one needed to be seen to have achieved status and influence. Within this elitist context, the automobile was as much a badge of office as mere transportation.

A 1933 advertisement, devised by Campbell-Ewald Co., set the pattern for later decades:

> Just as certain types of habiliment are made practically obligatory by the occasion, so does the event of unquestioned refinement dictate a motor car of unquestioned refinement.... For years, it has been Cadillac's privilege to build for the select occasions of American society a motor car eminently befitting the need.

Ownership of the car was declared to be "eloquent of its owner's position in life," its value resting less in pure mechanism than in the "general impression of elegance" imparted to onlookers. The advertisement was aimed at those who, in their own estimation at least, had already "arrived" and knew it, rather than at social aspirants who wished to disguise inauspicious origins. It was brave copy for the middle of a depression, and was aimed at a very small minority that had been conspicuously depleted since 1929.

In the postwar years, Cadillac underlined its supremacy by citing common knowledge: that Cadillac was the leader in its price class. In 1952, the "Golden Anniversary Cadillac" was described as a "New Goal for Twenty Million Motorists!" An assurance of objectivity followed: "Research as to motor car preference indicates that some twenty million motorists would like to own a Cadillac, if they felt it within their economic means." Aspiring owners were offered a new "heart's desire" which they could see at any Cadillac showroom.

A similar message was couched in different terms in another 1952 advertisement for the Coupe de Ville:

Overt elitism from Lincoln in one of a series of 1967 advertisements that described aspects of the "Continental life" (January 1967).

> It's a 'Who's Who' of the highway.... If you could see a list of all the distinguished persons who own and drive the Cadillac car — you would know, beyond any question, that the statement ... is true. For the roster of Cadillac owners comprises a virtual listing of the best known and most respected names of our day....

It was surely pure coincidence that the Nash Ambassador was also "a new 'Who's Who' of the highway" in a headline of the same year. In 1955, Cadillac identified with social aspirants, already in early middle age but young in Cadillac's terms, who would now join the elite: "Maybe This Will Be The Year!" Packard's earlier theme was echoed in the illustration, which showed a "handsome couple" who had "just made a very wise decision ... to get the facts about Cadillac — to see if, perhaps, the time has come for them to make the move to the 'car of cars.'" Not surprisingly, the makers believed that 1955 was "the *perfect* year to discover the joys of Cadillac ownership!"

The message appeared to have been heeded, as a 1956 advertisement crowed that "During the current year, Cadillac has welcomed a greater number of new owners to its motoring

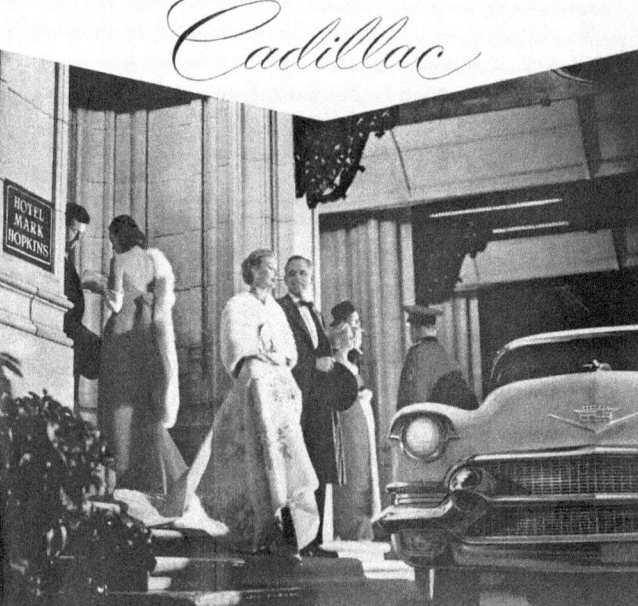

Above and opposite: "A single glance" reveals a consistency of style and outlook in Cadillac advertising of the 1950s. The social implications of Cadillac ownership were relentlessly stressed. In *The Status Seekers* (1959), Vance Packard recalled that one country club committeeman "seeking to recruit a new member boasted that [his club] had eight members who owned Cadillacs, while the rival club only had two members with Cadillacs, 'the newest three years old'" (June 1952, May 1956, and June 1957).

family than ever before in its history." Both 1955 and 1956 were record-breaking years for the Division, and, 1955 being a boom year for car sales generally, any successful marque could be expected to have reaped its fair share of first-time buyers.

Cadillac's confidence was reflected in another 1956 advertisement which built upon 1952's theme: "... for through the years, Cadillac has been the consistent and overwhelming choice of those who choose without restriction." In 1957, the social climber was again openly targeted in an appeal to his idealized self-image:

> A Single Glance Tells the Story ... when it reveals a gentleman and his lady in the company of a new Cadillac car. It tells you, for instance, that they are probably the kind of people you would enjoy knowing ... people of character and substance.

In this context, of course, "character" meant inherited wealth and "substance" its continued accumulation. According to a 1958 advertisement, Cadillac's "association with the world's leading citizens" indicated its owner's "standing in his world of affairs." The "his" here was clever, as the real, public, world of affairs was much too small to accommodate nearly 120,000 1958 Cadillac owners. But by paying approximately $5,000 for a Cadillac, one could acquire social distinction the easy way. Was it a price worth paying for the fleeting, impersonal admiration of other motorists as one sped along the highway? And how secure was the target reader's "standing," that he needed to be reassured of its value by buying a Cadillac — or any car?

In 1959, Cadillac's logic was carried a step further:

> The 1959 Cadillac car speaks so eloquently — in so many ways — of the man who sits at its wheel. Simply because it *is* a Cadillac ... it indicates his high level of personal achievement. Because it is so beautiful and so majestic, it bespeaks his fine sense of taste .... Why not visit your dealer tomorrow — and arrange to let a new Cadillac tell its wonderful story about *you*?

In the early 1960s, Cadillac combined elaborate illustrations with minimal — if grandiose — copy. Perhaps the most memorable line appeared in 1961: "A new Cadillac car is one of the few material possessions for which there is no completely acceptable substitute." In 1962, more directly comparative copy took over in captions such as "Cadillac craftsmen build only Cadillacs — a circumstance that is unique among America's fine cars;" "You can buy a new Cadillac for less than the cost of eleven models of less eminent makes of cars;" and "There are thirteen Cadillac body styles for 1962 ... more than twice the selection available with any other car in Cadillac's price range."

From 1963, greater emphasis was placed on the tangible qualities of the car and, between 1963 and 1966, buyers who could not afford a new Cadillac were encouraged into the fold by a series of advertisements which stressed the prestige that accrued even from ownership of a used model. Once the car buyer had got used to the social benefits of Cadillac ownership, he would be unwilling to give them up, and might be persuaded more rapidly than otherwise to buy a new model.

Such advertising relied not only on wishful thinking, but also on the genuine esteem in which the marque was then held. It was up to the copywriter to nurture that perception by balancing descriptions of the car itself with overt snobbery and, in some cases, portentous prose. This return to a duplex simplicity reflected earlier approaches which had been largely absent from Cadillac copy since the early 1930s.

The quest for public admiration and an upmarket ambience was not confined to upmarket cars. In the 1950s, Plymouth showed a Belvedere Convertible Club Coupe in one advertisement, remarking, amid the assurances of quality and advanced engineering, that "It's only human to get a glow when others view your car with admiring eyes." In 1956, Chevrolet's headline, "More people named Jones own Chevrolets than any other car" humorously echoed Cadillac's headlines of 1952.

In 1957, Chevrolet promised that "You'll feel a very special kind of pride the day you park a new Chevrolet in your driveway.... And when the neighbors drop by to 'look 'er over,' you'll be prouder than ever." But this was a sociable one-upmanship, as both the owner and his neighbors would appreciate the car's "fine construction and finishing touches everywhere." In this respect, Chevrolet's copy echoed the functionally based upmarket copy of the 1920s, but the tenor of the advertisement was inclusive, highlighting features of general interest. Despite appearances, the main purpose of this advertisement was to demonstrate the car's value for money in practical, rather than social, terms.

In the early 1960s, Buick modified established patterns in upmarket automobile advertising. Rather than seek to superimpose an upmarket car on the buyer's lifestyle in order to transform him into a sophisticate overnight, Buick urged the reader to buy a car that conformed to his own, pre-existing high standards, whether or not those standards had yet been acknowledged by the world. Inherently distinguished, he would one day be "discovered."

Buick's affluence was dynamic and actively ascendant: The social ascent was not claimed to culminate in Buick ownership, but was attempted in partnership with the car. This attitude was consistent with Buick's status as a lowlier marque than Cadillac, and it was also appropriate for advertising aimed at the professional classes who were Buick's principal customers, and who were generally ten years or so younger than Cadillac's clientèle. Success, for Buick, did not consist simply in looking elegant at a fashionable party; instead, Buick glamorized business. Glamorizing the *means* of social ascent as well as its prize, this copy marked a distinct change in the tempo of aspirational advertising.

A series of similar advertisements illustrated the theme in 1963: "Today's look of success is a look of action — in men and in motor cars. The 1963 Buick Electra 225 is built for men who put performance above position...." There were variations on this quasi-meritocratic theme: "Today's man of action instinctively sets standards for others to follow. For this man there is a new (and most necessary) luxury: 1963 Buick Electra 225...." Above all, the modern perfectionist was energetic and forward-looking: "Today's man of action puts performance

A relaxed, sociable one-upmanship was the keynote of these advertisements from Plymouth and Chevrolet (1953 and 1956 campaigns).

before prestige ... is impatient with yesterday's standard of excellence...." Which, given Cadillac's "Standard of the World" slogan, suggested a certain amount of inter-divisional rivalry.

Each advertisement in the series showed a "man of action" in dynamic pose, striding along a corridor, or working out a deal with a colleague. For Buick, "class" was no longer something one did or did not have; it had to be achieved, the means of achievement being made visible, and consisting in more than being born into a rich family, or the acquisition, by exertion or benign fate, of a large amount of cash.

There remained an underlying tension in much elitist copy between individualism and the need for a recognized symbol of status. If the car buyer bought an instantly recognized, mass-produced status symbol, it was *ipso facto* impossible for him to be a genuine automotive individualist, with the prestige that such individualism entailed. Yet if he bought what was claimed to be a truly exclusive car, while remaining within the American "fine car" tradition, it might not easily be recognized on the road as the prestigious indicator of "discrimination" that it set out to be.

The supposedly exclusive Cadillac was a common car, built in hundreds of thousands, and the difficulty was not permanently overcome by the introduction of successive Eldorados, culminating in the distinctive, personal-luxury, front-wheel-drive Eldorado of 1967. In a climate that increasingly associated success with individualism and originality, and taste with exclusivity, it was not surprising that confused — and confusing — copy frequently appeared in advertisements.

The confusion was particularly apparent in a 1967 advertisement for, of all cars, the low-priced Plymouth Valiant:

> More Valiants are bought internationally than any other American car. So buy one. That way you can be different without taking chances.... Owning a distinctive '67 Plymouth Valiant is a rare and exciting experience. True, there are more Valiant owners around to confirm the wisdom of your choice of imported American car. But they're still a distinguished few. You may not see one of them in days. And when you do, the chances are that his Valiant will be little like yours.

In this frenzied attempt by Plymouth to have every cake and eat the lot simultaneously, logic and persuasiveness were

Get 'em while they're young(ish), and with luck they will stay loyal for years. Owners of 1961 and 1963 models exchange compliments (April 1963).

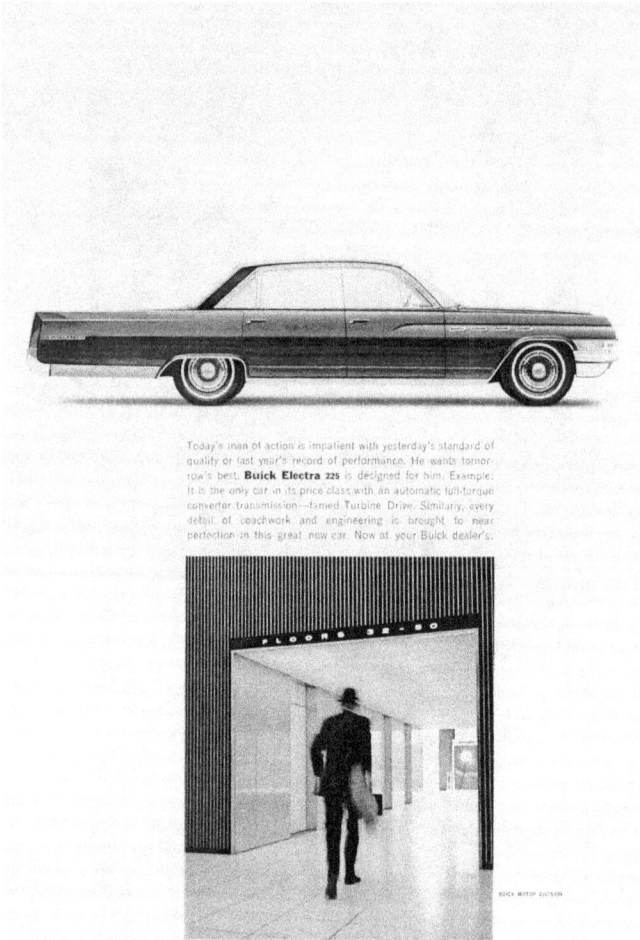

Buick glamorized office work as the means of social ascent in 1963 (December 1962).

The confusion apparent in this 1967 advertisement for the compact Valiant reflected a wider dilemma, as buyers of economy and prestige cars turned to imports for individuality and social kudos (February 1967).

thrown to the wind. The resulting copy was meaningless, and did not convey confidence in what proved to be a reliable product.

It was at this point, after all, that the automobile advertisers' myth broke down, and it was perhaps inevitable that the real individualists, sensing the contradiction, increasingly chose to buy foreign cars—a trend acknowledged by Plymouth's would-be-humorous description of the Valiant as an "imported American car." By buying an imported car, the wealthy consumer avoided the difficulty. Any expensive foreign car was prestigious and instantly recognizable as such, yet there were so many different types available that individuality was assured.

Ironically, it was BMW who resolved the dichotomy in 1978 by altering the agenda:

> The decision to buy a large BMW shows a preference for technical perfection — above all without ostentation — and the identification with a concept that is clearly modeled on the more vital forces in society. This outlook has nothing to do with age, profession or position — it can be found wherever people see their car as a perfect piece of workmanship rather than [sic] as a symbol of their wealth and status.

Thus the consensus among upmarket American automobile advertisers about the social function of a prestigious car — a consensus that had existed since the early 1930s — was undermined. American car manufacturers themselves were undermined by the importers when the car that could be promoted as showing that its owner was socially "beyond the fray" ceased to be American. The confidence of earlier Cadillac copy, in particular, appeared unlikely to return. It was by a renewed emphasis on engineering and on the efficiency of their products as functional mechanisms that the copywriters eventually found a way forward. The wheel had turned full circle, but with an important change: Never again would an American automobile be enough to satisfy every consumer's automotive dream.

Chapter 7

"Plymouth — The Car That Likes to be Compared"

Plymouth's advertising, from the marque's creation in 1928 until well into the 1950s, was predominantly factual and "copy-heavy." Illustrations, whether paintings, photographs, or line drawings, were realistic. The first Plymouths were based upon the cheaper models in the Chrysler line, and Plymouth advertisements represented the antithesis of Chrysler's earlier, flamboyant style.

The marque therefore acquired a distinct, and distinctive, identity which served it well during the Depression and until the outbreak of war in 1941. Plymouth made rapid and permanent inroads into territory which had formerly belonged to Ford and Chevrolet alone, combining the functionalism of Ford's Model T with the mechanical refinement and vigorous promotion of novelties which had ensured Chevrolet's success at Ford's expense in the mid–1920s.

Plymouth's was a philosophy to which comparative copy — a form of advertising which had declined since the end of World War I — was peculiarly well suited. An informal ban on "knocking copy" within the advertising industry, which extended to implicit comparisons that denigrated the competition, ensured that early Plymouth advertisements did not name the marque's rivals, preferring instead to let the reader make up his own mind.

"See the Plymouth. Compare it, try to equal it for the price — and inevitably you will rank it first and foremost in every element that determines true motor-car value" invited one 1929 advertisement. The car was claimed to incorporate the features found in higher-priced Chryslers in an implied challenge to Plymouth's immediate rivals. This was combined with a favorable comparison with more expensive cars: "In quality, Plymouth now advances to even higher levels, while it retains the sound Chrysler principles which have given it an international repute for economy of operation and upkeep."

Late in 1931, Plymouth placed its introductory 1932 campaign with a rapidly rising agent, J. Stirling Getchell, who, with Jack Tarleton, an art director formerly with J. Walter Thompson, had recently secured the De Soto account. Tarleton eventually devised a headline which would become famous: "Look at All Three!" Chrysler executives were skeptical at first. It was understandable that one should ask, "Why the hell do I want to sell Fords and Chevies?" Walter Chrysler decided that the advertisement should be run regardless of the risk; the rival manufacturers would not be named, but their identities would be obvious.

The first advertisement of the new campaign was published in April, 1932, and Plymouth's sales rose by 218 percent in the following three months compared with the April–June quarter of 1931. Getchell was then given the entire Plymouth account, and Plymouth's share of the low-priced car market rose from 16 percent in 1932 to 24 percent in 1933.[7]

Not all of Plymouth's advertisements were directly comparative. Some carried personal messages from Walter Chrysler, such as a 1934 piece in which Chrysler wrote:

> Why I believe Plymouth is the *Best Engineered* Car in the Low-price Field.... Our business has been very good. At this time, I believe people will be interested in knowing why. To put it as simply as I know how — our engineers have built into Plymouth the *things people want!*

Chrysler went on to describe the new car's features, some new, some long-established in cars of the marque, and concluded:

> I credit our present position in the industry to these engineering achievements. I sincerely believe Plymouth is the best

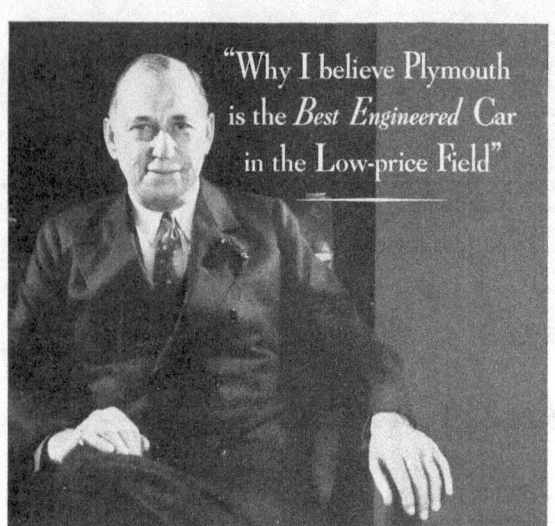

Above and opposite: Three typical advertisements from J. Stirling Getchell's famous campaign which combined realism with human interest. The comparative theme was incorporated into two principal forms: personal assurances from Chrysler Corporation personnel, including Walter Chrysler himself; and the contented-ordinary-user testimonial. In each case, the photographs used were chosen with care from a vast number taken by professional photographers at great expense, so that a modest slice-of-life tableau often cost more to create than the most elaborate conventional artwork (March 1934, June 1936, and March 1937).

engineered car in the low-price field — because it is the only low-priced car that has all of them.

A June, 1936 advertisement quoted a "certified interview with Gary Evans, Arcadia, California": "Only Plymouth has the size, comfort and performance I wanted for long trips. And it's the only one of 'All Three' with *both* 100% Hydraulic brakes and Safety-Steel body!" Both points were necessary in a year when General Motors was promoting Fisher Body's Turret Top, while Ford retained mechanical brakes until 1939 in the face of buyers' increasing skepticism. The advertisement then encouraged readers to "Compare 'All Three' ... on price, terms, features. *Drive* this new Plymouth! Ask your Chrysler, Dodge or De Soto dealer." The advertisement included photographs of Gary Evans and his Plymouth which, if not glamorous, looked the rugged and serviceable car that it was.

In 1937, promises of dependability were highlighted in a "newsprint" layout that combined several pictures with blocks of copy, slogans, and prices. Getchell insisted on advertisements that:

... came off the page fast.... We believe people want realism today.... Events portrayed as they happen. Products as they really are. Human interest. People. Places. Told in simple photographs that the eye can read and the mind can understand.[8]

"See how Plymouth savings pile up!" began a March, 1937 advertisement, in letters an inch high: "Here's the biggest and most beautiful of 'All Three' low-priced cars ... and the most economical full-size car in America!" There followed a list of features and specifications, such as a "new, Hypoid rear axle, formerly in high-priced cars only." The advertisement concluded with the slogan, "Plymouth Builds Great Cars" and a reminder that the 1937 model was still "The Best Buy of All Three!"

Advertisements for the 1938 model year consisted mainly of captioned photographs of special features. In November, 1938, paintings joined the photographs to promote the 1939 Plymouth in a "newsflash" style: "Plymouth's Got It! — more value, beauty, luxury than any other low-priced car in history." A competitive edge was maintained with "New Lower

"Massiveness and lowness distinguish the front end of Plymouth's Finest. The car is long, wide, roomy ... with concealed running-boards ... new-styled interiors." This was marginally more exciting, perhaps, than the pedantry of 1939, and it was a sign of how far Plymouth's styling had come in the intervening years that a 1942 model was used in one of General Tire's glamorous color advertisements of 1945.

Plymouth's 1942 style would be perpetuated in outline on Britain's postwar (1947) Standard Vanguard, whose advertising copy, with realistic photographs and minutely detailed copy in catalogs, reflected that which promoted the parent idiom, while 1942's slogan, "Buy Wisely, Buy Plymouth," turned up in pre- and postwar copy for the upper-middle class British Wolseley as "Buy Wisely, Buy Wolseley."

After World War II, the comparisons resumed with a wider variety of styles, and 1939's hysterical newsprint was banished. An October, 1948 advertisement took the form of a story told by a proud, if mythical, Plymouth owner: "Buying a new car is a big decision for a family," he began:

> And, in my little family, everybody has an equal voice. That's why Mother and Johnnnie went along with me as we started out to find the one car that would be the best car for us.

And so they set out, Family Man in his suit, Mother and Johnnie in judges' robes, ready to give their verdict. So that the story would not drag on for several pages, Family Man was shrewd enough to look at the most competitive car first:

> We stopped first at the Plymouth dealer. That's because we know people who have Plymouths, and they tell us this is the greatest value car of them all. We saw the new Plymouth Quality Chart and got the facts and figures for accurate comparisons. Then we took a ride.

The tale unfolded, and Johnnie expressed delight at the "Airfoam Cushions" as Mother "just sat back ... kept saying 'I feel so safe and secure,'" which must have been unsettling for the demonstration driver. Safely at rest, she got out of the car and "got real practical." She inspected the big luggage compartment. "Why, the lid opens with a finger-touch," she exclaimed, "and it's so balanced that it *can't* fall down and crack your head."

Finally, Family Man took the wheel and found "this Plymouth was the easiest-handling car I ever drove.... After the ride, I looked at Mother and I looked at Johnnie and I knew we had arrived at a verdict." At the end of the story, the inevitable family dog, also in judicial attire, delivered the family's unanimous verdict by banging his gavel on a board which said, "There's a lot of difference in low-priced cars and PLYMOUTH makes the difference!"

By contrast, a December, 1948 piece showed a painting by Norman Rockwell of a little boy standing forlornly on stage at his school's Christmas play. His mother, in the audience, explained to an anxious-looking Family Man: "I knew he'd forget ... all he can think of is our new PLYMOUTH." A seasonal

Prices!" (from $645) and "convenient terms," which reminded readers that the cost of motoring, in real terms, was decreasing. There followed the usual recital of standard equipment.

There were half-hearted attempts to sell the car on its style: "So beautiful you can hardly believe it's a low-priced car!" declared one 1939 copyline, unconvincingly, in a speech-box coming from a passenger within. The copywriter was not helped by a dull monochrome photograph that made the car look distinctly utilitarian when compared to rival Chevrolets and Fords. This was largely the fault of the car's radiator grille, which was made up of alternating painted and chromium strips that were reminiscent of a domestic heating appliance. The Plymouth was, however, "the biggest of the leading low-priced cars: 5 in. longer than one, 6 in. longer than the other!"

A great number of variations on the theme appeared in magazines and newspapers to prove beyond doubt that "Facts Show It — Owners Know It — Plymouth is the most for low price." In 1940, the strategy was elaborated with a "1940 Quality Chart ... you get a clear picture of the size, safety, long life and all-round value in 'all 3.' Of 22 quality features found in high-priced cars."

By 1942, "the car that stands up best" had become more attractive, and a picture was even reserved for styling features in a typical advertisement. According to the caption,

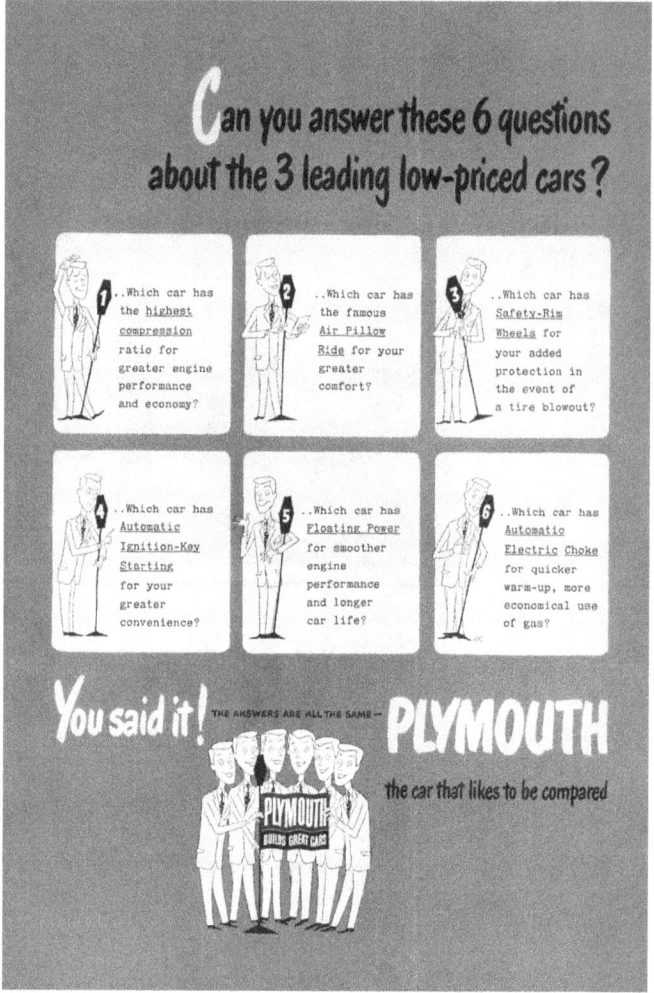

The comparative theme continued after Getchell's death in 1940. Cartoon strips were briefly popular in the late 1940s (Ford used them as well) and with Rambler in the late 1950s, although 1949's "quizmaster's challenge" was an oddity, representing a kind of advertising rarely used with automobiles and leisure goods (October 1948 and November 1949).

equivalent in 1950 was more cheerful. A family, laden with presents, bustled through a front door: "Merry Christmas Grandma ... we came in our new PLYMOUTH!"

In November, 1949, pedantry returned in the form of six questions, typewritten in white boxes against a dull grey background, suggesting stills from a television show. "Can you answer these 6 questions about the 3 leading low-priced cars?" began a cartoon quizmaster, optimistically. "Which car has Automatic Ignition-Key Starting for your greater convenience?" asked one question. "Which car has the highest compression ratio for greater engine performance and economy?" demanded another. At the end of the interrogation, 1949's new car buyers were given the answer: "You said it! The answers are all the same — Plymouth — the car that likes to be compared."

Other Plymouth advertisements of 1948–49 were more attractive, and less taxing on the reader, especially once the full-width "true" 1949 Plymouths had replaced slightly updated 1948 interim models in the spring of 1949. Convertibles and station wagons were shown in country settings, and color was used more widely than in the 1930s. Copy lightened up as well, even if the theme did not. In an August, 1949 piece a bright red convertible sped along a deserted beach, but there was no suggestion of fun or escape in the copy. Instead, there was the inevitable injunction to analyze the product in depth:

> The best way to tell new car value is by comparison. Compare the new Plymouth — feature for feature, dollar for dollar, mile for mile — to any car in any price range. Of 22 quality features found in most high-priced cars, low-priced Plymouth has 21 — low-priced car "A" has 13 — low-priced car "B" has 4!

This approach was understandable with a sedan delivery or station wagon, and desirable with commercial trucks, but it was surprising when applied to the one glamorous car in Plymouth's line-up, even if it was acting as a "draw" for the sedans in a sellers' market. Moreover, the arrival of new cars from Ford and Chevrolet, over whom Plymouth had enjoyed genuine technical advantages until 1948, made continuous use of the "comparative" theme increasingly hazardous,

"I knew he'd forget...all he can think of is our new PLYMOUTH"

Imaginative Christmas advertising in the kind of small-town setting that matched Plymouth's longstanding marque values (December 1948).

Two colorful, conventionally illustrated pieces for a new Plymouth range. The copy was relentlessly functional (August and September, 1949).

particularly when both rivals had modern and attractive styling.

The comparisons receded in 1950, and although Plymouth was still claiming "You can't match it anywhere else in the low-price 3" even in 1956, there were no lists of bumpers and ashtrays, and the main emphasis was on style and power. The "Aerodynamic Plymouth '56" with "Push-Button Driving ... Hy-Fire V-8 and ... 90–90 Turbo-Torque getaway for Top Thrust at Take-Off" was far removed from the marque's earlier, more stolid incarnations.

Plymouth was not alone in inviting comparison with competitors. Less aggressive challenges were commonplace. Lincoln understandably crowed in 1937 that "the first feature that sets a dividing line between the Lincoln-Zephyr and all other cars in the field is the V-12 engine."

Most 1954 Mercury advertisements promoted that car's power-assisted controls and easy handling, but one piece for the whole range showed a Sun Valley, a regular Monterey hardtop and a Monterey convertible, assuring those who traded up from low-priced cars that "It pays to own a Mercury." Selected statistics were given to show that economies of scale helped:

> With a 480% increase in Mercurys on the road since 1946, Mercury dealers sell more cars per dealer than their competition. This higher volume means they have lower overhead expense per car sold, can give you a better deal....

The copy purported to let the buyer "in on the act" to give him information that allowed him to realize his advantage, but the information given was highly selective and raised more questions in an inquiring or cynical mind than it answered. Did Mercury sell more cars per dealer than the opposition because those dealers sold more cars than their competitors, or because there were fewer dealers— who might be overworked when it came to service? What, exactly, was a "better deal?"— was it a better deal than Mercury might otherwise have given, or was it better than those actually offered by the competition? Given that the Mercury marque had been created as recently as 1938, and allowing for the general shortage of new cars until 1950–51 which encouraged the continued use of pre-war

Rationalism in retreat. The comparative theme was still present in 1956, but no longer made headlines (February 1956).

models, it was to be expected that the number of Mercurys in use would have increased since 1946!

The supposed information, therefore, did not equip the reader with the information needed to make a rational and informed choice, but rather simply enabled him to *feel* that his choice was rational or (more cynically) just that it was time to buy a new car. It was an ingenious form of pseudo-objectivity, ostensibly taking the reader for a shrewd businessman of the world, but containing his supposed wisdom within convenient limits. Not that the American consumer was, in fact, easily led, as Ford found out three years later when the Edsel flopped.

Chevrolet invited comparison in 1956:

> Pick out a '56 Chevy owner — one who recently switched from another make of car — and ask, in a comparative kind of way, about Chevrolet handling. Easier to park? Quicker reflexes in traffic? Holds the road better taking corners and curves? We'll bet you get 100 percent affirmative answers.

It was a safe bet, too, as many of those buyers would have traded from 1952–54 Plymouths and Fords. It was a clever way to invite flattering comparison with the opposition of two or three years earlier.

While lower- and middle-priced marques compared features and "roadability," upmarket copywriters made prestige and styling the primary factors in any comparison. Lincoln employed a variation on this theme in 1957:

> Be our guest — spend a weekend with a Lincoln. Yes, we invite you to drive a Lincoln for a whole wonderful weekend ... without the slightest obligation. Just stop in at our showroom, or give us a call.... With a Lincoln parked in your driveway, you can compare its long, low, clean-lined kind of styling with that of any other fine car in your neighborhood.

The comparison would invite conversation, and the neighbors would imagine that one owned the car. The "guest" might be tempted to buy it in order not to have to admit on Monday morning, as he got into his '55 Mercury, that he couldn't afford it, and only had the car on trial. And even if he could afford the car, the "neighborhood" might not be convinced unless he bought it.

Cadillac was more straightforward in 1959:

> We believe that a personal inspection will convince you — and that an hour at the wheel will add certainty to conviction. Why not accept your dealer's invitation to visit him soon — for a ride and a revelation?

During the 1960s, comparative copy became more widespread. A 1965 Rambler advertisement concluded: "FREE!

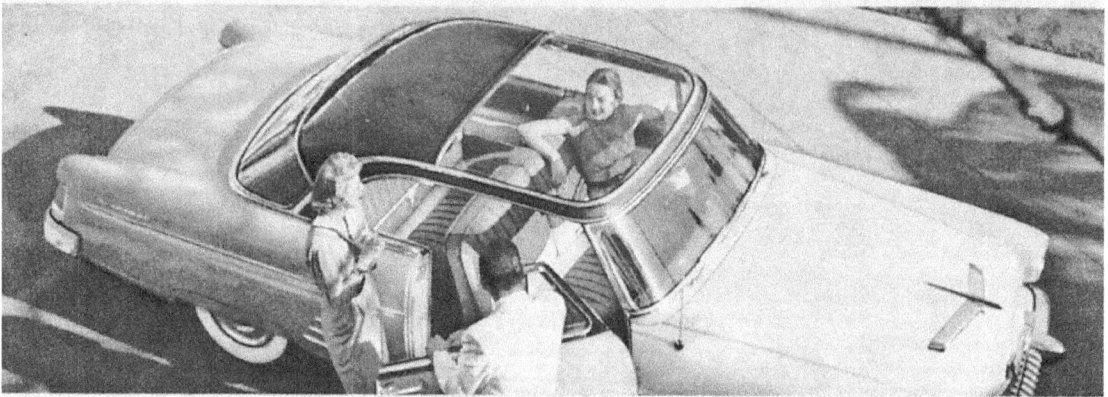

Selective statistics from Mercury in 1954. The consumer was not encouraged to think for himself, but merely to think that he was thinking... (September 1954).

LINCOLN

UNMISTAKABLY... THE FINEST IN THE FINE CAR FIELD

SPRING BONNETS BY JOHN FREDERICS LINCOLN PREMIERE LANDAU—PICTURED AT THE CARLYLE HOTEL, NEW YORK CITY

Be our guest – spend a weekend with a Lincoln

Yes, we invite you to drive a Lincoln for a whole wonderful weekend... without the slightest obligation. Just stop in at our showroom, or give us a call.

If you've ever talked to a new Lincoln owner, you've probably heard the comment that we hear over and over: "If everyone could just *drive* this Lincoln, they'd know it's even greater than it looks!"

Well, now you *can* drive this Lincoln. We want you to take a Lincoln home... for a day, for an evening or for a weekend – make your own arrangements. But by all means, get to know Lincoln on a "first-name" basis.

With a Lincoln parked in your driveway, you can compare its long, low, clean-lined kind of styling with that of any other fine car in your neighborhood. But best of all, you'll have the opportunity to really *drive* this car – and that's why we extend you this unique invitation.

We know that once you've driven a Lincoln as though it were your own, you'll understand why more fine car buyers are turning to Lincoln than ever before in history.

Call us today, and make arrangements for *your* Lincoln weekend. Remember, there's no obligation.

YOUR LINCOLN DEALER

"Without the slightest obligation"— but how do you admit to neighbors that you have only borrowed it? (May 1957).

A confident, if implicit, invitation by Cadillac to compare the flamboyant 1959 Series 62 Coupe with its rivals. Fin height varied slightly from car to car, as handwork was employed during construction (May 1959).

1965 Car X-Ray Book! 48 pages of comparisons of the leading '65 cars. Hundreds of illustrations, many in full color. It can save you hundreds of dollars. Get yours at your Rambler dealer." In 1966, AMC disingenuously claimed to consider comparison of the AMC Ambassador with the Chevrolet Impala and Ford Galaxie unfair because neither car was fitted with air conditioning as standard equipment. The Ambassador was compared instead with one car that did have air conditioning — the Rolls-Royce Silver Shadow. Having caught the reader's attention, AMC then pointed out that "the Rolls-Royce has less headroom than a Cadillac. The Ambassador has more."

Increasingly, it was feature-for-feature comparison, rather than general "knocking" or comparative copy, that was employed. Chrysler stayed in the front line with the Dodge Coronet 500 Wagon in April, 1968. The Coronet was promoted on its own merits but, at the end of the copy, it was pointed out that air conditioning could be fitted to bring the Dodge's price up to the level of unconditioned Impalas and Galaxie 500s. By 1968, all three makes were competing in the middle price range, low-priced status being confined to smaller Chevrolets, Fords, and Valiants.

A danger with mentioning Ford and Chevrolet as the marques to beat, however, as Chrysler's executives realized in 1931, was that such advertising might have the effect of reinforcing the images of those cars rather than that of the advertised product in the public imagination. Being the one to beat might, from the consumer's point of view, mean being the one to buy. In order to avoid such own goals, AMC and Chrysler had to tread carefully. Plymouth knew this in the 1940s, and if the reader was temporarily frustrated by the copywriter's designation of Chevrolet and Ford as car "A" and car "B," it was Plymouth's name that remained in his mind after the page was turned and not — for good or ill — the names of Plymouth's rivals.

In 1962, Chrysler Corporation took the comparative theme a stage further in a series of advertisements, mainly in black and white, that issued "a forthright challenge to everyone who plans to buy a luxury car this year." The invitees were selected by Imperial, who assured VIPs that "in a few days, you will receive, by mail or telephone, a personal invitation to drive a 1962 Imperial." There was a catch-all at the end: "R.S.V.P. Even though our invitation may somehow miss you,

Imperial lured "eminent" motorists from other makes during 1962-63 in a distinctive campaign (February 1962 and April 1963).

"It isn't very likely that you'll run out and buy the new '69 Imperial just because the headlights see you to your door." Just so — but is it any more likely that you'll buy a conventional luxury car for its hidden engineering features? Imperial crosses its fingers in 1969 (October 1968).

an Imperial comparison-tour may easily be arranged by writing on your letterhead to: General Manager, Imperial Division...." Subsequent advertisements targeted specific groups of Americans who were successful in their fields. A "proposal to America's eminent attorneys" was typical:

> Within the month, you and your colleagues in the legal profession will be offered personal use of a new Imperial for a thorough driving test. You will be asked only to specify an hour of appointment. Our dealer will deliver the car at your home or office; he will brief you on operation of its controls; he will answer any questions you may have. Then the Imperial is yours ... for as long as you need to make a full and private evaluation of Imperial motoring.

It was up to Imperial to decide who was "eminent," and there was a provision in case an invitation "should fail to reach you": The attorney who had been passed over, but who found the offer of a road test intriguing, needed only to write to the makers for arrangements to be "made promptly." Similar invitations were sent to "America's 5,344 leading M.D.s." A later advertisement reported the doctors' collective approval: "Leading doctors accept new Imperials for comparison testing." In another piece, the "chief executives of the 100 top banking firms" were promised invitations to drive the new car in language less exaggeratedly formal than that used to address the lawyers, and snappier than that used for the doctors, whose invitation concentrated more on engineering features. It was in many ways a subtle campaign and an imaginative variation of Plymouth's earlier, more abrasive development of the strategy. The car sold better during 1962–63 than in 1961, and 1963's invitations were sent to "America's most successful independent businessmen" and "principals of America's 6500 leading architectural firms," among others.

The essence of marque loyalty as stated by Cadillac in the mid–1970s (February 1976).

Yet by the late 1960s, Imperial's sales were declining, while Cadillac, and to a lesser extent Lincoln, enjoyed increased production and continued prestige. Imperial had suffered over several years from too close an identity with Chrysler cars, which frequently looked similar to the prestige line of the Corporation's range. For 1969, Imperial advertising continued to invite comparison with rivals, but the copy was unusually earnest, reflecting a lack of social, if not mechanical, confidence. "Introducing the all new 1969 Imperial. And several things you should know before you buy any luxury car" began a typical piece for the Le Baron 4-door Hardtop in October, 1968. After several hundred words of descriptive prose which ranged from the principles of unitary construction to "a stereo system with 5 speakers," the fine car buyer was reminded of the weighty decision he made when choosing a car: "Before you spend $6000 or $7000 for a new '69 Imperial, or any other luxury car, you should know what you're spending $6000 or $7000 for. This year spend a little time with all three of them."

But, as Imperial knew, no one bought a luxury car for its "unitized body" for which there was "no better insurance against rattles," or even "torsion bars instead of coil springs." And when Imperial's copywriter concluded that "... you should have been adding it up. These are the things you buy a luxury car for," he displayed a startling naivety. For these were exactly the mundane details that most luxury car buyers sought to escape. The copy might convince those who were actively dissatisfied with their current (rival) cars, which was partly its intention, and it was true that Imperial was the best-handling American luxury car. But Imperial did not convey the necessary element of prestige; the copywriter, unlike his counterparts at Lincoln and Cadillac, did not invite the luxury car buyer to be flattered by his own aspirations. Imperial sales slumped in 1970.

It was left to Cadillac to state a more convincing case in 1976, for a marque whose prestige, among its limited target market, was less in doubt:

> You'll buy your first for what you think it is. And your second for what you know it is. Maybe that's the reason Cadillac repeat ownership is consistently the highest of any U.S. luxury car make.

Even if, by 1976, those letters "U.S." in Cadillac's copy spoke volumes for the success of luxury imports, Chrysler's comparative strategy was turned on its head by General Motors, whose low-priced car had been so consistently, if anonymously, targeted by Plymouth in the 1930s. Imperial, meanwhile, had been discontinued as a marque in 1975, re-emerging only in 1981 as a notionally independent adapted Chrysler before disappearing again after 1983, while Plymouth continued until 2001.

The "comparative" strategy was most effective in the low-price field when used with an emerging marque which enjoyed tangible advantages over its opposition. The comparison was anchored in factual, feature-by-feature analysis, which lent it the necessary credibility. It was least effective whenever functionalism and practicality were less important to the consumer than social credibility or participation in a wider automotive fantasy. Applied indiscriminately, it could, indeed, "unsell" a product. Imperial's mistake was never made by Cadillac, who, insofar as it acknowledged any opposition, did so only in general terms before asserting its own supremacy, and who, by diversifying its range while retaining a distinct identity, survived the fuel-crisis era.

Colorful, and only a little fanciful: During the Depression, tangible mechanical features were described even in aspirational advertising. *See* Chapter 6 (May 1933).

Color photography made the motorist's heart beat faster, too, when it was a rarity. *See* Chapter 1 (May 1934).

IN TUNE

• To those who take pride in their homes, their surroundings, their standards of living, a fine motor car is an essential. For thirty-five years Pierce-Arrow has been a symbol of social standing . . . has fitted naturally into a well-ordered mode of living.

• And so today, with a new spirit in the air, with people everywhere again gratifying their desires for the finer pleasures of life, the supreme comfort and luxury and the distinguished excellence of a Pierce-Arrow are eminently in tune with the times.

America's Finest Motor Car for America's Finest Families

THE ENCLOSED DRIVE LIMOUSINE

PIERCE·ARROW

The indoor color photograph used for the dinner table in this *Fortune* magazine advertisement was very advanced in 1935. Other papers ran a black-and-white version. *See* Chapter 1 and Chapter 6 (September 1935).

American-style advertising from the British arm of N.W. Ayer & Son in the mid–1930s. *See* Chapter 12 (May 1935).

Modernists in paradise: a slightly Teutonic-looking advertisement for the streamlined Lincoln-Zephyr. *See* Chapter 2 (August 1937).

Nash combined illustration and copy to elegant effect during 1939-40. *See* Chapter 1 and Chapter 13 (February 1940).

This morale-boosting campaign lifted servicemen's spirits at a time when tire mileage mattered. *See* Chapter 10 (February 1945).

J. Walter Thompson created one of the best-known campaigns of its era for Ford. *See* Chapter 10 (November 1945).

Lincoln evoked a pre-war elegance in Continental advertising of the late 1940s. *See* Chapter 6 (July 1947).

Buick's simple side view echoed Continental advertising a few years earlier. *See* Chapter 1 (1953 campaign).

Freudians, look away now. The fantasy seems far-fetched today, but how else to frighten off those UFOs? Oldsmobile's late-starting 1951 model year allowed the '50 "88" this imaginative finale. *See* Chapter 3 (November 1950).

Peaceful, family-oriented escapism from Nash in 1953. *See* Chapter 5 (1953 campaign).

Gentle advertising in an impatient era — yet many Americans did equate value with long-term reliability. See Chapter 12 (January 1954).

Not just a myth: Pink Cadillacs really did appear in a few advertisements. *See* Chapter 1 (1957 campaign).

Sociable leisure was a long-running theme in Chevrolet advertising. *See* Chapter 1 and Chapter 6 (July 1958).

Pontiac's advertising illustrations of the 1960s, typified by this 1964 Grand Prix, became famous, and surviving artwork is highly prized today. Many settings, like this one, were European. *See* Chapter 1 and Collector's Note (December 1963).

Top: Dark, moody backdrops were popular in the late 1960s for both sporting and luxury cars. Length could be exaggerated photographically, too, if the wheels remained round. *See* Chapter 1 and Chapter 13 (November 1966). *Bottom:* The double-spread as a miniature poster for a clean and sculpted design, beautifully photographed. *See* Chapter 1 (October 1968).

1970 Chevelle SS 396.
It's getting tougher and tougher to resist.
The standard V8 has been kicked up to 350 hp.
A new air-gulping Cowl Induction Hood awaits your order.
You can also order your choice of a floor-mounted 4-speed or the 3-range Turbo Hydra-matic.
Under that lean and hungry look is a lean and agile suspension. F70 x 14 white-lettered wide oval treads. 7"-wide mag-type wheels. And power disc brakes.
Your mission is to infiltrate your Chevy dealer's and escape with this car.
It will go willingly.

Putting you first, keeps us first.

In ten seconds, your resistance will self-destruct.

"But Mom, I'm reading *National Geographic*!" But which page? A fantasy for boys young and old, then and now. *See* Chapter 3 (December 1969).

You can get one for the price of a Toyota.

At first glance, the Toyota Celica ST might come off as a rich man's sports car.
That's the nice thing about it.
However, in real life, it's an economy car.
That's the nice thing about it.
The Celica ST has hood vents and rally stripes. Standard.

It comes with a four-speed synchromesh transmission and radial tires. Standard.
A high revving overhead cam engine, tachometer (redline at 6300 rpm), and front disc brakes. Even an AM radio. Standard.
All this and more for $2848*
That's the nice thing about it.

For your nearest dealer, call 800-243-6000 toll-free. (In Connecticut, 1-800-882-6500)
*Mfrs suggested retail price. Freight, local taxes, dealer prep, and options extra.

Practical yet sporty: Toyota picks up an American theme and runs with it. *See* Chapter 18 (June 1972).

An investment in badge-engineering for an economy-minded era — and the cityscape outside recalled Lincoln-Zephyr advertising of forty years earlier. *See* Chapter 1 and Chapter 14 (May 1977).

Chapter 8

The Objectivity Factor

The "objectivity factor" of an advertisement was increased by comparing a product with its immediate rivals. Otherwise, with advertising for cars, as for other products, a lingering doubt might remain in the reader's mind that the features selected for analysis had been chosen less than impartially. And when, as in Plymouth's copy, the automobile in question was declared to have a greater number of features than its rivals, the question remained — What was a feature? In the early days of the automobile, a steering wheel, rather than a tiller, was a feature. So was a pneumatic tire or, in the early 1930s, a pressed-steel wheel. By 1939, however, the general design of the American automobile was established, and apparently similar products needed to be differentiated. There then arose the danger that, by laboring details, a copywriter would bore the reader and appear to damn the product with faint, if protracted, praise. What was the car, in its totality, really like?

One response to this challenge was the contented-ordinary-user testimonial. As an advertising motif, it appeared sporadically. The independent testimony of the consumers cited by Plymouth in its long-running "Compare All Three" campaign was convincing because it was derived from down-to-earth experience, rather than any supposed expertise or vested interest. Even if Plymouth's interviewees all sounded remarkably similar, the all-important appearance of objectivity was given, and the objectivity of demonstrable difference provided by comparisons with Ford and Chevrolet was augmented by the objectivity of disinterestedness guaranteed by the independence of the testimonials. At the very least, Plymouth was seen to value the opinions of its customers. Plymouth preferred the testimony of conspicuously worthy, dependable individuals—the people who reflected Plymouth values: engineers, small businessmen, firefighters, police officers—above all, people who were realists. In April, 1936, Plymouth cited "Deputy Sheriff Pat Enos" of Oakland, California:

> As Sheriff, I Needed A Tough Car! I didn't have to look at "All Three".... My three brothers did it for me. I got in their cars—saw how easily they rode — how easy they were on gas— how 100% dependable.... A man in my line of work has to have a car he can count on all the time. You can't speculate on how quick your car will start — how fast it will pick up — or how sure it will stop — no sir, not when you're a sheriff in this country!

"America is full of families that own more than one Plymouth," added the copywriter, challenging the longer-established opposition. An August, 1936 piece quoted Mrs. William Pitt of Stamford, Connecticut, who was shown with her new sedan beside her husband's 1935 Plymouth convertible—a clever way of showing off 1936's updated styling. "The first time I rode in my husband's Plymouth ... I knew I wanted one, too.... And, since interior decorating is a practical hobby of mine, I am quite in love with the beauty of this new Plymouth ... both inside and out!"

In May, 1936 Walter Zepke, an aircraft development engineer, declared: "A Sweet-Running Motor is Music — to Me" and went on to say how impressed he was with Plymouth's "Floating Power" rubber engine mountings: "Aviation puts a premium on vibrationless operation. So Plymouth's Floating Power impressed me tremendously. As did the economy and power of the engine." For 1937, the theme was continued with slightly updated layouts and typefaces. "Miss Beth Hower, Director of Public School Bands" was pictured with her Plymouth, which she had driven through water so high that it flowed over the floorboards. "But my car ran perfectly ... and I've *never* had any real mechanical expense!" she assured readers.

As an advertising strategy, this series of testimonials had

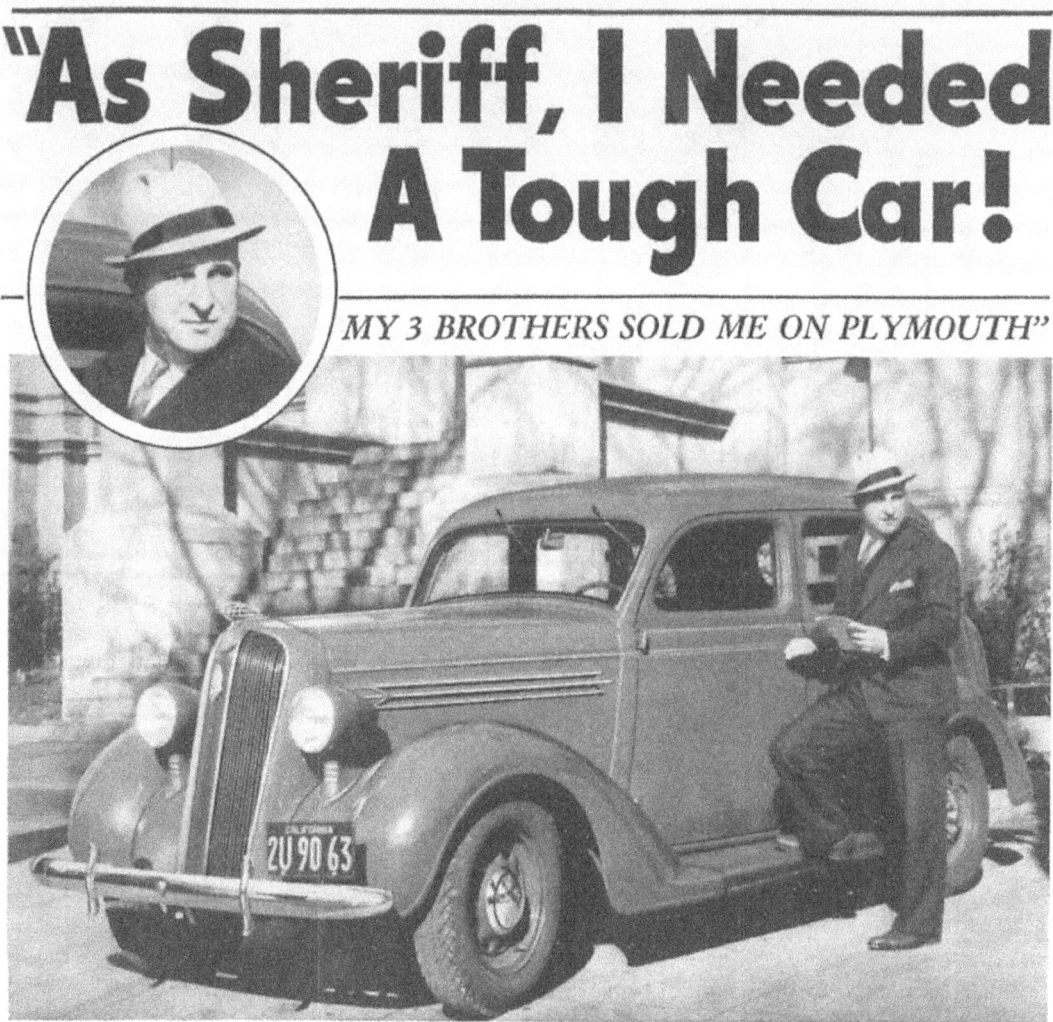

Deputy Sheriff Pat Enos was typical of the solid, mature citizens cited by Plymouth in the mid–1930s (April 1936).

the merit of being memorable for their human interest, and Plymouth's rising sales figures suggested that they were more persuasive to the people who bought low-priced automobiles for solid, day-to-day service than any vague assurance of the product's competitiveness. Compared with Chevrolet and particularly Ford, Plymouth lacked a tradition of service in mobilizing America, but made up for that deficit in copy that was imaginative and, above all, plausible.

Dodge, known as a producer of solid, dependable automobiles since 1914, and part of the Chrysler Corporation since 1928, used longer copy than Plymouth's to cite the experiences of well-known people who were admired for their practical skills, such as "Frank Buck, Famous Explorer" and "Major M.E. Trull, Noted Marksman," in a series of half-page advertisements which perpetuated Plymouth's distinctive newspage layout. As in a newspaper story, Major Trull's testimony was peppered with expressions which reflected his own field of expertise:

> Dodge Scores a Bull's-Eye With Me.... My experience as a marksman has made me intolerant of anything mechanical that is not efficient.... I have had no mechanical trouble.... [I]t rides and drives like a dream. I haven't found another car that has all the safety features combined in one car that my Dodge has ... sure-fire, trigger-quick genuine hydraulic brakes ... safety-steel bodies ... and there's the "clincher" ... record-smashing economy....

During 1963–65, Rambler — like Plymouth in the 1930s, a manufacturer of simple, worthy automobiles — ran a series of "Love Letters to Rambler" from contented ordinary users of its cars; and like Plymouth thirty years earlier, Rambler cited the testimony of reliable, middle-aged citizens who valued quality and reliability over pushbutton gadgets. They ranged from "Naval Firefighter John E. Simeon of Silver Spring, Maryland" to "Chief Engineer of the Barbizon Plaza Hotel in New York City, Malcolm Anderson." Others included a manufacturer, a sportscaster, a mechanic, a U.S. Coast Guard and a buffalo rancher. One television advertisement featured a learner driver, whose attempts to cope with stick-shift and traffic hazards caused chaos, but did not destroy the car.

In 1968, Buick deployed the genre in several advertisements, among them a piece for the Sportwagon. "Mrs. Graham Brown, Mother of five" explained how the car was ideal for the sailing enthusiast: "Any given weekend, we carry boats, sails, masts, five or six children ... we even pack a nine-foot dinghy in the back of our Buick Sportwagon."

The luxurious Electra 225 Limited, on the other hand, was praised by a real estate investment counselor for its comfort and prestige: "You should have just as beautiful a feeling in an automobile as you do in your living room. My Electra Limited gives me that feeling. The interior is nicely done — not a bit gaudy.... I've had clients get in the car and say, 'I didn't know they're building a car like this today.'"

Distinct from, and more common than, the ordinary-

Dodge prices started $130 higher than Plymouth's but, like Plymouth, Dodge appealed to conservative, practical folk (May 1936).

Love Letters to Rambler

Lt. David A. Corey

U.S. Coast Guard Lieutenant David A. Corey of Quaker Hill, Conn., has owned many different cars—is now driving his first Rambler. But you can bet it won't be the last, to judge by his enthusiastic comments on his Classic Sedan with stick-shift. He writes:

"Needed no corrections on the 2,000-mile checkup"

"I have owned at least one each of the cars of all the so-called 'big three,' and the success I had with them could not even approach that which I have had with Rambler.

"I have just driven my 20,000th mile...(with an outstanding mileage of just over 22 miles per gallon). Aside from the gasoline, oil and lubrication costs, the only money I have spent has been for one fan belt.

"These have been the most enjoyable miles I've ever driven. Too bad more people don't experience this 'delightful driving'."

But thousands and thousands of people *are* discovering Rambler's "delightful driving"—year after year. Proof: more than 2 million of them have made the switch to Rambler.

Why? Simply because Rambler gives them more in value and comfort and economy. See your Rambler dealer!

Love Letters to Rambler

Carl L. Klocker

The Klocker family are Rambler experts. They have thirteen Ramblers in their past and present and are still buying. Read why they remain so loyal.

"Dependable transportation— low mileage costs are essential in my business."

"I appreciate the extent to which American Motors goes in making Rambler owners happy. I drive approximately 50,000 miles a year and I turn my Rambler in every year or 50,000 miles, whichever comes first. This is my 10th Rambler and my wife is driving her third. None of my nine previous Ramblers has cost me more than $100.00 for repairs, including tires for the 50,000 miles I drive them... my new one is a four-door sedan. The increase in horsepower is much appreciated. One would think he was driving an eight-cylinder car."

Here's the 1965 version of the 4-door sedan Mr. Klocker is now driving happily. It's the Classic 770 with the Torque Command 232 Six. It's the Six that comes on like an Eight. Try it now!

FREE! 1965 Car X-Ray Book! 48 pages of comparisons of the leading '65 cars. Hundreds of illustrations, many in full color. It can save you hundreds of dollars. Get yours at your Rambler dealer.

AMC echoed Plymouth's campaign nearly thirty years later in a long-running series of "Love Letters to Rambler" (July 1963 and June 1965).

Contented-ordinary-user testimonials featured prominently in Buick's 1968 advertising (December 1967).

user testimonial was the celebrity endorsement, in which a well-known film star, writer, or other celebrity posed with the product and said how good it was, while not necessarily owning or knowing very much about it.

In 1937, Goodrich Tires employed well-known authors to write graphic accounts of accidents caused by faulty tires. In a piece written by "well-known author Rex Beach," the reader was told the "thrilling True Story of the man who is living on 'Borrowed Time,'" in which a motorist suffered a blow-out at an inopportune moment: "His wife was ill. He was rushing to her ... when BANG!... A BLOW-OUT!" The story appeared to be an account of a documented incident, although the true story could — cleverly — have been that of any man who is presently living on borrowed time rather than that of the particular character who felt he was after the blow-out brought him to his senses. But it was a parable of what could happen to any motorist. It concluded with an earnest injunction to keep tires in good condition, and to buy Goodrich tires, of course.

In another advertisement, S.S. Van Dine, "celebrated author of popular mystery thrillers and creator of Philo Vance," was drafted in to write about a police chase in which the pursuing car suffered the inevitable blowout. There was the inevitable homily, too, though credibility was enhanced, in this case, by the use of a story "suggested by an actual occurrence," though it was not mentioned whether the occurrence had involved a police car and an eyewitness or a bicycle and a vivid imagination. Both advertisements were signed by their respective authors and they ensured, if nothing else, that the next time a reader picked up a mystery thriller, he would also think of his tires.

Showbusiness celebrities endorsed all kinds of improbable cars in the 1930s. The technique was a particular favorite with De Soto, whose cars were acclaimed by such luminaries as Gary Cooper, Ginger Rogers, Jack Dempsey, and Deanna Durbin. Shirley Temple and her safety-conscious mother endorsed a 1936 Dodge, and a 1937 Studebaker was shown with Bob Hope.

Copy reflected the stars' individual specialties. Bing Crosby

Rex Beach was one of several popular writers who endorsed Goodrich tires in 1937. It was not stated whether he actually used them (1937 campaign).

"sang the praises" of the 1938 De Soto, although in 1939 he sang "In My Merry Oldsmobile" in "The Star Maker" which dictated a change of allegiance. He went on to endorse the year's new Oldsmobile convertible in the *Saturday Evening Post*, and readers were invited to send to the makers for copies of the music from the movie. Popular songs were savaged mercilessly; in the case of Kate Smith, the adaptation was less than subtle: "The moon comes over the mountain no more serenely than the 1937 Studebaker does" was typical of the square-wheeled lyricism sometimes achieved by copywriters who strayed off their natural turf.

Contrasting with Plymouth's contented ordinary users and De Soto's showbusiness stars was a series of illustrious clients paraded by Buick in 1937. It was an old theme in upmarket copy, but it had fallen into disuse since the Depression. A Buick sedan, shown in China, was declared to be "Number One Boy for transportation in many an honorable household," and a list of Buick-owning Chinese military and civil dignitaries was included in the middle of the page. In another advertisement, the Buick was trumpeted—only four years before Pearl Harbor—as "long a favorite with Japanese of most exalted degree .... Many branches of the government, including the army, navy, home department and foreign department; a score and more of prefectural offices; municipalities; schools; provinces—these as well as private citizens show by repeated purchases the high esteem in which Buick is held the whole world over."

In February, 1940, the illustrious client testimonial gave way to an indirect but impliedly expert assessment by a British automobile manufacturer. The Buick Limited was declared to be a pattern for one of the best cars in the world:

> In England is built a motor car which is recognized around the world as an illustrious example of craftsmanship, a car priced high in five figures for its least expensive model. Once each year the builders of that car buy an American automobile, not to be driven, but to be torn down to provide part-by-part precision standards to be matched by the methods of British workmen.

The car was a standard production Buick, and the boast was not an idle one. King Edward VIII had owned several successive Buicks, and it seemed that no amount of hand-built care could supplant the advances brought by the best American mass-production technology. Buicks were popular among British buyers of American cars in the 1930s, and as early Rolls-Royce Phantom IIIs suffered hydraulic tappet failures, Buick

The illustrious client testimonial was rare by 1937, when Buick revived the theme in this most ironic of automobile advertisements (May 1937).

went from strength to strength. The Phantom's independent front suspension was licensed in England under General Motors patents.

With the increasing popularity of domestic radio in the 1930s and 1940s, a relationship of mutual support developed between the automobile makers and radio stations through commercial sponsorship of programs. In 1939, for instance, Plymouth encouraged readers of its advertisements to "Tune in Major Bowes' Original Amateur Hour, Columbia Network, Thursdays, 9 to 10 P.M. E.D.S.T." Major Bowes endorsed the related De Soto in a late 1938 press advertisement, and he ordered a special Chrysler Airflow Custom Imperial for his own

Rolls-Royce quality at a fraction of the cost? American engineering gave many European luxury car makers pause for thought in the 1930s. Behind the car is Nelson's column, 169 feet high, in Trafalgar Square, London (February 1940).

Bennett Cerf was one of many famous personalities featured in Hertz advertising during 1958. The convertible is a Chevrolet Impala (March 1958).

An old-fashioned advertisement for an old-school Oldsmobile 98 hardtop sedan (January 1976).

use. Constructed by LeBaron, it had a uniquely luxurious interior designed by Chrysler's head of interior design, Fred A. Selje.

Radio sponsorship continued through World War II. Patriotic listeners could "tune in on Major Bowes' Program every Thursday, 9:00 to 9:30 P.M., Eastern War Time" according to a 1945 De Soto advertisement showing a 1942 model. In the same year, NBC offered "General Motors' Symphony of the Air" every Sunday afternoon, while Nash devotees were promised a "New Radio Hit Show!" with "'The Andrews Sisters' and Guest Stars Sundays 4:30 P.M. E.W.T. Blue Network." Alternatively, there was the Friday night "Ford musical program," also on Blue Network, succeeded later in 1945 by "The Ford Show" with "Brilliant singing stars, orchestra and chorus. Every Sunday, over Coast-to-Coast NBC Network." Times were given for different time zones.

In the 1950s, television increasingly supplanted radio and film in the public imagination, and copywriters adapted their scripts as automobile companies began to sponsor television programs. In 1953, Buick offered a "Television treat, the Buick Circus Hour every fourth Tuesday," while De Soto-Plymouth dealers presented "Groucho Marx in 'You Bet Your Life' every week on Radio and Television ... NBC Networks." By 1954, Plymouth were inviting viewers to "Tune in Medallion Theatre every week on CBS-TV" with a helpful rider for low-priced car buyers who had only just acquired a set: "See TV page of your newspaper for time and station." Ford, meanwhile, now offered "Great TV! Ford Theater, NBC-TV."

From being confined to the small print, television moved center-stage in a striking 1955 advertisement for the Lincoln Capri hardtop, as talent-spotter "Ed Sullivan, M.C. of 'Toast of the Town,' and Julia Meade introduce New Lincoln." The setting was a television studio: "Camera one! Close up! Take the new Lincoln for 1955." The reader saw the car through a gallery window, while other images, taken by different cameras, appeared on small screens below: "Monitor sets show new rear deck, new longer body, new front assembly." The rest of the copy was completely conventional, emphasizing the car's styling features and performance.[9]

In 1954, the celebrity endorsement was combined with

old-fashioned snobbery and a specific appeal to women in Nash's "She drives a Rambler" campaign. Prominent women such as "Mrs. Philip Armour III" endorsed a compact which had been substantially updated in 1953. An equivocal-looking Mrs. Armour was seen at the foot of a staircase with her household dog, in a revival of the kind of portrait popular with upmarket marques in the 1920s, and which had been used by Packard as late as 1953.

In 1958, Bennett Cerf was one of several celebrities who endorsed Hertz Rent-A-Car: "Every Sunday night you can see Bennett Cerf on CBS-TV's 'What's My Line?' At Hertz, however, we see him many more times. On one of his visits, we asked this well-known publisher, author and columnist to pose for us. Afterwards, he told us: 'It's no secret what your line is. I caught on first time I rented one of your new cars. It's service!'" He was shown climbing into a 1958 Chevrolet convertible, to keep "a campus speaking engagement on time." The copy concluded with a brief description of the Hertz service. Norman Rockwell, according to another 1958 advertisement, found the Lincoln of that year ideal for his pictures.

By the end of the 1950s, the celebrity endorsement was losing favor as an effective theme for press advertising, and it would recur only sporadically in the 1960s and 1970s. It was therefore surprising to see the genre fleetingly resurrected for large cars in the 1970s, as by Oldsmobile in January, 1976: "We built this Olds 98 for Walt Lecat, who expects the car he buys to make him feel like a king. Or better." In the same year, the singer Jack Jones smiled suavely from the velour-upholstered back seat of a Chrysler New Yorker Brougham: "It's the talk of the town.... Everybody's talking about the New Yorker's elegant styling and comfort." It was an old-fashioned strategy for an old-style hardtop sedan, and the nostalgic flavor was reinforced by a television program announcement at the foot of Oldsmobile's copy: "Tune in the Bing Crosby Pro-Am ABC-TV Sat. and Sun., Jan. 24–25."

It was almost like old times.

Chapter 9

"Remember How You Hungered for It?"

Nostalgia was one of many advertising themes that never dominated copy at any one time, but which periodically reappeared in advertisements for all kinds of American cars. In the early days, advertisers appealed to the memories of pioneer motorists—memories of motoring in a period when the automobile was still a novelty; when skeptical onlookers would cry "Get a horse!" at the first whiff of an impending breakdown. Once the automobile had been established in America for several decades, nostalgia became an effective element in the copywriter's repertoire. In the postwar years, it appeared regularly in automobile advertising.

In many advertisements, the value of the "American tradition," the heritage of the marque represented, and the recollections of the target readership were addressed simultaneously in an effort to inveigle a car into the public imagination and private affection. It was hoped that while the prospective buyer was still overcome with that sense of well-being which came from a life enjoyably spent participating in the American dream, he would reach for his pocketbook, make the first payment and drive away in a new car before the delirium wore off. This participatory angle was generally considered to work best on a male audience, and while many nostalgic advertisements were aimed at men, very few, if any, were targeted at women. Marque loyalty, in particular, was considered a male phenomenon.

Nash rekindled forgotten dreams in August, 1953, in an advertisement for the Ambassador Country Club hardtop. The copy was addressed "To the Boy who wanted a Stutz Bearcat," a car that had been one of America's most famous sports cars in the years immediately before World War I:

> Remember how you hungered for it? Remember how your pulse raced to its engine throb? That was it ... that old Stutz Bearcat, Heaven-on-wheels to that boy you used to be!

In the Ambassador, "styled in the continental manner by Pinin Farina" in advertising copy if only minimally so in life, the new car buyer could assuage the disappointments of middle age by traveling more comfortably than any Bearcat owner, his memories kept alive by a "Hood ornament by Petty." If he ordered the optional "Dual-Jetfire" engine, the buyer could own a car powered by the engine that "holds the top American record in the 24-hour road race at Le Mans, France." It was not a very sporting enthusiast who needed to be reminded where Le Mans was, and the Ambassador's styling, while influenced by a Pinin Farina prototype, had been so extensively modified from the Italian original that little of Farina's expertise was evident in the production versions.

A similar car was shown in smaller Statesman sedan form by the pressed-steel body pioneers Budd of Philadelphia in a December, 1952 advertisement which congratulated Nash on fifty years of car production, and pointed out Budd's own contribution to the success of the American automobile in general:

> The life of a pioneer in business, as we have reason to know, is ... never dull. We first discovered it when trying to sell the idea of an automobile body built entirely of steel.... With Nash, we have been partners in adventure ... adventure that has built the Budd business to world-wide proportions and has profoundly influenced many other industries.

In another advertisement of the series, Budd tapped more deeply into the collective memory with "A Toast to the Model T," a car for which Budd had made body panels from 1918 onwards, and whose pioneering spirit and subsequent success

Wishful thinking: The 1952–57 Nash gained a reputation as a ladies' car, and was neither sporting nor European in flavor, Pinin Farina's actual contribution being minimal. The record-breaking engine was faster in the Nash-Healey sports car than in a full-size unitary Airflyte (August 1953).

Budd made body components for numerous manufacturers, and could justly claim to be pioneers in the field, having supplied all-steel closed bodies to Dodge as early as 1914, and licensed their production by European manufacturers such as Citroën and Morris between the wars (December 1952 and January 1953).

were claimed to be analogous with Budd's own development.

More than a decade later, Buick invited would-be owners of the 1965 Electra to look back not on past happiness, but on a lifetime of automotive mediocrity, so that the Buick might provide long-overdue contentment:

> In a lifetime, you have just so many chances to buy a car. Make this one count.... Think back over the years. Were all your cars as good as you deserve?... Did they come equipped with every last thing needed to make driving (or just riding) an unmitigated pleasure? No? Then don't settle for anything less, from now on. Your Buick dealer is waiting to introduce you to the car that will make it up to you for all those disappointments.

The slogan, "Wouldn't you really rather have a Buick?" involved readers' emotions as others' catchphrases often did not, and worked particularly well with Buick's more charismatic personal-luxury Riviera.

Several copywriters traded on a burgeoning public interest in old cars. If the Stutz Bearcat was considered worth preserving in 1953, the same could be said of many pre-war cars by 1968, "a vintage year for Wide-Tracking" according to Pontiac, who showed a number of old cars, such as a 1940 LaSalle, with a Bonneville coupe. "So there's really no doubt," said the copy, "that 1968 Pontiacs will be talked about for years to come. And lucky you. You can own one without paying classic car prices."

Few genuine automotive novelties arrived in the early 1970s, and increasing interest in nostalgia of all kinds was reflected in advertising. After several years of unmemorable copy, Chevrolet revived an old and popular jingle, "See the USA in your Chevrolet," which had been associated with a TV show hosted by Dinah Shore. Chevrolet's marque identity, at a time when it produced many ranges of cars which appealed to distinct consumer groups, was under threat, and the 1972 slogan, "Chevrolet — Building a better way to see the USA" worked well with an "Impala at the beach south of Miami, Florida" or a Chevelle Malibu Sport Coupe "at the

Taos Pueblo in Northern New Mexico," with copy in each case that linked the location into a discussion of the car. The campaign capitalized on marque loyalty and, with an eye to the growing market for imports, suggested that the car was ideal for use in all landscapes and associated Chevrolet with traditional American values.

In 1975, Cadillac promoted its Coupe de Ville alongside a 1930 Roadster, and its Eldorado convertible with the 1933 355 Phaeton. Chrysler, in its fiftieth anniversary year, showed a New Yorker above a sepia-tinted photograph of an early-1930s sedan, the 1974 car "a totally new expression of an idea that has never changed." In a 1976 advertisement, Buick traded on readers' recollections of its Roadmaster of the early 1950s. It seemed surprising that Buick should show a regular Roadmaster sedan rather than the glamorous top-line Skylark, but too attractive an early car would have detracted from the modern one. Moreover, in this case the makers wanted to trade on public affection for a car that was the the subject of shared experience and aspiration, rather than on a glamorous image. Over 50,000 Americans had bought new ($3,254) Roadmaster sedans in 1953, but the Skylark had sold in very small numbers—fewer than 1,700 in that year, at a price only given "on request" according to the model's advertising (actually $5,000, which was top-line Cadillac territory).

Ford suggested in 1974 that the subcompact Pinto might one day prove to be as desirable a collector's item as a Model A or Thunderbird: "Will Pinto turn out to be another classic? We'll have to wait to find out." It was a humorous way to remind readers of Ford's heritage, but the verdict on the Pinto was sensibly left to posterity. Even thirty years later, with memories of "exploding gas tank" litigation still fresh in many minds, the Pinto had not yet troubled the collector-car market except as a curiosity.

By contrast, copywriters for "the sports car America loved first" positively wallowed in nostalgia during 1971–79 in advertising from Bozell & Jacobs that was both very different from, and more extensive than, British copy for the same cars. American MG advertisements, with photography by a Canadian, Marce Mayhew, showed pre-war and early postwar models alongside the latest MGB roadster—and occasionally the Midget—to combine a celebration of the company's sports and racing history with a specifically American nostalgia for the MGs of 1940s and 1950s.[10]

This nostalgia was collective and cultural rather than personal, as the late-twentysomething and thirtysomething professionals targeted by MG had not yet reached their motoring anecdotage, and were much too young to have experienced early MG ownership first-hand—although their parents might well have done. "When they write the book about sports cars in America MG will be chapter one" said a 1972 headline, with a TC in the background in front of a library. "First on the scene. And still one jump ahead" declared MG in 1974, above a dark blue roadster parked with a red TC in a meadow, the long grass cleverly drawing the eye away from the year's new and huge, rubber-over-metal "Sabrina" bumper guards.

In 1975, with the bumper of the "B" now

Buick, unusually, invited readers to recall past disappointments in 1965, and to make up for them with an Electra 225 (April 1965).

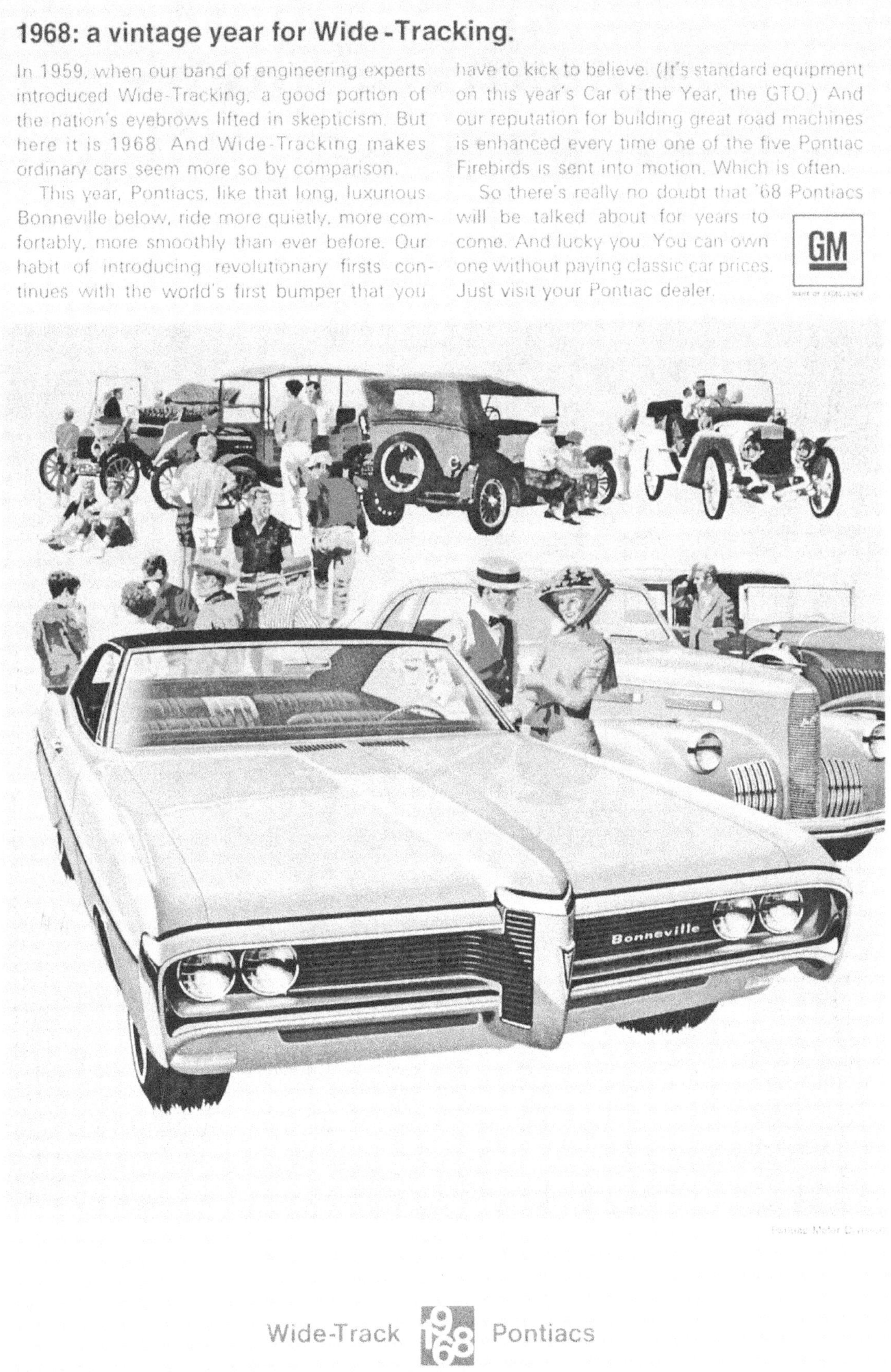
1968: a vintage year for Wide-Tracking.
In 1959, when our band of engineering experts introduced Wide-Tracking, a good portion of the nation's eyebrows lifted in skepticism. But here it is 1968. And Wide-Tracking makes ordinary cars seem more so by comparison.
This year, Pontiacs, like that long, luxurious Bonneville below, ride more quietly, more comfortably, more smoothly than ever before. Our habit of introducing revolutionary firsts continues with the world's first bumper that you have to kick to believe. (It's standard equipment on this year's Car of the Year, the GTO.) And our reputation for building great road machines is enhanced every time one of the five Pontiac Firebirds is sent into motion. Which is often.
So there's really no doubt that '68 Pontiacs will be talked about for years to come. And lucky you. You can own one without paying classic car prices. Just visit your Pontiac dealer.
GM
Bonneville
Wide-Track 1968 Pontiacs

Pontiac capitalized on a growing public interest in old cars in 1968 (April 1968).

Chevrolet reintroduced an old slogan in 1972 in order to strengthen its marque image after the Corvair débâcle, engine mounting problems with late–1960s full-size cars, and a Vega début beset by strikes and quality control lapses. The campaign was successful, and sales improved (May 1972).

entirely in rubber, British Leyland Motors Inc. announced "The Golden Anniversary MGB" in a double-spread which showed the latest American-market model alongside six photographs of MGs from 1925 to 1957. Each was posed outside an ancient English church, the early models with English license plates. "Since 1925, MG has espoused a simple but unconventional philosophy: that driving can and should be enjoyed, not just endured," said the copy. Another advertisement in the series reminded readers that "From our first Gold Medal in the 1925 London–to–Lands End Trial to our latest SCCA victories, MGs have been racing and winning for 50 years," before describing how such experience had influenced the design of the latest model.

Not that the latest MGB was quite as invigorating as its chrome-bumpered predecessor. In March, 1966 that car — with an invocation of the "Octagon spirit" but no explicit nostalgia — had been shown with knobbly rear tires and skis strapped to the trunk as "a car that keeps its feet on the ground — free of the vicious, unpredictable tricks that careless design can lead to." Ralph Nader's *Unsafe at Any Speed* was by then well known to enthusiasts, and if a convertible Corvair Monza was only an indirect rival, the Triumph Spitfire, with swing-axle rear suspension of a type no longer fitted to the Corvair, was almost a direct competitor.

In the late 1970s, accompanied by famous pre-war and postwar models, the MGB appeared in atmospheric, American-style countryside-at-sundown photographs to emphasize the car's suitability for when "the road narrows to two lanes and begins twisting through rolling mountain meadows," as a 1973 copywriter put it. In 1979, MG invited readers of *Time* and other magazines to visit its showrooms and enter a draw for a prize: "You could win a classic 1948 MG TC worth $17,000!... (The car cost $1,875 when new, which should tell you something about how gracefully a well-maintained MG grows old.)" An immaculate TC took center stage in the company's double-page spread as a new Midget and MGB stood demurely behind. The best way to sell an antiquated car was, perhaps, to show it with an even more antiquated predecessor. Yet as a brand-new convertible the MGB was, in its last years, a rare commodity, and therefore still desirable to sports car fans.

Chapter 10

"There's a Ford in Your Future"

The war years and their aftermath provided a unique opportunity for automobile manufacturers to present themselves as a force for the national good. Patriotism and a sternly optimistic outlook were combined in advertising. Civilian car production ceased on February 9, 1942, and factories were converted to war production under the guidance of the Automotive Council for War Production, which had been created on December 31, 1941 to coordinate the use of manufacturing facilities within America's car plants. If copywriters could not illustrate new cars, they could demonstrate how hard their respective companies were working for the war effort, and much imaginative copy resulted.

Advertisers could also trade on the fact that their last pre-war models were still running, enabling civilian life to continue with the minimum of disruption. Of course, if the wartime motorist had been foolish enough to buy an unreliable 1942 model, he was stranded, with no possibility of finding a new replacement until the war ended.

In 1945, De Soto could claim that "of all the De Soto cars ever built, 7 out of 10 are still running." In one advertisement, a mother was shown arriving at a school gate in her 1942 De Soto, complete with concealed headlights. It was raining hard and the road was slippery, but:

> Rain or shine, Mother never fails them. Neither does the family car. De Soto cars are rolling up 100,000 miles ... 200,000 ... even more. Because in all our 17 years in business, we've had this thought foremost in our minds: *keep making a better car*.... Today, De Soto manufacturing skill is going into bomber sections, airplane wings, guns and other war goods. But when we're making cars again ... better decide on De Soto. It's the car that's *designed to endure*.

America and her allies were winning the war in Europe by 1945, but advertisers did not slacken their pace. Most advertisements in the early part of the year showed military equipment rather than automobiles. General Motors depicted tanks, aircraft, and other military hardware in its advertising. "Where have we met before?" asked Fisher Body (whose peacetime slogan, "Body by Fisher," had been amended to "Armament by Fisher") in March, 1945:

> It was at Tarawa — on the beach at Anzio — in Normandy — in bombers over Berlin.... These are the recent places where the craftsmanship symbolized by this emblem has been meeting up with the men who are winning the war.... Major assemblies for the B-29 and other bombers ... delicate aircraft instruments ... tanks — the flood of Fisher Body armament knows no end until final victory.

Buick Division, whose long-running slogan, "When Better Automobiles Are Built Buick Will Build Them" at last seemed appropriate, pointed out that "Buick powers the Liberator.... She's got four 'Bs' in her bonnets!" In May, 1945 it was the turn of the M-18 Hellcat tank destroyer. A mock newspaper cutting was shown: "Buick M-18 Hellcats score in 21 days of Steady Action." The text lauded the Army's war effort and the contribution that Buick's machines had made:

> Long ago we decided something about the American fighting man. Give him good weapons to fight with — and he'll do the rest. That thought ... guided us when we sat down to design the M-18 as an answer to the German Tiger Tank.

Studebaker was less triumphalist: "What flyers say counts most with us" began one piece showing the Boeing Flying Fortress, for which Studebaker provided engines. A few

A 1945 prestige advertisement showing a 1942 model. The purpose of the piece was as much to keep the marque name in the public mind as to prime the market for peacetime production (1945 campaign).

Above and opposite: Contrasting war-time styles. As teenagers in the 1930s, many World War II soldiers had built models of the Napoleonic coach for the Fisher Body Craftsman's Guild competition. Nash described the war effort in unusually personal, human, terms (Nash: February, Fisher: March, Studebaker: April, and Buick: May 1945).

Buick M-18 Hellcats Score In 21 Days of Steady Action

Mounting evidence that the Buick Hellcat M-18 Tank Destroyer is the "hottest thing in armored warfare" recently described in Army news...

Valley, Okla., commands Company B of the 604th Tank Destroyer Battalion. In his outfit there are 12 M-18 'Hellcats.' His company was recently...

BUICK POWERS THE LIBERATOR

BUICK BUILDS THE M-18 HELLCAT

LONG AGO we decided something about the American fighting man.

Give him good weapons to fight with—and he'll do the rest.

That thought guided us in building the big Pratt & Whitney aircraft engines that keep the B-24 Liberator boring relentlessly through the skies.

It guided us, too, when we sat down to design the M-18 as an answer to the German Tiger Tank.

Shortly after the breakthrough out of Normandy, stories began to trickle back about what the Tank Destroyer Battalions were doing with this lightning-paced slugger.

Typical of these exploits is the tale of a single battalion—12 Hellcats—that spent 21 days in continuous action. Score: four Tigers, two Mark IV's, four armored vehicles knocked out—and hundreds of enemy troops killed, wounded or captured!

It seems that the men like to keep busy—especially with the Hellcat. For in all this action only two M-18's were damaged—neither beyond repair—and the crews suffered only minor injuries.

That's what Buick men and Ordnance officers were after when they joined hands to perfect the M-18.

They gave it hitting power—in a high-velocity 76-mm. cannon. They gave it traction to go anywhere and speed to outrace any other land vehicle.

It now appears they also gave it ability to take care of itself.

And given tools like that, you can count on the boys who use them to do the job!

Every Sunday Afternoon
GENERAL MOTORS SYMPHONY OF THE AIR—NBC Network

The Army-Navy "E" proudly flies over all Buick plants

WHEN BETTER AUTOMOBILES ARE BUILT BUICK WILL BUILD THEM

BUICK DIVISION OF GENERAL MOTORS

YOU LEND A HAND WHEN YOU LEND YOUR DOLLARS. INVEST IN MORE WAR BONDS

LET'S FINISH THE JOB
Buy Extra War Bonds

WHERE HAVE WE MET BEFORE?

IT was at Tarawa—on the beach at Anzio—in Normandy—in bombers over Berlin—in tank battles, dog fights, and on the high seas—on every fighting front.

These are the recent places where the craftsmanship symbolized by this emblem has been meeting up with the men who are winning the war. And every day sees a new meeting on other fronts as the output of Fisher Body factories moves into the battle lines.

Major assemblies for the B-29 and other bombers, delicate aircraft instruments, big guns of various calibers, tanks—the flood of Fisher Body armament knows no end until final victory.

Into every single piece go the skills and techniques that have always made the Fisher Body coach a symbol of fine craftsmanship throughout the length and breadth of our land.

Every Sunday Afternoon
GENERAL MOTORS SYMPHONY OF THE AIR
NBC Network

The Army-Navy "E" flag flies over six Fisher Body plants for excellence in aircraft production and flies over seven for tank production, while the Navy "E" with five stars is flown by still another Fisher Body plant for its metal stamping work.

armament
BODY BY Fisher

DIVISION OF GENERAL MOTORS

What flyers say counts most with us

MEMBERS of the crews of many a Flying Fortress have written Studebaker about the fine performance of that mighty bomber's Studebaker-built Cyclone engines. Studebaker prizes the comments of those intrepid men far above any of the official commendations its war plants have received.

The senior civilian test pilot at an important army aircraft modification center says: "I've flown and tested over 200 Studebaker-powered Boeing Forts. Nothing could be tougher on engines than the workouts I've given those ships."

Famous for its peacetime motor cars and motor trucks, the Studebaker organization has but a single purpose right now—to back up our fighting forces with all the military equipment its factories and workers can provide.

The war's "surprise" vehicle—it's the Army's new Weasel personnel and cargo carrier—built by Studebaker and powered by the famous Studebaker Champion engine.

Save for the future with
★ WAR BONDS ★
THEY'RE THE BEST INVESTMENT IN THE WORLD

Awarded To All Studebaker Plants

Studebaker WARTIME BUILDER OF WRIGHT CYCLONE ENGINES FOR BOEING FLYING FORTRESS

months later, Studebaker emphasized the important role of the "father and son" production-line teams who would reappear in postwar copy. Many such teams had been split up by the exigencies of war. "They're half the world apart but still 'working together'" said one advertisement, which described the careers of "Edward and Roman Kowalski" and their father, who remained in America to carry out skilled manufacturing work on equipment which his sons used abroad.

A more personal — and sentimental — approach was favored by Nash in February, 1945. A soldier was shown contemplating his fate as he stood in front of a heavy bomber:

> Back here ... Back home ... With our missions done and the roar of guns and the bombs fading and faint in my ears ... I don't want to kill any more ... I don't want to destroy ... I want to work and build and make things live and grow.... Now I know this war will not be fought in vain ... this Victory can be made real for all of us ... if we keep on working together not to destroy but to create ... if we turn all the power we have gained in war, to peace ... there can *always* be for me and every man a boundless opportunity ... to build *our* America the way we want it to be....

The copywriter then took over in his own voice, and promised cars to come:

> When Victory comes, Nash will go on ... from the building of instruments of war to the making of two great new cars designed to be the finest, biggest, most comfortable, most economical, most advanced automobiles ever produced for the medium and low-priced fields ... the new Nash Ambassador Six and the new Nash "600."

There followed a very small picture of a 1942 Nash to remind the reader of the car he was longing for.

Peace had returned by December, 1945, and Studebaker was jubilant. Beneath a painted street scene in which cars drove in the snow past a lighted Christmas tree, the copywriter summed up national relief that war was over:

> This year, the beautiful old Yuletide sentiment — "peace on earth" — means something far more real to most of us than it did at any previous Christmas.... [P]eace is a dearly won and precious acquisition we know we must treasure vigilantly .... [A]s the lights of this inspiring Christmas twinkle at our hearthsides ... our nation hopefully, confidently and resolutely faces the opportunity to shape its destiny.... Studebaker, Builder of cars worthy of America's homes.

Within months, that destiny would include some startling new Studebakers.

If saccharine prose was an inevitable concomitant of traumatic circumstances, it was not universal. A 1945 Plymouth advertisement from N.W. Ayer & Son showed a man at home in his armchair, holding an imaginary steering wheel with a smile of pure contentment: "Just wait till you get your hands on the wheel of the Latest, Greatest PLYMOUTH." Buick was more modest in the summer of 1945. It illustrated a car, too:

> No, the fighting isn't over.... But victory in Europe is releasing many fighting men to come home — and permitting the country to turn, at least in part, to the making of things they will find nice to come home to. To many a fighting man, this will

A Christmas to remember...

This year, the beautiful old Yuletide sentiment — "peace on earth" — means something far more real to most of us than it did at any previous Christmas ... In this ever-memorable year of 1945, peace is a dearly won and precious acquisition we know we must treasure vigilantly ... And so, as the lights of this inspiring Christmas twinkle at our hearthsides, as carolers sing their joyous roundelays and community trees gleam with friendliness, our nation hopefully, confidently and resolutely faces the opportunity to shape its destiny.

Builder of cars worthy of America's homes

Studebaker captures the national mood for the first peace-time Christmas since 1940. Cars were not mentioned at all in the body copy (December 1945).

Anticipating postwar demand. The car is a 1942 convertible, one of the most modern-looking of its year (September 1945).

mean such pleasures as an open road, a glorious day — and a bright and lively Buick.

Admittedly, the car shown was a 1942 model, but it heralded the "high standards to be surpassed in new models now being made ready." A yellow Roadmaster convertible stood under the gaze of a military searchlight, with tanks and low-flying aircraft dimly visible in the background.

By December, the new model had arrived, reassuringly familiar: "Yes, its Engine is still out Front" said the headline. The car was similar to the 1942 model, but there were improvements to the engine, which employed:

... matchless valve-in-head principle used in the engines of every American warplane. It's a power plant, indeed, which in a fistful of vital dimensions is actually *made to closer tolerances than modern aircraft engines are.*

This was perhaps risky, but the good reliability record of American aircraft precluded misinterpretation, and service personnel would know that in aeronautical use tolerances varied according to design and materials. In 1946, the same Buick would be sold with the mixture of euphemism and hyperbole that characterized most postwar advertising.

Amid the patriotic fervor that accompanied the end of hostilities, one campaign stood out by capturing the national mood, and for imaginative artwork. Early in 1945, Ford's advertising agency since 1943, J. Walter Thompson, released the first advertisement of a new series. It showed a clear, blue-green crystal ball, held in the palm of a hand. Across the ball was written the legend, "There's a Ford in your future!" Beneath the illustration was the single copy line, "Ford has built more than 30,000,000 cars and trucks."

This advertisement, which was widely published, immediately caught the public imagination. The theme was developed during the year in many different pieces, each of which emphasized a particular virtue which the new Ford would possess.

In March, 1945 the slogan was taken out of the crystal ball and placed underneath it. Within the ball could be seen pedestrians looking down a street, all in one direction, apparently startled by a vehicle that had just passed, but which was now out of view:

Whoosh! And you're out in front.... You will scarcely know it's running when it idles. Yet when that smooth, soft-spoken motor springs into action, you'll go surging out ahead.... This

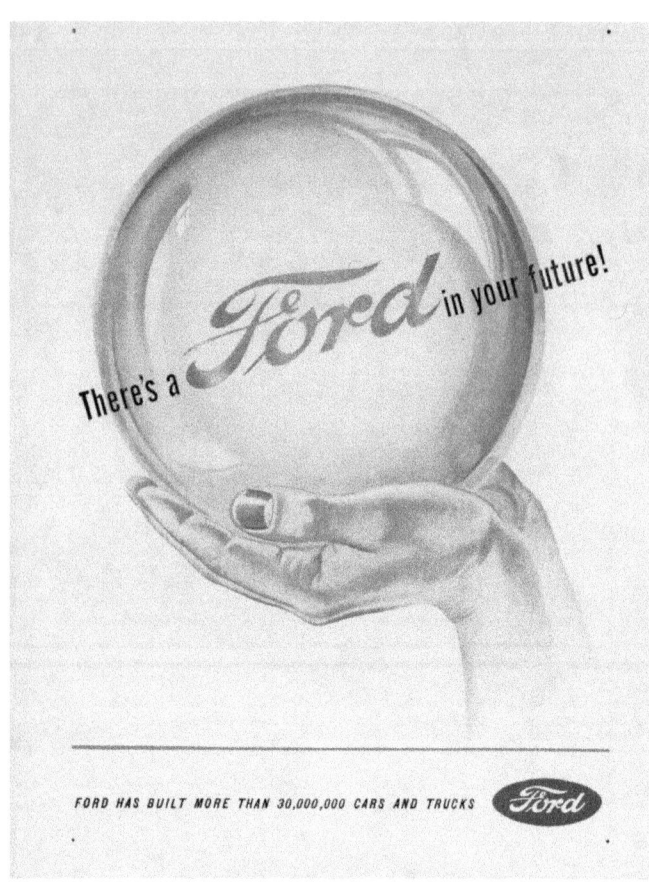

FORD HAS BUILT MORE THAN 30,000,000 CARS AND TRUCKS

IT'LL BE THE PRIDE OF THE FAMILY

There's a *Ford* in your future!

COUNT on it! One day, you too will know the joy of owning a new Ford—a car that will be eager to take you traveling in style.... Then you'll look with pride at a car that's big—inside and out. It will be smart appearing. You'll hear a motor that whispers of power.... And when you get underway—what pleasure! It will be so smooth and easy- riding—wealthy with comfort. Thrifty and reliable, too, in the finest Ford tradition.... More Ford cars are coming soon. Production has started but is very limited. America needs all available transportation, so take care of your present car by seeing your Ford dealer regularly.
FORD MOTOR COMPANY

"THE FORD SHOW". Singing stars, orchestra and chorus. Every Sunday, complete NBC network. 2:00 P.M., E.W.T., 1:00 P.M., C.W.T., 12:00 M., M.W.T., 11:00 A.M., P.W.T.

There's a *Ford* in your future

"FORD'S OUT FRONT WITH CROSS-COUNTRY COMFORT!"

A day behind the wheel of the big new Ford will show you what real comfort means! Here's a car with solid sureness on any road... a car that's easy to handle, fun to drive. The stabilized chassis rides steadily even in cross winds and on curves. New multi- leaf "Rest-ride" springs cushion the miles. Deep, soft, correct-posture seats give you perfect relaxation. Plenty of room all around you. And that flexible, smoother, quieter, more powerful Ford V-8 engine levels the hills and thrives on distance! See your friendly Ford Dealer today!

The only 100 h.p. V-8 in the low- priced field!

Only Ford gives you 100 horsepower, only Ford gives you the extra smoothness of an eight, only Ford gives you a "V" type engine—the kind used in America's costliest cars!

THERE'S A *Ford* IN YOUR FUTURE

Above and opposite: Evolution of a successful campaign: Ford promotes 1942's style with new trim, grille, and engine in 1945–46. The "teaser ads," in particular, were novel and effective. (*This page and opposite, upper left to right:* January, September, and November 1945 and January 1946. **Opposite,** *lower:* September and November 1946).

is not wishful thinking. When the green light is given, we will be ready to start production plans. In the meantime, the full resources and energies of Ford are engaged in turning out war goods to help speed the day of final VICTORY!

A similar advertisement was prepared for May; the theme was ride comfort, and within the crystal ball could be seen a mother with her child and dog playing in the back seat of the new car as it glided across the countryside. "You'll take your ease in style," began the copy, "Some day — when America's biggest job is done — peace will return. And with it will come a big, new Ford.... Then you'll have the kind of gentle ride you've always hoped for. So smooth, so packed with comfort ... you'll find yourself at ease and completely relaxed." The copy concluded with a description of the planned improvements to the pre-war Ford in the new model, and the usual assurance of Ford's continued contribution to the war effort.

The new 1946 Ford was scheduled for introduction in September, 1945, but production difficulties delayed its appearance until October. By September, however, the car which would be "the pride of the family" could at last be seen in the crystal ball. A proud family took center stage, and, in one corner of the picture, the tip of a maroon fender was visible.

October 26, 1945 was designated "V-8 Day" at Dearborn, and the new model was finally announced. "1946 Ford — with many advancements now in production!" declared a November advertisement. For the first time, the crystal ball contained only a maroon Fordor sedan:

> Here is the most beautiful Ford car ever built — with more improvements than many pre-war yearly models.... Under the broad hood there's new and greater power.... Colorful interiors invite you to relax in luxury.... New-type springs assure a full-cushioned level ride.... Ask your Ford dealer about the smartest Ford cars ever built.

Smartness was enhanced by a newly restyled radiator grille, and "greater power" (100 bhp rather than 1942's 90 bhp) came from the adoption of a Ford truck engine, modified for installation in a car which had been technically outmoded even in 1942. But in car-starved postwar America, such shortcomings did not matter.

During 1946, the car and crystal ball were separated. The new sedan was shown speeding along, while in a separate illustration 1945's expectant family could be seen within the crystal ball, dreams fulfilled. Eventually, conventional copy took over, with both crystal ball and slogan retreating to the foot of the page and the maroon sedan, now widely available, taking price of place and occasionally being replaced by a maroon convertible. Towards the end of the year, in a related but distinct campaign, "Ford's out front with ...," the car was surrounded by proud owners while individual features were demonstrated in separate illustrations. Cartoon demonstrators added a light touch. The overall theme continued into the 1947 model year with the slogan, "There's a finer Ford in your future." In June, 1948, Ford's first new postwar car was announced for the 1949 model year. The slogan was extended to "There's a New Ford in your future" and, for 1950, to "There's a Ford in your future with a future built in!"

The continuation of 1945's advertising theme into the 1950 model year was an indicator of the campaign's success, and it was much better remembered — and more affectionately recalled — than Plymouth's earnest cross-examination of low-priced car buyers during the same period. In the late 1940s, Americans wanted not only a product, but a promise of future happiness as well, and Ford provided both.

Chapter 11

"Lady, Relax!"

> It is positively uncanny how a woman senses style.... Mere beauty never deceives her ... unless the subtle scent of her perfume ... the cut of her bob ... the curve of her brows ... unless all these things are in vogue her day is utterly ruined.... It was men who christened Paige "The Most Beautiful Car in America" ... but it is women who have seen beyond that beauty a smartness and exclusiveness that stamp Paige motor cars style leaders of the season.... Drop into a Paige-Jewett showroom when next downtown.... Your visit will prove quite as engaging as an hour along the Rue de la Paix.

With these words, a well-known but relatively minor American manufacturer enticed affluent, upper-class readers of *The Ladies' Home Journal* into contemporation of a colorful and carefully styled product in 1927. The advertisement itself was elegantly composed. A modish rendering of a fashionable woman was placed in the center of a display of fourteen highly colored coachwork designs, whose variety was intended to beguile her into believing that her car, though fashionable to the highest degree, was nevertheless an extension of her own personality. She would conform to dominant aesthetic mores, yet exhibit originality and taste in her choice. General Motors was not the only company whose awareness of the value of style in car choice had consolidated into considered policy by 1930.

For Paige's target buyer, the car was not merely a means of transport. It had to be integrated into an immaculately nurtured world-view whose values were determined largely by appearance. Those values—together with promises of comfort and handling ease—would characterize most attempts to sell cars to women for the next forty years.

Economic independence was enjoyed by few women in the 1920s, and it could be assumed that the cost of the car was ultimately derived from the fruits of male economic labor. But in this upmarket corner of the automobile market, the car was nevertheless intended to be chosen as well as driven by its female owner, and the use of it brought freedom, if only on a limited scale. By 1927, it was expected that the car would work reliably, allowing the copywriter to escape from technicalities. Paige's copy was an extreme example of a genre which had persisted in upper-class American magazines for several years, and which percolated downmarket in the 1930s.

In 1936, Ford was more overtly patronizing, as copy by N.W. Ayer & Son sought to persuade the female buyer that the modern V-8 was not an unruly mechanism whose efficiency in traveling fifty miles without mishap was largely a matter of luck. The mechanical niceties which brought about this reassuring state of affairs were nevertheless largely unmentioned. (It may be debated whether women were assumed to be uncomprehending of them, or merely uninterested.) "Lady, Relax!" invited one headline:

> A ride in a Ford these days [sic] is a journey in contentment.... Everything is just as you would like to have it. Many times you will find yourself leaning back and saying—"It's a grand car to drive".... You drive relaxed in the roomy, comfortable Ford V-8—sure of its safety—confident of its performance and dependability over many thousands of miles.... [T]his kind of driving adds a great deal to motoring enjoyment—explains the popularity of the Ford V-8—tells why it is the first choice of so many women nowadays....

Omit the explicit appeal to women, add a few performance statistics and describe the features which gave the car its safety and poise on the road, and the copy could have been aimed at anyone—and in generally targeted copy these aspects of the V-8 were usually mentioned in some detail. But their omission here was typical of advertising that was aimed deliberately towards women and, indirectly, towards the men who, by purchasing the product, would provide for their safety and well-being. Unlike Paige in 1927, Ford's copy was essentially practical, but it was practical in a limited sense, and reassurance, rather than explanation, was considered appropriate for the female reader.

Fisher Body, promoting its "Turret Top" construction in Chevrolet guise in 1936, appealed more overtly to male protective instincts. In an advertisement headed, "Just between us Girls," safety was included more insistently in the maker's canon of desirable virtues, with an eye to the well-being of a little girl, shown with her parents admiring the new sedan:

> To this curly-haired young lady, the solid steel "Turret Top" may be merely a new and more exciting place from which to view the world. But to her parents, it's the crowning glory of a car chosen for style, for safety, for sturdiness, for comfort.

It was implied that the parents chose the car together, but their underlying points of view differed. While Family Man looked on mother and child indulgently, his wife, at the wheel, beamed grateful thanks to him, with the clear implication that he was the provider, and she the supplicant upon his responsible nature. Her motorized independence was granted, not assumed.

Insofar as their respective roles in choosing the family's car differed, the man's was usually portrayed in automobile advertising as the more active, purchasing the product and thereby ensuring his family's well-being. His wife's involvement was largely receptive, once she had expressed her preference. When both were shown in the car, it was the man, in most cases, who drove.

In the 1930s, one car sufficed for the average family, and if the man had overall charge of it, his wife would nevertheless be expected to use it from time to time, and Ford was not alone in realizing that her opinion of the automobile in question would be instrumental in its purchase.

In 1939, Buick ostensibly appealed to women in an advertisement which appeared to be written from a woman's point of view, but which was also intended to bring indirect pressure to bear on any husband by holding out the prospect of a loyal and contented wife: "She married an Angel," began the copy above a photograph of the new sedan:

> You can tell from the car she drives, she has a husband approaching perfection as nearly as any mortal can!... Hence the Buick in the family, smart of line and brilliant of behavior ... and comfort-cushioned for life with the soft, slow spirals of BuiCoil Torque-Free springing. A car, in short, to delight any woman — and to thrill any man by its action and life and ability to travel.

The angelic husband was clearly looking over his wife's shoulder in the matter of car choice, and would need to be assured that her preference, if heeded, would not force him into a sluggish, unexciting automobile. Custom dictated that the female motorist rarely spoke for herself in copy; in most cases, as here, she was spoken for, either by her husband or by an impliedly male copywriter.

The prevailing view expressed in advertisements of the period—that men and women thought in different automotive categories and consequently were attracted to a given car for different reasons—was stated with unusual clarity and conciseness by Mercury in 1946:

> Women judge a car mostly on its beauty, comfort, safety, ease of handling, and its perfection of detail. To men — power, economy, and how it's put together are most important.

Whether this confident statement of the sexes' respective concerns was accurate or not, it was a representative account of what copywriters, overtly or otherwise, chose to portray as accepted wisdom.

These advertisements typified copy aimed at those sectors of the market in which men and women chose cars together for the family's use. Where the independent woman was explicitly targeted (usually in the upper and upper-middle sectors), she was encouraged to choose a car as much for the impression it would create among her social peers as for the sensual enjoyment — or lack of discomfort — that came from actually driving it. And in the realm of the truly upmarket automobile, the car might be chauffeur-driven, which meant that there was little point in boring the prospective owner with mechanical mundanities in which she would have no practical interest — such things could safely be left to the back pages of the catalog. In this context, it was irrelevant whether or not women were assumed to be able to understand them.

There were, however, some striking exceptions to the prevailing trend. Several of Plymouth's ordinary-user testimonials of 1937 came from independent women. "Miss C. Eleanor Hinkley ... drove over 7,000 miles in her Plymouth" in the summer of 1936, "through mountains, deserts, sandstorms. In all, she's driven 31,025 miles ... and her car has never been touched for repairs ... is still on its original tires." Another Plymouth, used by rural nurse Margaret W. Davison of Maryville, Montana, was "Never on sick list in 166,000 miles ... goes through in all kinds of weather." Nurse Davison had "averaged over 20 miles per gallon of gas ... never had the head off an engine!... Never yet ... has Plymouth failed me."

The purpose of these advertisements was not, in fact, to appeal to the woman driver as such, but Plymouth's decision to cite the experiences of realistic independent women indicated that public portraiture of female motorists did not always follow private reality. By 1937, women habitually drove high mileages, particularly in rural areas where potential buyers would not be impressed by metropolitan fads.

Throughout the 1930s and beyond, women — whether or not specifically targeted as consumers — retained an important, decorative role in automobile advertising across the

Happy is the woman who marries a responsible man, for she shall drive a new Chevrolet. Sexism was not an issue in 1936 (April 1936).

SHE'S THIRD IN FAMILY TO PICK PLYMOUTH AS MOST RELIABLE LOW-PRICED CAR

The Car that Stands Up Best— Miss C. Eleanor Hinkley has driven 31,025 miles...spent only about $20... gets 20 to 23 miles per gallon of gas ...and she's delighted with Plymouth performance.

New 1937 Plymouth has still greater reliability and over-all economy

LAST SUMMER Eleanor Hinkley drove over 7,000 miles in her Plymouth... through mountains, deserts, sand-storms. In all, she's driven 31,025 miles...and her car has never been touched for repairs...is still on its original tires.

Plymouth *stands up!* And *new* features make it *more luxurious*. Scientific sound-proofing. New airplane-type shock-absorbers, rubber body mountings and Floating Power engine mountings. *All*-steel body. 100% hydraulic brakes. And *owners* report 18 to 24 miles per gallon!

Compare "All Three"...and compare *resale values*. You'll want Plymouth—the car that stands up best. PLYMOUTH DIVISION OF CHRYSLER CORPORATION, Detroit, Michigan.

PRICED WITH THE LOWEST

YOU'LL FIND the big, 1937 Plymouth is priced with the lowest and offers very easy payment terms. The Commercial Credit Company has made available—through Chrysler, De Soto and Dodge dealers—terms as low as $25 a month.

BEAUTIFUL 1937 Plymouth De Luxe 4-Door Touring Sedan, with spacious built-in trunk.

PLYMOUTH BUILDS GREAT CARS

Plymouth's female motorists were tough, realistic, and independent (April 1937).

social spectrum. The appeal of a glamorous model, artfully posed, transferred itself to the product advertised, which was sometimes sorely in need of vivification.

The model who posed with a Buick in a 1939 Fisher Body advertisement to set the "Style note for Spring" could have been dispensed with without any great loss of impact, but she was altogether more necessary in the realm of the car tire, an object which possessed no inherent aesthetic or social appeal.

General Tires showed its "Squeegee" tires on a wide variety of upper-middle market cars in 1938 and 1939. Each car was painted white in order to lend it a sense of glamour (differentiating it from the unexciting norm in paint colors of black, blue, grey, and green), and to complement the fashionable furs worn by posed models. White bodywork also allowed the black tire, with or without whitewall, to dominate the artwork. The advantages of the product itself were explained in the copy, rather than by illustration, and the overall effect was attractive, upmarket, and instantly recognizable. In many cases, General's advertising was more distinctive than advertisements for the actual cars depicted (such as Packard, Oldsmobile, and Lincoln-Zephyr)—a result not seriously compromised by an occasional surfeit of copy.

In 1945, General's use of fashion models was taken to its logical conclusion in a colorful series of wartime advertisements in which the tire/woman relationship was more than one of mere proximity. "Just alike? Not when you know them" ran the slogan, above pictures of apparently identical babies, female Service personnel, brides and, most notably, invitingly posed chorus girls sitting at a bar. Intimate acquaintance with the tire, explained the copy, revealed that, in spite of superficial appearances, it was quite unlike any other, just as (the reader inferred) closer acquaintance with the chorus girls would reveal beguiling diversity. Automobile use was restricted in America during much of 1945, and with little likelihood that readers would themselves often be able to buy tires, General's name was kept alive in the minds of servicemen by mock-erotic artwork and suggestive copy which demonstrated, as the pay-off line put it, that General "goes a long way to make friends."

Peace brought consolidation of earlier advertising themes in many areas and, from around 1950, it brought increased middle-class affluence and rapid expansion of out-of-town suburbs. Automobiles became cheaper in real terms, and more

Fashion models, stylishly photographed in color, were widely featured in Fisher Body's advertising of the late 1930s. A 1939 Buick is shown here (1939 campaign).

families were able to afford two cars, of which one, in many cases, would be used almost exclusively by the housewife for access to town from a suburban home.

Given that more women owned cars, and used them more often, copywriters increasingly targeted the woman motorist exclusively, without attempting to balance the male and female appeals of a car by trying tortuously to reconcile diverse priorities within a single advertisement. A few advertisements for a marque during a model year could be devised to appeal to the female driver alone, and, in the 1950s, the car makers placed several series in women's magazines. If a man bought the car for his wife to use, it did not matter whether he would

Tire advertisements were frequently utilitarian and sometimes alarmist, but General's were more imaginative than most (1939 campaign and February 1945).

necessarily have chosen it for himself. "Show this to your husband ... when his mood's just right!" advised Chevrolet in 1956, beneath a photograph of a pale green and black Bel Air Sport Coupe. "If he complains about those last-minute dinners, put this next to his napkin," advised another advertisement in the series.

Thus there emerged a distinct style of feminized copy which emphasized color and trimmings and the automobile's potential as a fashion accessory — the very preoccupations which had hitherto been mainly confined to upmarket magazines with a female readership. In August, 1946, Studebaker advertised its new Champion in *The Ladies' Home Journal*:

> Here's "fashion on wheels" that mirrors your personality as effectively as a Bruno costume.... It's an eager-to-go, low, long lovely melody in metal, agleam with gay, exciting color. It's richly upholstered in soft, harmonizing fabric.... It's a dream of a car to handle — steers, stops and parks with delightful ease — and the comfort of the ride is really beyond description.... Don't miss seeing what it does to you and for you....

The car was shown alongside a painting of a woman in a fashionable Bruno tweed ensemble, with close-up drawings of her shoes, hat, and handbag. The overall tone of such copy was carefully devised to appeal emotionally to the female reader. Studebaker's advertisement was a mild foretaste of what was to come in the 1950s, when women were enticed into consideration of the latest cars with plenty of exclamation marks, scrupulous avoidance of technicalities, and frequent use of selected words and phrases ("thrilling," "delightful," and "utterly" for example) in a variety of combinations. Though concentrated by 1955 in copy for medium-priced cars, this trend was occasionally evident further upmarket, even in magazines and papers with a general readership of both sexes.

Cadillac advertisements continued to be targeted principally towards men, and sometimes to the affluent couple, but one 1952 advertisement typified its genre. The latest Sixty Special, costing $4,323 and resplendent in salmon pink and chrome, was shown outside an elegant suburban house. The copywriter set out to demonstrate the social potentialities of Cadillac ownership:

> Perhaps it's to be a visit to a friend's home ... or perhaps she's meeting the man of the house in town ... or, again, it may be only for the day's shopping. But whatever the trip — for the

woman who enjoys possession of a Cadillac car, *this* is the highlight of the day's activities.... Out on the highway there's nothing for her to do but —*relax*! She merely *preselects* the type of performance she wants for the miles ahead ... and the car does her bidding as if by magic.... She just leans back, with a queenly sense of well-being, and listens to the quiet lullaby of the passing breeze.

Unlike her compatriot in the 1936 Ford, who had to cope with the vagaries of stick-shift and transverse springing. If one believed the copywriter, driving a Cadillac was an almost passive activity, demanding no energy, little intelligence, and no interaction with the outside world. Driving pleasure in this context lacked any suggestion of the excitement to be had from operating a powerful machine, and in this anaesthetized interpretation of handling ease, Cadillac echoed equivalent upmarket copy of the 1920s.

There was a strong suggestion in much feminized copy that while men drove cars, women formed relationships with them. In 1952, Mercury:

> ... built a new car and made this challenge: Match Mercury *if you can*. Now we know we've got the sweetest thing on wheels since the ladies began to drive ... this is a love affair you can afford.

Nash acquired a reputation as a ladies' car in the early 1950s, in spite of 1953's appeal to "the boy who wanted a Stutz Bearcat." The 1952 Ambassador, "upholstered in Mediterranean Blue needle point and striped homespun," was promoted as the means above all others by which "your golden dreams can come true!"

De Soto fielded an implied testimonial in 1955. The caption, "Anne Fogarty, famous fashion designer, drives a De Soto Sportsman," appeared underneath a studio shot of the designer looking out of the car towards the camera. As the copy made apparent, the "Sportsman" name was in this case misleading:

> There's no word in the English language that quite describes the utter satisfaction, the thrill, the delightful ease of driving a De Soto.... Here is a car that translates your wishes into action almost with the speed of thought itself.

In the spring of that year, a special-edition sedan was announced, called the Coronado. It was available only in three-tone white, turquoise, and black, at a $100 premium over the regular Fireflite, and the copy gushingly highlighted its role as fashion accessory as much as transportation:

Suburban ecstasy in 1952. Not every man could afford to buy his wife a Cadillac, as many British "GI brides" discovered after World War II (May 1952).

> Have you ever dreamed of a car so handsomely crafted, so distinctive in concept and color that it would stand out like a rare jewel?... A glamorous new three-color treatment, exciting and exclusive new fabrics .... No detail has been spared to bring you a car that is a distinction to own ... a car to turn heads wherever you drive.

A fashion model was posed beside the car, her clothes carefully coordinated to the paintwork and to matching white and turquoise interior trim.

If any doubt remained about who was the target audience, it was necessary only to compare this advertisement with equivalent copy for the regular Fireflite, shown in two-tone blue, on which the Coronado was based:

Above and opposite: An implied testimonial from a fashion designer and a luxuriously trimmed Coronado invited women into De Soto ownership in 1955. A man was in charge of the regular Fireflite, however. (Sportsman: 1955 campaign; Coronado: May 1955; Fireflite: April 1955).

Take a turn at the wheel of a De Soto, and it's certain you'll be spoiled for other cars.... Not only has its mighty V-8 engine the sheer power you need for instant response — but there is ... a sureness of control, a solid feel, that puts De Soto in a class by itself among American cars.

The Coronado buyer was urged to "make a date with your De Soto dealer and see and drive the fabulous Coronado today." The prospective (male) Fireflite owner, on the other hand, was much more dynamic, and interested primarily in power, rather than fabrics: "Take a Firedome or Fireflite out on the road. Try a stretch of cobbles, the steepest hill in town, a bit of heavy traffic .... See if the De Soto isn't the finest car you've ever driven.... De Soto Division, Chrysler Corporation."

In a 1956 advertisement, Plymouth emphasized color, upholstery, and a conspicuously fashionable appearance, offering, in the "Aerodynamic Plymouth '56," a "Dream car ... dream deal! Women love this dream car ... and, with a vital stake in family budgets, love the 'dream deal' that Plymouth dealers offer...." The copy pointed out useful design features such as "wide doors that never snag frocks ... generous headroom, so hairdos stay beautifully in place ... rich fabrics ... and utmost safety for the children...."

A supposedly female perspective was thus tacked onto such advantages as interior roominess, and it was noticeable that "children" of neutral copy became "the children" when it was feminized in order to entwine the product within the panorama of the reader's own emotional relationships. It was not considered sufficient just to assume that the reader would apply relevant features to her own circumstances unaided, and an underlying belief that a woman would remain unmoved unless the product were overtly integrated into her personal world-view, and into the circumstances of her own particular life, was widely apparent.

By the mid–1950s, this pattern was most noticeable in copy for those types of car which would be chosen by the prosperous suburban housewife for her own domestic and leisure use: in other words, convertibles and station wagons. A 1955 Ford advertisement promoted the "Two-Ford family," showing a man in charge of a low-priced station wagon, while his partner sat in a luxurious black and yellow Fairlane Sunliner convertible.

A year later, Pontiac's top-line Star Chief Custom Convertible was promoted in flowery, cocktail-party-invitation script as "a Very Special Car for a Very Special Person!" A metallic purple and white car was shown outside an exotic, upmarket venue, tended by the obligatory femme à la mode.

Where women were shown with station wagons they were

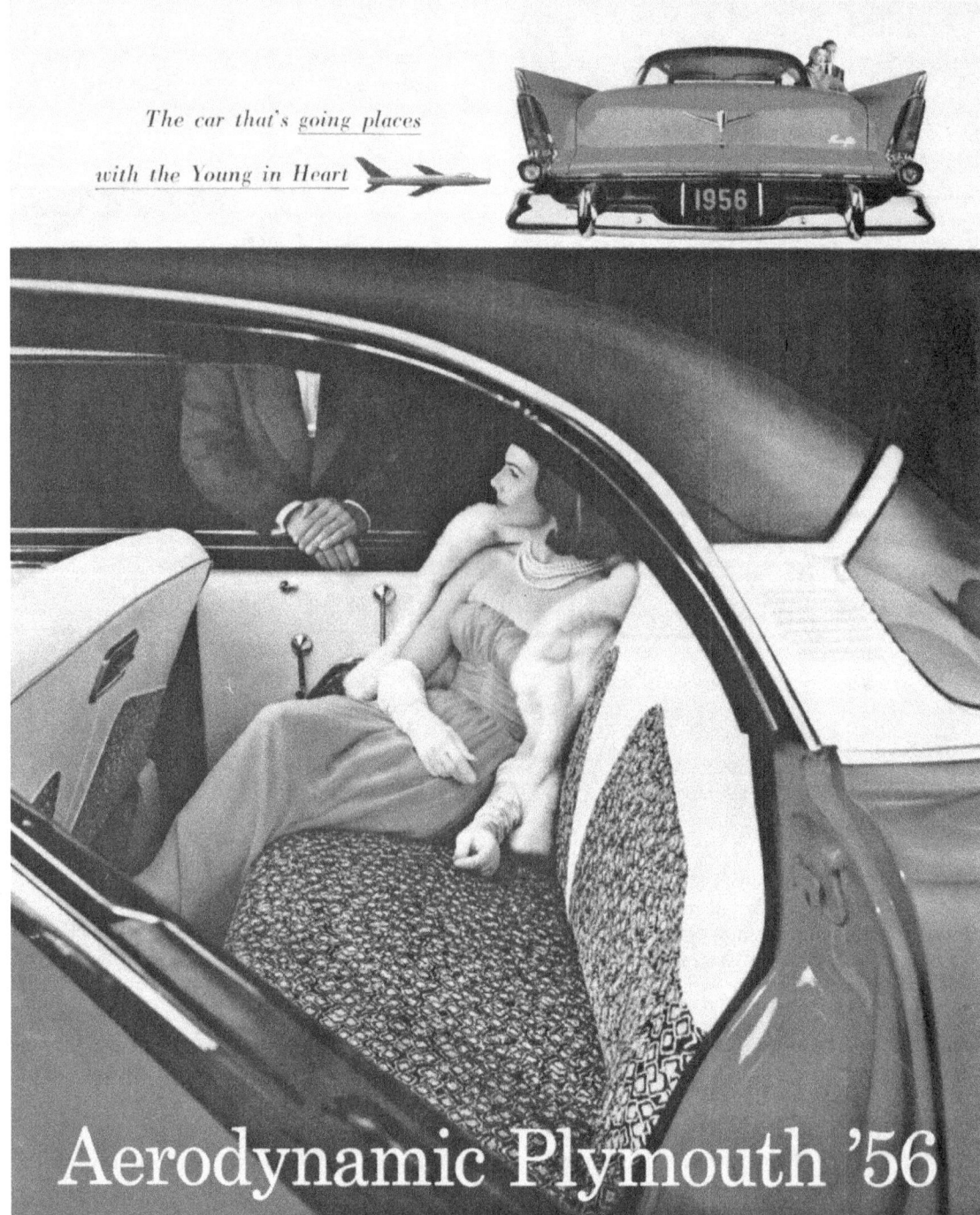

Plymouth appeals to fashion-conscious women in 1956 (March 1956).

Spoked wheel covers, a continental kit, bumper guards, and a pillar-mounted spotlight enticed would-be sophisticates in 1956 (May 1956).

usually luxury versions, and suburban rather than rural locations prevailed. By 1958, luxury wagons were commonplace, the type having lost all vestige of its austere ancestry for good. Chevrolet Nomads, Brookwoods, and Kingswoods were photographed in "fun" and "family leisure" contexts, with mothers and children outside supermarkets and antiques shops.

Given prevailing assumptions, it was not surprising that where women were depicted as drivers in automobile advertising, they were almost invariably seen gazing out of side windows, talking to passengers, or waving to their partners or friends in the distance.

The archetypal male driver, by contrast, usually looked forwards, conspicuously concentrating on the road ahead, undistracted by passengers or admiring neighbors. While his wife might recline elegantly in the bench front seat, he would sit up straight, decisively grasping the controls. If women steered effortlessly with two fingers, men drove with both hands on the wheel. Where a woman sat in a stationary car, and her husband was present, she usually looked up at him standing beside the car; she smiling, seeking admiration; he indulgent and solicitous, proud to be the means of his wife's contentment. These visual codes transcended socioeconomic boundaries, and were apparent whatever the "statusphere" of the car advertised. There were few exceptions to the stereotype until the late 1960s.

From the earliest days of automobile advertising, women — as models, drivers or passengers — had one more active role: that of gadget demonstrator. The theory ran (although it was rarely stated as such after around 1925) that if a girl could operate an automobile's controls, it would be effortless and simple for anyone else. In 1911, the Star Starter Company of New York had offered women motorists relief from the painful and potentially dangerous hand-cranking which had led many towards electric cars with the slogan, "Any Woman Can Start Your Car" and, in the years that followed, the theme of effortlessness became firmly established.

In some cases, the demonstrator of gadgets was included in order to appeal to the female buyer, but the idea had a much wider application. Occasionally, the gadgets were not easily operated at all, a fact from which the reader's attention was diverted by the operator's well-practiced smile which, if unconvincing on film, could be touched in by an artist later.

In 1946, for instance, Buick showed a woman of medium height operating the "venti-heater" control of a Roadmaster sedan. The necessary switch was located under the dashboard and the operator, in order to reach it, needed to lean against the steering wheel for support. Since the wheel rim was approximately level with her forehead, she had to turn to the side, in which position it was impossible either to steer or to see out of the windshield. Had the "driver" been facing forward, she probably could not have reached the switch at all. It was characteristic of the period that such disastrous ergonomics — planned around the average male frame — were actually promoted as advanced and convenient for women as well.

In 1953–54, optional power steering, brakes, seats, and windows arrived on low-priced cars, and the gadget operator was drafted

Can't drive, can pose: a Chevrolet owner wanders all over the road and looks everywhere but in front in 1958. The stereotype survived into the 1960s (May 1958).

HOW WILL YOU HAVE YOUR WEATHER? *Summer or winter, Buick's venti-heater means springlike comfort inside your car. Ask your dealer about this temperature conditioner.*

How far away will you have your heater control? 1946's Buick driver smiles bravely during a move best attempted while at a standstill (October 1946).

in to explain their advantages. A 1954 advertisement for the Ford range, and especially the Crestline, included four illustrations. The first showed the car's interior, with Family Man driving his wife and mother through lush green countryside, rejoicing in the "no shifting — no clutching" that that came with "Fordomatic Drive." In the back seat, his mother operated a window switch with exaggerated delicacy. In the remaining pictures, it was a female leg which demonstrated the car's power brakes and her finger which moved the electric seat adjustment. In the final picture, another woman maneuvered a two-tone pink and black Crestline hardtop out of a parking space with the aid of newly optional power steering.

Examples of such advertising were legion, and when the Chrysler Corporation promoted its station wagon range to family car buyers in a concentrated campaign during 1960–62, maternal priorities, little different from Chevrolet's in 1936, infiltrated the mixture of established clichés as an anxious mother protected her children in the back of a Dodge Dart or Plymouth Suburban by flicking the electric lock activator switch.

In the mid–1960s, the gadget operator was increasingly combined with the "seductive passenger" who demonstrated hazard warning flashers and cassette decks from the comfort of a sporty bucket seat. The seductive passenger had the merit of appealing to both male and female buyers, particularly in the sports and personal-luxury sectors of the market.

Several factors combined to encourage the modification of long-lived stereotypes. The growing sexual and economic liberation of women meant that more of them bought cars. Increasing numbers of those buyers were single, self-support-

ing, and young, and were able to choose their cars without deferring to male patronage of one kind or another. Lacking families, they were not solely motivated by practical considerations and, being socially mobile, they were not much concerned with the admiration of suburban neighbors; the consumer saw little point in keeping up with the Joneses if she neither knew nor cared who they were.

The diminution of male influence in the automotive market-place also meant that, from being largely a symbol of male dynamism, the powerful automobile could be promoted, albeit subtly, not only as a giver of freedom but also as an element in a woman's sexual equipage as it had not been, except intermittently within the highest income groups, in the 1930s. Add to these developments a growing informality in advertisers' social tableaux and a rejection by many younger buyers of old snobberies and social habits, and it became necessary for automobile advertising, in relation to women as in other areas, to evolve rapidly.

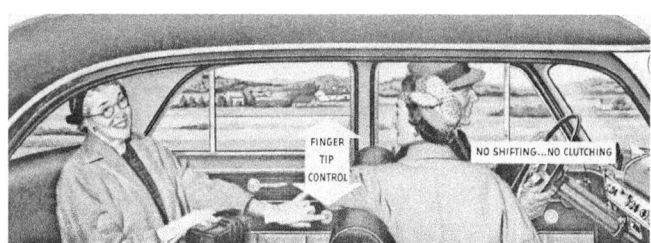

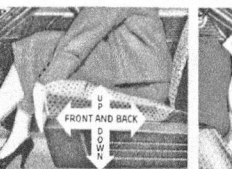 

The woman as gadget demonstrator: Ford employed an age-old theme in 1954. The man (hands on wheel, looking ahead) drives a dark-colored car, while the woman has a two-tone hardtop (May 1954).

By the mid–1960s, the male benefactor was in retreat as more women chose their own cars and enjoyed a measure of autonomy (June 1966).

Earlier, distinct images of women in relation to automobiles—as fashion models, drivers, and gadget demonstrators—became intermingled and, by 1965, the woman who owned a car was assumed to understand and be more interested in what made it enjoyable to handle. The bland, patronizing assurances of earlier years were no longer enough. Little now distinguished a woman who drove from her male equivalent; both desired power and comfort, and Mercury's earlier statement of the sexes' respective priorities, plausible in 1946, had little application twenty years later. Moreover, the cars of 1965 were easier to drive: Power steering and brakes removed the need for strength; and larger windows, combined with lower hood lines and rear decks that were visible from the driving seat, made height less of an advantage when maneuvering a full-size car.

A 1966 advertisement for the Chevrolet Caprice Custom Coupe illustrated the vinyl-topped car with a bikini-clad model lying on the roof. She was not looking at the reader and, intent on applying her make-up, suggested that the car was her own domain. She was as feminine as her forebears, but independent. The car—in contrast to equivalent station wagons—was portrayed as a liberator and not merely as an ameliorator of domestic drudgery.

In 1967, a mink-clad model promised that the Oldsmobile Toronado was "next to mink ... the most exciting animal around.... The kind of car a man buys for his kind of girl!" Was this a reversion to the assumption of male patronage? Perhaps—but in this advertisement it was very definitely the girl who took the initiative. The copy added, in a pointed aside, "Who says it's a man's world?" It also revealed changing expectations of both car and driver:

"Who says it's a man's world?" Oldsmobile's girl would not be satisfied with a dull sedan or, perhaps, with the kind of man who would choose it (April 1967).

> Now take the wheel. Toronado's front wheel drive negotiates tight turns, deep snow and rugged terrain effortlessly. And makes pulling into a parking place as easy as pulling on a kid glove.

Promises of driving ease and age-old obsessions with parking were apparent, but technical features (such as front-wheel drive) were considered, along with the challenge of driving in the potentially difficult conditions which, in 1952, Cadillac had ignored. Oldsmobile's driver was more dynamic than her predecessors, and the copywriter had arrived at a point roughly midway between De Soto's male (Fireflite) and female (Coronado) priorities of 1955.

The seductive passenger, who appeared in advertisements for Pontiac GTOs, Chevrolets, Mercury Cougars, and any number of Thunderbirds and Mustangs, was an ambiguous motif—intentionally so. Was she the car's owner, or the owner's partner, or—where the copy was aimed partly at men—the kind of girl that a male buyer of the automobile in question might attract if he drove the new car? Or was the car simply a means by which a woman's attractiveness, to herself as much as to any man, was enhanced? Or did the car interpose itself between man and woman, providing that independence and excitement which, in earlier years, a man alone would have been able to provide? It was impossible to determine which was the case unless the copy made it clear—which it did rarely — but the female motorist unquestionably enjoyed a greater physical and mental autonomy than did her predecessor of 1935, or even 1955.

It would be a mistake to infer from this development that the social climate changed overnight — it did not, and the trends depicted by copywriters were not equally prevalent in all states, or in rural, as opposed to urban, communities. A buyer's social class and level of education mattered, too. But among those traditionalists who maintained that it was, and should remain, a man's world, the automobile advertisers were less and less common. A successful appeal to independent women could have a significant impact on an automobile's sales.

Images of women in automobile advertising did not change radically after 1970, and the liberation which was bound up in the wider climate of the 1960s was increasingly taken for granted. Housewives continued to load groceries and children into station wagons, but women were habitually portrayed at the wheel of other types of car, without a man in sight, and their body language grew noticeably more confident. Models were still posed in and beside cars, but it was taken for granted by all involved that many women bought cars for fun and for business use as well as for domestic convenience. Compared with the changes that had taken place between 1930 and the mid–1960s, it was a relatively small step from Oldsmobile's Toronado theme to the Mercury Capri owner in 1991's catalog who declared, as she got into her red convertible, that "the end of my workday opens up endless possibilities."

PART THREE : REALITY SUPERVENES

Chapter 12

Justifying the Indulgence

The new 1938 Plymouth celebrates *10 years* of building great cars! Plymouth started in '28, a newcomer. Today Plymouth owners number *millions!* Because Plymouth offers *more value*.

Out on the General Motors proving ground — in the research laboratories— along the assembly line — men are busy working to the same broad purpose. Their steady aim is to give the public *extra value*. The benefits of these activities are clearly shown in what you get for what you pay when you buy any car in the GM family.... The next time *you* buy a car, remember — General Motors means Good Measure.

Both of these advertisements appeared in December, 1937. One was typical of its marque, and consisted of captioned photographs which demonstrated particular features of a new low-priced model. The second advertisement had a similar purpose within a corporate framework, underlining the value for money inherent in General Motors cars of all class categories, from Chevrolet to LaSalle and Cadillac. Such copy encouraged value-conscious buyers to trade up within the Corporation.

Whatever the particular merits of individual marques and models, the new car buyer had to be convinced that he was getting value for money. This applied to second-hand cars as much as to new ones, for marque loyalty nurtured by a used car often led to the purchase of a related new model.

General Motors published corporate advertisements from 1922, when it was found that "people throughout the United States, except at the corner of Wall and Broad streets," did not know anything about the parent company of so many popular marques.[1] The Ford name, on the other hand, was associated with a man, a company, and a product line.

Thus General Motors' two-tier advertising structure was born. Corporate advertisements were necessarily general in content, but they often featured (with divisional consent) individual marques, or particular features such as Fisher bodies and 1934's new "Knee-Action" independent front suspension. The underlying message of such advertising was that the Corporation, with its unmatched production resources, offered unbeatable value for money. More fanciful advertising themes were generally confined to copy for particular marques with specialized features and carefully defined (and often mutually exclusive) target markets.

Beneath the fantasy, therefore, lay a conservative and value-conscious attitude to the automobile as mechanism. Even the overt anti-functionalism of the early postwar period would be rejected by many consumers in the 1960s and, more comprehensively, in the 1970s. In the 1920s, the automobile, though widespread, was much more of a novelty to individual buyers, and styling in its modern sense had not yet obscured the car's essential purpose.

For Henry Ford, that purpose was simple. It was expounded in Ford's *My Life and Work*, published in 1923, which, though autobiographical, served also as a statement of personal ambition and corporate policy. Ford cited his first advertisement as a concise account of what he set out to achieve:

> Our purpose is to construct and market an automobile specially designed for everyday wear and tear ... an automobile which will attain to a sufficient speed to satisfy the average person without acquiring any of those breakneck velocities which are so universally condemned; a machine which will be admired by man, woman, and child alike for its compactness, its simplicity, its safety, its all-round convenience and — last but not least — its exceedingly reasonable price....[2]

The identification of the product with its manufacturer's personal ambitions and desires was a popular advertising

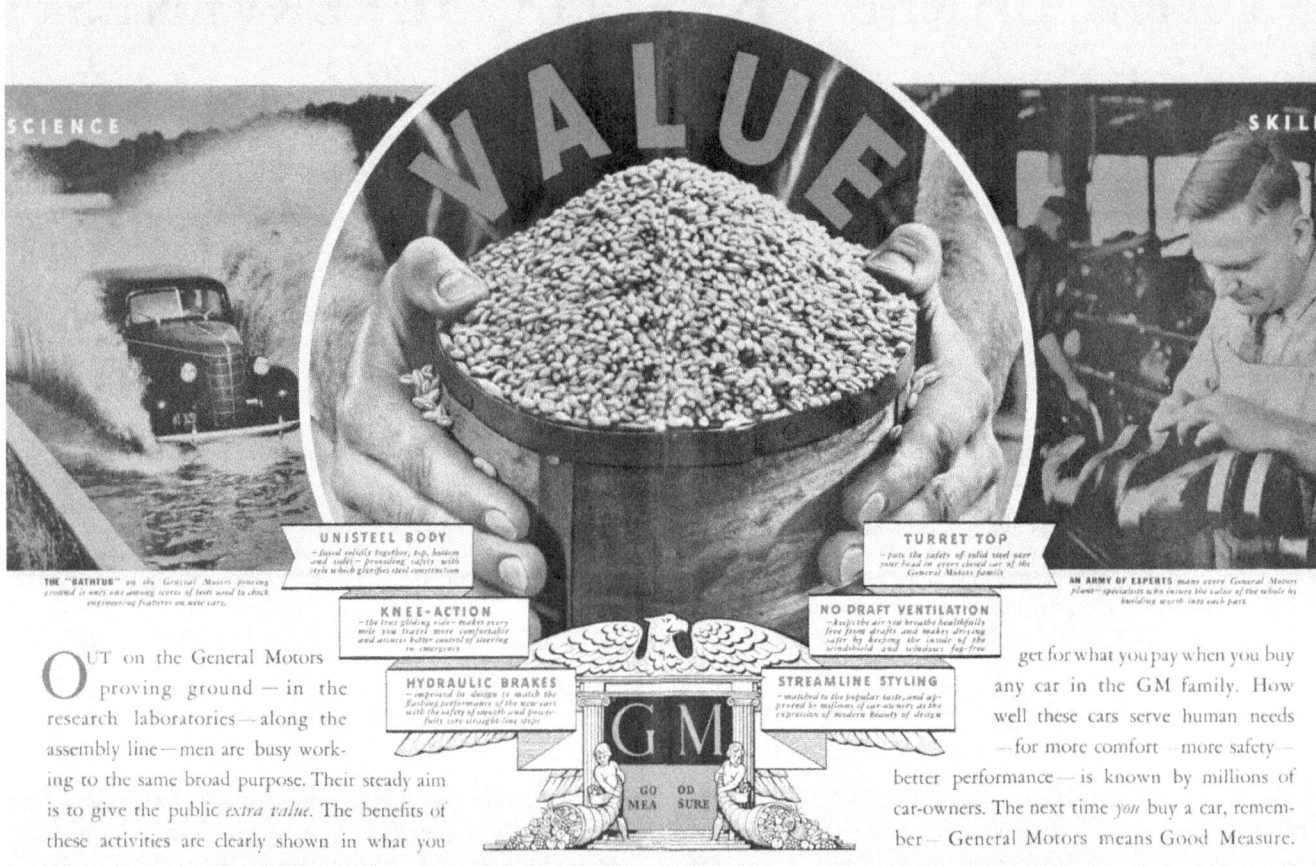

Above and opposite: Practical advertising in a recessionary model year, when competition amongst the "Big Three" was intense (Both ads: December 1937).

strategy of the 1900s; it suggested a personal commitment to buyers which had not yet been rendered foolish and improbable by the complexities of mass-production. It was ironic that Ford, a pioneering mass-producer, should have been able to trade on that personal reputation, directly or indirectly, until well into the 1930s. Ford, however, occupied a unique position in the automotive arena, and such advertising techniques could not safely be attempted by any other popular manufacturer.

Chrysler tried a similar trick in 1936, by writing a Plymouth advertisement around one "P.C. Sauerbrey, Plymouth's vice-president in charge of production." The narrative took the reader round the Plymouth factory, describing the equipment and machinery used to produce Plymouth cars to a consistently high quality. P.C. Sauerbrey kept "in personal touch with the job. Because his chief concern is to get a superbly engineered car superbly built. And from the boss down that's true of every Plymouth worker."

This personalization of advertising was intermittently popular as a counteracting force to the perceived depersonalization of the industry through mass production. It was also, perhaps, a cynical attempt to appeal to the "small-town values" of Plymouth's target market. The Plymouth name had been chosen for the marque in 1927 because it was familiar to American farmers through Plymouth Binder Twine, and advertising for the marque reflected the associations which the name already held in the American mind. It was therefore perhaps not surprising that buyers of regular Chryslers and Chrysler Imperials were not introduced to Mr. Sauerbrey's colleagues in the Corporation's other plants.

Overall value for money was a nebulous characteristic. Even disregarding the purely emotional element in a new car purchase, priorities varied from buyer to buyer and were not always easy to place in order. Quality, initial cost, reliability, and refinement were all desirable; in each area of the market it was necessary to create a tailor-made combination of virtues, and copywriters had to ensure that buyers were convinced that the best possible compromise had been achieved.

By 1927, the determinants of what the public perceived as value for money had changed, and they included an element of style. For this reason, as much as for its mechanical crudity, Ford's Model T was no longer viable, and it was discontinued in that year. While many new car buyers might have admired Henry Ford personally, and even his Model T as a contributor to American progress, they actually went out and bought Chevrolets in increasing numbers.

In 1928, Ford replied with the mechanically more conventional and up-to-date Model A, a car which was deliberately styled as the Model T had not been. A new Tudor sedan was declared to be "roundly at home in any company ... distinguished by its low, trim lines and the quiet good taste of every detail of finish and equipment." It was not merely cheap transport, but "the advanced expression of a wholly new idea in modern, economical transportation." It was apparent, even to Henry Ford, that utilitarian virtue alone was no longer enough to sustain sales. Value for money was a more complex amalgam of features in 1928 than in previous years, and the aesthetic component had come to stay.

In 1930, with competition intensifying, particularly from the Chrysler Corporation's new Plymouth, Ford staff began discreet work on a new V-8. The first engine was laid out in May, 1930, and by early 1931 an experimental motor was running. It was followed by further prototypes, and once Henry Ford had become convinced of the type's worth as a replacement for the Model A after a meeting with his son Edsel in December, 1931, the company worked frenetically to prepare the new car for launch to the public at the beginning of April, 1932.[3]

The V-8 was a long way removed from earlier Fords, and advertisements for the car traded on the company's reputation as a general provider of transport for the people, while at the same time promoting the stylistic and technical merits of the latest models compared with the Model A and — by indirect implication — the four-cylinder Model B. If Henry Ford had once scorned V-8 engines, he now wanted to consolidate the single obvious advantage that his new model had over the six-cylinder Chevrolet. Light bodywork enabled the V-8 engine — of little more than average power for its time, at 65 bhp — to propel the new car fast and smoothly. By 1938, streamlined V-8 sedans were shown in dramatic poses which drew attention to the low-priced Ford's resemblance to the glamorous, middle-market Lincoln-Zephyr.

The V-8 was marketed in Europe as well as America. Ford realized that European-assembled V-8s would occupy different areas of their markets from their American equivalents at home. Yet within their target, upper-middle class markets in Europe, they could still be promoted as offering better all-round value for money than their competition which, in most cases, was domestically designed and produced in small numbers by American standards. Ford could never sell its cars on exclusivity, but it could, and did, draw consumers' attention to the economic advantages of large-scale production.

Advertising strategies were adapted accordingly by Ford's agency between 1927 and the early 1940s, N.W. Ayer & Son:

> It was evident that American-made advertising and selling methods could not be successfully transplanted to England.... The firm decided to have a British staff under an American manager who had proved himself in the parent organization...[4]

This policy was reflected in British copy for the V-8, which was made palatable to its market without being complacent and insular. It was largely devoid of the smugness and diffidently expressed snobberies with which many British advertisements for the V-8's competition were infused. Where social climbing was attempted, it was attempted boldly, veering occasionally into self-parody, but never to the extent that the virtues of the car itself were obscured. The most exaggerated forms of this genre were reserved for the smaller "Eight" and "Ten" models of the late 1930s, which were not sold in America.

Unlike these smaller Fords, the V-8 was never perceived by British motorists as anything other than an American car,

Plants and Products of GENERAL MOTORS

STOCKHOLDERS of General Motors should be informed with regard to the constituent parts of the Corporation, including the extent of its interests in and control of other companies.

A complete list of the divisions that make up General Motors and how the Corporation coordinates its subsidiary and affiliated companies will be found in a booklet entitled "Plants and Products of General Motors."

A copy of this booklet will be mailed free upon request to Department K-6, General Motors Corporation, Broadway at 57th Street, New York.

"A car for every purse and purpose"
CHEVROLET · PONTIAC · OLDSMOBILE
MARQUETTE · OAKLAND · VIKING · BUICK
LaSALLE · CADILLAC · *All with Body by Fisher*
GENERAL MOTORS TRUCKS
YELLOW CABS *and* COACHES
FRIGIDAIRE—*The Automatic Refrigerator*
DELCO-LIGHT *Electric Power and Light Plants*
D *Water Systems* · GMAC *Plan of Credit Purchase*

Corporate advertising increased the likelihood that, when he traded up, the motorist would choose another General Motors marque (June 1929).

and British buyers of American cars in the 1930s bought them primarily for their low initial cost in relation to the performance offered. At a time (1935–37) when the cheapest saloon car in Britain, the Ford "Eight" (Model Y), cost £100, the Dagenham-assembled American sedan sold for a modest £230, which was superb value for a large V-8. But the car's fuel consumption, and the annual "horsepower" tax payable on the V-8 "30" engine, were in the luxury car league.

British copywriters consequently found it difficult to target the V-8, promoting it both as a luxury car whose first cost happened to be extraordinarily low, and as a mid-priced car with the performance of an expensive "sports saloon." Body styles changed every year or two from the V-8's introduction in 1932, but the flavor of N.W. Ayer's copy stayed the same. A September, 1936 advertisement for the Model 68 was typical:

> Really "De Luxe" Touring Comes Easy to the owners of the Ford V-8, universally conceded to be the luxury car for the economically-inclined, generous in pleasure-giving, miserly in fuel consumption, running and maintenance generally.

A new, streamlined 1937 Model 78 was shown outside an antiques shop in a March, 1937 advertisement:

> Hunting Period "Pieces," Pictures, Silver, Up and Down the Kingdom, you could have no better car than the New Ford V-8 "30," whose appearance indicates your judgement of value, whose performance is equally gratifying to amateur or expert, every seat a front seat in restful, comfortable roominess. It costs very little to buy, run and maintain, over a term of years, always in prime condition.

Not all advertisements for the V-8 were as high-flown as these color pieces. According to a small black and white advertisement taking up just one sixteenth of a large magazine page of *The Field* in September, 1937:

> With accommodation for seven passengers—in addition to the driver—the Ford Utility Car [1937 wooden-bodied station wagon] is the ideal vehicle for country house, station or hotel service. Amply powered with an 8-cylinder engine, the car will perform heavy duty at moderate cost. Prices from £275 (ex works). Obtainable from South London's oldest estd. Ford dealers, F.H. Peacock Ltd. 219–221 Balham High Road, S.W.17.

A full-page monochrome advertisement for the equivalent sedan was almost as down-to-earth in April, 1937:

> After even forty years of motoring, you still have something to learn unless you have tried this new Ford V-8 "30." You may take its wonderful engine "for granted," because of the designers' unique experience of V-8s. You expect much: You are not disappointed. But its clutch, gear-box, steering, suspension, particularly those really remarkable brakes, have to be personally tried before you can understand such an improvement upon those of other cars.... This Ford V-8 "30" gives you multi-cylinder luxury-car motoring at a cost you can contemplate undisturbed.... We put price last. Satisfy yourself on every other point. Then consider the price, permitted only by the matchless production-resources of the Ford Works at Dagenham [England].

The reader was not told that the "really remarkable brakes" were operated by cables, rather than the increasingly widespread hydraulic cylinders fitted to Plymouths and Chevrolets since 1928 and 1936 respectively, or that the suspension was by transverse leaves, as fitted to the Model T. Fuel vaporization in hot weather was left unmentioned, too, though such weather did not usually trouble British motorists for more than a few weeks in a year.

Copy for the 1939 Model 91A de Luxe claimed value for money, but was disingenuous:

> An entirely new car ... it possesses elegant, roomy bodywork of a class and distinction usually associated only with far costlier cars.

This was certainly true of the bodywork, if not of the machinery underneath. The copy continued:

> ... its typically Ford power-to-weight ratio makes it a car of incredible economy of running and maintenance, apart from its very conservative first cost.

Convenience of servicing apart, this was less true. The "Saloon de Luxe" cost £280 by March, 1939, when this advertisement appeared. Curiously, no mention was made of the Model 91A's new hydraulic brakes, although much was made of Ford's production methods in a spirit of English eccentricity:

> Did you know...? King Henry I of England decreed that a lawful English yard was the measure of the distance from the tip of his nose to the end of his thumb, the arm fully extended. His word was law, but Ford precision gauges, in hourly use at Dagenham, measure rather more exactly, if required to a two-millionth of an inch.

N.W. Ayer & Son understandably played it both ways, comparing the V-8's initial cost favorably with the luxury eight-cylinder car norm, yet also comparing its running costs with those of cars whose purchase prices were two or three times the £280 asked for a Ford V-8. To Britons, the car was either the best of all possible worlds or an ignominious collapse between every possible stool, as in England the V-8 was still expensive to run for so inexpensive a car.

Compromise was attempted in 1936 with the V-8 "22" (Model 62), a 136 cubic inch "small" V-8 with a Dagenham-designed body which was never sold in America. The new model was heavily promoted with lavish color advertising in upmarket British magazines such as *Punch*, *The Illustrated London News*, and *The Field* from late 1936 onwards. American influence was immediately apparent in the layout and artwork of such pieces which, set against the contemporary norm in British automobile advertising, were uncluttered and distinctive.

The V-8 "22" was announced at £210, at which price it was only marginally cheaper than the "30." Yet running costs were

Above, left and opposite: The Dagenham-built Ford V-8, as advertised to cost-conscious, middle-class British motorists. Minor details distinguished British models from their Dearborn sisters, of which the most noticeable were electro-mechanical semaphore turn signals, or "trafficators," in boxes beside the front door hinges on the 1936 and 1937 cars, and hidden in recesses between the doors in 1939. The 136 cu. in. "22" was a British-market special, heavily advertised as the ideal compromise for that country's needs. All Ford V-8s were sturdy, and surviving "30" variants were popular in the postwar years with British motorists who could find the fuel to run them (October 1936, August 1937, February 1938, and March 1939).

claimed to be significantly reduced, and much was made of the annual tax of £16 10s (16 pounds and ten shillings) payable, which was little more than twice the £7 10s charge for a Model C "Ten." "You have to see, examine at close range, test on the road, this New Ford V-8 to realize how fine, handsome, dependable — and, above all, how *economical* a car it is," said a typical announcement advertisement. In February, 1937 it was "...just as fine a car as its bigger sister, but attractively less costly to buy, run and maintain...."

At the end of 1936, the V-8 "22" was advertised as the ideal Christmas present, repeating a theme used in copy for the Model Y "Eight" in 1935: "The Season of Peace and Goodwill, of hospitality at its most lavish, coming and going at their busiest, calls for this New Ford V-8... the magic carpet of engineering!" The car was shown, chauffeur at the wheel, parked outside a stately home as Christmas party-goers gathered

around. Beneath the picture was the pay-off line, "There is No Comparison! More Miles per Gallon is Good: Fewer Pence Per Mile is Better!" and an offer: "No Motorist Should be Without The New FORD Book of Maps! Handy in Size — Easily Read, 1s [one shilling], From any Ford Dealer." Another piece in the series showed the V-8 "22" outside a more modest town house, the ideal gift from an affluent man to his wife:

> Merry Christmas.... The Best Gift of which I could think.... The New Ford V-8 ... the multi-cylinder luxury car of outstanding dependability, economy and efficiency.... There is No Comparison.

Two years later, aware that detractors considered the V-8 "22" a "gutless wonder" which lacked the performance of the larger V-8 but which was almost as expensive to run, Ford traded on the larger car's performance image: "Sample V-8 performance! No cost! No obligation! Until you have driven a Ford V-8, you don't know what twentieth-century motoring can mean.... Watch the Fords go by!"

Yet the "22" was not a success, selling only 9,239 copies as a single model between June, 1936 and February, 1941, while nearly 12,000 of the "30" were sold in four successive editions (Models 68, 78, 81A, and 91A) between November, 1935 and January, 1940. More compact than the American product, the "22" was still a large car by British standards, and it did not offer such good value for money as the original. Nevertheless, eight months after the horsepower tax was abolished for new cars in January, 1947, the regular 221 cu. in. engine was fitted into a facelifted V-8 "22" body (called the Pilot) that owed nothing to America's latest incarnation of the parent idiom, which had been around since 1941. The Pilot, sold from the outset as a luxury car, was more successful than the V-8 "22," and more than 21,000 were produced between 1947 and 1951.

On both sides of the Atlantic, Ford pursued the value-for-money theme relentlessly. In America, the company had long been a part of the country's social and industrial fabric, and could play the role of general provider much earlier, and more convincingly, than was possible in Britain. Ford was able to trade on the reputation of a company whose position was not only established in the annals of motoring history, but also firmly planted in the fertile substratum of America's cultural consciousness.

In 1937, an American advertisement for the Ford V-8 combined elements of the popular contented-ordinary-user testimonial with an appeal to the reader's common sense. The speaker was a (mythical) retired farmer, who sat in the sunshine surveying the land, his new Ford parked a few yards away:

> Seems to me, nothing ever takes the place of experience. You learn to do a good job by going out and doing it. The more you do it, the more you learn about it. Take cars for instance. They tell me Henry Ford has built more than 25 million. Nobody else ever had near that much experience. So, the way I figure, Henry Ford's the man I want to build my car. Besides, all those cars weren't sold — most of them were bought. Bought because folks got more for their money — because Henry Ford did a better job every year....[5]

The cult of Henry Ford's personality was employed to the full. Everyone knew that he had been born on a farm, and that he had been motivated by a desire to provide transport for farming communities so that they would not suffer the rural isolation in which he and his contemporaries had grown up. But it was significant that the advertisement made no appeal at all to the farmer's understanding of automobiles; the homespun philosophy so eloquently contrived required absolute trust on the part of the new car buyer. It was true that many people did trust Henry Ford to cater to their motoring needs, but Ford was essentially a paternalist, and it showed.

The onset of economic depression in 1929 reduced advertising budgets in all sectors of the market. For their clients to remain loyal, agencies needed to demonstrate an ability not only to cultivate marque images over the long term, but to sell as many of the present year's cars as possible. Automobile production fell by 40 percent between 1929 and 1930, and one result was a renewed concentration among copywriters on the operating costs and serviceability of their products, at the expense of whimsical and "artistic" types of advertising. Value for money became a fashionable theme and, particularly

American advertising for the V-8 was less fanciful than the British equivalent, reflecting the car's low-priced status and an essentially practical approach to motoring (February 1938).

within the low and medium price fields, it remained dominant for many years, and only faded once again in 1941–42.

The independent manufacturers, which lacked the production resources of the Big Three, had to try particularly hard. Hudson declared in 1934: "You won't believe your ears when you hear the price" of its eight-cylinder model. The recommendation was earnest:

> With due regard for the value of each word, Hudson believes that the following statement cannot be successfully challenged: "The new 1934 Hudson Eight will out-perform every other eight-cylinder stock car ever built."

The small print continued with a careful, if pedantic, analysis of the car's superior comfort and economy ("the lowest fuel and oil cost per horse-power ever achieved"). In the absence of any one remarkable characteristic, and aware that the low-priced Ford V-8 offered eight-cylinder competition, Hudson strove, like many others, to offer the best of all possible worlds.

The Depression reached its nadir in 1932, and car production rose steadily thereafter until 1938, when sales fell again by 40 percent compared with 1937's total of nearly four million. Recovery was evident by the end of the model year, but uncertainty—and new competition from Mercury in the middle price range—was reflected in the noisily persuasive copy that surfaced in 1939. According to Oldsmobile, for instance, "America rides and decides—'THIS YEAR, IT'S OLDSMOBILE!'"

As one of GM's mid-range marques, Oldsmobile was vulnerable to fluctuations downwards towards top-range Chevrolets, Fords, and Plymouths, and those who had previously been content with cars of the "low-priced three" were encouraged to trade up. Oldsmobile's starting price of $777 was prominently displayed in the company's 1939 advertising, and even if most cars that left the factory would not be stripped business coupes selling for less than $800—a six-cylinder Series 60 four-door sedan cost $889, with the equivalent eight-cylinder Series 80 at $1,043—the low starting price acted as a psychological incentive to those who thought a middle-range marque beyond their means. Advertisements reassured buyers that even the most basic model came with "safety glass, bumpers, bumper guards, spare tire and tube," but such luxuries as a second windshield wiper were relegated to the options list. Oldsmobile's tactics were common to many other low- and lower-middle priced mar-

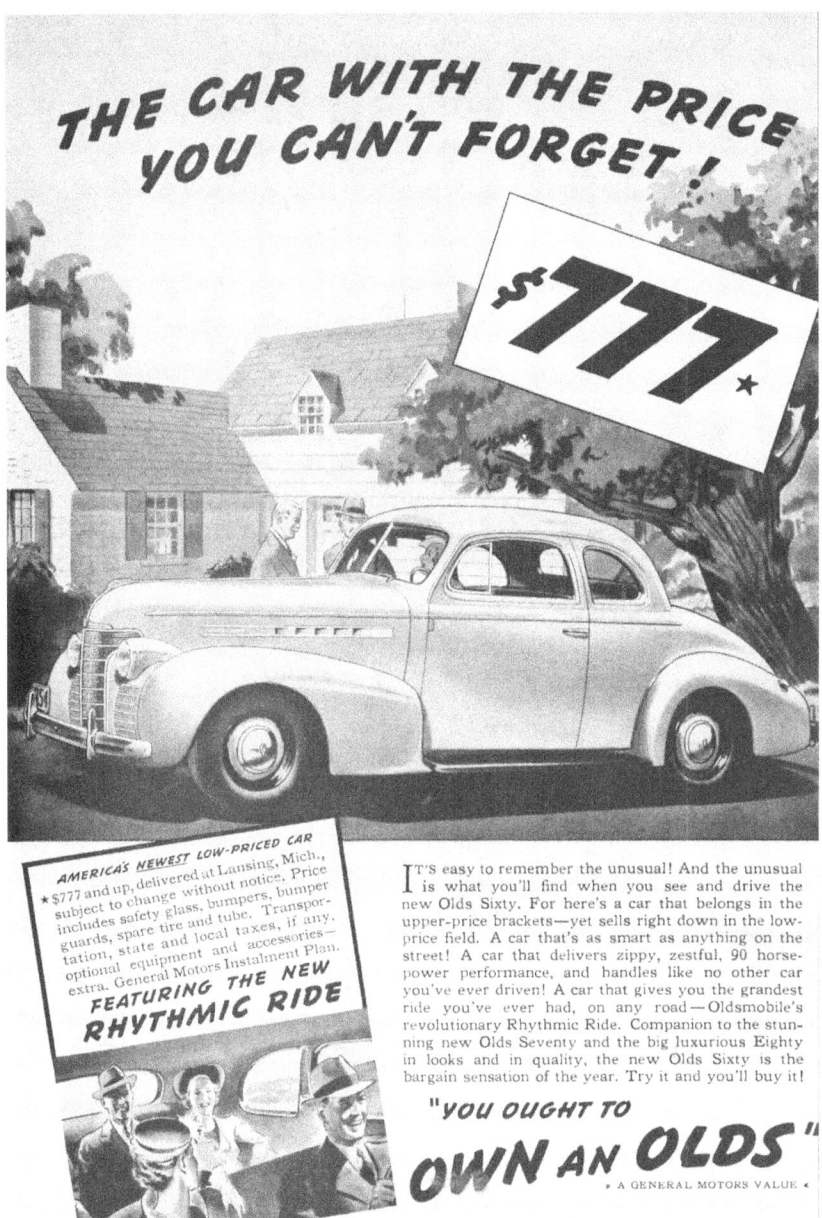

Oldsmobile encouraged owners of the "low-priced three" to trade up in 1939. Modest artwork reflected the functional copy (February 1939).

ques, but, above the $900-$1,000 level, lists of fittings made way for less starkly factual copy.

By the late 1940s, the mundanity of much pre-war copy was mitigated by a more widespread use of color and elegant language, even in advertisements whose primary purpose was to promote their products' value for money. In most cases, "value" continued to be defined as an accumulation of detail advances and features, rather than an overall package. The 1950 Plymouth was "packed with value and ready to prove it!" but photographs and myriad captions had given way to simple color illustrations and a single block of text. J. Stirling Getchell, creator of Plymouth's starkly photo-realist campaign of the 1930s, had died, aged 41, in December, 1940.

Contrasting conceptions of value from Plymouth in 1950 and 1954 (March 1950 and January 1954).

Chevrolet had been producing cars since 1911, and commanded marque loyalty that was as fierce as Ford's and numerically wider than that enjoyed by Plymouth. That loyalty rested on a reputation for simplicity and reliability and, for the low-priced field, an element of style that was not matched by Ford until 1932. The aesthetic component of the value-for-money equation was largely responsible for Chevrolet's ingress into former Ford territory in the 1920s, and it was a lead which GM fought hard to maintain. Thus, while a typical 1952 advertisement for the Chevrolet range showed ten particular features to prove that Chevrolets were the "Only Fine Cars Priced So Low," the main illustration depicted a two-tone Bel Air hardtop rather than a stripped sedan.

Among Chevrolet's cheaper models, which benefited from the glamour of the Bel Air but which sold in greater numbers, the clean-lined and attractive De Luxe Sport Coupe was shown in several advertisements. Chevrolet's copywriters of the late 1940s and early 1950s consistently sought to demonstrate that the car combined all the important virtues of high-priced cars with low actual cost. Chevrolet buyers did not wish to feel that they were buying cars that said "utility" and therefore "cheapness" to the world at large. The 1952 two-door De Luxe sedan in "Regal Maroon," for example, was promoted as the way to "Keep Up Your Quality Standards and Cut Down Your Motoring Costs," suggesting a regular acquaintance with "quality" motoring which, however improbable, flattered and reassured the low-priced car buyer.

In the anti-utilitarian climate of the 1950s, value for money was not always claimed explicitly, but even in an atmosphere that was far less congenial to the "nuts-and-bolts" school of copywriting than that of the early 1930s, car buyers still wanted to rationalize their purchasing impulses. Plymouth offered reassurance in 1954:

> The deep satisfaction that is part of the everyday life of Plymouth owners results from a unique engineering concept. A concept that blends beauty with safety, combines elegance with economy, permits no compromise with mechanical excellence. No other low-price car has such a heritage, nor offers as great a measure of value.

The brutality of earlier copy was thus relinquished, and the principal appeal was to a satisfaction felt, rather than to the reader's analysis of the car as mechanism. No longer was value to be measured purely in terms of a car's functional equipment, styling, and price. What had been described in Chrysler's earlier corporate advertising as engineering was now promoted as an "engineering concept," and the reader was implicitly encouraged to form his response to the car on the basis of how he felt about the "concept," rather than what he thought about the car's engineering, as demonstrated to him.

Thus the value of the automobile as mechanism was incorporated into, and subsumed within, its perceived value as a bringer of emotional fulfillment and satisfaction to the consumer. Ironically, while this development in Plymouth's copy style clearly indicated a recognition by the copywriter of recent developments in the way consumers were encouraged to think about automobiles (and, in some cases, did think about them), the 1954 Plymouth, lacking the style of its rivals, was not a great success. By the mid–1950s, the aesthetic component of the value-for-money equation was not only unavoidable, but dominant.

Copywriters continued to claim that their cars offered "value" during the remaining years of the decade, particularly in relation to low-priced versions of full-size sedans, and the success of the mischievously named Studebaker Scotsman of 1957–58 (from $1,795 in 1958, compared to $2,013 for a Chevrolet Delray utility sedan) demonstrated that a stripped sedan, if priced low enough, would find a ready market. But "value for money," other than as a bland catchphrase, was largely sidelined by copywriters until the arrival of the modern American compact cars in 1959.

Chapter 13

The Sybarite's Progress

Whether he was an automotive fantasist, a realist, or drawn uneasily between the two, the American car buyer demanded comfort. By 1930, the automobile had proved itself as a reliable form of transportation, and much effort was taken thereafter to ensure that the motorist's journey was made as effortlessly as possible. In Europe, even in the 1930s, a trip of fifty miles or so was considered long; in America, it was short. If the European buyer of a small car rarely found out how uncomfortable his thinly padded seat could be after three hours at the wheel, his American counterpart discovered such shortcomings quickly. Most Americans would willingly sacrifice a few dollars' worth of gasoline, not to mention race-car cornering, in order to arrive at their destinations feeling refreshed, rather than sore.[6]

From the early 1920s onward, America's automobile manufacturers became interested in the individual and combined effects of space, seating, ventilation, and silence. The closed sedan body, an expensive novelty in 1919 which accounted for no more than ten percent of new car sales, was in most cases cheaper than a similar open car by 1925, and was fitted to more than 90 percent of new cars by 1930. The science of ergonomics was then in its infancy, but the driver's environment was given increasingly careful consideration, and the results were not always haphazard. Copywriters sometimes chose particular features for emphasis, particularly if they were genuinely novel; more usually, the combined benefits of parallel improvements were highlighted.

General Motors made much of a new ventilation system in the mid–1930s. A February, 1934 advertisement for Fisher bodies showed three elaborately dressed women in the back of a chauffeur-driven Buick sedan:

> These fortunate people have forgotten it is night, forgotten they have miles yet to journey, forgotten a chill and importunate world outside.... The smart Fisher Ventipanes controlling No Draft Ventilation ... the new breadth and depth of seats and cushions, the new and richer beauty of appointments all contribute to a complete sense of well-being almost beyond price....

Buick offered a variety of features in the same year:

> To ride in [the 1934 Buick] is to know a relaxed ease such as you have never known before ... because Buick alone combines Knee-Action wheels [here, non-Dubonnet independent front suspension], Balanced Weight and Springing, The Ride Stabilizer and Air Cushion Tires—the four factors which produce the gliding ride as Buick gives it.

In May, 1936, Fisher Body showed an Oldsmobile sedan with two children sitting on the running-board, examining a pet tortoise:

> These two young moderns have made a great discovery which we hope will not be lost on any fond parent who drives a car. Nature herself applies the same principle of protection you enjoy in the one-piece solid steel "Turret Top" body by Fisher.... Under this guardian crown of steel, thanks to Fisher No Draft Ventilation, you ride in the deep comfort of a car that's independent of the weather — always draft-free, yet ever amply supplied with fresh air in cold or hot weather.

Improvements were enthusiastically demonstrated, whether they had been designed for comfort alone, or offered on the way to providing other, separate advantages over earlier models or the opposition. Independent front suspension was vigorously promoted by General Motors and, to a lesser extent, by the Chrysler Corporation during the mid–1930s, at a time when the Ford Motor Company stayed resolutely with the transverse leaves that were ideal for rough ground, but which gave a comparatively bouncy ride. They would be fitted to all Fords, Mercurys, and Lincolns until 1949.

Weight distribution was improved on most cars too, by moving the engine forward over the front axle line. Chrysler

Draft-free ventilation was promoted vigorously in Fisher Body advertising of 1934 (February 1934).

capitalized on the innovative design of the new Airflow in this respect in 1935 Plymouth advertising:

> If Plymouth's looks give you a thrill, what a thrill you'll have from Plymouth's luxurious *Floating Ride!* Weight is redistributed like in the famous "Airflow" cars. New soft-action springs "iron out" the bumps. A sway eliminator keeps you steady on curves.

In a 1937 advertisement for the regular, conventionally-styled Chrysler line, the wife of a new Chrysler owner explained the advantages of independent front suspension from a female (and therefore subjective, non-technical) point of view:

> I think we both made up our minds when we got to the railroad tracks on Sixth Street. We braced ourselves as usual ... but that love of a Chrysler just glided over them as if they weren't there at all. So John took up weight distribution, and hydraulic shock absorbers and independently sprung front wheels ... and I just asked him gently if Chrysler engineering wasn't reputed to be the best in the industry. He said it was. So I told him we could probably accept what everybody knew.

By 1940, independent suspension was no longer a novelty, and Studebaker declared simply:

> Your Commander's sound, solid, dependable Studebaker craftsmanship enables you to keep any travel schedule you set. And you cover every mile with the velvet smoothness and sure-footedness that only exclusive planar independent suspension can give a car.

Silence was a matter of engine design as well as sound deadening, and Buick, avoiding the mundanities that filled advertisements for some other marques, was euphoric in June, 1936:

> So hushed is the oil-cushioned action of the great Buick valve-in-head engine that even in full flight this marvelous car seems "ghosting" along — its silky mobility matched only by the ease and certainty of its fingertip control.

The car was shown in the bottom left-hand corner of the page, photographed at bumper level. Gulls soared above the car, flying with it as it sped across the ground. It was one of the first in a successful series of advertisements by Buick's new

"Weight re-distribution"—moving the engine forward to increase passenger room and lessen a tendency to oversteer—was not confined to Chrysler Corporation products. Plymouth capitalized on public interest in the Chrysler Airflow two years before it was discontinued (June 1935).

agent, Arthur Kudner, who had left Erwin, Wasey and Company in 1935 to set up his own agency and who did much to revitalize Buick's image in the 1930s. Comfort and power, usually in euphoric combination, were the marque's selling-points.

Nash consolidated a reputation for imaginative copy in 1940, promoting the sophisticated "Weather Eye" ventilation system first fitted in its 1938 models. A September, 1939 advertisement was headed "Night Flight" and described a long winter journey: "There's magic in the air tonight. Fleecy clouds sail high above, and your road is a ribbon of glistening moonlight. Keen and crisp is the whistling wind. But inside your Nash, you're sitting snug and coatless, in the never-changing June of the 'Weather Eye.'"

The system drew fresh air into the car through a cowl vent, keeping dust and drafts at bay by lightly pressurizing the interior, and included a replaceable pollen filter. A February, 1940 advertisement was devoted to the feature:

Weather Eye Magic.... The mercury tumbles ... the wind howls louder — but stop or go, fast or slow — your comfort is automatically kept the same. That little thermostatic sentinel just inside the windshield never lets a chilly breath slip by. Yes— it's Weather Eye magic that even outguesses "old man Winter"!

Until the advent of power features in mainstream cars in the early 1950s, postwar copy consolidated earlier themes. Ford's early postwar advertising was strongly comfort-oriented, but copywriters were hampered by the company's continued use of non-independent transverse leaf springs, front and rear. General Motors' "Knee Action" front suspension gave far greater highway comfort, even if Ford's "multi-leaf 'Rest-ride' springs" were more suitable for really rough ground. "A day behind the wheel of the big new Ford will show you what real comfort means!" declared one 1946 advertisement which showed the new car speeding along a country track. By 1948, however, roads were improving and sturdiness alone was not enough to remain competitive, and the 1949 model, with independent coil-spring front suspension, marked the end of a Ford tradition.

For Plymouth, true comfort was achieved in 1948 with "Airfoam Seat Cushions" and "Super-Cushion Tires" together with that perennial Chrysler Corporation feature, "chair height [seats] so a man can sit up like a man." In the early 1950s, this requirement would play havoc with body styling, as rival Chevrolets and Fords became longer and lower, while Plymouths stayed boxy and comparatively upright.

The early postwar Buick was more modern than its rivals in its styling and engineering, and was promoted as an effortless highway cruiser. "What other car has so much that clicks for Forty-Six?" asked a Canadian advertisement in October, 1946, which listed several features designed to increase the passengers' comfort. Old-fashioned euphoria featured, too:

You build up the miles—five hundred, eight hundred, a thousand. Faultless miles they are, cradled on the gentle action of all-coil springing.... The soft, floating action of BuiCoil springing becomes gentler, it seems, with each hour on the road....

The Nash Airflytes of the late 1940s and early 1950s were sold on comfort and gadgets rather than speed. In 1954, "the world's first

Mild euphoria from revitalized Buick advertising in 1936 (June 1936).

Rarely was so much copy expended on so small a component — in this case an adjustable thermostat. Nash cars containing lightly clad models were driven about in winter to push the point home (February 1940).

INCH BY INCH... MILE AFTER MILE It's PLYMOUTH for <u>Roomy</u>, Pillowed Riding Ease

The big, roomy Plymouth won't knock your hat off. And even for the lanky, there's legroom to spare.

This low-priced car is *engineered* to give you extra inches where inches do the most good. But Plymouth's great ride comes from more than space to move around in. It's an *Air-Pillow Ride* — pillowed comfort built into mile after mile.

Seats are chair-height—so a man can sit up like a man. And you literally ride on air when you ride on Airfoam Seat Cushions, available on Special De Luxe Plymouths at moderate additional cost. Millions of tiny air pillows give to your slightest body pressure, mold themselves to you for restful support.

You ride *between* the axles, not over them. That's a difference, a comfort difference. Bigger, fatter Super-Cushion Tires, standard equipment on Plymouth, soak up road shocks from sides *and* below. The longest wheelbase in its price field makes for a still more *level* ride.

And these are only a few of the dozen and more major Plymouth features that speak up for a great ride—and a great car. There is a difference in low-priced cars, and Plymouth makes the difference!

PLYMOUTH is <u>still</u> the low-priced car most like high-priced cars

PLYMOUTH BUILDS GREAT CARS . . . GOOD SERVICE KEEPS THEM GREAT. *Your nearby Plymouth dealer will provide the service and factory-engineered parts to keep your present car in good condition while you're waiting for your new Plymouth.* PLYMOUTH Division of CHRYSLER CORPORATION, Detroit 31, Mich.

Seats that were "chair-height — so a man can sit up like a man" featured in all Chrysler Corporation products in 1948 — as did old-fashioned tall and bulbous styling. A new Plymouth would arrive in the spring of 1949 (September 1948).

combined *cooling-heating-ventilating* system" was offered on the Rambler, Statesman, and Ambassador under the name of "All-Weather Eye" to provide "Year-'round Air Conditioning." Nash's system was a good and remarkably inexpensive version of the refrigerated air conditioning which had first appeared on Packards and Cadillacs in 1940 and 1941 respectively, and which, by the mid-1950s, was becoming an increasingly popular option elsewhere even if it was not yet commonly ordered on middle- or low-priced cars. In the Nash, all of the major components were located under the hood, obviating the need for any bulky equipment in the trunk or transparent ducts inside the rear window. To underline the point, an Ambassador sedan was shown "in scenic Arizona." Also described in detail were the long-established "Nash Airliner Reclining Seats" which could be quickly turned into "Twin Beds." Optional extras included plastic window screens for repelling insects. Nash sales nevertheless fell from over 140,000 in 1952 to fewer than 110,000 in 1953 and a mere 77,000 or so in 1954, at a time when national car production was increasing. In May, 1954, Nash merged with Hudson to form American Motors Corporation, or AMC.

The horsepower race of 1952–57 diverted copywriters' attention from comfort features for a few years. Effortless control was nevertheless allied with increased power and a proliferation of pushbutton gadgets—particularly transmissions. These were offered by, among others, Packard and Chrysler from 1956 and, in the middle price field, by Edsel and Mercury in 1958.

The universal de-emphasis of performance as an advertising theme in 1958 encouraged copywriters to turn to comfort once again. Chevrolet fitted "Full Coil suspension" to give the "extra-soft cushioning of deep coil springs at every wheel," while a "real air ride" from "Level Air suspension" was an option on Chevrolets and other GM cars. The craze for air suspension, which was not confined to General Motors, was shortlived, as owners complained that their cars bottomed easily over undulations and bumps, bounced and floated too much even when fitted with self-leveling equipment and, crucially, that the systems were unreliable. Packard's 1955–56 "Torsion-Level" torsion bar suspension, with self-leveling at the rear, had been much more satisfactory. The new 1959 Chevrolet came with conventional suspension and "foam-cushioned seats that feel like they're riding on a sunbeam."

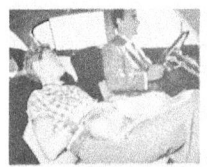

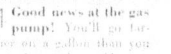

Clutching at straws — Weather Eye ventilation, even in improved form as one of America's most advanced air-conditioning systems, was not enough of a novelty by 1954, when refrigeration was becoming more widely available (June 1954).

Chrysler combined power and dynamism with comfort in 1959's New Yorker four-door hardtop, billed to highly stressed businessmen as the car that "Lets you relax <u>before</u> you get home." (A similar copyline, identical even in its emphasis—"For those who like to sit down and relax <u>before</u> they get home"—would be used by GM's British subsidiary, Vauxhall, in a 1976 advertisement for its VX 2300, which was aimed at much the same market in Britain.) Chrysler elaborated:

> At day's end your Chrysler invites you to relax. The newly available Swivel Seat turns into the car with you. You lounge in your own private world. Tasteful colors and fabrics and clear tempered safety glass windows surround you.

Comfort and space were Chevrolet's priorities in 1959 (May 1959).

Power was taken for granted, and was available more for peace of mind than for wheel-churning thrills, if one believed the copy.

Another 1959 Chrysler advertisement, for the Windsor hardtop sedan, explained how Chrysler's designers had increased the car's roominess at a time when rear-seat headroom, in particular, had in many cars taken second place to styling: "The big news in '59 is roominess ... and Chrysler's got it!" No longer was the Windsor a dowdy concoction with out-of-date looks; it was low, long, and sleek, and its makers reassured long-term adherents of the marque that although Chrysler had "the style that set the standard for an industry" with its second-phase Forward Look, old-fashioned comfort had not been sacrificed.

By 1960, full-sized low-price cars were imitating traditional "fine cars," and the 1960 Chevrolets were claimed to be "sumptuous." The 1961 models would glide "over the bumpiest byway with the kind of poise and stability you'd expect only in the most expensive makes" while a 1963 headline made the point forcefully: "There may be something more comfortable and luxurious at the price, but it isn't a car!"

In the early 1960s, the compact Chevrolet Corvair catered to the "utility" end of the market which, ten years earlier, would have been offered an austere full-size Styleline sedan. The 1963 Impala convertible was described as the "Most comfortable thing since grandmother's lap." Even copy for the Sport Sedan version, which seemed at first glance to recapture the spirit of 1957, was mild: "You don't take a back seat to anybody!" suggested speed and handling, but the true emphasis was made clear in the small print, which described how the car moved "effortlessly, quietly" with a "Jet-smooth ride."

It seemed inevitable that Chevrolets would one day be as comfortable as Cadillacs, and Chevrolet advertisements for the early part of the 1967 model year made that leap. The full-size Caprice explicitly set out to offer Cadillac standards of refinement at Chevrolet prices. Instead of being shown in traditional Chevrolet settings—on beaches, in the countryside, on freeways—Caprices appeared outside hotels and fashionable upmarket resorts, their passengers in evening dress. "Squint slightly. Now couldn't this Caprice almost pass for a you-know-what?" asked an April, 1967 advertisement for the Caprice Custom Sedan.

The layout, copy, and theme of the advertisement were pure Cadillac, and while the strategy might have flattered and amused Chevrolet buyers, it did not entertain Cadillac's marketing department, which ensured that General Motors' president, James Roche, instructed Chevrolet to abandon the campaign. He was not convinced by the plea that the "you-know-what" was, in fact, a Lincoln or Imperial.[7]

"Just you and your new Chrysler humming the miles aside." Chrysler targeted tired executives with "Swivel Seats" and "Auto-Pilot" cruise control (February 1959).

In 1965 Ford moved upmarket, too, with a super-luxurious LTD based on the full-sized Galaxie 500. Impressed with the quietness of Ford's prototypes, a member of J. Walter Thompson's team on the Ford account wondered aloud whether they might be almost as quiet as Rolls-Royces. Shortly before the new model's announcement, the agency asked the independent acoustical consultants Bolt, Berenek, and Newman to test three of the cars—none specially prepared—against two new Rolls-Royces bought for the purpose. The Fords actually proved *quieter* than the British cars by 4.9, 5.5, and 2.8 decibels at 20mph, 40mph, and 60mph respectively.

A national TV, radio, newspaper, and magazine campaign followed, and was consolidated in light-hearted TV and press advertising for the revised 1966 models. "Lots of people find it hard to believe," said the most famous piece in the 1965

Advertising for the full-size Chevrolets focused on size and comfort during the 1960s and 1970s. The 1967 piece deliberately aped earlier Cadillac copy (March 1963, April 1967, and October 1976).

series, which showed an LTD owner in conversation with the chauffeur of a Silver Cloud parked beside him, "But it's a fact — in tests by a leading acoustical firm, a 1965 Ford LTD with a 289-cu.in. V-8 and Cruise-O-Matic rode quieter than a Rolls-Royce. This quiet does not mean Ford *is* a Rolls-Royce. But it does mean Ford is strong, solidly built, designed to give you luxury, comfort and convenience...." A conservative layout reinforced the upmarket look of the dark-colored LTD in the photograph. Bill Bernbach thought it the best campaign of the year.

In the early 1970s, traditional large cars were regularly advertised with photographs of velour upholstery and special features, as by Oldsmobile in April, 1972 for "The Limited-Edition Regency. A very special Ninety-Eight with the Tiffany touch to mark Oldsmobile's 75th Anniversary.... The exterior is painted in Tiffany Gold.... Even the face of the electric timepiece has been specially styled by Tiffany's, and bears the famous Tiffany name .... each Regency owner will receive a distinctive sterling silver key ring as a gift. If ever lost, the keys can be dropped in a mail-box, and Tiffany's will return them to the owner... Oldsmobile Ninety-Eight. Quite a substantial car."

An October, 1972 advertisement for the 1973 model featured an endorsement from "Walter Hoving, Chairman of Tiffany's," who declared that "The Ninety-Eight Regency is a car that people with good design judgment will appreciate." The copywriter took his cue: "The Regency interior is extraordinary. Seat cushions and backs are tailored to create a soft, pillowed effect, like that of fine furniture. Zippered storage pouches are sewn into the front seat-backs. And a distinctive limousine-quality velour is included among your upholstery choices."

Such huge cars were out of fashion by 1977, when the Chevrolet Caprice Classic offered enough imposing spaciousness for many in an age of downsized automobiles. With "More head room ... More leg room ... More trunk room," it was far from glamorous, and compromised with the spirit of the decade: "We made it right for the times without making it wrong for the people." There were gas mileage figures to prove the claim to frugality.

Moderately large, comfortable cars were still in demand, but the copywriters who promoted them were more than a little nervous of the increasingly hostile, Honda-infested climate. The full-size car was not yet dying, but it kept its head down.

Chapter 14

"Get More 'GO' From Every Gallon!"

In America, paragraphs of fuel consumption figures were largely a development of the 1970s. Yet economy was by no means a new preoccupation, albeit that it had not always been a priority. Even large car buyers preferred their chosen automobiles to be competitive within the full-size luxury category.

The economic trauma of the early 1930s produced a spate of advertisements which stressed, or at least quantified, their products' fuel consumption. This was to be expected from Plymouth, whose unfanciful approach to copy during the 1930s lent itself to gas mileage statistics and other indications of mechanical worthiness which, in later years, would be deemed too mundane to mention. According to a March, 1937 advertisement, Plymouth owners "report 18 to 24 Miles Per Gallon of Gas," and, with phrasing that varied only slightly, the claim was repeated in much Plymouth advertising of that year.

Ford consistently combined style and thriftiness not only in copy for the Ford marque itself (as with "Economy is a Ford Word" in 1938) but also in advertising for the Lincoln-Zephyr. Having drawn attention to its V-12 engine, copy reassured those with aspirations beyond their pocketbooks that twelve cylinders did not necessarily entail the ruinous gas mileage of an earlier big Packard or Cadillac. "The new engine is even smoother, quieter, with the same economy of 14 to 18 miles to the gallon!" crowed a typical advertisement in December, 1937 for the 1938 model year.

Once the reassurance had been given, the copy could discuss the car's comfortable interior and sometimes— in a country where buying on credit was not encumbered with the social stigma that prevailed in Britain — the "convenient terms" which could be obtained through "Authorized Universal Credit Company Finance Plans." With the Lincoln-Zephyr's reputation established by 1938, the inevitable Greek chorus of owners was drafted in, so that in March, 1938 it could still be claimed, with a nod to objectivity, that "Owners report 14 to 18 miles to the gallon under a wide variety of driving conditions." This "variety," of course, might be simply in the weather on level roads rather than in styles of driving, speeds, or steepness of hills. Some owners also reported oil starvation, too, but in spite of the engine's questionable reliability in its early years, the message evidently worked, as production rose steadily after the sales hiatus suffered by everyone in 1938.

Oldsmobile did not always quote figures, but promised that, however much gas was used, it would be well-spent: "Get more 'GO' from every gallon!" shouted a 1939 headline, in keeping with the year's value-for-money theme in advertising for the marque's low-priced "60" series sedans. The year's slogan, "You ought to own an Olds," combined a hint of snobbery with the suggestion that the car was a rational and sensible choice.

Studebaker capitalized on a reputation for economy in 1940:

> When you travel this winter to new vacation places or old favorites, go in this smartly styled, restful riding, new 1940 Studebaker Commander. You can do so for less gasoline expense than in many lowest price cars because this Commander is powered by the same thrifty Studebaker engine that scored an overwhelming gas economy victory over all cars in the Gilmore–Yosemite Sweepstakes of '39.

After World War II, economy was not a popular theme among copywriters outside the world of the compact and sub-compact cars, but Studebaker, with an established reputation for economy and with 1947–50 models that were smaller and lighter than most, was able to capitalize on the additional benefit of its new shape. The 1948 Land Cruiser not only rode

The "nuts and bolts" school of copywriting worked well with the theme of fuel economy. This realistic illustration shows just a single windshield wiper (1939 campaign).

Low gas mileage was a Studebaker preoccupation before and after the war (September 1939 and May 1949).

"low, wide and handsome straight into the heart of discriminating America," but was also "America's cost-cutting luxury car!" A 1949 advertisement pointed out that the Studebaker's "flight-streamed designing bars out all burdensome excess bulk — there's no squandering of gasoline." Frugality was made palatable for the consumer by the undeniably modern styling of the Starlight coupe shown above the copy.

For 1950, a measure of objectivity was re-introduced in Studebaker's copy. The Champion Regal De Luxe four-door sedan with overdrive was billed as the car that "convincingly proved Studebaker gas economy in this year's Mobilgas Grand Canyon Run." The car "averaged 26.551 miles per gallon to beat 30 other cars of 16 makes in straight-out gasoline mileage." The styling may have been only three years ahead of its time in 1947, but Studebaker's economy-biased copy was more typical of the 1970s.

Chevrolet's assurances of good gas mileage were more typical of their period, as was the Chevrolet itself. Rather than promote fuel consumption as a separate issue, copywriters combined it with escapism and suggestions of technical modernity. One 1953 advertisement was headed, "How Chevrolet's new high-compression horsepower takes you more places on less gas...."

The theme was a concise way of killing at least three birds with one headline, and it was continued for the similar 1954 models. An April, 1954 advertisement showed a Bel Air Sport Coupe easily climbing a steep hill on an unmade road above the headline, "How the new Chevrolet wrings more <u>power</u> and more <u>miles</u> out of every gallon of gas...." Under the subtitle, "It's a long way from 'full' to 'empty,'" the technicalities were explained in non-technical language for the benefit of the widest possible audience:

> Higher compression means simply that the fuel mixture is squeezed more tightly in the engine to get more power and more work out of the same amount of gas. That is why the Chevrolet gas gauge takes such a long time, and so many miles, to move from "full" to "empty."

It was assumed that readers would not be familiar with automobile jargon, and that they did not mind admitting to ignorance so that the advantages of the product could be explained simply. This was a risky ploy, as one reader's helpful

Spelling it out. Chevrolet promised improved gas mileage and increased performance in 1953-54, although no figures were given (August 1953 and April 1954).

guidance might appear to another as disdain for his intelligence. This approach was expressly rejected by Doyle Dane Bernbach in advertising for the Volkswagen from 1959.

The imagined abyss between those initiated into "autospeak" and the ordinary consumer was bridged in another advertisement, this time for the Bel Air sedan seen at a Sunday social event outside a town or church hall:

> Frankly, what would these people really say about the new Chevrolet? We're frank to admit it. Most people really don't talk about cars the way the manufacturer would like them to.... No-one up there is likely to go in for technical engineering talk about "higher compression ratios resulting in increased horsepower and finer performance with outstanding fuel economy." But that new Chevrolet owner would probably point out the same things to his friends in his own words. Something like this, maybe: "This new Chevrolet's got a lot more stuff in it. And it's the easiest car on gas I ever owned."

But one way to get him to "talk about cars the way the manufacturer would like [him] to" was perhaps to tell him that, in doing so, he was using the "technical engineering talk" that marked him out as an expert. Yet it was always difficult for a copywriter truly to imitate an expert or even an ordinary human being, as an attempt at either could very easily end in a mixture of bowdlerized jargon and language-school informality that sounded more contrived than conventional copy, for which the reader would make mental allowance at the start. Volkswagen—no mean promoter of economy in cars—would start afresh at the end of the decade.

Gas mileage figures returned with a vengeance after the Arab oil embargo was enacted by OPEC in October, 1973. Gasoline rose from 30 cents to $1.20 a gallon, fuel sales restrictions and speed limits were imposed, and it became apparent that fuel might be expensive in the future and that oil supplies were unlikely to last forever. Legislation which required the products of each manufacturer to conform to a stated mean consumption figure focused the attention of automobile makers and their customers on the subject. High fuel consumption in a manufacturer's large cars would have to be offset by frugality further down the line.

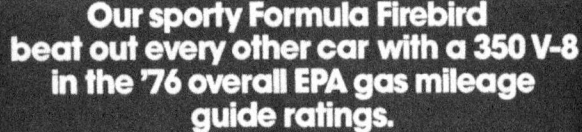

Above and left: Vague assurances of economy were not enough by 1976, when official test figures were given in advertising. Dodge took a swipe at the opposition, too (Chevrolet and Pontiac: February 1976; Dodge: March 1976).

Many consumers were happy to buy small cars, but others wanted the space of a large car with the fuel mileage of a small one, and the satisfaction of these apparently contrary goals preoccupied copywriters in the mid–1970s as never before. Figures became headlines. In February, 1976, a typical advertisement for the Chevrolet Chevelle was headed, "Two roomy Chevelles priced under $3671. 26 MPG Highway, 18 MPG City, EPA." The EPA figures could only ever be a guide, however, and advertisers added a qualification, of which Chevrolet's form was typical: "That's nice mileage, but *remember:* EPA ratings are estimates. Your actual mileage will vary depending on the type of driving *you* do, your driving habits, the car's condition and available equipment." It made for sober copy. Sandwiched between the mileage figures were earnest descriptions of the Chevelle's passenger space and reasonable first cost.

The Dodge Aspen was another mid-sized car that tried to be all things to all buyers. A March, 1976 advertisement reassured readers that compactness also meant style: "The Aspen has the look of a fine European road car.... The Aspen was de-

Introducing their Excellencies the internationally renowned AMBASSADORS

AT your command – their prestige, power, comfort and quietness *and* outstanding space, all for these unbelievable prices – right-hand drive saloon £3261.86, right-hand drive station wagon £3532.12. Where else can you buy such luxury at such prices? The internationally recognised AMC V8 engine requires minimum maintenance during all its long life. It will run on regular grade petrol and has achieved 21.94 mpg in varied motoring conditions, as documented by BSM High Performance School drivers in a 300-mile road test (copies available on request). In addition, the Ambassador Estate has a unique rear door giving access for an extra three passengers and allows it to be used for a multitude of commercial purposes.

Your AMBASSADOR distributor

American Car Centre	Notting Hill London W11 Tel: 01-229 8231
Clarke & Simpson Ltd	49 Sloane Square London SW1W 8AU Tel: 01-730 0436
Delta Car Sales Ltd	Mannamead Garage Elm Road Plymouth Tel: 0752 64777
Endcliffe Motors Ltd	Bramall Lane Sheffield Tel: 0742 24092
Hamblins of Peterborough	17 Oundle Road Peterborough Northants Tel: 0733 54044 & 63643
Howes Motors	High Street Eaton Bray Dunstable Bedfordshire Tel: 0525 220508
Ottershaw Motors Ltd	Spinney Hill Addlestone Weybridge Surrey Tel: 719 2326
Reekie Motors (FS) Ltd	South Road Cupar Fifeshire Tel: Cupar 2481 & 2445
Russell Bates Garages Ltd	High Street Sandyford Stoke-on-Trent Tel: 0782 88688
Sports Motors Ltd	250 Plymouth Grove Manchester Tel: 061 224 335/6/7

AMERICAN MOTORS CORPORATION (Great Britain) Ltd
PO Box 32 Techno Trading Estate
Bramble Road Swindon SN2 6HB Wiltshire
Telephone Swindon (0793) 692 327

Big American cars, and some Australian Fords and Chryslers, were occasionally advertised in Britain in the early 1970s. They did sell, albeit in small numbers, despite rising fuel prices and the improbability of achieving, in day-to-day driving, the kind of mileage claimed here (August 1974).

signed with as much attention to its outside appearance as to its inside engineering." Even in an advertisement concerned with styling, ride comfort, and convenience features, a paragraph was devoted to fuel consumption: "According to EPA estimated mileage results, the Aspen sedan and coupe got 27 MPG on the highway and 18 city. The wagon got 30 MPG highway and 18 city." And then there was the catch: "All were equipped with a 225 six and manual transmission." Add air conditioning and automatic, let alone a V-8, and the figures would not be as impressive. Californian drivers, with their own emissions regulations to meet, were advised to "see your Dealer for mileage results."

Even the Pontiac Firebird, one of America's most sporting cars, was shown speeding along a freeway below a headline which read, "Our sporty Formula Firebird beat out every other car with a 350 V-8 in the 1976 overall EPA gas mileage guide ratings." It was not mentioned how many other 350 V-8s took part, or whether an optional high-ratio back axle had been used, although the car's comparatively light two-door body must have helped. The purpose of the advertisement was to invite the reader to "just imagine what our small cars can do." The smaller cars' mileage figures were given, and the copy concluded with a brave attempt at recapturing the carefree climate of ten years earlier: "So if you want your car to look exciting, drop in at your Pontiac dealer's. He's got cars that'll take your breath away. Without taking away all your fuel."

Chapter 15

Padding and Prejudice

If you are one of the millions of Americans with a soft spot in your heart for the original Buick Roadmaster, portholes and all, this is for you. The new Buick Roadmaster and Roadmaster Limited 6-passenger sedans will be available in the spring of 1991 as 1992 models.

With this announcement, General Motors revived an old name. Beside the text in Buick's 1991 catalog was a picture of a sleek new sedan with roof-pillar mounted portholes, together with a soft-focus shot of a nostalgic enthusiast with his immaculately preserved 1953 Roadmaster. But the earlier "Custom Built Roadmaster by Buick" had not been universally loved. Indeed, it was not loved at all by one Robert Comstock, a garage mechanic whose leg had been crushed by a runaway Roadmaster with defective power brakes which, in his and other cases, did not "lighten the task of quick, sure stopping" as promised in 1953's advertising.[8]

The accident, and the subsequent court case, became famous in Ralph Nader's 1965 book, *Unsafe at Any Speed*, which criticized faulty design in the American automobile and launched a vitriolic attack against what were considered by the author to be inadequate recall procedures for cars, like a number of 1953 Buicks, which were known to be potentially hazardous through manufacturing defects.

By the time that Buick's 1991 catalog was published nearly forty years later, American motorists were protected by "lemon laws," mandatory recall procedures and, in the Roadmaster itself, "lap and shoulder belts for driver and outboard passengers, plus a Supplemental Inflatable Restraint System (air bag) for the driver."

It was not always thus. In the early days of American motoring, a "safe" car was one that could be relied upon not to explode under its owner, break his wrist while being started, or veer out of control while being driven at moderate speed along a smooth road. Rapid braking was achieved by imaginative, and usually terminal, use of the transmission.

In the inter-war period, safety was not ignored, but it was usually promoted as a facet of generally improved design. The "safety feature" which had no other purpose or benefit than to protect passengers in an accident was rare. General improvements included four-wheel (and, later, hydraulic) braking, reliable electric lamps, and "Safety Plate Glass," the latter noisily heralded as a feature of General Motors' Fisher bodies in the 1930s, though not confined to them.

There was the occasional gadget, such as Hudson's "Dash-Locking Safety Hood" of 1939—a front-hinged hood which could not be blown open by the wind at speed or unlatched from outside the car. The safety of the Lincoln-Zephyr's steel-truss body frame received mention alongside its other advantages, and similar claims were made for the GM "Turret Top" and the Chrysler Airflow's "new conception of strength and safety." Anything that contributed to an automobile's structural integrity or ability to avoid an accident was promoted as safe.

Occasionally, entire advertisements were devoted to the theme, as in one piece for the 1936 Chevrolet, in which a wife and mother said: "I want them to have the SAFEST CAR that money can buy!" allowing the copywriter to describe the delights of hydraulic braking, a valve-in-head engine and the manifold advantages of a Fisher body. All with a gleeful over-the-shoulder glance at the year's Plymouths and Fords, of course.

From a modern perspective, however, safety promotion was half-hearted and fragmentary, and there was little evidence that aesthetics were sacrificed to safety considerations as a matter of course, if at all. According to Nader, pedestrians

Power brakes lightened the "task of quick, sure stopping" in a 1953 Buick Roadmaster — in most cases (May 1953).

were being impaled on the tail fins of Cadillacs built as late as 1962. A child — such as nine-year-old Peggy Swan of Kensington, Maryland in 1963 — did not have to hit such a fin very hard to be killed.⁹

There was one area in which a more robust approach would be taken, and that was in the field of tire design. Advertisers who wanted to persuade new and used car buyers to change brands pulled few punches. "Do You Want to Keep Your Daughter?" asked a 1937 advertisement for Goodyear "Lifeguard" tires. "Accidents are no respecters of persons" threatened the copy, "Your daughter ... your wife ... yourself ... all are in equal danger of serious accident if a tire should suddenly collapse...." The implication was clear — no man who had the best interests of his family at heart should drive on any but the best tires; to do less would be culpable and immoral. He would be a disgrace to his family, his church, his neighborhood; he would be known as the Father Who Did Not Care. Pseudo-scientific diagrams, and the assurance that Lifeguard Tires were easily obtained and fitted, offered the motorist a way out of social and moral oblivion.

In the same year, General Tires offered the "Dual 10," a tire which allowed quicker stopping and resistance to wet road skidding with a "flexible tread" that "wrinkles into squeegee-like action when you apply the brakes." In case the reader still wondered whether to bother changing his tires, he was shown a picture of some children crossing a road, who had been narrowly missed by the large and expensive Dual 10–equipped car behind them.

For those who were willing, but unable, to buy a set of Dual 10s outright, a "convenient payment plan" was available. These aggressive advertising tactics — which were more commonly associated with patent medicines, detergents, and life assurance — were not usually deployed on the motorist, as the car manufacturers, whose copy made up most automobile-related advertising, were not promoting products whose absence would lead to illness, injury, or the death of the consumer's family. Gentler strategies had to suffice; in the absence of an effective stick with which to goad the consumer, the carrot had to be made as tempting as possible.

The first postwar car to be sold consistently on its safety was the rear-engined Tucker, introduced in 1948. According

Where safety was mentioned in pre-war advertising, it was usually as a facet of generally improved design (April 1936).

to one early advertisement for the car, "Riding beside the driver, the front-seat occupants ... are immediately conscious of the extreme roominess, the excellent vision, and a feeling of safety and solidity. Then, too, it is a comfort to notice the soft crash pads that line car and dash." There was a padded cell into which passengers would fall in the event of a frontal collision, rather than being impaled on a conventional dashboard. If the windshield were hit from inside, it sprang out, preventing severe head injuries.

The Tucker's safety features received much publicity, but as only a prototype and fifty cars were completed before the new model was discontinued, the impact of Tucker's advertising

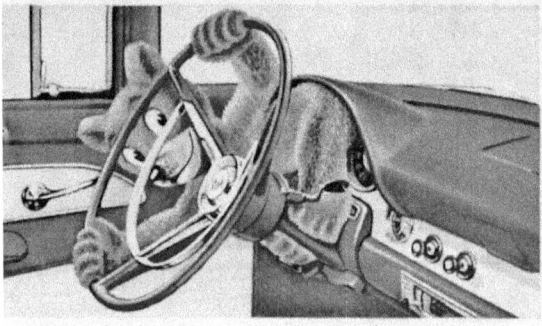

Above and opposite: Three typical advertisements from the most famous and controversial of automobile safety promotions (*Above:* April 1956. *Opposite:* November 1955 and December 1955).

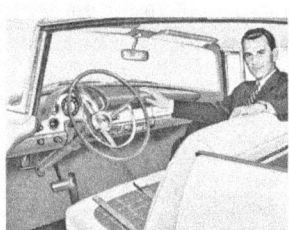

was limited. It became clear, however, that the rest of the industry was unhappy that Tucker had tried to bring the issue to the forefront of consumers' minds.

Crash padding was not confined to Tucker. In 1949, Chrysler offered "A safety feature of major importance! Front passengers, especially children, are given new protection against possible injury in the event of sudden stops or collisions by the new sponge-rubber Safety-Cushion [which] extends across the top part of the dash, and is upholstered in leather to match the interior." But this description was given in the catalog, rather than in advertising, and it did not constitute a major component of Chrysler's 1949 publicity campaign. The 1951 Kaiser gathered sales with a dashboard from Brooks Stevens which combined a "new Safety-Cushion Padded Instrument Panel" with recessed instruments and control knobs, and the car also had a pop-out windshield within its thin pillars. But fewer than 140,000 Kaisers were built that year, and the make disappeared for good in the United States in 1955.

Almost twenty years after Goodyear warned motorists how easily they could lose their children, the Lifeguard name reappeared under the aegis of J. Walter Thompson, Ford's advertising agency, in the fall of 1955. The first modern safety-led automobile advertising campaign was launched for the 1956 model year. "You'll be safer in a '56 Ford!" crowed an early headline.

The strategy immediately attracted controversy. The implication was clearly not only that the Ford was safe, but, by extension, that the rival Chevrolet was less safe. This suggestion was reinforced by the photographs that dealers were instructed to display in Ford showrooms, which claimed to show that passengers in a new Ford were more likely to survive a given accident than those who traveled by Chevrolet. Traditional advertising priorities were replaced by earnest injunctions to social responsibility which threatened to undermine Detroit's entire promotional apparatus. The fantasy was not simply being bypassed — it was threatened with destruction.

The actual features offered were modest. A dished steering wheel whose "deep-center structure ... provides a cushioning effect under impact" was fitted as standard equipment, as were a "Lifeguard rearview mirror that 'gives' on impact and resists shattering" and "new Lifeguard door latches," which were claimed to reduce the possibility of "doors springing open under strain and occupants being thrown from the car." The remaining major features, "new Ford seat belts," and "Lifeguard padding" on the dashboard and sun visors, were optional extras at $9 and $16 respectively, representing less than two percent of the $2,274 which bought a Lifeguard-equipped Fairlane Victoria hardtop sedan. It was this new body style that featured most prominently in advertisements.

There was a widespread belief among Ford personnel, and in the automobile industry generally, that the campaign would not sell cars, and it became apparent, to the industry's relief, that most consumers did not wish their automotive fantasies to be eroded by the suggestion that they might crash at all. Any manufacturer who promoted passive safety features (that is, features that minimized the harm to passengers in an accident, but did not help the driver to prevent it) ran the risk that an association would be created in the consumer's mind between the trauma of an accident and the marque name of the manufacturer who, for whatever reason, brought such trauma to mind in safety-related advertising.

It was this association that was believed to be critical, regardless of whether or not the motorist would survive a crash in the advertised vehicle that would be fatal in another car. Moreover, such an association could harm sales even if the consumer, if asked, acknowledged the advertised marque's superiority. It was the juxtaposition in the consumer's mind of "crash" and the marque name that was held to be critical. At the parochial level, General Motors vehemently disputed Ford's claim to make a safer car than the 1956 Chevrolet.

As Ford's campaign progressed, the message was made more palatable by the introduction of "Grizzly," Ford's cartoon bear who, with the aid of colorful diagrams, pointed out the new car's features while clambering over the steering wheel or grinning at the padded dashboard. Headlines ceased to suggest that any other car was necessarily less safe than the Ford, although any mention of Ford's precedence in offering advanced safety provision carried such an implication, if only indirectly.

Features from the low-priced Ford found their way into Lincolns and Mercurys. Lincoln offered "important safety advances: retracted steering column with safety-flex steering wheel ... triple strength safety-plus door locks ... optional safety belts" in one advertisement and, in another, safety and styling were combined in "the largest windshield of any car."

Early in 1956, the campaign was dropped, and J. Walter Thompson was instructed to stress performance, styling, and other conventional inducements. Little was remarkable in the advertisements which followed, and "Lifeguard Design" was henceforth mentioned only in passing, although the features themselves remained available. Performance became a dominant theme. "Call out the reserves *with a touch of your toe!*" began a May 1956 piece which showed a Fairlane sedan pulling out to overtake a truck. The safety advantages of the "225-h.p. Thunderbird Special V-8" were obliquely suggested in the slogan that followed, which suggested that power was there for "instant go when instants count!" Ostensibly underlining the safety advantages of good acceleration, the advertisement also suggested excitement and danger only just avoided. There was nothing novel about the assurance in a July advertisement, for the Fairlane Fordor Victoria, that "The GO is great in a Ford V-8."

Was the campaign successful? In later years, Ralph Nader maintained that it had been cynically torpedoed by vested interests within Detroit, and that it was deliberately prevented from continuing long enough for objective results to be obtained. According to Nader, Ford Division chief Robert McNamara was ordered to reinstate more conventional advertising by senior personnel in the Ford Motor Company, who in turn had been put under pressure by former colleagues of theirs at General Motors who objected both to the comparison with the 1956 Chevrolet, and to a campaign — any campaign — that highlighted public awareness of an issue which it was not in the commercial interest of the automobile industry as a whole to promote.

Nader cited a Ford press release of November 18, 1956, which suggested that the campaign had been at least moderately successful:

> Since two of the five features — crash padding and seat belts — were optional with the customer, it was possible to measure demand.... No optional feature in Ford history caught on so fast in the first year ... 43% of all 1956 Fords were ordered with safety padding.[10]

Nader went on to draw attention to McNamara's testimony before a House of Representatives subcommittee in the summer of 1956, in which he stated that seat belts had been so much in demand that the belt manufacturers could not supply the 1,000 belts required every day. Apparently, Ford Division officials estimated that the safety campaign was directly responsible for selling 200,000 Fords that would otherwise have remained unsold, out of a model year total of 1,392,847 units.[11]

Nader's citations were impressive, but they left several questions unanswered. It was not clear, for instance, whether or not the 14.4 percent of sales attributed to the campaign could equally have been achieved by another imaginative campaign which made no claims to safety on behalf of the product. Were all sales of the safety padding achieved through public awareness of its advantages, or did its appeal lie partly in novelty alone — a novelty-value which might have been achieved by other means? And how much of the apparent consumer interest in "Lifeguard Design" was generated by the advertising, and how much by dealers' enthusiasm for the optional features? In how many cases could Lifeguard-equipped cars be supplied more rapidly to customers than otherwise identical non-equipped models? In short, how many consumers were motivated towards Ford because of the campaign, and how many would have bought Fords in spite of it, or regardless of it?

If Ralph Nader believed that the Lifeguard campaign had been strangled soon after birth, one of those involved at the time remembered it differently. Lee Iacocca, who later became President of the Ford Motor Company before joining Chrysler in 1978, was assistant sales manager for the Philadelphia district when the 1956 Fords were announced. Taking his cue from an experiment in a promotional film that had been circulated to sales managers, Iacocca decided to demonstrate the effectiveness of the dashboard safety padding to his salesmen. The padding was claimed to be "five times more shock absorbent than foam rubber." In his autobiography, Iacocca recalled that the demonstration did not go entirely as planned:

> Instead of having the salesmen learn about the safety padding from the film, I would make the point far more dramatically by actually dropping an egg onto the padding.... I had spread strips of the padding across the stage, and now I climbed up on a high ladder with a carton of fresh eggs. The very first egg I dropped missed the padding altogether and splattered on the wooden floor. The audience [of about 1,100 men] roared with delight. I took more careful aim with the second egg, but my assistant, who was holding the ladder, chose this moment to move in the wrong direction. As a result, the egg bounced off his shoulder.... The third and fourth eggs landed exactly where they were supposed to. Unfortunately, they broke on impact. Finally, with the fifth egg, I achieved the desired result, and got a standing ovation.... [I]t turned out to be a prophetic symbol for our 1956 cars. The safety campaign was a bust. Our campaign was well conceived and highly promoted, but the consumers failed to respond.[12]

The campaign remained a conspicuous one-off, and advertisers continued with their existing priorities. Chevrolet drew attention to a "new X-built Safety-Girder frame" in 1958, and Goodyear had long since abandoned the blood-curdling scenarios of 1937 for an innocuous "There is no more distinctive way to travel" in support of the "New 3-T Nylon Cord Double Eagle." The tire was shown on a 1958 Continental Mark III, in atmospheric soft-focus, tended by a couple in evening dress.

As in earlier days, where safety was a side-effect of improvements introduced for reasons of styling or handling ease, it was emphasized in otherwise conventional copy. The 1958 Oldsmobile was available with "Safety Power Steering" so that the consumer could "trust the wheel with the safety feel" according to an advertisement which showed a pink convertible being conducted effortlessly along a cliff-top road by a fashionable mother with her two children. It was an indication of how much ground remained to be covered that one of the children was shown standing up on the front seat, his head only inches away from a projecting vent window frame.

Safety continued to be attributed to a variety of engineering and styling features in the 1960s. In the roof of the 1966 Ford Thunderbird, above the windshield, was an "overhead Safety Convenience Panel" of control switches and warning lights. A seat belt warning light was built into the panel, but the intention was primarily to glamorize the driving experience by association with aeronautical practice.

Tire manufacturers had abandoned blood-curdling scenarios by 1958. The car is a Continental Mark III, a behemoth whose relative failure was tacitly acknowledged by the makers when they called the 1968 Lincoln Continental a Mark III, too (August 1958).

On the other hand, Buick encouraged passengers to use the seatbelts which had been standard equipment in its cars since 1964. With controversy over *Unsafe at Any Speed* in full swing, a February, 1966 advertisement for the Electra 225 mentioned within brackets: "(The following safety items are standard on all Buicks: front and rear seat belts, inside and outside rear view mirrors, padded dash and sun visors, dual-speed windshield wipers and washers, back-up lights. Our suggestion on the subject of front and rear seat belts: Use them.)" Not that every Buick advertisement for the year went into such detail, but this time the subject was here to stay. Announcing its 1968 models in October, 1967, Pontiac mentioned that "two shoulder belts are standard in the front seat of every new 1968 Pontiac." In the same month, Buick reflected increasing public (and political) awareness of the issue, and of the controversy affecting GM, by stating even in an advertisement with short copy for a sporty new Skylark that "All Buicks have the full line of General Motors safety features as standard equipment.

The "Safety Convenience Panel" of the 1966 Ford Thunderbird recalled aeronautical practice, and made the subject glamorous (December 1965).

Passive safety was firmly established in the minds of all automobile manufacturers by 1968 (October 1967).

Chrysler promoted — and capitalized on — public concern in 1968 (June 1968).

For example, seat back latches and padded windshield corner posts." These advertisements were typical of their year.

In the summer of 1968, Chrysler Corporation described a safety awareness campaign in which a group of young Americans, called the Spurrlows, visited high schools, carrying with their "Music for Modern Americans" a "special message about safe driving.... As America's fifth largest industrial corporation, we feel that our responsibility doesn't stop at the end of a production line. As music lovers, our favorite records are the ones about safe driving." European car fans would have noticed that the list of Chrysler marques at the foot of the page now included Simca and Sunbeam.

In a long-copy advertisement of June, 1971 Cadillac asked:

> [W]hat could be more practical than the host of safety features that are an integral part of every new Cadillac? From side-guard beams to the energy-absorbing instrument panel and steering column. From dual-action safety hood latches to easy-to-use seat and shoulder belts.

Now that certain safety provisions were mandatory, and the issue was irreversibly on consumers' agenda, it was worth stressing the competitiveness of one's product. The features which had been promoted so vigorously by Ford in 1956 were taken for granted by the end of the 1960s.

By the 1990s, whole advertisements were regularly devoted to the safety theme, as in 1993: "We have seen the future and are prepared to meet it, side on.... The 1993 Buick Roadmaster Sedan meets the 1997 federal side-impact standard — four years in advance" declared a typical Buick advertisement of that year, which included a "freeze-frame of actual side-impact safety test" being conducted on the car. But at the bottom of the page, a small slogan, "Buckle up, America!" reminded readers that not all motorists actually wore their seat belts.

Chapter 16

From Utility to Suburban Chic

The station wagon was an integral part of the American automotive scene by 1935, but the angular, wooden body of the average wagon was expensive to build and looked ungainly when attached to the streamlined front of a regular sedan.

Chrysler recognized the difficulty in 1941, when the first Town & Country was introduced. Advertised as having a "swank appearance" (two years after British Ford V-8 copy claimed that the possession of two Fords was not "swank" or vulgarly ostentatious!), the Town & Country was promoted as "the smartest station wagon on the road ... designed for the discriminating owner who wishes exclusive, distinctive transportation." It also promised "handling ease, particularly for women drivers" — a theme to which promoters of station wagons, including Chrysler, would often return.

The Town & Country combined the partly wooden construction of a wagon with the more streamlined form of a conventional sedan which, depending on the buyer's point of view, was either a combination of virtues or of vices, as wooden bodywork demanded maintenance that conventional steel paneling did not.

In 1947, Mercury promised: "One day in the life of your Mercury Station Wagon shows you why it's just about the most useful car that you ever owned!" A picture story showed the owner picking up guests from the station and taking them to the beach, adding, "Nice part of it is— your Mercury Station Wagon is the smartest car wherever you go— at the beach, the club, the local playhouse or even in town." If the "even" suggested that social acceptability could not yet be taken for granted, the wooden look was nevertheless considered attractive in its own right by 1947–48 and had spread to convertibles. Among them were the Ford and Mercury "Sportsman" models and Chrysler's own Town & Country convertible, which was briefly fashionable enough to form the centerpiece of an advertisement for General Squeegee tires in December, 1947.

The vogue for wooden luxury bodies—fueled in part by the upmarket ancestry of the British shooting brake bodies fitted to elderly Rolls-Royce chassis for estate work — proved to be strictly a phenomenon of the late 1940s. There were some interesting variations on the theme by Packard ("Station Sedan") and Nash ("Suburban" sedan), as well as by Chrysler and Ford. The conventional wooden-bodied station wagon lasted a few years longer, but became extinct in the early 1950s.

Plymouth's unpretentiously named "Station Wagon" of 1949 was typical of the breed. Practicality, a theme which fitted more easily into the general tenor of Plymouth's advertising than any other, was emphasized:

> This great new Plymouth Station Wagon sets new standards for beauty, utility and long life.... Comfortably seats eight full-sized passengers. Both rear seats quickly and easily removed for maximum loading space. Handsome, easy-to-clean vinyl plastic seats and seat backs. Natural-finish bonded plywood body panels with long-life finish on all wood surfaces.

This sounded more like copy for café décor, yet it did not come cheap. The copy was unassuming, but Plymouth was able to capitalize on the element of "chic" which percolated down from the "wooden" Chrysler convertibles. For true utilitarians there was the DeLuxe two-door, steel-bodied wagon which, at $1,840, was $532 cheaper than the Special DeLuxe wooden four-door. By 1951, the steel version had taken over entirely, as the wooden wagon was offered for the last time in 1950.

But steel did not inevitably mean only the barest utility, as Nash proved with its compact but well-finished 1950 Rambler wagon, and Plymouth's 1953 two-door Savoy, costing $2,207, was targeted upmarket: "Dignity of design, quiet good taste in styling and appointment, assure this car's welcome in any company." It was illustrated at Long Island's Meadow Brook Polo Club, rather than in the countryside of earlier years, and the advertisement as a whole indicated Plymouth's desire to integrate the wagon into the mainstream of automobile fashion. The car was shown in a smart metallic red rather than in the somber brown cellulose that had been adequate in 1949.

Between 1949 and 1953 Kaiser-Frazer offered "Vagabond" and "Traveler" utility sedans which, like the early Town & Country, aimed to offer in one package the combined advantages of sedan and station wagon. But while Chrysler's priorities had been largely stylistic, the 1951 Frazer Vagabond (which took its name from a 1949–50 Kaiser) was a more genuinely practical vehicle. Often said to have prefigured the hatchback of later years, the Vagabond (and its closest American precedent, a similar De Soto of the late 1940s), were in fact much more akin to the pre-war French *commerciales* which, like the Frazer and De Soto, looked like the sedans on which they were based.

Late in 1950, Frazer's copywriters tried to inject some excitement into their product. In one advertisement for the whole Frazer line, the Vagabond was trumpeted as "the famous 2-cars-in-1—converts in 10 seconds from luxurious 6-passenger sedan to spacious carrier ... for sports or business equipment!" A later piece for the Vagabond alone called it "beautifully new as a sedan!" which was true semantically even though it had been lifted from the earlier Kaiser line. A half-hearted attempt was again made to sell it to the "sportsman," but its principal market was the "estate owner or commuter," particularly the latter.

The Vagabond was claimed to supersede conventional wagons: "... here is the *1951 successor* to the station wagon ... truly a car *built to better the best on the road!*... For merchant, farmer, technician or professional man the Vagabond serves double use in transporting products or equipment." As a parting shot, it was claimed to be "the year's smartest buy for smart people," although, in this case, smartness had more to do with sound commercial sense than cocktail-party credibility. The word was usefully ambiguous.

Frazer's 1951 model year ended early, when it was decided to market all future large Kaiser-Frazer cars as Kaisers, with a new Traveler succeeding the Vagabond. Only about 3,000 Frazer Vagabonds were sold; even allowing for mid-market targeting, this did not compared well with Plymouth's 34,457 steel-bodied and 2,057 wooden wagons produced in 1950. Vigorous copy and novelty alone could not revive a car that, at $2,399, was even more expensive than Plymouth's top-line wagon.

Nor was the Vagabond helped by advertisements that were less than attractive. "The new handcrafted 1951 Frazer Vagabond" was not only nothing of the sort; it was also shown in uninspired tinted monochrome illustrations which suggested a lack of funds and, therefore, a less than successful product. Amid a rash of V-8s from the Big Three, the Frazer's "new Supersonic Engine," a 115bhp L-head six, was comprehensively outclassed, and promises of power—and the copy styles that went with them—were out of the question.

The result was novelty by default. The car was illustrated in the hand of a craftsman, as if it were a scale model. The motif was reminiscent of the hand-held crystal ball with the "Ford in your future" of 1945–46, and was almost identical to British artwork of 1938 for the compact Ford V-8

General made the most of the glamour of Chrysler's Town & Country (December 1947).

16. From Utility to Suburban Chic

Above and right: Station wagons lost their wooden body framing and were gradually integrated into the mainstream of automotive fashion in the early 1950s (October 1949 and August 1953).

"22." The theme was original for 1951, and undoubtedly suggested that the Vagabond was a "car apart." But it was also at least ten years out of date.

By the mid–1950s, the steel-bodied station wagon had taken over from its wooden forebears, and most advertising for the breed was conventional and unadventurous. Maturity brought diversification, however, and styling — which had been rudimentary on the Plymouth Savoy — became more important. "Luxury" and "sporty" wagons complemented the conventional two- and four-door utilities. The 1955 Pontiac Safari, for example, was promoted in an advertisement of almost Continental-like restraint and clarity. "Pontiac creates an entirely new type of car combining Catalina smartness and station wagon utility," said a headline which introduced copy and studio photographs that owed nothing to the rest of Pontiac's 1955 campaign.

Chevrolet's 1954 Nomad concept car combined racy Corvette styling with a novel, ribbed roof and raked B-pillars that were successfully echoed in production two-door Nomads during 1955–57, and on the Pontiac Safari. The Nomad was essentially a revival of the original Town & Country theme. As that car had marked a rebellion against the utilitarian functionalism of most boxy, wooden wagons, so the Nomad represented a deliberate move away from boxy, steel wagons towards something more luxurious and distinctive.

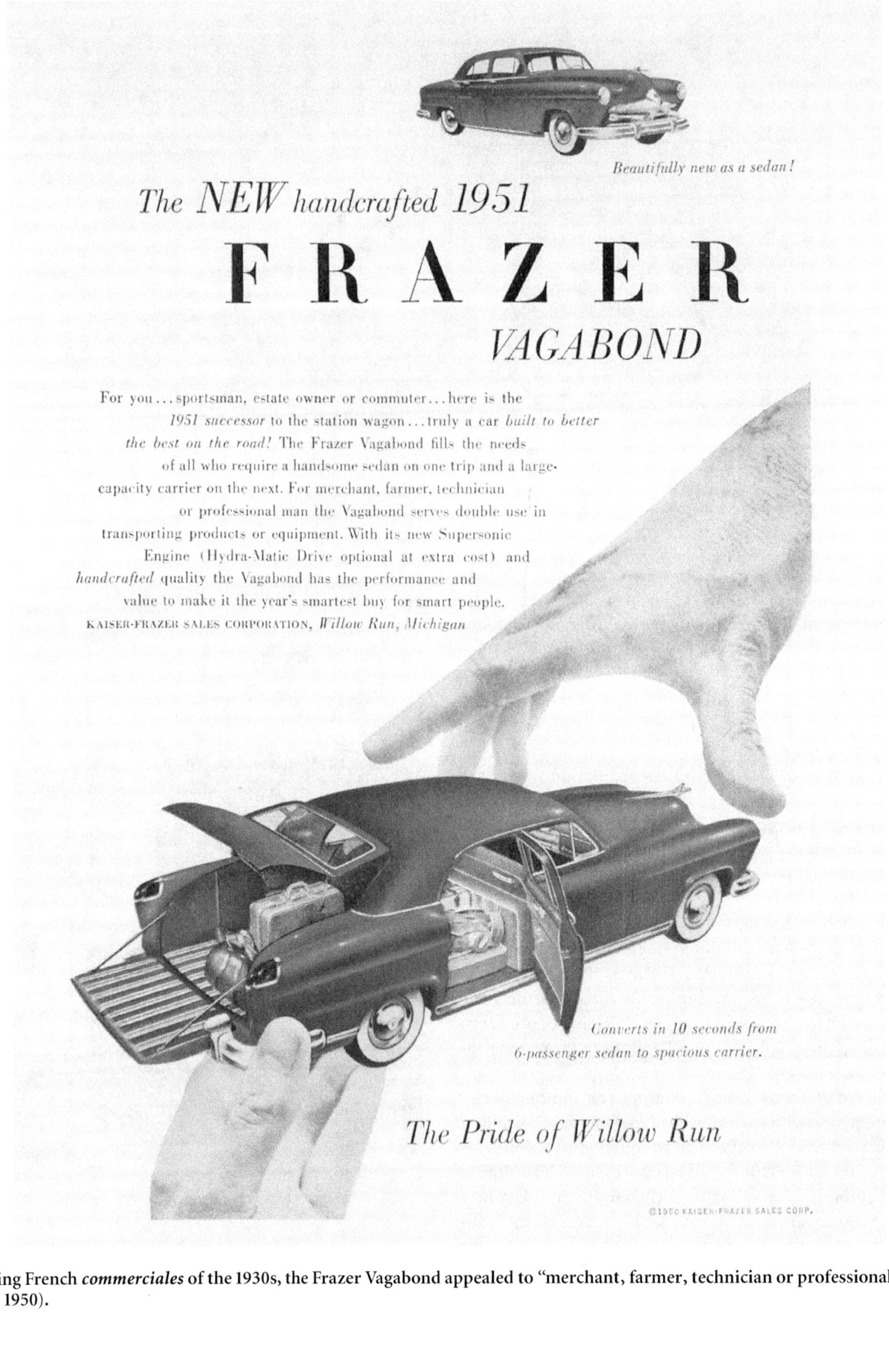

Echoing French *commerciales* of the 1930s, the Frazer Vagabond appealed to "merchant, farmer, technician or professional man" (June 1950).

There was, however, an obscure stylistic link between the two. In 1954, the British coachbuilders Abbott of Farnham converted an Austin Atlantic convertible into a station wagon. The rear body was part-metal (retaining the rear fender profile of the convertible) and part wooden, with raked B-pillars and a sloping tail; it was sporty, practical, and good-looking. It was an interesting coincidence that both the Atlantic and the prototype Nomad were based on their respective makers' sporting models, and they both combined similar, novel styling features to dramatic effect.

If the production Nomad, "Long, low and very different," glamorized Chevrolet's station wagon range, 1955's best-selling two-door wagon, the Two-Ten Handyman, was resolutely boxy and practical. Copywriters attempted to inject some glamour:

> Never have you seen Station Wagons as wonderful as the new Chevrolets! You can have your cake and eat it too—with Chevrolet's spanking-new line of Station Wagons! For here is sophisticated big-city style ... plus pack-horse performance and astonishing new utility features.

By 1955, it was "big-city style" rather than bucolic charm that impressed buyers, who had to be reassured that a workhorse need not be crude or démodé. The rest of the copy described new practical and mechanical features and the optional "Turbo-Fire V8" engine which had revitalized the whole Chevrolet range.

In the same year, the long-established "two-Ford family," which had even appeared, albeit tongue-in-cheek, in pre-war British copy, made a come-back in a distinctive advertisement. A black and yellow Fairlane Sunliner convertible and a red and white Custom Ranch Wagon were proposed as the ideal combination for the affluent suburban family. The theme was perpetuated in a 1956 television advertisement in which a man got into his Ford sedan to drive to work while his wife went shopping in her new station wagon.

In 1956, Ford and Chevrolet each offered six models in their full-line wagon advertising. Ford's selection include a hastily contrived answer to the Nomad, called the Parklane. It was added to the Fairlane line, and promised "limousine comfort" in a car that still did not mind "rolling up its sleeves." It was slightly cheaper than the Chevrolet Nomad, and with bodywork shared with lowlier versions it was more practical. A raked B-pillar effect was achieved by artful use of stainless trim rather than with a genuinely novel configuration. The Parklane outsold the Nomad by almost two to one, but it lacked the Nomad's individuality and trend-setter status.

Chevrolet's station wagon advertising for 1956 focused not so much on the Nomad as on a four-door luxury wagon called the Bel Air Beauville. A typical advertisement illustrated the Beauville at the top of the page, while smaller color pictures showed the five other wagons in the range, including "the distinctive, luxurious Nomad." Ford's Parklane was seen outside the latest in modern, suburban supermarkets; Chevrolet accommodated a baseball team "beautifully" in the Beauville, in keeping with the marque's new, dynamic image.

Between them, Ford and Chevrolet highlighted the two areas of modern suburban American life—shopping and recreation—that would feature in most subsequent advertising for station wagons of all sizes and prices for decades afterwards. The similarities between these particular 1956 advertisements also graphically illustrate the intensity of the competition between Ford and General Motors in every sector of the market. Direct model-for-model duplication within specialized areas of complex product ranges became commonplace, particularly in the low-price field, and these rivalries would grow in the 1960s.

By 1958, the station wagon was firmly entrenched as an integral part of America's expanding suburban landscape and, to remain socially acceptable, it had to become fashion-conscious. Copywriters emphasized the fun, freedom, and recreational activities that wagon ownership facilitated. The wagon was, above all, a family car, and children figured prominently in artwork. It was implied that the man who provided for his family ought not to deny his wife and children the independence and convenience that ownership of a wagon could bring.

De Soto showed children playing happily in the back of a Fireflite Explorer, finished, according to the caption, in "Wedgwood blue and pearl white with matching interior." It was a far cry from the 1957 sedan that could "flick its tail at anything on the road." Unfortunately for De Soto, the color-matched interior, "heap plenty room," and "convenient steps ... on the tailgate" persuaded only 1,734 buyers to choose either this or the equivalent Firesweep Explorer in 1958. By 1961, "De Soto—the exciting look and feel of the future" was extinct.

Dodge combined suburban leisure with upmarket aspiration in copy for its similar Sierra wagon in the recessionary market of 1958. Two couples were shown in a park with the new car, picnic basket balanced on the open tailgate:

> What the Millionaire said to the Bystander.... "How much does it cost to own a yacht like that?" a millionaire sportsman was asked about his 200-foot luxury vessel. His answer was simple: "If you have to think about costs, you shouldn't own one...." Now maybe you have that attitude about a Swept-Wing '58 4-door station wagon. Certainly this "land yacht" costs more [$3,354] than other body styles.... But here's a new way to look at the cost: If you divide the purchase price *by the number of times* you'll use this wagon, it may be the least expensive car you could buy. Because, you see, you'll use it for everything: It's that great.

Chevrolet also pursued the recreational theme during 1958–59. For 1958, buyers had a choice of five "new wagons with wonderful ways." The Nomad, by now a four-door, was shown with several boys and their balsa wood toy airplanes, about to set off for flight trials in the countryside. In the same

In 1956, Ford and Chevrolet competed head-on in an expanding sector of the market (February and May 1956).

advertisement a Brookwood, in two-tone blue, was parked outside an antiques shop, with the predictable (and hideous) grandfather clock being loaded into the back. In the absence of genuine novelty, the copywriter clutched at straws:

> Notice that the larger liftgate curves clear around at the corners. It's hinged into the roof and raises completely out of the way for easier loading and maximum-size loads.

The idea was not confined to Chevrolet, or even to General Motors, and a wrap-around liftgate had appeared on American Fords in 1957. Surprisingly, a similar wrap-around rear window had also been seen in 1956, on another English prototype by Abbott of Farnham, called the Frensham (after a nearby village). Abbott built it onto the rear of a Ford Zephyr Mk II before opting to adapt its existing "Farnham" conversion, with a side-opening tailgate, for that car; while Britain's Rootes Group, always alert to American influences, fitted a roll-down tailgate window, in the style of an early–1950s Chrysler Town & Country, to its Humber Hawk Mk VI Estate Car of late 1955.

For 1959, Chevrolet's Brookwood was either a four-door or a two-door. "The car that's wanted for all its worth" could hold "everybody and his brother" according to copy for the two-door. The car was shown in a suburban driveway; a young mother sat on the wagon's open tailgate, reading to a toddler as other children played in a paddling pool. According to another advertisement, a four-door Nomad was the "Handiest helper a family ever had.... All five '59 Chevrolet wagons are as beautifully at ease with a delicate bit of greenery as they are with a rough-and-tumble cargo of kids."

By 1960, the station wagon market had expanded enough to allow Chrysler, in its corporate advertising, to offer "27 wagons built with families in mind." The Corporation ran several advertisements for its wagon range; in another, it was claimed that "The 1960 wagons from Chrysler Corporation put space in its place — inside, not out.... They give you more room inside than ever before, yet fit in the same parking space as last year's models." In another piece, Chrysler explained that the Corporation's wagons were "built by people who know what parents are up against," and promised that in a new Dodge, Plymouth, or Chrysler, "Even the kids seem quieter."

A dying marque offered "the exciting look and feel of the future" in 1958 (March 1958).

Classical station-wagon advertising from Chevrolet in 1959. With sharp fins and corners everywhere, this was not the safest place to play (July 1959).

One of a series of Chrysler Corporation advertisements from 1960. The Valiant, in particular, was distinctively styled (April 1960).

If anyone feared a return to drab and boxy wagons, they were reassured by the fins and chrome highlighted in the accompanying photographs. The cars' "New Unibody Construction" and "Torsion-Aire Ride" with torsion-bar suspension — the former new to Chrysler but not unique to it and the latter a Chrysler feature since 1957 — were promoted heavily. The early 1960s, like the early 1950s, were years in which Chrysler's corporate styling was fussy and out-of-date when set against prevailing trends. Even in 1961, a Chrysler's wagon's "smart looks" included enormous fins when General Motors had abandoned them, and Ford had reduced 1960's sweeping horizontal blades to miniature proportions. In station wagon advertising, however, Chrysler's copywriters could, with some credibility, ignore styling that was conspicuously outdated and concentrate on the cars' practicality.

Although wooden-bodied station wagons had been costly to make and time-consuming to maintain, the wood looked attractive if carefully styled, and it gave an upmarket feel to a car — partly because of its actual cost, and partly for its "traditional" connotations. Mock-wood trim was fitted to obviously steel Fords and Mercurys from the early 1950s onwards, and to a handful of prestigious Cadillac conversions by Hess & Eisenhardt in 1955–56; it also enjoyed widespread popularity on other marques in the 1960s. During its transitional year of 1949, Chevrolet replaced the wooden upper body framing of its Styleline DeLuxe wagon with steel that was carefully shaped and painted to look almost identical to the original wood. The price was unchanged.

A 1964 advertisement for the Mercury Colony Park, headed, "Imagine calling anything as elegant as this a 'wagon,'" typified the trend. The car was shown outside a fashionable apartment at night, where "warm, mahogany-like paneling" gave it a distinctive appearance. The idea was even used by Ford of Britain, at first with modest strakes on the flanks of its small 1955 Squire wagon, and then with the full Di-Noc treatment on the sides and tailgate of the 1963 Consul Cortina Super Estate Car. But what was elegant and sophisticated to the American motorist was vulgar in Britain, not least because mock-wood trim looked fussier on a small car than on a large one, and this version of the Cortina was quickly abandoned.

Mercury and Chrysler offered mock-wood paneled luxury wagons in the 1960s. A Mercury Colony Park and Chrysler Town & Country are shown here (April 1964 and April 1968).

The British still had a genuine if antiquated "woody" in 1964, in the form of the Morris Minor 1000 Traveller, a 1953 style which looked either appealing and unpretentious or like a dodgem car sticking out of a shed, depending on the viewer's taste.

The idea continued to thrive in America, however, and 1965's Mercury wagons, "for people who don't mind being looked at," were joined in 1968 by a Di-Noc trim option for the Park Lane convertible and hardtop. The similarly decorated 1967 Pontiac Executive wagon was claimed to be a trend-setter in one advertisement which declared, "It looks like a lot more people will be driving station wagons this year," echoing Dodge's appeal in 1958.

Chrysler, whose top-line 1968 model revived the Town & Country name after a sabbatical in 1966–67, billed its full-size luxury wagon as "sort of the penthouse of luxury cars ... a world apart from the plain-vanilla wagons." Unusually for a station wagon, this car was targeted at the male buyer, and was promoted not merely as a socially acceptable commuting car, but as a status symbol in its own right. There was a similarly finished full-size Dodge Monaco, and even the less exalted 1967 Chevrolet Chevelle Concours Custom Wagon with a "look of hand-rubbed walnut panels," and Dodge's mid-size contender, the Coronet 500, indicated by their fake-wood trim a loyalty to big car priorities.

Comfort and novelties dominated copy for the majority of station wagons in the late 1960s. The 1965 Chevrolet Impala offered an under-floor "stowage compartment," together with comfort-oriented suspension: "Some bumps get through Chevrolet's new suspension. But when a bump gets through those 4 double-acting shock absorbers, 4 coil springs, 1 Girder-Guard frame and over 50 rubber shock cushioners, you must be off the road." The smaller 1965 Chevelle included a more modest "improved suspension system incorporating a softer coil spring at each wheel to take care of the rough spots."

In the mid– to late–1960s, Ford chased Chevrolet by introducing a number of new models to cater to expanding specialty sectors, and several new features in its regular models. Many were highlighted in the highly successful "Ford has a better idea" campaign. Among the most noteworthy of the

Chevrolet's Impala was a far cry from the utilitarian wagons of the 1940s (March 1965).

Ford's "better idea" campaign of the late 1960s included an advertisement highlighting the two-way tailgates of Ford and Mercury wagons (March 1967).

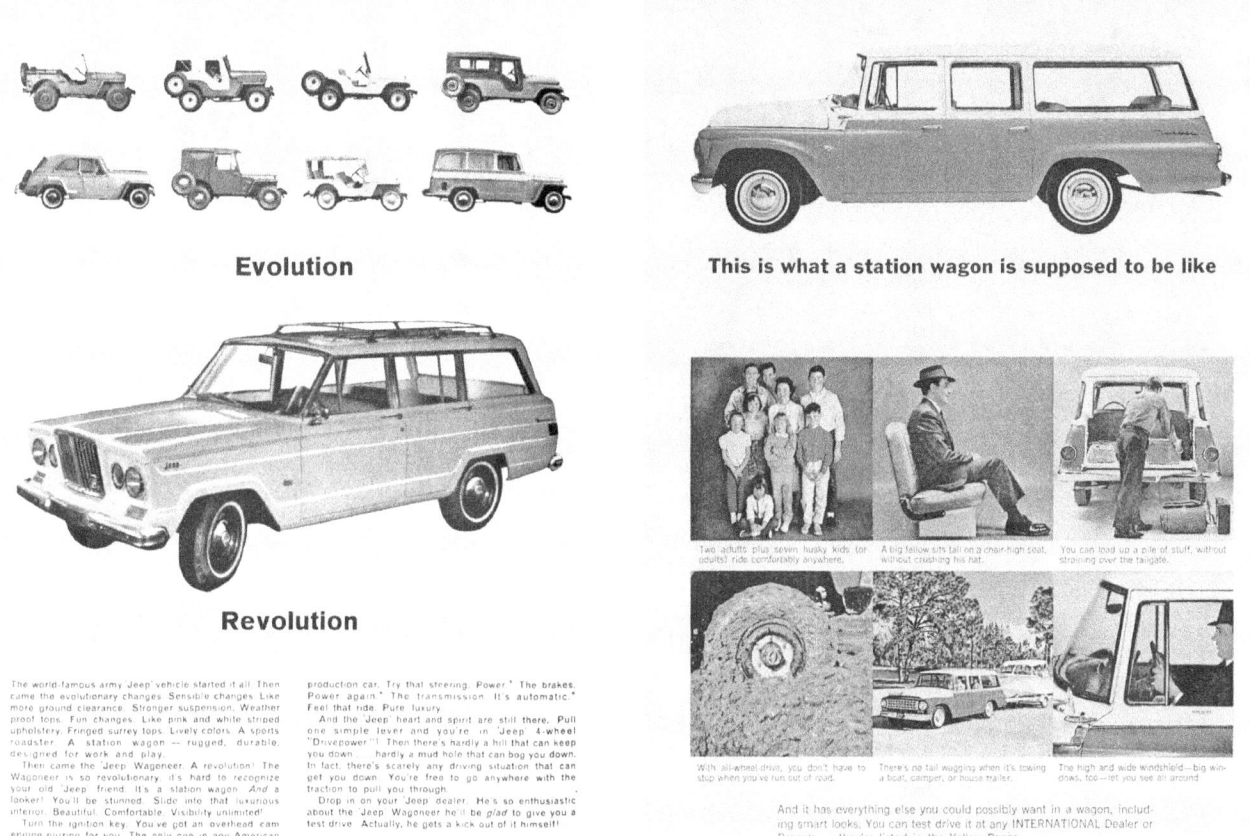

Modest precursors to the SUVs of later years. Of the two, the Jeep was the better known and more car-like, while copy for the Travelall, which was visibly related to International's light trucks, recreated the practical flavor of much 1930s advertising (April and June 1964).

new ideas was a "two-way tailgate" promoted in a 1967 advertisement in the series which showed a Ford wagon: "Exclusive! Only Ford and Mercury wagons have it. Use the handle on the side, it opens like a door. Use the handle in the middle, it operates as a tailgate." The idea was well received and was soon adopted elsewhere.

In 1966, Ford showed a wooden-bodied 1946 Station Wagon ("Classic") with a modern Country Squire ("Son of Classic") and reminded car buyers that it had been a pioneer: "Since 1929, when Ford invented the mass-produced station wagon, Ford wagons have been the standard of quality ... the prime innovators year after year.... Even apart from the unique Magic Doorgate (swings down for cargo, swings open for people), these '66 Fords are classics. Best-selling. Best of Breed!"

Other innovations included the multi-window roofs of the Buick Skylark Sports Wagon and Oldsmobile's Vista-Cruiser, the latter promoted as "All new from the top down" in 1964 and in 1965 as a "family-room-on-wheels" with a "New sky's-the-limit look in station wagons!" Brooks Stevens' Studebaker Wagonaire of 1963–66 had a novel retracting rear roof section to accommodate long or tall loads.

There were two main exceptions to the generally anti-utilitarian trend. The Kaiser Jeep Corporation's Jeep Wagoneer of 1963–92 was seen by many as a semi-truck at first, but it soon lost its early, commercial-looking frontal styling to become a familiar suburban sight in the 1970s. It was a forerunner of sport utility vehicles of later years which included its own successors. "Stop running scared," began a March, 1964 advertisement depicting a Wagoneer climbing a steep hill at night: "The rain is wet ... the road is slippery ... the wind is fierce ... but that doesn't trouble the 'Jeep' Wagoneer.... 'Jeep' 4-wheel 'Drivepower' is what ... keeps all four wheels gripping the road, providing the kind of traction that you can't get with any ordinary vehicle.... So for the love o' your family — get a 'Jeep' Wagoneer!"

An April, 1964 advertisement showed a row of Jeeps and Jeepsters from the 1940s and 1950s above the caption "Evolution" with the "All new 'Jeep' Wagoneer" captioned "Revolu-

Plymouth combined small-car dimensions with big-car styling in the compact Volaré wagon. Its poor build quality soon had Americans cursing, however (December 1977).

tion.... The world-famous army 'Jeep' vehicle started it all.... And the 'Jeep' heart and spirit are still there. Pull one simple lever and you're in 'Jeep' 4-wheel 'Drivepower' ... Wagoneer station wagon's new, improved and exclusive 4-wheel drive system ... there's hardly a hill that can keep you down ... hardly a mud hole that can bog you down." The copy style was straight from the mid–1930s.

In the same year, the International Harvester Company rebelled against luxury wagons with multiple photographs of its upright, four-door Travelall:

> This is what a station wagon is supposed to be like.... Two adults plus seven husky kids (or adults) ride comfortably anywhere.... A big fellow sits tall on a chair-high seat, without crushing his hat.... With all-wheel-drive, you don't have to stop when you've run out of road.... And it has everything else you could possibly want in a wagon, including smart looks.

This was trying hard, and one sensed a copywriter resenting the need to mention looks when the car itself was so useful. But it did have two-tone blue and white paint. In another piece the Travelall was, like Oldsmobile's Vista-Cruiser, a "Family room on wheels.... Mom, Dad, seven kids ... and the family pooch — plus a load of camping gear — can ride in comfort.... You can get in without twisting yourself up like a pretzel." The Travelall was "strong enough to pull a boat trailer or house trailer without wagging its tail." When the makers asked in April, 1964, "Will you buy it for LOVE ... or MONEY?" the love was for "hunting, fishing, boating, skiing, camping, exploring" rather than for the car's styling. And, like the Frazer Vagabond, it was for the small businessman, too: "If you make money delivering parcels, cartons, hard goods ... workers, kids — the TRAVELALL will do a lot of work for you." This was a station wagon in the spirit of the 1940s.

By the late 1970s, huge luxury wagons were no longer fashionable, and producers of mid-size models emphasized their products' convenience and space efficiency. "It convinces you," assured an advertisement for the 1977 Dodge Aspen, "that it's a much bigger wagon than it really is," while the larger Chevrolet Caprice Classic Wagon "[e]liminates excess inches and ounces. Uses space more efficiently." Plymouth returned to practicality for the 1978 model year with the Volaré. This was not the "extraordinary" wagon claimed, but "the wagon that has America singing" was nevertheless the "No. 1 selling wagon in America" according to the makers. It was efficient and economical by comparison with the finned Sport Suburbans of 1960, but by 1978 the competition included not only domestic rivals, but increasing numbers of imported cars.

Chapter 17

Back to Basics

Americans did not take easily to small cars. The pre-war Austin Seven-based Bantam was not a success, and the post-war Crosley enjoyed only a brief vogue in the late 1940s before extinction in 1952, thirteen years after the marque's first car had been produced. Even the Crosley Hotshot roadster, which was of a similar size to imported British sports cars, attracted only around 2,500 buyers between 1949 and 1952.

The "compact" car, large to Europeans but small by American standards, enjoyed greater, if initially fragile, success. During and immediately after World War II, Detroit tinkered with compact prototypes. The Chevrolet Cadet, designed by Earle MacPherson, was technically advanced when the first prototypes were tested in 1947.[13] But the car would only have been profitable with sales, beyond those of regular Chevrolets, of at least 300,000 a year, and the project was quietly sidelined.

The Cadet's creator joined Ford in England, where many of the prototype's design features, including "MacPherson strut" front suspension, saw fruition in the British Consul and Zephyr sedans. Both British and American road testers were impressed with the result.[14] Ford's American division also experimented with a light car in the late 1940s, but, like the Cadet, it did not see production, although unlike the small Chevrolet it reappeared in recognizable form, as the French Ford Vedette.

Apart from the long-established Willys, three new compact cars did reach American buyers in the early 1950s, and all were produced by "independent" manufacturers. The Nash Rambler was deliberately conceived as a luxury compact rather than an austerity model, and it was successful; it survived for fourteen years, in Nash Rambler guise from 1950 to 1955, lightly modified as the Rambler American during 1958–60, and continuing with new outer bodywork from 1961–63. Promoted in 1950 as "Something completely new," it was claimed to offer more in "Beauty, Custom Luxury, Economy and Ease of Handling than ever before!" It was cannily introduced in station wagon form and as a convertible, which gave "all the thrill of the open car with the comfort and safety of a sedan," thanks to unitary construction and fixed roof rails in the style of West Germany's Opel Olympia.

The Hudson Jet was conceptually less radical than the Rambler, but it was a car that squandered its maker's limited resources. While undoubtedly practical, it was made available only as a two-door or four-door sedan. In England, *The Autocar*, testing a four-door in July, 1953, found it "in many ways a car with a European character. It is trim and compact, has good performance, and is well finished." Few were sold in Britain, or in the rest of Europe, although it was enthusiastically advertised in Italy. Crucially, however, it lacked the novelty and attractive appearance of the Rambler; it was altogether too rational for the American market of its period, and was sold for only two model years, during 1953–54.

Kaiser's "Henry J" (named after Henry J. Kaiser) was a slightly smaller car than the Hudson Jet but, unlike the Hudson, it showed "no sign of having been influenced by European thought" and had "a character quite different from European cars of similar overall dimensions" according to *The Autocar*, which tested an example in December, 1951. The Henry J suffered in its home market from being too utilitarian, with little compensating appeal to the motoring enthusiast. Trumpeted in 1951 as "the most important new car in America," "the car for today!" and "America's smartest new car!" it achieved no lasting success. Its first model year, 1951, was easily its best, with just under 82,000 sales; eventually just over 130,300 were produced overall. Like the Hudson Jet, it did not survive beyond 1954. It had no successor, although a modified version was badged and sold as the Allstate through Sears' department stores during 1952–53. This venture was an even greater failure, as only an estimated 2,363 Allstates were built,[15] although it prefigured the combination of car showroom and sales/leisure complex that re-emerged intermittently in the late 1980s.

Of the regular Henry J, Joseph W. Frazer, Kaiser's erstwhile partner in the Kaiser-Frazer combine, said: "I would have brought it out dressed up, and undressed it later." It became apparent that, in the climate of the early 1950s, it was wiser to produce a utility version of an established compact with a luxury or semi-luxury image than to add gee-gaws and two-tone paint (or, in the Henry J's case, a "continental kit" and opening trunk lid) to a car whose first association in the public mind was one of austerity.

It was against this variegated background that the modern generation of compacts was announced by Studebaker, Chevrolet, Ford, and Chrysler Corporation, the first in 1958 for the 1959 model year, the others in 1959 for 1960. Chrysler's Valiant — initially a stand-alone model and from 1961 a Plymouth — was slightly larger than the others and more obviously related to its maker's regular lines. Even in 1960 the Valiant was advertised in a style closer to that used for the Corporation's other cars. Further compacts followed with the Falcon-based Comet in March, 1960 (as a stand-alone model at first and as a Mercury from 1962) and, from General Motors, with the Buick Special, Oldsmobile F-85, and Pontiac Tempest in 1961. A Valiant-derived Dodge, the Lancer, arrived in the same year.

The Studebaker Lark, with "scads of scamper, marathon mileage, common-sense cost," was visibly an abbreviated version of the regular product, although it offered a measure of charm and individuality and, if one believed the copy, "more luxury and good taste per dollar" than the opposition. Curiously, its "unique, lively styling," with a semi-classical grille that mimicked that of the Hawk coupe, together with large wheels and wheel cutouts, a short hood, and a stumpy tail, all combined to make it look even smaller than it actually was.

The principal contenders came from the Big Three, who had hitherto shunned compact cars, preferring to offer stripped versions of full-size sedans. By 1959, a growing proportion of the motoring public desired not only a reduction in the first cost of its automobiles, but also a reduction in their size, which had been growing steadily since the early 1940s. Moreover, a stripped full-size Studebaker Scotsman with painted hubcaps suggested poverty, while a well-equipped Lark indicated merely a disinclination to be ostentatious. Many families bought compact cars not only as second cars, but as their principal transport, deserting traditional full-size sedans completely.

The Hudson Jet was compact, spacious, fast, and handled well for its time. But it was the kind of functional design that had fallen from grace since the mid–1930s, and it sold badly in America and only in penny numbers in Europe. It was a good concept introduced at the wrong time (1953 campaign).

Ford competed in this sector with the Falcon. It was mechanically conventional, and combined simplicity with neat styling that distinguished the car from the regular full-size Fords, but was in no way unusual. It was advertised in late 1959 as "the easiest car in the world to own," and was promoted as an economy vehicle with all the advantages of a larger car.

An early advertisement was headed, "Introducing a wonderful new world of savings in the new-size 1960 Ford Falcon." A painting of the car surrounded by a crowd of admirers was shown above a cutaway diagram, of a kind unusual since the early 1950s, that illustrated the amount of room in the car. "Up to 30 miles a gallon on regular gas" were promised (although in real life 23–24 mpg were more usual), along with ruggedness, something for which the Volkswagen had become famous.

Three of the modern compacts announced in 1958–59. The Lark (boxed in here by a Studebaker Hawk and a 1957 Packard Clipper) was an adaptation of a 1953 design; the Falcon was new, but conventional; and the Corvair was a controversial car that only a skilled driver could handle at high speeds. Sales of imports fell by 45 percent between 1960 and 1962, with only the Volkswagen unaffected (1959 campaign, November 1959, and November 1961).

Americans needed to be reassured that a small car was not necessarily a delicate one, and the Falcon was claimed to have been "proved over every mile of numbered Federal Highway in Experience Run, U.S.A., a grueling demonstration climaxing Ford's 3 years and 3 million miles of testing and development." The Falcon proved to be the most reliable of the compacts, but servicing was encouraged: "The Falcon is a product of Dearborn, Michigan, automotive capital of the world. Every part of the Falcon has been designed for maximum durability and dependable performance. Falcon service is available at over 7,000 Ford Dealers across the country." In other words, it was not an obscure foreign Lilliputian that no one could fix.

If the Falcon held few surprises, the same could not be said of General Motors' challenger. As anticipated by its name—which blended "Corvette" with "Bel Air" and derived from a 1954 Corvette fastback show car—the air-cooled Chevrolet Corvair was sold from the outset as an automobile for the enthusiast, as in its first model year, 1960:

> In a Corvair even a ho-hum trip through town can be a happy experience.... It's a kind of challenge to your Corvair's light-hearted handling and nimble reflexes ... you'll get a real boot out of driving this car ... we know why you'll really want this car. Just drive one and you'll know too.

In June, 1964, General Motors settled out of court a suit brought by Mrs. Rose Pierini of California, whose Corvair had overturned, leading to the loss of her left arm.[16] It was one of many accidents attributed to the early Corvair's unpredictable handling, which included an unusually lethal version of the snap-oversteer for which a handful of imported, rear-engined cars were well known.

While he had criticized particular Ford, Chrysler, and General Motors automobiles in passing, a major part of Ralph Nader's invective in *Unsafe at Any Speed* was reserved for the Corvair. His attack became famous. A camber compensator was fitted to its swing-axle suspension in 1964 models—aftermarket compensators were also available for imported, swing-axled Triumph Spitfire sports cars—and the suspension as a whole was substantially redesigned for 1965.

In the meantime, the families of those who had been "Corvaired," together with nascent consumer protection groups, sought a reevaluation of automobile makers' responsibilities for their products. Was it always up to the consumer to beware? Was a safe car one which could be controlled by an expert, or must it protect, as far as technically feasible, the most reckless of drivers? Did "safe" mean only as safe as immediate rivals or contemporaries? Did tougher standards apply to cars that were promoted as "sporty"? And how far should a design allow for owner neglect? The debate over the Corvair's design continued for several years. Eventually the National Highway Traffic Safety Administration decided that, properly maintained, the 1960–63 Corvair was adequately safe by the standards of its time, notwithstanding that correct tire pressures were crucial to its performance.

In the early 1960s, the car was advertised not only for its practical virtues, but on fun-value. A 1962 advertisement promoted the Corvair as "The Sporty Car in Chevrolet's New World of Worth.... Built for budget-minded people who go for sports car driving." By 1964, convertibles were established in the Corvair range, and this body style featured prominently in Chevrolet's full-line advertising. A more conventional compact, the Chevy II, joined the Corvair in 1962 to compete more directly with the Ford Falcon. Thus Chevrolet was producing two distinct compact ranges alongside its full-sized Impalas, Bel Airs, and Biscaynes and, from 1964, medium-sized Chevelles.

The entrenchment of the compact, at General Motors and elsewhere, was the first stage in the subdivision of the new car market which continued, with ever-increasing elaboration, throughout the 1960s and 1970s. Advertisers increasingly placed different models in their own market niches. Blanket coverage of a price field with several versions of one basic product was no longer possible as it had been in the 1950s.

Chrysler's 1960 Valiant was less obviously a utilitarian compact than the Falcon and Corvair. Conventionally engineered for the most part, it was a car which, in its early years, sought to imitate the stylistic flamboyance of larger models as far as its size and price would allow. Ironically, when the Falcon and Corvair grew larger in the mid–1960s (ultimately to be "undertaken" by new compacts and subcompacts), the Valiant was advertised in 1967 as the rational car *par excellence*, which had remained true to its compact credentials:

> Compact cars sure were a good idea. Valiant still is. In case you've forgotten, the original idea was to skip the doodads and concentrate on the most car for the least money possible. But compacts have been getting chromier and less economic lately—even the foreign economy jobs. Meanwhile, Valiant

Chevrolet returned to the conventional fold with a direct Falcon competitor, the Chevy II, in 1962 (July 1962).

Compact cars sure were a good idea. Valiant still is.

In case you've forgotten, the original idea was to skip the doodads and concentrate on the most car for the least money possible. But compacts have been getting chromier and less economic lately—even the foreign economy jobs. Meanwhile, Valiant's stuck to its guns. Which is why its percentage of repeat owners is highest of any American compact. And its depreciation rate is among the very lowest. So much for the highlights; now let's get to specifics...

Our sticking to—and perfecting—the basic compact car involves a lot more than just size—it's a whole philosophy we're committed to.

In fact, while others have been adding GTs, SS's, etc., we've dropped all hardtops, station wagons and convertibles from our line. *Because we found they required compromises we don't like.*

Sure, we'll lose some sales to sporty-car buyers. But we figure to win over more of you who *want* what a compact car was intended to be in the first place.

Uhh—what *is* a proper compact, anyway?

It's sort of like a perfect marriage—hard to describe, rarely found, but a delight to experience.

Specifically, a compact is big enough to hold six without pinching, plus a fair stack of luggage—but small enough to maneuver and park with ease.

It's heavy enough to hug the road at 70 mph. Light enough to give you every break on license fees and insurance.

It's lively enough to keep up with any traffic. Yet thrifty enough to save you good money on gas.

And it's deluxe enough to give you all the comfort you need. But never at the expense of becoming expensive.

Valiant *is* all these things. And more.

Now, what it isn't...

Valiant is not a sports car—even though it has options like vinyl roof coverings and bucket seats and 4-on-the-floor. (The last is to help our ex-foreign-car owners enjoy their new surroundings.)

Valiant also is not the absolutely lowest-priced car in the world to buy and feed. The foreign economy cars have us beat on that point—until you figure out their *total cost-to-own*.

When you factor in the extras ... the more frequent service usually recommended ... the repair costs you can figure on after the warranty runs out (assuming you can get parts)... you'll find Valiant, figured on the same basis, comes out a whole lot closer than most people would guess. (And we have a few engineers who swear their figures prove Valiant *beats* the bitty ones.)

Could Valiant win you over to compacts?

If you've gotten this far into our ad, it just might. Because people do manage to become very devoted to it.

Item: Valiant is winning its owners back

Above and opposite: Worthy virtue at its worthiest: Chrysler took on the imports in 1967 with this essay in automotive philosophy (June 1967).

for seconds and thirds at the highest rate of repeat ownership among all American compacts. And their used Valiants bring back one of the highest returns on original investment.

Now you *know* that doesn't happen by accident. Obviously, something is fundamentally very right about this car.

What are the ground rules?

Some of Valiant's biggest advantages start in closest to the ground. Its wheelbase is 108 inches—long enough for riding comfort, short enough for easy handling and parking. Its suspension has never varied from the originally computed ideal—torsion bars up front, multi-leaf springs in the rear. And its extra weight helps give you a great sense of man over machine.

The brakes are self-adjusting; a chassis lube job is recommended only every 36,000 miles—you can see we're still thinking of your budget every minute.

Mileage, schmileage.

Inevitably, someone will ask what kind of mileage you're getting in your Valiant. When that happens, it's only natural to feel a bit smug. For usually you're getting better miles-per-gallon than you have a right to expect. Because economy is a Plymouth specialty. (Witness its class wins in 10 straight Mobil Economy Runs.)

Another thing to remember, while we're on engines. Valiant's Sixes and V-8s were the first in the field with a 5-year/50,000-mile warranty.* Which tells you something about their stamina and durability. And, of course, we didn't quit perfecting just because they were ahead.

Care about safety? Money?

If you're Valiant's kind of people, you do. That's why such basic safety measures as engine in the front and safety rims on the wheels (in case of flats) were part of the first Valiant ever built. Now that everyone's safety conscious, we still do a little extra for our kind of customers. So we have the

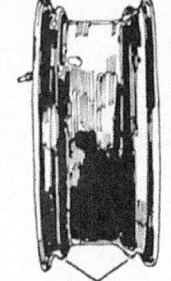
Safety Ridges

conventional features—and go on from there. With super-silent door latches that are now 50% stronger than ever before. And new Safety-Action inside door handles.

As for money, we've saved the best for last: with all we've accomplished here, we still keep our Valiant 100 2-door sedan list-priced at $2,117†— which happens to be lower than 74 models of foreign economy cars.

That ought to give you something to think about until you can get down to your Plymouth dealer's. It's his turn to prove we're out to win you over this year. He's ready and waiting.

†Manufacturer's suggested retail price for standard six-cylinder Valiant 100 2-door sedan. Destination charges, state and local taxes, if any, and optional equipment (including whitewall tires, wheel covers, bumper guards and deluxe interior) extra.

*Here's how Valiant's new Customer Care Warranty protects you: Chrysler Corporation warrants against defects in materials and workmanship and will repair or replace without charge for parts or labor at any Imperial, Chrysler, Plymouth or Dodge Authorized Dealer's place of business, the engine block, head and internal parts, intake manifold, water pump, transmission case and internal parts (except manual clutch), torque converter, drive shaft, universal joints, rear axle and differential, suspension system (except shock absorbers), steering gear and linkage system, wheels and wheel bearings of its 1967 Valiants for 5 years or 50,000 miles and all other parts for 24 months or 24,000 miles, whichever occurs first, excluding only tires, normal maintenance replacement of spark plugs, condensers, ignition points, filters, brake and clutch lining, etc., and normal deterioration of hoses, belts, upholstery, soft trim and appearance items. Maintenance services required under the warranty are: change engine oil every 3 months or 4,000 miles, whichever occurs first, and replace oil filter every second oil change, clean carburetor air filter every 6 months and replace every 2 years, lubricate front suspension ball joints and tie rod ends at 3 years or 36,000 miles, whichever occurs first; and every 6 months have an Imperial, Chrysler, Plymouth or Dodge dealer certify (i) receipt of evidence of performance of the required services and (ii) the car's then current mileage.

Mildly humorous, anti-obsolescent advertising for the 1971 Chevrolet Vega. Early versions were overweight, overpriced, and unreliable, but the car was eventually improved (July 1970 and July 1971).

stuck to its guns. Which is why its percentage of repeat owners is highest of any American compact. And its depreciation rate is among the very lowest.

The copy continued for several hundred words, discussing the advantages of the compact car in general, implicitly knocking the competition which had deserted the breed's original rationale, and inviting owners of imported economy cars to try the latest model.

Among the cars which had been getting "chromier," if not a great deal less economic, was the Rambler. Yet its expansion was still modest, and in 1958 Rambler mocked the Big Three's addiction to large cars with illustrations by famous cartoonists which showed caricatured "dinosaur" models stuck in places a Rambler could get through easily. "Get the Best of Both," said Rambler, "1. Get American big car room and comfort. 2. Get European small car economy, handling ease."

By the early 1960s, the Rambler moniker was comfortably established as a marque rather than a model name within the American Motors Corporation, and AMC would become a marque in its own right in 1966. Rambler promoted its smaller American, successor to the 1961–63 model, in several "Love letters to Rambler" during 1964–65. The emphasis was on gas mileage and reliability. In one such letter, "Rolf Haefner of Newark, New Jersey" wrote: "Rambler has really gone out to give their customers something good for their money. The American [220 sedan's] styling is pleasing.... It is bigger, more powerful, has more trunk space and is still economical in gas consumption." It was advertising of a kind which had last been seen in quantity during the Depression, but in its pursuit of an unglamorous niche rather than the whole compact car market, Rambler's was a strategy of its time. The "ordinary-user testimonial" would be used in almost identical form by Datsun ten years later.

In the 1970s a new generation of American small cars emerged, including a 1971 débutante, the Chevrolet Vega. Early copy echoed Volkswagen's disdain of planned obsolescence. Under the sub-heading, "No shiny new ashtray knobs," Chevrolet declared in an early advertisement: "Before we tell you anything about the car itself, we think you should know that once it comes out, it's going to stay out. We don't plan to change it for at least four years." The piece was headed, "Chevy's new little car: If you like the 1971, you'll like the 1975," and went on to mention the car's specification and practical features—but only in outline as "Naturally, all these things are ads in themselves, so stay tuned to this magazine."

A year later, the Vega had become established, and a more conventional advertisement introduced the Vega Kammback: "The Vega Kammback wagon is three things. It's a Vega. It's a Kammback. And it's a wagon." "Kammback" was "not just another fancy word. It refers to the aerodynamic shape of our little wagon." The housewife, who was the target market, was promised that "while it's no giant, it'll easily hold plenty of groceries and rose bushes and antiques and cub scouts," if not all at the same time.

It was not easy to inject excitement into ownership of a subcompact station wagon, but an "overhead-cam aluminum engine, front disc brakes, front bucket seats and lots lots more" combined with the Kammback name to give it a hint of quasi–European sophistication. No hint was given in advertisements of the problems which had beset the Vega from the outset. Early models were heavier, more expensive, and less well-equipped than originally intended, and the aluminum engine was prone to oil leaks and overheating. Factory strikes, bad publicity, and competition from the Ford Pinto, Volkswagen, Datsun, and Toyota meant that it was only in 1974 that the car started to compete more strongly against its opposition before falling back in 1975. Imaginative advertising had not saved it, and disillusioned buyers of early models, having given the American product one last chance before turning to imports, deserted it. The Vega name was discontinued at the end of 1977.

The Ford Pinto, by contrast, was advertised as a simple car in 1972, with a dose of nostalgia under a picture of a Model T, and an eye to the imports bought in haste by economy-minded motorists who later struggled with inaccessible engines and metric bolt sizes that their spanners would not fit: "If you find yourself staring whenever you see a Model 'T' go by, we don't blame you.... It was simple. It was tough. And if something went wrong, you could probably fix it with a screwdriver and a pair of pliers. Pinto has many of those same qualities. Which is good to know if you're the kind of person who likes cars, and likes to work on them. Pinto is the kind of car you *can* work on, without having to be some kind of master mechanic.... When you get back to basics, you get back to Ford."

It was realistic advertising for the kind of person who would not consider references to home servicing as admissions of unreliability, but Ford adopted it only after an earlier, more traditional approach had proved unsuccessful. As Vance Packard recalled in 1981:

> When Ford first introduced the Pinto as a sub-compact to compete with the flourishing foreign small-car market, it called its entry the Pinto for a special reason. Its creative image-makers pictured the car as a carefree, frisky vehicle. A galloping pony was superimposed over it in TV commercials. The début was disappointing, and Grey Advertising called in the psychographic experts for help.... It turned out that [potential buyers] were not in a carefree mood.... [R]ather they were sick and tired of high gas costs, planned obsolescence, etc. So the Pinto was re-imaged into an economical, efficient vehicle, reminiscent of...the Model A, famed for its sturdy efficiency .... It was soon the largest-selling subcompact in the USA.[17]

Yet the typical American compact still remained appreciably larger than the average European sedan—a fact highlighted by comparing American and British advertisements for the 1965 Rambler Classic 770 sedan. This car was promoted in one of AMC's "Love Letters" as "dependable transportation" with the "low mileage costs essential to my business," according to "Carl L. Klocker," who, true to his name, drove about 50,000 miles a year and who, with his wife, had owned thirteen Ramblers. For the British market, the same car, advertised in upmarket magazines in August, 1965 with the same illustration that had graced American copy, was described as "amongst the most sought after prestige vehicles today" which would be "elegantly at home in the most distinguished company."

The Classic 770 cost a middling $2,436 in its home country but, as a specialty import from Canada, it was expensive for Britons at £1,719 from Rambler Motors (AMC) Ltd. in London. For the time being, America imported many more British sports cars than Britons bought Ramblers, even if the Rambler was among the most popular non-sporting American cars in Britain. In the 1970s, Japanese imports would outnumber both.

Chapter 18

Fantasy Under Siege

In the 1930s, America imported almost no cars, and exported hundreds of thousands. In 1938, for example, the United States and Canada exported 161,612 and 40,284 cars respectively, representing eight percent and 33 percent of those countries' annual production. But in 1953 American manufacturers exported only three percent of their production with Canada exporting eight percent, which amounted to 7,153 and 12,307 fewer cars than 1938's export totals. Yet the world market was expanding rapidly. This decline was only partly accounted for by America's status as a creditor nation at the end of World War II. By 1980, American exports in relation to world production were negligible, and domestic automobile manufacturers were fighting for survival against a three-pronged attack from imported luxury, sports, and economy cars. From being a world provider, America gradually ceased to provide even for all of her own needs and, from the early 1970s, increasing numbers of imported Japanese cars made up the deficit.

In the 1950s, the American automobile became a more and more specialized product, suitable for the wide, flat highways of its home country, but inappropriate for the rugged colonial conditions in which pre-war Chevrolets and Plymouths had survived for decades. Electrical complexity and low ground clearance did not make a car easy to repair with minimal tools, or suitable for use on unmade roads and isolated farms. A smashed double-curved panoramic windshield could not be repaired by the local glass-cutter with the aid of some putty. Livestock and machinery were not easily carried in a hardtop sedan body less than five feet high.

Britain's progress was in the opposite direction. Forsaking small, underpowered, and fragile designs that many colonial Britons had deserted in the 1930s for the rugged American product, the British automobile industry gradually usurped America's former role as the world's provider, exporting 594,808 cars in 1953 — or just over half of its total output for that year.[18]

The battle for colonial markets had intensified in the 1930s, when a few British adventurers drove across inhospitable landscapes, demonstrating their cars' (and their own) durability. In 1932, T. Yates Benyon drove a Hillman Minx from London to Calcutta in 44 days, covering 8,600 miles. Humphrey Symons and Bertie Browning took just under 32 days to drive 10,290 miles across the Sahara and down to Cape Town in a medium-sized sedan, the Wolseley 18-85, in 1938–39. The car fell off a bridge near Niangara in the Belgian Congo, but was retrieved from the water by a gang of 100 local men and driven away, battered but intact, towards Juba, and then to Nairobi, 750 miles away, at an average speed on vicious roads of 25mph. In 1951, Alan Hess, George Coates, Ronald Jeavons, and Ralph Sleigh drove 9,263 miles round the world in three weeks in an Austin A40 Sports, which gave no trouble, consuming one tire and two pints of oil.

All bolstered the reputation of British cars, and led to increased sales in postwar years, necessarily at American manufacturers' expense. As Hess remarked of Yates Benyon's trip in his book, *Wheels Round the World*, in 1951:

> Few solo motor trips can have had such sweeping economic effects. Here was a convincing demonstration that British cars could perform just as successfully over the difficult Indian terrain as the larger American automobiles generally in use there. This lesson has been remembered to this day and India is now one of the world's best customers for British cars.[19]

The subsequent long continuation in India of Britain's 1956–59 Morris Oxford Series III as the Hindustan Ambassador became famous, and, if Britain's was not a lead that could be maintained forever, for twenty years or so a wide variety of British automobiles could be seen on American roads. The majority were specialist sports and luxury models — MGs,

Triumphs, and Jaguars in particular — although several small family cars gained a temporary toe-hold in the sellers' market of the late 1940s. The $1,660 Austin Devon, for instance, was advertised as the ideal present from a father to his son when he graduated from college.

Austin's rival, the Nuffield Organization, was jubilant in January, 1953: "We're part of the American scene, too!" crowed a British advertisement showing a Morris Minor and an MG TD darting amongst the conventional large cars in New York traffic. From the copy, it appeared that British cars were all but indispensable to Americans:

> You might think that a country with 39 million cars and a production of 6,680,000 more every year would be able to supply all its needs. But the fact remains that since the war Nuffield products have become extremely popular in the U.S.... The reason for our success is simple. The U.S. does not produce anything in their class quite as good as, or quite like ... the Morris Minor and the M.G. Sports, which have formed the bulk of Nuffield's car exports to the Americas.

Given that Crosley, who produced the only comparable domestic sedans and wagons, had expired following a merger with General Tire and Rubber in mid-1952, Nuffield's claim could be confidently made. The MG developed a niche in the early postwar years, including among returning servicemen, and its TD was depicted as a symbol of youth, fun, and vigor by Coca-Cola in its advertising.

On the other hand, America developed no lasting affection for the Morris Minor, and even enthusiastic Anglophiles who were well disposed towards what appeared little more than a miniature utility car to most Americans wrote to British motoring papers to complain that it was too slow for American conditions. Sales declined from over 2,000 in 1952 to fewer than 500 in 1956, before rising, when the car gained a new engine, to a peak of nearly 15,000 in 1959 [20] on the crest of an import boom. Imported by Hambro Automotive Corporation, it sold for $1,495. Buyers were "smart to be curious about ... Morris '1000' ... Now, more than ever, your biggest small car buy!" But sales declined rapidly after 1960, and, apart from a modest, fleeting revival in the late 1960s, enthusiasm for the Minor was largely confined thereafter to automobile hobbyists. With the arrival of the inexpensive American compacts, imported miniatures (as opposed to luxury and sports cars) suffered stiff competition. Annual import sales had risen from approximately 27,000 in 1952 to about 100,000 in 1956 and more than 600,000 in 1959, before falling by 45 percent to 1962's low point of fewer than 340,000.

One imported small car that did give Detroit serious pause for thought in the 1950s was the Volkswagen sedan. Early postwar auguries had not been favorable. In 1947, Bill Swallow of General Motors Overseas Operations reported to engineers in Detroit that he thought the design had potential as the basis of an austerity model to be sold in developing countries, but his findings were not taken seriously, and the general view was that the car would survive for a few years at most. The Volkswagen was not considered worth adopting in any form, and Swallow was apparently considered lucky to retain his job.[21]

In fairness to General Motors, what was viable to an importer was not necessarily viable for a major domestic producer to make, particularly when it had nothing in common with established production models, with which it could share only limited manufacturing facilities. Moreover, British experts were of a similar opinion; according to a report prepared by Humber in Britain, the car was "not to be regarded as an

The dream car for car-haters. Doyle Dane Bernbach made the most of a unique product in a long-running campaign for Volkswagen in the 1960s. Advertisements in the series became instant collectors' items (October 1963).

example of first class modern design to be followed by the British Industry."[22]

By the mid–1950s, however, the Volkswagen was selling steadily in America, making up half of the country's imports by 1956, and it was assisted from 1959 by an imaginative advertising campaign from Doyle Dane Bernbach and a carefully structured service organization. The advertising used was humorous, cleverly illustrated and, almost uniquely among automobile advertising campaigns, it had a huge readership which waited eagerly for new advertisements to appear, even if many enthusiasts for the advertising had no intention of buying the car itself. As William Bernbach recalled in the late 1960s:

> When we were awarded the account, the first thing we did was to go to the factory in Wolfsburg.... We spent days talking to engineers, production men, executives, workers on the assembly line.... We were immersed in the making of a Volkswagen and [from the] off knew what our theme had to be.... We had seen the pride of craftsmanship in the worker that made him exceed even the high standards set for him. Yes, this was an honest car. We had found our selling proposition.[23]

Volkswagen deliberately rejected the conventional advertising techniques suggested by other agencies: "Car ads are all full of mansions, horses, surf, mountains, sunsets, chiseled chins, chic women, and caviar — anything but facts," said one art director whose agency failed to win the account.[24] Bernbach's view was clear:

> Cleverness for the sake of cleverness is the worst thing in the agency business. When an agency gets preoccupied with the techniques of advertising, these get in the way of the message.... There's a feel and tone to a page. And these too were used in the VW ads to convey honesty. The layouts are utterly simple and plain and clean, the type classic and unadorned, the copy style factual and straightforward: subject, verb, object.... We've had five writers on the account and I defy anyone to tell the difference in Volkswagen copy over the years.[25]

Timing mattered, too. According to Dr. Carl Horst Hahn, head of Volkswagen's American operation from January, 1959: "We made a rule not to advertise when Detroit introduced its new models. While Detroit shot off its big guns and rockets, we didn't want to come in with our pistol. We decided to fire our pistol when it could be heard." Bernbach agreed: "[Hahn] had an intuitive sense of what we were trying to do when we got started."[26]

The result was a campaign that appealed to a wide range of people which included those who could afford more expensive cars if they chose. According to Huston Horn, writing in *Sports Illustrated*, Volkswagen drivers "... tend[ed] to have two or more cars, to live in the suburbs, to have college education, to be younger than the average car buyer and to be slightly more inclined to outdoor sports than to bowling or going to the movies."[27]

Which perhaps explained a 1966 advertisement for the equally air-cooled and rear-engined Corvair that took up the theme: "If you perked up when you turned this page, our research computer says you're probably well informed, earn above average income and have more or less 'in' type tastes."

One 1963 Volkswagen advertisement parodied Detroit's obsession with the annual model change by suggesting that, in order to update a Volkswagen from one model year to the next, it was necessary only to give it a coat of paint. The car was shown, covered in masking tape and primer, awaiting its annual freshening-up. Indulgent dismissal of such iconoclasm developed into genuine interest within Detroit when annual American VW sales exceeded 150,000 in 1959, as overall imported car sales peaked at nearly 615,000.

By the late 1950s a vast range of imports could be seen on American roads. Some, such as the BMW Isetta bubble-car and the two-stroke DKW 3=6 ("Surefooted as the cast of the Ice Follies ... on three cylinders and seven basic moving engine parts") were improbable novelties. Others were more serious: "Mercedes-Benz motor cars are distributed exclusively in the United States by the Studebaker-Packard Corporation and sold and serviced through selected dealers franchised by Studebaker-Packard," announced Studebaker in 1958. Buyers were offered "an executive motor car of regal proportions" in the 300d pillarless sedan, while a 300SL roadster came with a "legacy of perfection ... a tradition of excellence unrivaled by any other motor car." A 220S convertible, "companionable" as a four-seater, was "also available as a coupe and a 4-door sedan," and the 190SL roadster promised "joie de vivre" in convertible or hardtop form. All were shown in stylish white-on-black drawings with borders in the style used for Studebakers and Packards. But the Mercedes-Benz cars were mechanically sophisticated, very expensive, and in striking contrast to what detractors called "Packardbakers," of which only about 2,600 were sold alongside approximately 50,000 Studebakers in 1958. These were tiny numbers by American production standards.

The sale of imports was not a strategy reserved for ailing companies. General Motors imported Vauxhalls and Opels from its European subsidiaries to be sold through Pontiac and Buick dealers, some of whom viewed their task with misgivings. Opel, through its association with Buick, gained a slightly more upmarket cachet than Vauxhall. Both small cars were styled in the contemporary American idiom, and were promoted as junior versions of the domestic product.

The Vauxhall Victor was sold for $1,988 in 1959 on the back of a perceived Anglophile sentimentality, and was illustrated in a pastiche English setting, albeit with left-hand drive. Pontiac tried to combine novelty value with a reassurance of familiarity: "Built by General Motors in England, the Vauxhall is becoming an extremely popular import among Americans who want something distinctive in a small car." The copy included the reassurance: "And, most significantly, your Vauxhall can be readily serviced by authorized Pontiac dealers located in practically every village and hamlet throughout the States."

The Victor's styling had been deliberately contrived as a reflection of American trends, and when the body clay was damaged in transit to Fisher Body in Detroit, Harley Earl's team effected a few "finishing touches."[28] The car was not a great success in Britain, and, even in its spiritual home in America, fewer than 50,000 were sold between 1958 and 1961. It was, however, successfully exported to many other countries.

In 1959, Opel capitalized on the reputation of Germany for thorough engineering and solid build quality which had grown with the Volkswagen. The Opel Rekord was advertised as "German made" with "American style" in a series of distinctive black and white advertisements. It was a "practical family-size, economical small car import with American big-car ideas"—and, as Opel did not say, it was better built than the first Victors. Copy included a list of specifications, invited the reader to send ten cents for a "full-color Opel brochure," and concluded, as had Pontiac with the Vauxhall, that the car was "sold and serviced all over America," in this case by Buick dealers. At around 55,000, Opel's sales were greater than those of the Victor.

In 1958, a small, unattractive, and crude-looking car won its class in the Round Australia Rally. It was one of the first modern Datsuns, a 210 sedan, of a type imported into America from June, 1958 and advertised as "The Foreign Car Classic, built to last for 20 years." It was certainly solid; so solid that when the rally car suffered an accident, straightening the front fender proved unexpectedly difficult. Unlike earlier Nissan products, it was not simply a modified or license-built Austin. Advertising for the car was unpretentious, and concentrated on facts and specifications.

In the same year, Toyota exported a few Toyopet sedans to America, and by 1959 was selling them from Los Angeles as the "world's greatest automotive value." The Toyopet was claimed to be "inexpensive to operate and maintain" in an advertisement whose layout was more polished and mock-refined, but also more obviously of its period, than that for the smaller and cheaper ($1,616) Datsun. But the Toyopet, although physically tough, turned out to be a mechanical disaster. Designed for winding Japanese roads, it was too slow

Sports and luxury cars from Mercedes-Benz were sold through Studebaker-Packard dealers in the late 1950s and early 1960s. This is the 300SL roadster (October 1957).

for American freeways and proved so unreliable that cars belonging to the company had to be dismantled to provide replacement parts for customers.

Japanese economy cars were not alone in attracting criticism from automotive traditionalists. Many British sedans of proven suitability for their home market were considered bizarre by mainstream American opinion. The MG 1100, for instance, advertised as the "MG Sports Sedan" at $1,898 in 1963, was dismissed by Henry Ford II as less than sophisticated in an American context:

The Opel Rekord and its British equivalent, the Vauxhall Victor, both featured toned-down American styling, and were sold by Buick and Pontiac dealers respectively (1959 campaign).

It's got a top on it like a box. Americans want a more graceful, more flowing line.... They had an engineering genius in there who was only interested in getting his ideas across.... The American people who buy the cars I manufacture don't want things like that. They want beauty and style and power, and they pay for it.[29]

The importers' long and attractive series of black and white advertisements echoed Volkswagen's humor and iconoclasm, but the cheapest 1963 Ford, a Falcon two-door sedan, cost only a little more at $1,985. Most American buyers preferred to sacrifice the MG's "Proud, defiant, staunch British grille" for this known, if conventional, quantity. It was therefore no surprise that in the early 1960s Datsuns and self-destructive Toyotas were not seen as a significant commercial threat to American automobile makers. The British did not take them seriously, either.

During the 1950s and 1960s, American advertising for British cars was very different from that which promoted those cars in their home market. American themes and layouts frequently crossed the Atlantic to reappear a few years later, in diluted form, in British copy, and many of the agencies used by British car manufacturers had American origins or connections. But this cross-fertilization was between equivalent market sectors rather than between copywriters promoting a single model. It was, moreover, almost entirely a one-way process as Britishness, as sold to Americans, was not the same as Britishness sold to Britons. In the late 1940s, American copywriters for small sedans from Austin, Ford, and Hillman concentrated cheerfully on economy and value for money in advertisements that were often colorful in a simple style, and which avoided the euphorics of domestic manufacturers. Smaller importers with low budgets advertised sparsely, and their black and white advertisements did not capitalize on the potential distinctiveness of monochrome illustration in the manner of Volkswagen and its imitators in the 1960s.

In September, 1958, the magazine *U.S. News & World Report* surveyed buyers of imported cars and found that, as a group, they were younger, better-educated, and slightly better paid than the average domestic car buyer, and often lived on the east or west coasts (in particular California). The survey found that nearly 60 percent of import buyers owned larger

The MG Sports Sedan, based on Alec Issigonis's Pininfarina-styled British bestseller, the Morris 1100, was sold on the reputation of MG's sports cars, but remained an oddity on American roads (November 1963).

domestic cars, too, although later research for the National Automobile Dealers' Association found that in 57 percent of cases an import was its owner's only car.[30] This mattered, as the American motorist who chose a British car over an American one made a distinctive choice and needed to be persuaded, against his natural conservatism, that he was buying something special. In dollars per pound weight, and in horsepower per dollar, a British car was expensive. This was not necessarily fatal for a specialist sports or luxury model — it could even be advantageous, ensuring exclusivity — but it militated against British family cars, which in American terms were usually unremarkable subcompact sedans.

Austin was among those who eventually fell foul of this difficulty, but as an independent company it was America's leading importer in the immediate postwar years and in 1954, as the senior marque of the British Motor Corporation (BMC) which had been formed in 1952, it enjoyed an Indian summer of distinctive copywriting from a burgeoning New York agency, Ogilvy, Benson & Mather. David Ogilvy's headline for the A40 Somerset was unusual and provocative: "I am sending my son to Groton [a prestigious private school] with the money I have saved driving Austins." Billed as part of a "Private Letter from [an] Anonymous Diplomat," the headline led into two pages of terse, factual copy that highlighted this slow but sturdily constructed car's low gas mileage, build quality, roadability, and complete equipment. The copy was written in a direct and unelaborate style which was ahead of its time, and which would not have been out of place promoting a domestic compact twenty years later. It was also disingenuous, as Ogilvy candidly recalled in *Confessions of an Advertising Man*, published in 1963:

> My first advertisement for Austin cars took the form of a letter from an "anonymous diplomat" who was sending his son to Groton with money he had saved driving an Austin — a well-aimed combination of snobbery and economy. Alas, a perspicacious *Time* editor guessed that I was the anonymous diplomat, and asked the headmaster of Groton to comment. Dr. Crocker was so cross that I decided to send my son to another school.[31]

Ogilvy does not record whether this advertisement sold many cars, but his slightly austere yet confident style was ideally suited to a super-luxury product. Ogilvy's advertisements for Rolls-Royce in the late 1950s, recognizably from the same pen, were masterpieces of calculated understatement. They described, in numbered paragraphs, facts about the car's construction and features, avoiding the twin perils of overt snobbery and utilitarian pedantry, yet deliberately selecting facts that were interesting and, above all, quotable.

The most famous in the series, which appeared in two magazines and two newspapers at a cost of $25,000, was headed with a quotation from an English road test report: "At 60 miles an hour the loudest noise in this new Rolls-Royce comes from the electric clock." The advertisement concluded: "The Bentley is made by Rolls-Royce. Except for the radiators, they are identical motor cars.... People who feel diffident about driving a Rolls-Royce can buy a Bentley." The reaction of Rolls-Royce's chief engineer in England to Ogilvy's copy was brief: "It's about time we did something about that damned clock."[32]

Ogilvy was surprised to discovery that the theme was not original. Charles Brower of the agency Batten, Barton, Durstine & Osborn wrote to Ogilvy, citing an advertisement he had written for Pierce-Arrow in 1933: "*The only sound* one can hear in the new Pierce-Arrows is the ticking of the electric clock." Ogilvy replied, "What a fascinating thing. I picked up that headline from an article in a British motoring magazine." Ford notoriously adopted Ogilvy's theme in a headline for its luxurious 1965 Galaxie 500-based LTD: "'Ford rides quieter than Rolls-Royce.' '*Oh come now, old boy!*'" The claim was true, but the Rolls-Royce in question — the Silver Cloud III — would be superseded by the new Silver Shadow during 1965.[33]

Ogilvy's advertisements for Rolls-Royce were unusual for their length as well as their style at a time when upmarket manufacturers, including Rolls-Royce in Britain under Dorland Advertising Ltd., preferred an atmospheric photograph and a line or two of grandiose prose. A 1957 advertisement, showing the radiator of a Silver Cloud beside a lake with "The best car in the world" printed in small capital letters below, was typical. By contrast, as Ogilvy remembered:

> When I advertised Rolls-Royce, I gave the facts — no hot air, no adjectives ... no gracious living.... In my first Rolls-Royce advertisement, I used 719 words — piling one fascinating fact on another.... Judging from the number of motorists who picked up the word "diffident" and bandied it about, I concluded that the advertisement was thoroughly read. In the next one I used 1400 words.[34]

Recalling the success of this campaign, Ogilvy — born in England of Scottish descent — criticized the established paradigms of American automobile advertising:

> I have never admired the *belles lettres* school of advertising, which reached its pompous peak in Theodore F. McManus's famous advertisement for Cadillac, "The Penalty of Leadership,"[35] and Ned Jordan's classic, "Somewhere West of Laramie." Forty years ago the business community seems to have been impressed by these pieces of purple prose, but I have always thought them absurd; they did not give the reader a single *fact*.... I share Claude Hopkins' view that fine writing is a distinct disadvantage. So is unique literary style. They take attention away from the subject.[36]

Ogilvy's approach, iconoclastic as well as individual, was expressed almost as a philosophy of advertising, which he applied to automobiles as to other products. But Ogilvy himself had initiated many "image-led" rather than factual campaigns, and, with Rolls-Royce as with Austin, was able to build upon the obvious uniqueness of the car itself — an advantage denied to the promoters of most domestic automobiles.

Moreover, Ogilvy's preference for facts was not founded on utilitarian disdain for emotion in advertising copy. Rather, he realized that the appearance of rationality, order, and restraint appealed to the emotions of the particular consumers who might buy Rolls-Royces. His campaign was of a kind that could only succeed in the most upmarket sectors. To this extent, it reflected the self-conscious classicism of much upmarket American copy of the 1920s — the difference lying in the fact that, in Ogilvy's case, the classicism rested in the writing itself rather than in the images and objects associated by the copywriter with the car. It was Ogilvy's method, rather than its underlying premise, that was distinctive.[37]

Despite the campaign's success in selling Rolls-Royces (sales for the year 1958, when it began, were 50 percent greater than in 1957), it did not make money for Ogilvy, Benson & Mather, and Ogilvy resigned the account when he became dissatisfied with the quality of the product. Rolls-Royce, however, was sanguine. According to Ogilvy:

> They went through a very bad two-year period.... I knew what was going on. Automatic gears had just come in and their automatic gearbox didn't work, so they had to go and buy one from [an American manufacturer] which did work. And then they put in air conditioning for Americans and other people who lived in hot countries.... The manager of the American company went down and got these new air-conditioned Rolls-Royces off the boat. The first one he drove around Central Park. He didn't go halfway round Central Park before the windows fogged up. He couldn't see out. Things like that happened all the time. I wrote this dreadful letter resigning. Even then I thought it was dreadful. Now I think it was unpardonably offensive. But do you know they didn't take offense at all. The head of Rolls-Royce, who was an engineer, wrote back and said I don't blame you at all. I think you have a point.[38]

Two years later, Ogilvy recalled in 1983, "we took Mercedes, and sent a team to interview their engineers in Stuttgart. From this sprang a campaign of long, factual advertisements which increased sales from 10,000 cars a year to 40,000."[39]

The "factual" Mercedes-Benz campaign stressed build quality, durability, and safety at a time when consumers were paying ever greater attention to those subjects. "You give up things when you buy the Mercedes-Benz 230S. Things like rattles, rust, and shabby workmanship," said a typical headline, and the theme and style of the series were continued through the 1970s. The elegant but superficial advertising of Studebaker-Packard days would not return; quality and safety had to be demonstrated, not assumed.

Concern about safety and reliability was not confined to Mercedes-Benz. Many American consumers believed that a small car was necessarily an unsafe one, but, in the aftermath of Ralph Nader's *Unsafe at Any Speed*, importers capitalized on increasing mistrust of the domestic product.

In 1966, Rover promoted the 2000TC Sports Sedan as "among [the] elite of the world's best-performing cars," adding, "It is also quite likely the safest," citing the provision of four-wheel disc brakes and "steel-cage construction" (that popular 1930s asset) as noteworthy features. Increasing public interest in automobile safety was reflected in a note at the end of the copy which challenged those die-hards who scorned the debate by insisting that all accident injuries were caused by drivers' mistakes: "In the recent furore over safety standards some spokesmen have pointed out that most accidents are caused by driver error. So? Is that an offense punishable by hurt or worse? And what of the innocents who aren't driving?"

Occasionally, public awareness could backfire on importers. The Renault Dauphine was the second-place import behind Volkswagen in the late 1950s, and was promoted in light-hearted, pun-strewn copy that made much of its nationality. It was "très agréable ... confortable ... manoevrable ... formidable ... budget-able" in one piece which showed a Dauphine and a fashionable mother and children with their

The Rover 2000 TC's *first* purpose is to be safe?

For the same reason that a light switch, first of all, shouldn't electrocute you.

NOT to be too stuffy about it, the Rover 2000 TC Sports Sedan is generally acknowledged to be among that elite of the world's best performing cars. It is also quite likely the safest.

The two go hand-in-hand, apparently: surely safety is part of performance. What good is a car that goes the limit if it can't stop within it? And if everything else goes wrong—including driver errors*—isn't it still the car's job to protect you? We do think so.

To this end the Rover 2000 TC has two sorts of safety.

1) **So nothing will happen.** For example: the 2000 TC has disc brakes all around so it can stop as fast as it goes; radial ply tires to hold the road and a revolutionary suspension and control system to give it *immediacy*.

2) **So if something does happen it won't happen to you.** To begin with, the 2000 TC has two separate bodies. The outer you see below. The inner is of steel-cage construction to protect you even should the car roll. (Please fasten your safety harness, though.)

It follows that the 2000 TC already *has* most of the sweeping safety features that the U.S. Government demands by 1968. One notable exception: a "standard bumper height." One can't very well be standard all alone. We will be happy to cooperate on this or any other industry effort. The safer other cars are the safer ours will be.

Now you know about safety. Buy a Rover 2000 TC and stop worrying about it.

*In the recent furore over safety standards some spokesmen have pointed out that most accidents are caused by driver error. So? Is that an offense punishable by hurt or worse? And what of the innocents who aren't driving?

The Rover Motor Co. of N. America Ltd.: Chrysler Bldg., New York, N.Y. 10017; 231 Johnson Ave., Newark, N.J. 07108; 1040 Bayview Drive, Ft. Lauderdale, Fla. 33304; 373 Shaw Rd., South San Francisco, Calif. 94080; 10889 Wilshire Blvd., Los Angeles, Calif. 90024; Mobile Drive, Toronto 16, Ont.; 186 W. Second Ave., Vancouver 10, B. C.

A white elephant, but a safe one. Rover capitalized on public disquiet about the safety of American automobiles a year after Ralph Nader published ***Unsafe at Any Speed*** (November 1966).

father, a pilot, beneath a huge hot-air balloon as colored party balloons rose from the car. Another advertisement used multiple typefaces in many colors to give a "leçon française de l'automobile or, how to make your driving fun again," and boasted, *inter alia*, of "Le Dealer Network: over 800 coast-to-coast sales, service and parts headquarters, 150 more in Canada."

In 1961, a little cartoon car chugged up a steep line of blue, sans-serif text: "Snow piles up, up, up. Who cares? Let it snow — on we go, on and on and on ...," leveling off as it reached the top of the page and continuing "and on" until it ran off the right-hand margin. The main copy, highlighting the one advantage of the Dauphine's otherwise disadvantageous rear engine, explained: "For six winters, Americans have watched the Dauphine meet every type of snow situation and conquer it as no other car in the history of cars. The Winter Wonder-Car has not been fazed by snow-clogged drive-ways, nor by sloshy, slippery slopes...."

But it was fazed by a good deal else, and Renault suffered in the 1960s from the Dauphine's reputation for fragility, unreliability (caused in part by a fragile fibre timing gear), and unpredictable handling. The Dauphine shared the early Chevrolet Corvair's rear engine/swing axle layout, and its reputation was further damaged indirectly by association with that car. American Dauphine sales fell from over 90,000 in 1959 to fewer than 30,000 in 1962, and, in a 1966 advertisement that came closer than any other to groveling apology, Renault urged car buyers to forgive the Dauphine its failings, and to try a new (but still rear-engined) Renault 10. Few did.

Among rear-engined subcompact utilities, only the Volkswagen enjoyed any real success, and that car, immune to the general fall in import sales after 1959 and perceived very much as a one-off by the mid–1960s, was helped by a fine reputation for quality, reliability, and a good service network. Unusual handling was not a handicap for Porsche, who sold the 912 and 911 as specialist products for enthusiasts at $4,790 and $5,990 respectively. The Porsche driver bought a 911 precisely because it did not behave like a regular American sedan.

There were nevertheless clouds on Detroit's horizon, among them the issue of quality control, at a time when Lincoln's 24,000-mile warranty of 1961 was very much the exception. *Automotive News* was critical in 1963:

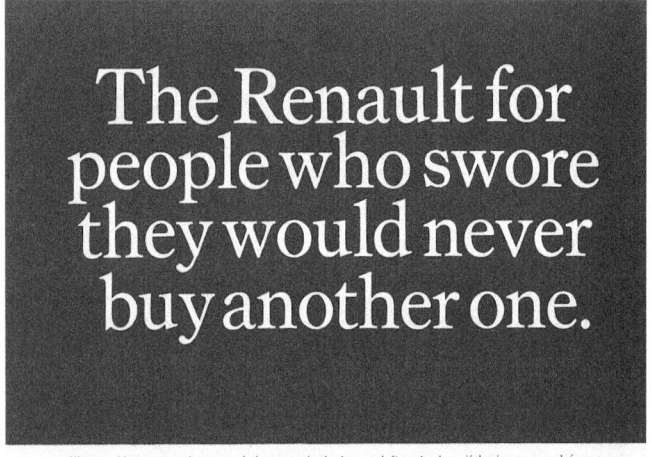

Once bitten, twice shy. The horse was a good deal more reliable and better-handling than an early Dauphine and, for most import fanciers, that was the point. Apologies, photographs of engine parts and half-hearted imitation of VW's iconoclasm by the Gilbert Advertising Agency did little for the Dauphine's successor (November 1966 and November 1969).

Move over.

From out of nowhere, a speck appears in your rear-view mirror, grows instantly larger, and you see the famed blue-and-white medallion on the hood. Mister, that's a BMW bearing down on you, and unless you're driving a BMW yourself, you'd best get out of the way.

For this is the car that's overtaking everything else on the road, and taking sportsmen everywhere by storm. This is the car that in Germany, where high-speed driving is a national sport, leads the pack.

What's BMW got? The most advanced high-performance engine in any production car, for a cruising speed of 100 mph. Head-snapping acceleration through the gears. A unique, fully-independent suspension for amazing roadholding that makes the car as safe as it is fast.

What else? Plenty of room for four big adults. Virtual freedom from repairs, and 30 miles to a gallon of gas. All constructed with the everything-fits, everything-works precision craftsmanship that is the pride of Germany.

And all for a remarkable under-$2,600 price.

Go to your BMW dealer, and take the wheel of the sportsman's car. Then kick the throttle hard, and watch the ordinary cars move over.

Suggested retail prices start at $2,597 P.O.E. New York. U.S. Importer: Hoffman Motors Corporation, 375 Park Avenue, New York, N.Y., 1862 S. La Cienega Blvd., Los Angeles, Calif. Dealers coast to coast. Advantageous European Delivery Program. Write for free brochure.

Bavarian Motor Works

The Sportsman's Car

This famous theme was used by BMW on both sides of the Atlantic. Such direct thematic transplants were rarely successful, but BMW's campaign was an exception, and is well remembered today (June 1968).

Surprisingly conventional advertising for a car that was too different for most consumers. Only a few thousand a year were sold in the United States before Citroën withdrew it in 1972 when safety and emissions legislation threatened (March 1967).

Sold on the back of the successful 356, this rear-engined Porsche was not intended to appeal to mainstream automobile buyers, and consequently prospered within its limited, affluent market (November 1966).

In the United States an MGB was not as not nearly as fast, relative to the cars around it, as in its home country, so American advertising in magazines such as *Time*, *Newsweek*, and *Scientific American* concentrated on its distinctiveness rather than on speed (May 1971).

The American public will not put up with the missing bolts and nuts, the malfunctioning parts, the squeaks and rattles and frequent return trips to dealers for adjustments — all of which are the rule and not the exception in present American cars.[40]

The industry had suffered quality control problems in the late 1950s, and they persisted for several years afterwards. While this did not precipitate a wholesale abandonment of the domestic product in favor of foreign competition — not least because America still made the best low-priced full-size family cars in the world — a residuum of dissatisfaction was built up against the increased costs engendered by planned obsolescence, and against a perceived complacency within Detroit. In the meantime, Datsun and Toyota had returned with products vastly more advanced than the Toyopets of 1958–59.

Datsun encouraged small-car buyers to have fun in 1970: "Get into a Datsun! Go like the wind in this sleeky [sic], high-powered machine! Styled in wind-tunnels, this exciting fast-back tunnels through the air smoothly... Responds like a compact tornado. Power/weight ratio: 10.3 kg per HP.... Eats like a sparrow, performs like an eagle." The imagery was confused and the car, a Datsun 1200 Coupe, was less than exciting, but by 1970 utility cars were promoted as vigorously as conventional large cars. Careful attention to stylistic details ensured that, though small, the 1200 Coupe did not look too out of place on American roads. The success of Datsun's real sports car, the 240Z, improved the image of lowlier models.

A 1973 Datsun advertisement used a cartoon of the car, in a style reminiscent of some muscle-car advertising of the late 1960s, to appeal to the twenty-somethings that were a large part of its target market: "New Datsun 1200 Sport Coupe. An original portrait by Peter Max.... Peter Max has captured the spirit of our 1200, a Datsun Original. Capture it for yourself in real, everyday terms at your Datsun dealer...." One copy line in particular — "For the ecology minded, it's a car that ... gets around 30 miles out of every gallon of gasoline" — anticipated a themes of thirty years later.

In 1976, Datsun concentrated on the low gas mileage of the B-210 fastback: "Built to keep its figure (41 MPG highway, 29 City)," and built a campaign around the slogan, "Datsun saves." In answer to skeptics who thought small cars insufficiently safe and rugged for American conditions, the B-210 was claimed to be "Tough all over" which, if less than specific, indicated its maker's priorities. Owners were encouraged to keep their cars: "Your Datsun is backed by nearly 4,000 factory-trained technicians and a computerized parts network. We figure the longer your Datsun survives the longer you'll save." And every new buyer's more conservative friends, colleagues, and relatives would, of course, watch closely before eventually taking the plunge themselves.

Toyota capitalized on a growing reputation in 1970 with the $2,126 Corona: "It led the new wave — economy cars that offer more than just a bare set of wheels." A list of detail features followed, and concluded with the slogan, "We're quality oriented." In 1971, an advertisement for the smaller Corolla listed 39 features, ranging from "thick, wall-to-wall nylon carpeting" and "coat hooks" *via* a "30-foot turning circle" to "up to 28 miles a gallon" which, if not remarkable, was better than an average domestic American small car and competitive with the Volkswagen.

The emphasis, in America as in other export markets, remained on the Corolla's equipment for the money, which, at $1,798, was substantially less than the $2,090 that bought the cheapest Chevrolet Vega. By 1972, Toyota's range included Corollas and a new Corona Mark II hardtop coupe, "the top of the Toyota line" for the American market and "the most comfortable. With leather-like padding. Reclining bucket seats.... All kinds of luxurious things. And all standard." Then there was the Celica ST: "At first glance, [it] might come off as a rich man's sports car. That's the nice thing about it. However, in real life, it's an economy car. That's the nice thing about it.... A high revving overhead cam engine, tachometer (redline at 6300 rpm), and front disc brakes. Even an AM radio. Standard. All this and more for $2848. That's the nice thing about it." Advertising for the new Carina of 1972 stressed its maker's durability program: "It might be new to you but we've been living with it a long time. We froze, drenched, buffeted, skidded and crash-tested the Carina prototypes without mercy. So just in case you don't show yours much mercy, it'll be better prepared."

By 1976, Toyota had established a reputation for build quality combined with value for money and, within its price class, an element of style. Even if relatively few of Toyota's exciting S800 and 2000 sports cars had been sold, they had injected a hint of glamour into the latest sedans and station wagons while demonstrating a mastery of modern automotive technologies.

An October, 1976 advertisement for the Toyota Corona wagon was typical of the increasingly sophisticated copy that accompanied consolidation within a growing market. "The wagon that thinks it's a sedan" included mock-wood paneling and a chrome-plated roof rack for the American market: "The outside looks like a sporty wagon. The inside rides like our quality sedan. A quality wagon with sedan comfort. You got it. The Toyota Corona Wagon."

Gas mileage figures were given prominence, and there was a photograph of a metallic pink car set against a lilac background, with the rest of the page a metallic greyish-blue on which headlines were white and the copy in black. The effect was one of parody, yet advertising history had shown that clever parodies often sold cars. Toyota's copywriters consistently underpinned the chrome and lilac with assurances of value for money, but utilitarian values were never thrust at the consumer. Toyota realized early on that utility had to be made palatable to its market.

Honda, always something of a maverick in design, did

Drive a wind tunnel! New DATSUN 1200 Coupe!

Get into a DATSUN! Go like the wind in this sleek, high-powered machine! Styled in wind tunnels, this exciting fastback tunnels through the air smoothly. Swiftly: 150 km/h! Handles like a breeze. Turning radius 4.1 m! Responds like a compact tornado. Power/weight ratio: 10.3 kg per HP! Takes off in a flash with a precision-engineered 4-on-the-floor. Stops on a dime with a newly designed brake system. Eats like a sparrow, performs like an eagle! The all new agile DATSUN 1200 Coupe!

NISSAN MOTOR CO., LTD.

Get Yourself inside the Big Little Car... **DATSUN 1200 Coupe!**

You can get one for the price of a Toyota.

At first glance, the Toyota Celica ST might come off as a rich man's sports car.

That's the nice thing about it. However, in real life, it's an economy car.

That's the nice thing about it. The Celica ST has hood vents and rally stripes. Standard.

It comes with a four-speed synchromesh transmission and radial tires. Standard.

A high revving overhead cam engine, tachometer (redline at 6300 rpm), and front disc brakes. Even an AM radio. Standard.

All this and more for $2848.

That's the nice thing about it.

Toyota Celica ST.
See how much car your money can buy.

The Toyota Corona was ahead of its time. It led the new wave — economy cars that offer more than just a bare set of wheels. We intend to keep it ahead.

So, we've improved it. Quite a bit.

First, we gave it twenty percent more horsepower. For greater acceleration and speed. We did this with an overhead cam engine that still gets up to 25 miles to the gallon. It's not only more powerful (108 hp), it lasts longer. Because of fewer moving parts.

Also, a lot of aluminum is used in our new engine — where it makes sense. To lighten the car and to dissipate heat faster (which also reduces wear).

It has a five bearing crankshaft, instead of the previous three. And dual exhaust manifolds, instead of one.

Then we gave the Corona a power braking system with front discs. For greater stopping power.

And a newly engineered suspension system, front and back, for a smoother ride. And also to deaden sound.

Inside, the seats come two ways. Buckets with the 4-on-the-floor stick shift. And with the column-mounted, 3-speed automatic, you get a full bench seat.

There's more leg room, more hip room and a bigger trunk.

The four doors are still there. So is the flo-thru ventilation, the nylon carpeting, the tinted glass, the courtesy lights, the whitewall tires and the locking glove box. All standard equipment.

And the options are the same. Factory air conditioning, AM/FM radio, stereo tape deck and automatic transmission.

What all this adds up to is the new Toyota Corona. For drivers who are in love with the best.

Until it's improved.

TOYOTA *We're quality oriented*

You loved it the way it was for five fantastic years. So we made it even more lovable!

This car is loaded with reasons why it shouldn't be under $1800.

1. Thick, wall-to-wall nylon carpeting.
2. Whitewall tires.
3. Tinted windshield.
4. Anti-rust undersealant.
5. Fully reclining and adjustable bucket seats.
6. Sealed lubrication system (no chassis lubes ever).
7. Up to 28 miles a gallon.
8. Up to 91 miles per hour.
9. Lined trunk.
10. Armrests front and rear.
11. Full wheel covers.
12. Unit body construction.
13. Flo-thru ventilation.
14. Front disc brakes.
15. Five-bearing crankshaft.
16. Bumper guards.
17. Vinyl interior.
18. Trip mileage meter.
19. 73 horsepower engine.
20. 161.4 inches in length. 59.3 inches in width.
21. Can of touch-up paint.
22. Glove box.
23. Tool kit.
24. Windshield washer.
25. Cigarette lighter.
26. Dome light.
27. 4-speed synchromesh transmission.
28. Curved side windows.
29. Parcel shelf.
30. 30-foot turning circle.
31. Swing-out side rear windows.
32. Double edge keys (go in either way).
33. Anti-freeze.
34. 2-barrel carburetor.
35. Heavy-duty battery.
36. 3-point front safety belts.
37. Spare tire recessed in trunk.
38. Passenger assist grip.
39. Coat hooks.

Everything you've just read is included in the price of the $1798 Toyota Corolla.

TOYOTA *We're quality oriented*

What increasing numbers of Americans were coming to by 1976 — the Honda Civic (March 1976).

not attempt to imitate American styling with the Civic. It became one of the best-known Japanese imports, emblematic of the changing car market, and was sold in 1976 on the twin merits of fuel economy and low price: "The 1976 Honda Civics.... We can explain how we did it in two words: brilliant engineering." A hint of social responsibility was given in the slogan, "Honda Civic. What the world is coming to," which taunted automotive philistines at a time when young Americans — particularly young professionals whose fathers had revered the names of Cadillac and Continental — deserted full- and mid-size sedans for tiny hatchbacks.

Many of those professionals were women, and a 1974 advertisement was headlined with a mock-quotation: "Women only drive automatic transmissions." The copy continued: "Some car manufacturers actually believe women buy cars for different reasons than men do. So they build a 'woman's car.' Oversized, hopelessly automatic and dull." Honda offered "a stick shift with an astonishing amount of zip.... Or, if you prefer, Hondamatic. It's a semi-automatic transmission that gives you convenience, but doesn't rob you of involvement. Neither one is a woman's car." Were they serious? Certainly serious enough to feel that they had to pretend, which was arguably progress of a kind.

By 1977, executives had begun to discard Buicks and Lincolns for imported luxury cars, among them BMW, billed as "one of the few luxury sedans in the world that wouldn't be laughed off the Nürburgring." It appeared that affluent Americans no longer wanted sports cars with sedan-like handling and ride, but preferred sedans that handled like sports cars while also offering, as BMW put it, "all the luxury one could sanely require."

BMW made no secret of its contempt for the old-style American luxury cruiser and, by implication, for those who liked it. To back up its claims, there was a quote from *Motor*

Opposite: Datsun and Toyota headed the Japanese sub-compact invasion in the early 1970s with astute marketing. The fuel crisis helped, too (1200 Coupe and Corona: October 1970; Corolla: July 1971; Celica: June 1972).

In the late 1970s, even Ford tacitly acknowledged that many Americans aspired to foreign car ownership — but should anyone unable to see the differences between a Granada and a Mercedes-Benz have been behind the wheel of any car? (December 1977).

Trend: "The reaction to a BMW is always the same. The first-time driver takes the wheel and after a few minutes no other automobile will ever be the same again."

Successful lawyers, financiers, and executives—the very groups that Imperial had targeted in the early 1960s—were buying BMWs and other imported luxury cars as never before. In the late 1970s, even Ford tacitly conceded that a Lincoln Continental was no longer the ultimate choice in prestigious motoring. Above a picture of a deep red Mercedes-Benz 450 SLC Sports Coupe in one advertisement was the headline, "Remarkable achievement. $23,976." Above a similar picture of a Granada Sports Coupe beneath the Mercedes was the headline, "Remarkable achievement. $4,189." A December, 1977 advertisement for the 1978 model year began: "Introducing the new Ford Granada ESS. Can you tell its looks from a Mercedes-Benz?" The reader was invited to identify details shown in ten close-up photographs as belonging to either the Ford or the Mercedes. Answers were given at the foot of the page, and it remained an unusual case of reader involvement in automotive advertising. At least by filling in the boxes, one would remember the advertisement, and, even if no Ford buyer would be in the market for a Mercedes, it was a poignant indicator of how much the American car market had changed since 1960.

By 1980, the European and Japanese importers' three-pronged offensive in the luxury, sporting, and utility categories threatened sales of the domestic product, particularly with new "compromise" models which did not fit neatly into existing sectors of the market, but which filled the gaps between them. Such cars offered combinations of style, handling, equipment, sportiness, and prestige which were not always available in domestically-produced rivals.

Thus the Detroit-based automotive culture which had appeared so strong and immutable in the 1950s was eroded by public demand for automobiles that were economical, soberly styled and designed with practicality, rather than any anti-functionalist fantasy, in view. This inexorable return to the rationality which had been deserted by automobile advertisers in the early 1940s was immortalized in advertising for that archetypally safe and sensible car, the Volvo, in 1970:

> Fat Cars Die Young!.... Some cars destroy themselves in the mere act of carrying themselves around. Burdened with tons of chrome and huge expanses of sheet metal, it doesn't take long for a car to collapse under the strain. So in building a car that will live a long time, you must begin by acknowledging one basic fact. Fat on cars, as on people, can be fatal.... Unfettered by fat, Volvos live to ripe old ages. We don't guarantee exactly how long that will be. But we do know that 9 out of every 10 Volvos registered here in the last eleven years are still on the road. If you don't believe us, look around. You can't miss an eleven year old Volvo. It looks a lot like a 1948 Ford. Only not as fat.

A 1977 advertisement portrayed the Volvo as the car for the motorist who not only had money, but who valued intelligence as well: "It takes more than just money to buy a Volvo 264. There are so many expensive, powerful cars around these days that the problem isn't finding one, but choosing one. To make it even harder, the real qualities of the Volvo 264 don't even show.... Volvo. For people who think."

Had the dream been shattered for ever?

Overview and Conclusion

The idea of the "American dream," as reflected in automobile advertising, is an elusive construct. It points to a social disposition, a corpus of ideas and aspirations, variously personal and abstracted, that are in a permanent state of flux. Over time, the automotive dream has changed its character beyond recognition. Even its principal element, a belief that the present is better than the past, and that the future can be better than the present, is not immune from disintegration. Yet that stubborn eschatology — the imaginative act of will towards a final, perfect, American society — has not wholly disappeared. It has grown older, subtler, wiser, occasionally disillusioned, and it may ultimately reject consumerism as we know it — but for the moment it survives.

At the beginning of the 1930s, the automobile was integrated into America's burgeoning technological consciousness as never before. Direct parallels could be drawn between new developments in automobile design, such as all-steel construction and streamlining, and developments in other spheres. Those innovations that made the automobile of 1933–39 work better than its forebears were in many cases the same innovations that allowed bridges and locomotives and airplanes to perform more efficiently. It was a time when automobile styling actually embodied wider technological advances. The automotive dream was integrated, as it never would be again, into the architectural dream and the aeronautical dream. All were bound up with a widespread belief amongst designers and social commentators that technology would improve the lives of Americans, and make them happier. Optimism was rife. As Norman Bel Geddes, arguably the most idealistic of America's early industrial designers, wrote in 1932:

> Of one thing we can be sure. All the industrial design we have had in the United States, as yet, is comparable in effect to a pebble dropped in a pond. The circles that have agitated the surface will continue to widen and spread with an ever-increasing sphere of influence. By the middle of the present century, I anticipate that we shall have begun consciously to achieve that complete mastery of the machine which is to-day a more or less unconscious goal. By that time, it will be one of the profoundest facts of our existence. It will make for our greater peace and contentment and yield not only purely physical but aesthetic and spiritual satisfaction.[1]

For the individual consumer, the automobile came to represent not only the technological novelties of the age and physical freedom, but, increasingly, the potential for the realization of a personal fantasy. In the late 1940s and early 1950s, advertisers concentrated on the satisfaction of that individual fantasy. This development was retarded, but not undermined or reversed, by World War II. Late wartime advertising, published in the early months of 1945, concentrated on the contribution of individuals to the war effort, and promised individual reward in the form of new cars. Americans would come home not to a new automotive order in general, but to their own new Buicks. There was a Ford in your (personal) future.

In the mid–1950s, advertisers appealed explicitly to the feelings of the consumer. If earlier copy had centered, by and large, on the satisfaction that would result from ownership of an automobile that was functionally superior to its predecessors, postwar copy frequently bypassed functionalism altogether. It was sufficient that ownership of a new automobile would make the consumer "feel good," and his (or, increasingly, her) feelings need have no rational, practical basis. Personal, sensual gratification was everything, and was achieved by the individual in isolation from other consumers.

Vance Packard, writing on this development in 1957, cited the findings of the Director of Research at the *Chicago Tribune*, Pierre Martineau:

The automobile tells who we are and what we think we want to be.... It is a portable symbol of our personality and our position ... the clearest way we have of telling people of our exact position. [In buying a car], you are saying in a sense, "I am looking for the car that expresses who I am."[2]

It took advertisers a surprisingly long time to realize that individuals differed in their feelings about any given product, and even longer to work out how to appeal with one product to different groups. And if individual self-expression was the consumer's credo, it therefore called for a diversity of products. Packard cited a study of 352 carefully selected car owners in the Chicago area:

> The investigators found that only a minority of the population, mostly men in the lower class, [had] any real interest in the technical aspects of cars.... People who want to seem conservative ... tend to buy Plymouth, Dodge, De Soto, Packard, four-door sedans, dark colors, minimum accessories and gadgets. People who want to seem sociable and up-to-date but in a middle-of-the-road sort of way tend to favor Chevrolet, Pontiac, Buick, Chrysler, two-door coupes, light colors, moderate accessories and gadgets.... People who need to express unusual status or individual needs favor Cadillac (ostentation, high status), Studebaker, Hudson, Nash, Willys, convertibles (impulsiveness), very bright colors, red, yellow, white, latest gadgets and accessories.... One of the interesting variations ... is what investigators call "conspicuous reserve." Those people want other people to know their status but at the same time want to express it modestly. This is a "frequent technique of people who are secure in their high social position. They show their superiority by displaying indifference to status—by purposely buying less expensive cars than they might be expected [to]. They love beat-up station wagons and old cars...."[3]

Thus the automobile buyer increasingly demanded a car that not only appealed to the emotions that he held in common with other Americans, but to his personal scheme of values. And so a fundamental assumption inherent in early, naive forms of consumerism — that every American thought in the same way and desired the same things as his compatriots — was revealed to be a myth. Two consumers with identical amounts of money might wish to buy different cars. To the dispassionate observer, this proposition might seem so blindingly obvious as hardly to represent an insight at all, but it did not appear obvious to automobile advertisers until large numbers of their audience bought imported cars. It was this, belated, realization that, from the advertisers' perspective, represented the point at which the old American automotive dream fragmented forever.

The problem was addressed in the early 1970s by the development of a pseudo-science of market research called psychographics—the categorization of consumers according to their attitudes, lifestyles, and likely emotional responses to advertised products. This innovation was graphically described by William Meyers in 1984:

> One of the most widely used psychographic approaches ... today ... is VALS (Values and Life-Styles), designed by SRI International (formerly known as the Stanford Research Institute), in Northern California. The world according to VALS is simple. There are essentially five basic groups of citizens in this nation — Belongers, Emulators, Emulator-Achievers, Societally Conscious Achievers, and the Need-Directed. Each segment of VALSociety is driven by its own special demons....[4]

Significantly for the automobile industry, a large percentage of one category in particular, the Societally Conscious Achievers, drove themselves in imported small and compact cars. Awareness of this was the demon that drove the domestic industry to conduct more detailed market research than hitherto in order to fight back. The success of a campaign's appeal to this group could determine the fate of a new product.

So have the advertising themes of the 1930–80 period finally been laid to rest, or are there only so many ways to swing an automotive advertising campaign, all tried before, and all destined to re-emerge from time to time for as long as Americans buy automobiles, whether or not of domestic design and manufacture? And how do advertisements of 1930–1980 compare with those of the 1990s and 2000s?

A sample of advertisements for domestically-produced 1993 models reveals that many old themes were far from extinct in the last years of the twentieth century, but that they had been adapted to modern preoccupations. Paranoia about foreign competition was as intense as it was in the 1970s, although the American industry was by then facing that competition on its own ground, rather than by trying to counter "foreign car values" with "American automotive values," except in the most traditional sectors. Chrysler's 1993 advertising for the Concorde typified this development: "You don't have to own a Mercedes, Jaguar, Lexus or BMW to appreciate the new Concorde. But it helps."

Another advertisement for the same car cited an independent endorsement from *AutoWeek* magazine: "... it renders meaningless such adjectives as European, American and Japanese." Old-fashioned traditionalism was renounced in announcement copy for the larger Chrysler New Yorker and LHS, which shared the novel "cab-forward" (short hood, long cabin) layout with the Concorde — a look which contributed towards what *Time* magazine described in November, 1992 as the company's "second amazing comeback."[5] "The Chrysler New Yorker has a huge trunk," said the copy, "But it doesn't come with a lot of Detroit baggage." With the LHS, Chrysler took a swipe at the established competition: "Judging from their products, a lot of people who design luxury cars must think you're an over-the-hill fogey."

Yet the "mature" buyer was courted with the suggestion that, in the excitement that ownership of a Chrysler generated, it would remind him of "the first car you truly ever cared about. What was it? A '49 Merc? A '57 Chevy? '65 Mustang? '68 Corvette? '70 'Hemi' Charger? Whatever it was, it's back."

So was nostalgia, 1953 Nash style, though by 1993 few motorists yearned for Nash's boyhood dream, a Stutz Bearcat.

Down-to-earth, feature-oriented copy dominated 1993 advertising for Chrysler Corporation's mid-market cab-forward sedan, the Dodge Intrepid, and in successive advertisements favorable citations from the motoring papers were arranged around photographs of the car. There were semi-technical diagrams of safety features, as in 1939.

Ford, too, concentrated on features in advertising for the front-wheel-drive Taurus, one of the first of the new generation of streamlined cars: "At Ford, quality, design and safety are at the top of our list." The car was shown in a moody, beach-at-sundown photograph, itself no novelty. Copy for the similar Mercury Sable explicitly reminded buyers who it was that had been first with the new look: "It Forced Other Car Makers Into The Copier Business."

Functionalism made a strong return in areas of the market where American cars competed head-on with imports. General Motors' Geo Prizm, the Toyota-based product of a marque created in co-operation with Japanese manufacturers, and aimed at buyers who might otherwise opt for small Japanese cars imported directly under their own names, was sold on its common-sense features and after-sale warranty.

GM returned to an old theme with the Saturn, its other small car contender, which was advertised to young, value-conscious buyers, and young women in particular. The car was promoted in a series of contented-ordinary-user testimonials from active, extrovert owners, such as "Dorsey-Gay Howser, a solo white-water canoeist" and "Suzanne Stehlik," a property tax analyst who bought a Saturn "because she didn't have enough fun in her life." (Her hobbies were sky-diving, scuba-diving, and skiing.) Saturn's women were described by reference to their occupations, rather than in relation to their husbands, boyfriends, social sets, or families. Above all, they were independent. Plymouth's "Miss C. Eleanor Hinkley" of 1937 would have been proud.

Another advertisement showed "Barry and Cynthia Nelson" who, discouraged by a fruitless search for their ideal car, "dropped into a Saturn showroom" and were bowled over by the Saturn: "I've never been a joiner," said Barry Nelson at the end of the copy, "I'm not into any clubs or anything. But this—you know, I wave at every Saturn that goes by. It feels like we're related or something. And the weird thing is—all I did was buy a car." In real life, early Saturn buyers proved highly enthusiastic about the brand and keen to spread the word. A survey found that more than fifty percent of them would otherwise have bought Japanese cars.

If Geo and Saturn were aimed at specific markets which the Japanese were targeting with ever more sophisticated model ranges, Oldsmobile's 1993 advertising gave the impression that it was aimed at everybody. One single-page advertisement for the compact Achieva sedan carried ten testimonials from the kind of solid citizens favored by Rambler in the 1960s. They ranged from a "homemaker" *via* an aerospace technician, a store manager, and a "retired military" who was "really impressed with the Achieva. It was the first American car I've seen in a long time I'd actually consider buying." Oldsmobile did not say whether he actually bought it. Similar uncertainty was apparent in an advertisement for the 88 Sedan: "Well, maybe there's a way of being traditional that's not so ... um, traditional, if you know what I mean."

But why should the reader bother to work out what the copywriter — or the mythical inarticulate car buyer — means? The difficulty with copy that tried to sound like "real people" was that when it failed it inevitably sounded artificial, yet when it succeeded it so easily made the people sound half-witted, as the rhythms of private conversation collided embarrassingly with the public, impersonal role of an advertisement.

Understated escapism was chosen for the Cutlass Supreme Convertible—"The breeze in my face. The wind in my hair. And I haven't even started the car." The would-be escapist was offered a hint of the old dream in the pay-off line: "And the feeling that you're as much a part of the universe as you are part of the road." No mention was made of the merits of the product itself in any of these pieces, and copywriters were no more unanimous in their preferences for "factual" or "inspirational" copy in the early 1990s than at the beginning of the modern period.

Buick alternated between several well-tried themes, including safety ("Years from now everyone will offer this much side-impact protection") with the Regal Sedan, snobbery ("Leave the sticker on and show everyone how smart you are. Or take it off and let them think you paid thousands more") with the LeSabre, quality ("Buick quality has never been so attractive. Or so affordable") in a Skylark Custom and the promise of easy payment for a luxury model ("If you're convinced money can't buy happiness ... consider leasing it") for the buyer of a Park Avenue. The last, in particular, reflected the new realism that had infiltrated the automotive dream. In 1963, no copywriter would have suggested, even in jest, that money could not buy happiness.

Visual techniques and layouts changed surprisingly little between the mid–1960s and the 1990s. Photography was universal in 1993 as it had been for twenty years or so, and backdrops were familiar. Neutral backgrounds prevailed in advertisements for mid-market automobiles, and realistic, everyday scenes were used for inexpensive cars. Moody, lakeside shots appeared with escapist copy, and to suggest sophistication, just as they had for Ford Thunderbirds over two decades from 1959. Buick showed a Park Avenue sedan in a snow-covered field, beside a lake, its owners dressed in winter clothes, replicating a Nash advertisement of 1940.

Of the themes which survived into the 1990s, the most robust seem to be those which concentrated on the functional virtues of the new car, whether by describing features, gleefully showing up the opposition, or citing ordinary users of the product. The contented ordinary user, in particular, enjoyed a revival, and the anti-rational themes of snobbery and escapism recurred sporadically, tending to decline in times of recession before reasserting themselves when consumers' confidence increased again. Fun seemed to be increasingly confined to the "leisure vehicle" sectors—sports cars, off-road vehicles, and minivans. Recession, in 1993 as in 1933, bred factual copy, which might explain the curiously old-fashioned air of 1993's copy, taken as a whole. It resembled the copy of the mid–1930s more than that of any other era.

When the fantasies and confidence of the 1950s and 1960s reappeared towards the end of the 1990s, they took new forms in a very different market. Several old themes continued into the twenty-first century. A sample of one hundred or so 2005 and 2006 advertisements reveals fewer assertions of basic quality, economy, and reliability than appeared in earlier periods, except from inexpensive comparative newcomers such as Hyundai, whose monochrome photographs of Sonata bodies rotating in a primer bath to demonstrate a "360 [degree] approach to quality" revived the pre-war spirit of J. Stirling Getchell. Safety continued to sell, particularly in cars long noted for it. "At our best when things are at their worst," from Mercedes-Benz, with a picture of a yellow-painted S-Class being crash-tested, conformed to a decades-long tradition.

Hard-pressed domestic marques such as Mercury periodically quoted independent consumer surveys and tests; a typical 2006 advertisement offered "a comprehensive 5-year/60,000-mile extended powertrain coverage and roadside assistance package" to recapture buyers increasingly convinced of Japanese cars' superior build quality. Well-known personalities appeared from time to time, such as the cyclist Lance Armstrong in advertising for the Subaru Outback VDC ("Everything must be engineered to the last detail").

Established visual traditions were maintained, too. Minivans and crossover vehicles, like the station wagons of old, were still seen with proud families in suburban driveways; and restaurants, mock-classical architecture, sports venues, and highways remained popular backdrops. Sports cars, such as the Saturn Sky, appeared on winding roads and in real or simulated motion shots; and twilight remained a favorite time of day. Yet there were few claims to outright beauty. Jaguar's international "Gorgeous" campaign remained conspicuously a one-off.[6]

With the recession of the 1990s long past and the arrival of improved computer-based graphic techniques, a visual and photographic exuberance accompanied copy which was usually much shorter than that of earlier years. Many an advertiser relied on a hard-hitting, self-consciously "witty" headline to capture both the idea in an individual advertisement and the essence of a product's intended appeal. In many cases the only writing apart from the headline was a list of electronics-based features, such as Chrysler's "[v]oice-activated ... Multimedia Infotainment System featuring a 20 gigabyte hard drive for storing digital music files and pictures" in the Sebring sedan, a car with "enough technology to be geeky. Enough style to avoid it."

Long copy could be used, with advantage, to describe advanced technology in cars of a luxury marque such as Acura, which demonstrated various active and passive safety features in a detailed double-page spread in 2006. It could also express a carefully reasoned case in a text-heavy magazine to readers whose preferences, occupations, and world-views were well known to the advertiser. But a disadvantage of long copy in a culturally fragmented new car market was that as many readers might be put off by its style, content, or apparent "weight" as were attracted by it; and there was always the risk of too-obvious banality. What could be said about a feature such as Chrysler's optional "heated/cooled cup holder" that was not adequately stated just by listing it?

In a few cases, however, the advantages of long copy were decisive: "How do you brag about a vehicle with low ego emissions?" asked Volkswagen in magazines such as *Vanity Fair* and *The New Yorker* about a sober and functional Passat standing beside an empty, spotlit podium. "You don't." In its layout, typefaces, long-copy style, and disdain for ostentation, the advertisement continued an honorable Volkswagen tradition and assumed for its humorous effect a familiarity with, and sympathy for, "green" concerns about global warming and the deleterious effects on the climate of non-functional consumption. But other, lighter advertising styles were often deployed for smaller cars of the marque.

Straightforward environmentalism appeared in advertising for individual hybrid cars as well as in corporate copy. Honda's "Environmentology," spelled out in letters made from stalks, leaves, flowers, and other plant matter promoted "the most fuel-efficient auto company in America" and promised that fuel-efficiency could be achieved by advanced technology. A 1974 Honda Civic CVCC appeared behind a modern hybrid: "[T]he CVCC demonstrated our spirited commitment to environmentally responsible technology. Many other firsts were to follow, such as the first hybrid vehicle sold in North America and the first government-certified fuel-cell car." And environmental idealism dovetailed naturally with Honda's international slogan, "The Power of Dreams."

General Motors, by contrast, promoted "FlexFuel Vehicles ... that can run on gasoline or E85 ethanol" in 2006 and invited readers to read a website to learn more about the fuel, "which GM vehicles can run on it, where you can get it and how you can make a difference. One car company can show you how." The headline, "Energy independence? The answer may be in our own backyard," offered the prospect of relief from dependence on Middle East oil, but debate continued among environmentalists about whether enough carbon-neutral crops could really be grown to feed America's populations of both cars and drivers.

Caught on the hop with huge new sport utility vehicles

in a period of rising gas prices and celebrity-endorsed hybrids, the "Detroit Three"— now too small, compared to Toyota, easily to be called the "Big Three"— adapted old escapist themes for a new market. SUVs were shown in macho-metallic shades of silver, grey, and black against rugged backdrops of urban concrete, industrial girders, cliff faces, shorelines, and deserts. Often a grey or beige plastic-and-leather interior was photographed close-up with countryside visible outside the car's windows. "Gives a whole new meaning to 'cabin in the woods,'" announced a headline for the Ford Expedition. "We have brains for rocks," declared another — perhaps riskily in a changing automotive climate—for the smaller Ford Escape. "It's That Big" promised DaimlerChrysler for the Dodge Ram Mega Cab. A standard shot of its grey interior, with ice-covered mountains behind, was made gently humorous by adding brown leather footstools between the front and rear seats.

Hummer's orange backgrounds and steel-grey cars were among the most distinctive: "Arrive fashionably" said one optimistic 2006 caption for the H3, cleverly implying performance with an omitted "late;" while "Nano-Hummer" as another caption appealed to technophiles. The Jeep Commander Overland was shown outside a restaurant, and a double-page spread from Nissan showed its Armada in an expensive-looking residential street at night and a Pathfinder with bicycles on its roof on a desert road. "Choices. Since birth, these identical twins have dressed the same and enjoyed the same activities— until now" said the copy about their owners in a variation of the "two lives in one" theme used by many SUV advertisers around the world.

The most difficult SUVs to advertise were the largest. Domestic copywriters often allied blatant ostentation to unspecified "American values" and hoped for the best, hoping too that gas prices would soon come down again. "Even the windshield washer fluid is hot" said Cadillac of its Escalade, which promised "403 HP, 417 lb–ft of torque. Unsurpassed highway fuel economy in its class [based on EPA estimated 19 mpg and 2006 GM Large Luxury Utility Segment]. 0–60 in 6.5 seconds. 22" chrome wheels available." It was— in a payoff line used for other GM marques as well — "Nicely equipped" at $60,485. Cadillac's slogan, "Life. Liberty. And the Pursuit," was not one for any reader unsure about what made him happy. The cheaper ($45,940) Cadillac SRX Crossover appealed to a wider audience: "It doesn't scream soccer Mom. It just screams."

The 2007 Chrysler Aspen, meanwhile, offered "a lot more bling for your buck," and the Infiniti FX45 appealed to the determined extrovert: "Don't just make the statement; scream it .... Move it. They look up. Not at you. But to you. If not you, then who? Being that brave, being that bold, takes something. It's the recognition of your own greatness. Your own power. And once you see it, all that is left to be done, is unleash it...." Lincoln's self-absorption was less frenzied for the 2007 Navigator, Mk X, and Mk Z: "Once, there was no road where I wanted to go. So I made my own. And I haven't looked back ever since. My dream is to carve my own path. I was never one to follow maps. Lincoln. Reach Higher.... Life's calling. Where to next?"

The copywriter-as-therapist could be either booster, as for Lincoln, or consoler, as in an appeal to the mainly female audience for the convertible Volkswagen Beetle. A dozen new Beetles in red, green, and blue were seen from above in plastic bubbles on a silver card: "Proven effective against negativity" said the only copy line. "Dare to be happy." This was a striking example of a growing trend — the arresting analogy or unexpected juxtaposition, in which the car was seen in terms of, or took the place of, something unconnected with automobiles or motoring.

Examples were legion. In 2006, Volkswagen showed its Rabbit RTS, or "Rabbit Transit System," at the top of a map set in a steel frame against white tiles, subway style. The aerial city view was overprinted with a green route and destinations such as "Leather Emporium" and "Hair and Makeup Supply Shop." The starting point was a bohemian loft, the destination a heavy-metal karaoke. Saab announced a "Jet Set Sweepstakes" competition with replica airline tickets attached to a conventional advertisement headlined, "Join the Jet Set." Toyota challenged *Fader* readers to "Scratch off and find two of the same" on a small card page containing multiple stratchcard images of its Scion hatchback. The reverse side showed a hand-decorated car with the caption, "Create one of a kind." Jeep depicted a 2007 Wrangler mounted in a wooden frame as "Unparallelicus [o]ffroadicus. A new species from Jeep." Characteristics such as "Increased horsepower and torque plus tougher axles" were described on printed cards pinned below the specimen.

Music became popular in appeals to younger car buyers. Pontiac showed rubber tire marks on grey asphalt, quavers and semiquavers neatly chalked between the treads in each black line: "The first 5,000 Pontiac G5's come with the digital mix: A year of XM Satellite Radio, plus an MP3 music download a day for one year." Nissan mixed musical and computing motifs with "The Next Nissan Maxima ... Fine-tuned instrument_2.0," seen in a velvet-lined instrument case. Photographs on the facing page showed a jazz singer, saxophone and bass players, and a percussionist. Hip-hop featured with vigorous khaki-toned graphics and an artist in full cry in copy for "the all-new Jeep Wrangler Unlimited ... the original certified vehicle of hip-hop.... The culture grew. So did we."

Other appeals to young car-buyers included Honda's brightly colored, cartoonish "Super Tail Action!... Move over mullet! You are no longer the undisputed king of stylish tail technology!" for the Honda Fit Sport. Virtual reality-style images depicted the 2007 Jeep Compass against a suburbia-and-skyscraper backdrop as figures with speech-bubbles such as "Side-curtain airbags!" and "All-new design!" capered around the car. "Keep it moving!" admonished a camp figurine in the foreground. As with Plymouth in 1948, there was a floppy-eared cartoon dog at the foot of the page. Advertisers targeted participants in diverse social and leisure cultures by using tailor-made styles of copy and illustration in magazines about music, sport, film, computer games, cartoons, and other interests and activities. The overall result was an increase both in the number of individual advertisements published, and in the range of advertising styles deployed at any one time.

Appeals to specifically female motorists were more subtle than in the early postwar years, but they still formed a distinct school of copywriting. References to shoes, coffee, handbags, and relationships, individually or in combination, were commonplace, as from Kia: "Attractive, dependable, good with money. If it made coffee you'd marry it.... You've just found The One. Sportage is strong and steady...." Mercury's young couple on a desert trip in a Mariner SUV "encountered their first bump.... Now Karen and Jack were at a crossroads. East or West? 'Monster Metal Hits' or 'Books on CD'?" A Mercury Milan driver almost missed a sign, "Designer Handbag Outlet This Exit," but — in an adaptation of greetings-card humor — jammed on the brakes just in time: "3:12 P.M. Exit 24. Nicole realizes she doesn't have as much control as her all-wheel drive."

More conventionally, Jaguar showed a fashion model with a "Selected Edition Pre-Owned Jaguar X-TYPE.... Jeannel got into her X-TYPE for under $22,000. It's all red carpet and velvet ropes from here. Can you resist separating yourself from the masses?" For *In Style*, a couch-bound model with a "keep our secret" finger to her lips dangled the keys of a Buick LaCrosse sedan parked behind her. Consecutive right-hand pages in *Marie Claire* showed a "Designed for action" Pontiac G6 Coupe ("Must have fun"), a Solstice sports car ("Must have sex appeal"), and a muscular Torrent ("Must have style"), each spotlit in black against a black-painted stage. "Let the sun worship you" enjoined the same company for a G6 sedan with an opening four-panel Panoramic Roof.

Typefaces were generally soft; copy concentrated on narrative rather than lists of electronic gadgets; backdrops were often in pale cream or light mauve; floors were usually tiled rather than concrete to suggest loft spaces; and grass was mown rather than wild. For the Toyota Corolla S, twenty-four pictures showed all the things that the driver could do in a day; venues included a bookstore, a cuddly animal shop, a café, and the inevitable beach at sundown. The driver was a girl-next-door; her boyfriend slightly idealized, but plausible: "Randomize your playlist" said the caption. Parenthood featured in Toyota's advertising, too, as when Toyota targeted a Highlander Sport, seen beside a lake, at mothers of teenagers: "Best thing to do when your kids leave home: Do the same." In another piece a hulking freshman stood beside a pile of bags and boxes, his computer keyboard, skateboard, and giant electric fan in hand: "5:15 P.M. Dropping the kid off at college. 5:17 P.M. What kid?"

Copy lines built around greetings-card or water-cooler humor appeared with both gender-specific and gender-neutral advertising. "From intern to mogul in 6.1 seconds," for a black Mercedes-Benz C 350 Sport Sedan set against a black background, played wittily to aspirant office workers with numbers signifying age and acceleration. If a late 2006 advertisement for the Dodge Caliber, "Respect the unexpected," made its orientation explicit by featuring "Lisa Bryant, 26 ... Newly Calibrated surfer girl," earlier advertising for the car appealed to anyone who fancied themselves mildly rebellious. The Caliber, "anything but cute," waited outside a door marked "Principal." The theme ran outside America, too. In Britain the same door was marked "Headmaster;" and in another British piece the Caliber's rump was balanced perkily on the edge of a flashing photocopier. In a parallel Russian advertisement, the rear of a bright red Caliber was lovingly decorated in a tattoo parlor.

Automotive advertising had become selectively international, and the new internationalism was multi-faceted. In the 1960s, most American car advertising was for American cars while copy from importers was almost always devised specifically for the American market. By the 2000s, however, many cars of "imported" marques were designed, or adapted for, or built in the United States. Only with a few cars, such as the largest SUVs, did advertisers generally set "American car values" directly against "import values." Export-oriented American manufacturers, such as the Dodge and Chrysler arms of DaimlerChrysler, bolstered their brands globally by employing the same styles of advertising in both domestic American and export markets. The same applied in reverse to specialist importers: Porsche's American advertising, for example, looked just like its advertising for other markets.

As advertising styles for non-specialist indigenous and foreign brands converged, however, direct competition between domestic and non-domestic marques, and between individual models, became more common. This did not always benefit the home team. According to industry analyst John Wolkonowicz of Global Insight, "Detroit spent 25 years copying the Camry and emasculating the American car.... Now they need to bring back real American cars for real American people, the folks who watch NASCAR and shop at Wal-Mart."[7]

So the question remains: How can a new domestic car be distinctly American and yet — without being huge or gas-guzzling or otherwise retrogressive — be competitive with, distinct from, and superior to its Japanese or Korean (or Chinese or Indian) rivals? Will America lead the world in inexpensive cars for the post-gasoline era as it did with conventional cars in the 1930s? If it can, will American manufacturers' intellectual property in their designs be safeguarded internationally for long enough to allow the domestic industry to recover? And how will advertisers persuade Americans to adopt such new cars?

It will be fascinating to find out. One thing seems certain, however: American automobile advertising will never be uniform, though it may, in recession or in times of increasing environmental consciousness, be subdued.

Perhaps the last word should go to Edward S. Jordan, creator of the most famous of all American automobile advertisements. Asked by *Forbes* magazine in 1926 to predict the course of the American automobile industry, he was optimistic: "Roughly speaking, it is safe to say that the saturation point for the automobile will never be reached until everyone has a car and none of them wears out.... In any business where there enters a style element, there need be no fear of monopoly. Just so long as women continually change their style of head dress and the length of their skirts, there is going to be a chance for every dressmaker. So it is with the car."[8]

Collector's Note

Magazine originals of pre–1980 American car advertisements are no longer as easy to find as they once were, but interesting material, particularly from the postwar period, continues to be discovered by collectors and enthusiasts. Finding a specific pre-war ad may take time, but it is surprising what still turns up, even in the 21st century.

There are two ways to build up a collection. The first is to buy either magazine originals or modern copies of magazine ads from the companies and individuals who advertise on the Internet or in the specialist press. A search under "historic car ads" or "vintage car ads" or similar words should yield several sources. These companies provide a valuable service by making available material which would otherwise remain out of reach. The alternative, which entails persistence, but which is arguably more satisfying and can be less expensive, is to check out every second-hand bookstore, junk stall, flea market, and charity sale in your area and to do so regularly. Most of the illustrations in this book are chosen from a collection of nearly 1,000 ads from the *National Geographic* (each ten inches deep by seven inches wide) which were gathered in this way between 1980 and 1995. If there is a large elderly population in your district who throw out piles of long-accumulated magazines from time to time, so much the better.

A question inevitably asked by collectors is: "How much should I pay for an ad?" There is only one answer: however much you want to. The prices asked by traders for individual ads, and by bookstores for complete magazines, can vary by a factor of ten or more. Many enthusiasts seek out ads for their favorite marques, and the collector who has found the ad needed to complete a set — say, the 1940 Lincoln-Zephyr ad which will complete a run of Lincoln V-12s from 1936 to 1948 — might well be happy to pay a high price for it. Generally speaking, attractive ads for popular cars will fetch more than unattractive pieces for unappealing automobiles, with the result that visually unremarkable but historically interesting black and white (monochrome) ads can be hard to find from specialists as there is little demand for them. Many specialists, however, will be happy to look out for such pieces for regular customers.

The serious collector will avoid color photocopies, except for reference or wall decoration, for which they are ideal. The reproduction, whether in color or in black and white, will not be as good as the original, and the "feel" of the original is lost. Similarly, avoid color copies billed as reproducing the "patina of age" of the original, unless faithfully reproduced coffee and mildew stains, *circa* 1955, have a special appeal.

Many professional traders offer framed ads. Find out whether the ad beneath the glass is an original or color copy, and do not pay over the odds for a cheap frame that you do not want, and will eventually throw away. Find out before buying whether the ad can be lifted out of the frame or whether it has been glued onto the board behind. Where this has happened the ad will not be easy to file and might be discolored by the glue over time. A collector will usually consider such an ad as damaged rather than enhanced by the frame. Some sellers, who frame their ads simply to appeal to casual buyers, will be willing to sell unframed ads at a reduced rate, particularly if you are buying several at a time.

Care should be taken if buying by mail order. You will not usually be able to see the ads you need before ordering in order to gauge their state of preservation, although the thumbnail pictures provided by Internet sellers are undoubtedly helpful in identifying the ads being sold. Be sure to check the model year of the car shown as well as the calendar year in which the ad was published. For example, when ordering, say, a "1948 Ford ad," find out whether the ad is for a 1948 (January–June) or 1949 (June–December) model. Remember, too, that some monthly magazines were dated to the

An advertiser's original will often contain information about where the advertisement was placed, and in many cases newspaper and magazine titles will be listed individually. This Lincoln-Zephyr piece was scheduled to appear "in rotogravure and black-and-white newspapers throughout the country during the weeks of December 12 and 19, 1937."

month following actual publication, so that a late ad for one model year could appear in a magazine dated to the first month of the new model year. Occasionally an inexpert seller might mistake one car for another, and send, say, a De Soto Airflow when you wanted a Chrysler, or even send a different car entirely. It is perhaps asking a lot of a general "nostalgia" dealer to expect them to know every subject in detail, and most are willing to exchange wrong orders quickly (as they should!). Some are experts, and funds of useful knowledge.

The purist might want to ignore completely ads taken from magazines, and to concentrate instead on "advertisers' originals" of ads supplied by automobile manufacturers and their agents to magazines and newspapers for reproduction in those media. These pieces are usually printed in a large size on good, often glossy, paper. They are necessarily of better original quality than the reproductions printed in magazines — though the margin might not be great — but such material is extremely scarce, is not always carefully stored (a magazine ad is protected by the pages that surround it), and may be creased where it has been folded over the years.

The advantage of an advertiser's original to the academic researcher is that, in many cases, a list of the publications in which it appeared is given at the top or bottom, or on the reverse side. Advertisers' originals were often pasted into agencies' guard-books as records of their work for automotive clients, and guard-books which have survived in car makers' or agencies' archives, or in museums or research organizations, can sometimes be made available for viewing by serious researchers. This may be the only opportunity for a marque enthusiast to see most or all of the ads in a series, and to discover which magazines and newspapers carried them when new.

Original magazine ads should be stored in a dry, stable environment, ideally in display files with plastic leaves which allow easy reference while preserving them from direct handling, moisture and, importantly, sunlight. Label each ad on its reverse side with a soft pencil, noting its date and source if known. Never frame and display either advertisers' originals or magazine ads, as even short-term exposure to sunlight — and ultraviolet light in particular — will cause fading and damage them irreparably. Display color copies instead.

Automobile advertisements have arrived late to the collector's market, but in recent years interest in the subject has increased, and continues to grow. It follows from this that even modern ads, now thrown away, will one day be rare and sought after by collectors and researchers. Car ads cut from newspapers and magazines today will be interesting to a whole new generation of enthusiasts and historians in decades to come. Only a real optimist, however, would collect ads as an investment; add up the cost of purchase, storage files and the fuel used to drive to second-hand bookstores and flea markets, and the money might more wisely be put in a bank. But where would be the fun in that?

The holy grail for many collectors is a piece of original advertising artwork or a photograph, painted or taken in period and used as the basis of an advertisement. In some cases — as, famously, with Arthur Fitzpatrick and Van Kaufman — one artist painted the cars while another painted their backgrounds. A few automotive advertising artists and photographers were, or have become, widely known, while others are little known today. Discreet signatures are sometimes visible on paintings in magazine advertisements. Dedicated collectors have worked hard to track down surviving artwork, and there have been inspiring exhibitions in recent years, as by the Detroit photographer and rescuer of much surviving work, Jim Secreto, at the Detroit Library in 2005; and by the Museum of Fine Arts in Boston, also in 2005. Photographs by numerous artists, including Mickey McGuire and Jimmy Northmore of Boulevard Photographic, and contemporaries such as Warren O. Winstanley and Walter Farynk, were exhibited at the Detroit Institute of Arts during 1996.[1] At the time of writing there is not yet an established market for such work and pieces still occasionally materialize for sale on the Internet, at autojumbles, and elsewhere. A "wanted" ad placed in car enthusiasts' and relevant professional publications might well yield unexpected results.

Notes

Part One

1. "Bauhaus-pastiche" describes a visual style in automobile advertising characterized by the use of artistic and graphic motifs derived from the Bauhaus movement which originated in Weimar Germany in 1919. A first-hand account of Chrysler's campaign in Britain is given in *Advertising and the Motor-car* by Ashley Havinden and Michael Frostick (London: Lund Humphries, 1970).

2. G.H. Saxon ["Bingy"] Mills. *There is a Tide..: The life and work of Sir William Crawford, K.B.E.*, p. 82 (London: Heinemann, 1954).

3. Harold Haliday Costain in F.A. Mercer and W. Gaunt (eds.). *Modern Publicity: An Annual of Art and Industry 1935-36*, p. 20 (London: Studio, 1935).

4. Ibid., p. 20.

5. F.A. Mercer and W. Gaunt (eds.). *Modern Publicity: An Annual of Art and Industry 1934-35*, p. 12 (London: Studio, 1934). For a selection of approximately thirty representative advertisements from the 1932 model year, see John A. Conde. "In the Face of Adversity: The Cars of 1932." *Collectible Automobile*, October, 1996, pp. 8–25.

6. I.e. copy which cites the demonstrable virtues of the product or appeals to the reader's understanding of the principles of automobile design, rather than appealing overtly to his or her emotions.

7. I.e. those manufacturers who were independent of the "Big Three," which were Chrysler Corporation (Plymouth, Dodge, De Soto, Chrysler, Chrysler Imperial, Imperial), General Motors Corporation (Chevrolet, Pontiac, Oldsmobile, Buick, LaSalle, Cadillac), and the Ford Motor Company (Ford, Mercury, Edsel, Lincoln, Lincoln Continental, Continental). The principal independents operating during the 1930–1980 period were, in alphabetical order, AMC (as Rambler from 1958–65), Checker, Crosley, Graham (as Graham-Paige to 1930), Hudson (to 1957), Hupmobile, Kaiser-Frazer, Nash (to 1957), Packard, Reo, Studebaker, and Willys. The histories of these and other companies, including minor marques connected with the Big Three, may be found in John Rae. *American Automobile Manufacturers* (Philadelphia: Chilton Company, 1959); and Consumer Guide (eds.). *The Encyclopedia of American Cars* (Lincolnwood, Illinois: Publications International Ltd., 2003).

8. For these industrial relations difficulties generally, see A. Nevins and F.E. Hill. *Ford: Decline and Rebirth, 1933–1962*, pp. 302–307, 334–338 (New York: Charles Scribner's Sons, 1963).

9. For two versions of this photograph, see the advertisement in the *National Geographic* for April, 1963; and David L. Lewis and Bill Rauhauser. *The Car and the Camera: The Detroit School of Automotive Photography*, p. 48 (Detroit: Institute of Arts/Wayne State University Press, 1996).

10. Rauhauser in ibid., p. 11.

11. Rauhauser in ibid., p. 19.

12. For the story of the two artists' association with General Motors (1953–73) and Pontiac Division (1959–71), see Vince Manocchi. "Arthur Fitzpatrick: Illustrious Illustrator." *Collectible Automobile*, April, 2004, pp. 68–79.

13. For a selection of muscle-car advertisements of this period, see M.J. Frumkin. *Classic Muscle Car Advertising: The Art of Selling Horsepower* (Iola, Wisconsin: Krause Publications, 2002).

14. Herbert Read. *Art and Industry: The Principles of Industrial Design*, p. 2 (London: Faber & Faber, 1934).

15. Richard Guy Wilson. "The Industrialist as Artist — The machine-age in America 1910–1945," in Angela Schönberger (ed.). *Raymond Loewy: Pioneer of Industrial Design*, p. 67 (London: Prestel Books, 1990).

16. The Times Motoring Correspondent. "8-Cylinder Airflow Chrysler," in *Cars of Today 1935: 65 Complete Reviews*, pp. 17–18 (London: Times Pub. Co., 1935). For the story of the Airflow see, for example, Karl S. Zahm. "1934–37 Chrysler/De Soto Airflow: Future Shock." *Collectible Automobile*, January, 1989, pp. 12–27.

17. Alfred P. Sloan. *My Years with General Motors* (2nd ed.), p. 266 (London: Penguin, 1986).

18. Ibid., p. 268.

19. Ibid., p. 273. For the story of Harley Earl's life and work for General Motors, see Paul Zazarine. "Harley Earl: 'Da Vinci of Detroit.'" *Collectible Automobile*, December, 2005, pp. 66–75 and February, 2006, pp. 72–82.

20. Alfred P. Sloan. *My Years with General Motors* (2nd ed.), p. 278 (London: Penguin, 1986). For a full account of the Edsel débâcle, see Robert Daines. *Edsel — The Motor Industry's Titanic* (London: Academy Books, 1994); and Thomas E. Bonsall. *Disaster in Dearborn: The Story of the Edsel* (Stanford, CA: Stanford University Press, 2002).

21. Raymond Loewy. *Never Leave Well Enough Alone* (2nd ed.), p. 307 (Baltimore: Johns Hopkins University Press, [1951] 2002).

22. Raymond Loewy. *Industrial Design* (2nd ed.), p. 148 (London: Fourth Estate, [1979] 1988).

23. Bruno Sacco. "The Studebaker Connection," in Angela Schönberger (ed.). *Raymond Loewy: Pioneer of American Industrial Design*, p. 123 (London: Prestel Books, 1990).

24. Tony Hossain. "Studebaker/Loewy Designers Come Home," in *The Best of Old Cars Weekly*, Vol. 4, p. 179 (Iola, Wisconsin: Krause Publications, 1982).

25. Cited in Joseph J. Seldin. *The Golden Fleece: Selling the Good Life to Americans*, p. 102 (New York: Macmillan, 1963).

26. "Planned obsolescence" was not at first meant derogatively. Brooks Stevens, the industrial designer who devised the phrase — though not the essential concept — in the early 1950s, recalled in a 1991 interview with Mike McCarthy of the British magazine, *Classic and Sportscar*: "I was asked to talk to the Advertising Club of Minneapolis [in 1954], and was looking for a

title. I eventually came up with the phrase 'Planned Obsolescence,' meaning the desire to own something a little newer, a little better, a little sooner than is necessary. It did *not* mean organized waste.... The average American earns enough not to have to run a refrigerator or car until the thing just stops.... Ironically, I designed the longest [running] concept [of] car ever apart from the Beetle — the Jeep station wagon, which went on year after year, and eventually became the Wagoneer and Cherokee. For 29 years we used the same set of tools, patching them and fixing them and making them over, but *using* them." Mike McCarthy. "Design Intervention." *Classic and Sportscar*, December, 1991, pp. 52–58. See also Glenn Adamson. *Industrial Strength Design: How Brooks Stevens Shaped Your World*, pp. 129–134 (Cambridge, MA: Milwaukee Art Museum/MIT Press, 2003). For Brooks Stevens' automotive designs, see Richard M. Langworth. "Brooks Stevens: The Seer that Made Milwaukee Famous." *Collectible Automobile*, June, 2005, pp. 68–77.

27. Cited in Joseph J. Seldin. *The Golden Fleece: Selling the Good Life to Americans*, p. 101 (New York: Macmillan, 1963).

28. Alfred P. Sloan. *My Years with General Motors* (2nd ed.), p. 265 (London: Penguin, 1986).

29. Vance Packard. *The Waste Makers* (2nd ed.), p. 100 (London: Longmans, [1960] 1961).

30. Michael Frostick and Ashley Havinden. *Advertising and the Motor-car*, pp. 20–22 (London: Lund Humphries, 1970). For Ashley Havinden's life and work, see Michael Havinden et al. *Advertising and the Artist: Ashley Havinden* (Edinburgh: National Galleries of Scotland, 2004).

31. Mark Haworth-Booth. *E McKnight Kauffer: A Designer and His Public* (2nd ed.), pp. 48, 52 (London: V&A Publications: 2005).

32. For the history from 1919–1990 of Britain's leading importer of General Motors cars (and of American cars) see Geoff Carverhill. "The Lendrum & Hartman Story [Parts I–III]." *Classic American,* June, 2006, pp. 60–62; July 2006, pp. 73–76; and August, 2006, pp. 68–69. See also Bryan Goodman. *American Cars in Prewar England: A Pictorial Survey* (Jefferson, NC: McFarland, 2004).

33. *The Motor Industry of Great Britain* [annual], 1955 ed., p. 270; 1956 ed., p. 260. (London: Society of Motor Manufacturers and Traders Ltd., 1955 and 1956).

34. For the history of American semi-automatic and automatic transmissions, see Byron Olsen. "Shifty Business: Detroit's Drive to Automatic Transmissions, 1930–55." *Collectible Automobile*, December, 2004, pp. 24–35. For an expanded version of this article, see Byron Olsen. "The Shift to Shiftless: Transmission Advances in U.S. Cars (1929–55)." *Automotive History Review*, Fall 2006, pp. 25–41.

35. Wernher von Braun in Cornelius Ryan (ed.). *Across the Space Frontier*, p. 12 (London: Sidgwick & Jackson, 1952).

36. For Mustangs and other American cars photographed in London during the 1960s, see Steve Miles. *Over Here: The American Car in England in the 1960s* (Northamptonshire: SGM Publishing, 2004).

Part Two

1. For the story of Jordan advertising and for reproductions in color and black and white of many Jordan advertisements, see James H. Lackey. *The Jordan Automobile*, pp. C1–C15 and 123–132 (Jefferson, NC: McFarland, 2005). See also "Ned Jordan: The Man Who Changed Auto Advertising," in *The Best of Old Cars*, Vol. 5, p. 79 (Iola, WI: Krause Publications Inc., 1981). For an interview with Ned Jordan, see B.C. Forbes and O.D. Foster. *Automotive Giants of America*, pp. 155–168 (New York: B.C. Forbes Publishing, 1926).

2. Alfred P. Sloan. *My Years with General Motors* (2nd ed.), p. 278 (London: Penguin, 1986).

3. The Hon. Maynard Greville in *Country Life*, April 22, 1939, pp. xxxvi–xxxviii.

4. See F.A. Mercer and W. Gaunt (eds.). *Modern Publicity: An Annual of Art and Industry 1936-37*, p. 82 (London: Studio, 1936).

5. Eoin Young in *Autocar*, May 4, 1967, p. 91.

6. See F.A. Mercer and W. Gaunt (eds.). *Modern Publicity: An Annual of Art and Industry 1938-39*, p. 29 (London: Studio, 1938). For a discussion of Packard's advertising of this period, and of the damage inflicted on a high-priced line by using its prestige to sell a lower-priced line, see James A. Ward. *The Fall of the Packard Motor Car Company*, pp. 32–33 (Stanford, CA: Stanford University Press, 1995).

7. Stephen Fox. *The Mirror Makers* (2nd ed.), p. 165 (William Heinemann, London, 1990).

8. Ibid., p. 166.

9. By contrast, Ford's television campaign for the Edsel of 1957-58 failed, despite the use of several celebrities and showbusiness stars.

10. My thanks to Taylor Vinson for a large selection of MG advertisements from this period. For a detailed account of American advertising for the MGB in the 1960s and 1970s under Reach, McClinton & Co., and from 1970 under Bozell & Jacobs with the same advertising team, see David Knowles. *MGB, MGC & MGB GT V8: A celebration of Britain's best-loved sports car*, pp. 44–46 (Yeovil: Haynes, 2004). In the present book the "MG" name is written without stops, as has been usual since the 1960s, except where the earlier form appears within a quotation.

Part Three

1. Alfred P. Sloan. *My Years with General Motors* (2nd ed.), p. 104 (London: Penguin, 1986).

2. Henry Ford. *My Life and Work*, p. 54 (London: William Heinemann Ltd., 1923).

3. A. Nevins and F.E. Hill. *Ford: Expansion and Challenge 1915–1932*, pp. 594–595 (New York: Charles Scribner's Sons, 1957).

4. Ralph M. Hower. *The History of an Advertising Agency: N.W. Ayer & Son at Work 1869–1949*, p. 142 (Cambridge, MA: Harvard University Press, 1949).

5. From F.A. Mercer and W. Gaunt (eds.). *Modern Publicity: An Annual of Art and Industry 1938-39*, p. 30 (London: Studio, 1938). Real farmers gave testimonials in Studebaker advertising in *Country Gentleman* and the *Farm Journal* during 1947.

6. A vivid account of American motoring conditions during the period up to 1939 is given in Maurice Olley's paper, *National Influences on American Passenger Car Design*, read before the Institution of Automobile Engineers in London in February, 1938. The paper is reproduced in the *Proceedings* of the Institution, Vol. XXXII, for the Session 1937/38, at p. 509.

7. Thomas D. Murray. "The Strange Beginning of the Chevy Caprice." *Classic American*, August/September 1991.

8. Ralph Nader. *Unsafe at Any Speed: The Designed-in Dangers of the American Automobile* (2nd ed.), pp. 36–43 (New York: Bantam Books, [1972] 1973).

9. Ibid., p. 192. For safety provision in early American cars, see Tim Howley. "Trial and Error: An Early History of Auto Safety in America." *Collectible Automobile*, February 2007, pp. 64–73.

10. Ralph Nader. *Unsafe at Any Speed: The Designed-in Dangers of the American Automobile* (2nd ed.), p. xi (New York: Bantam Books, [1972] 1973).

11. Ibid., p. xii.

12. Lee Iacocca: *Iacocca: An Autobiography* (with William Novak), p. 39 (New York: Bantam Books, 1984).

13. A detailed account of the Cadet's development is given in Consumer Guide (eds.). *Cars that Never Were*, p. 10 (New York: Beekman House, 1981).

14. As exemplified in tests such as those carried out by *Motor Life* in November, 1954 (Zephyr convertible) and November, 1955 (Zodiac sedan). For these and other tests, see R.M. Clarke (ed.). *Ford Consul, Zephyr, Zodiac Mk I & II 1950–1962* (Cobham: Brooklands Books, 1991).

15. Production figures from Consumer Guide (eds.). *Encyclopedia of American Cars*, pp. 13, 557 (Lincolnwood, IL: Publications International Ltd., 2002).

16. Ralph Nader. *Unsafe at Any Speed: The Designed-in Dangers of the American Automobile* (2nd ed.), pp. 2–3 (New York: Bantam Books, [1972] 1973).

17. Vance Packard. *The Hidden Persuaders* (2nd ed.), p. 228 (London: Penguin, [1981] 1991).

18. Production and export figures from *The Motor Industry of Great Britain* [annual], 1954 ed., pp. 23, 216; 1956 ed., pp. 23, 255 (London: Society of Motor Manufacturers and Traders Ltd., 1954 and 1956).

19. Alan Hess. *Wheels Round the World*, p. 70 (London: Newman Neame, 1951).

20. From figures in Jon Pressnell. *Morris Minor: Exploring the Legend*, pp. 97–100 (Yeovil: Haynes, 1998).

21. Maurice Platt. *An Addiction to Automobiles*, pp. 151–152 (London: Warne, 1980).

22. Cited in Tony Freeman. *Humber: An Illustrated History 1868–1976*, p. 51 (London: Academy Books, 1991).

23. Walter Henry Nelson. *Small Wonder: The Amazing Story of the Volkswagen* (2nd ed.), pp. 233–234 (London: Hutchinson, 1970).

24. Ibid., p. 230.
25. Ibid., pp. 237–238.
26. Ibid., p. 239.
27. Ibid., p. 251.
28. Maurice Platt. *An Addiction to Automobiles*, pp. 169–170 (London: Warne, 1980).
29. Booton Herndon. *Ford — An Unconventional Biography of the Men and Their Times*, p. 236 (New York: Weybright & Tulley, 1969).
30. See Tim Howley. "Into the Unknown: Imported Cars in Fifties America." *Collectible Automobile*, December, 2006, pp. 58–69.
31. David Ogilvy. *Confessions of an Advertising Man*, p. 111 (London: Longmans, Green, [1963] 1964).
32. Ibid., p. 107.
33. Stephen Fox. *The Mirror Makers* (2nd ed.), p. 237 (London: Heinemann, 1990). For Ford's "quieter than a Rolls-Royce" campaign of 1965, see Chapter 13, pp. 179–180; and Tim Howley. "1965-66 Ford: Quieter than a Rolls-Royce." *Collectible Automobile*, April 1994, pp. 44–57.
34. David Ogilvy. *Confessions of an Advertising Man*, p. 109 (London: Longmans, Green, [1963] 1964). See also David Ogilvy. *Ogilvy on Advertising*, p. 216 (London: Orbis, 1983).
35. This advertisement was published in the *Saturday Evening Post* of January 2, 1915. For its genesis, see Stephen Fox. *The Mirror Makers* (2nd ed.), pp. 71–72 (London: Heinemann, 1990). The ad is reproduced in Jane and Michael Stern. *Auto Ads*, p. 17 (New York: Random House, 1978).
36. David Ogilvy. *Confessions of an Advertising Man*, pp. 111–112 (Longmans, Green, London, [1963] 1964).
37. For an account of Ogilvy's life and best-known campaigns, see Stephen Fox, *The Mirror Makers*, pp. 225–239. Examples of Rolls-Royce advertising of this period are shown in ibid., p. 247; and in David Ogilvy. *Ogilvy on Advertising*, pp. 10, 59.
38. David Ogilvy. *The Unpublished David Ogilvy*, pp. 164–165 (London: Sidgwick & Jackson, 1988).
39. David Ogilvy. *Ogilvy on Advertising*, p. 11 (London: Orbis, 1983).
40. See Joseph J. Seldin. *The Golden Fleece: Selling the Good Life to Americans*, p. 97 (New York: Macmillan, 1963).

Overview and Conclusion

1. Norman Bel Geddes. *Horizons*, p. 293 (London: John Lane, The Bodley Head, 1934).
2. Vance Packard. *The Hidden Persuaders* (2nd ed.), p. 50 (London: Penguin, [1981] 1991).
3. Ibid., pp. 50–51.
4. William Meyers. *The Image Makers*, p. 15 (London: Orbis, 1984).
5. William McWhirter. "Chrysler's Second Amazing Comeback." *Time*, November 9, 1992.
6. This campaign certainly — if perhaps inadvertently — followed the spirit of the Jaguar XK's conception. According to its designer, the Scottish engineer Ian Callum, "[A] Jaguar should be sensuous and voluptuous, very sculptured and when I was thinking about it [the actress] Kate Winslet came to mind.... She is naturally a very shapely woman, very British with an underlying integrity and ability. Like a car, she has got substance, she is not just a pretty face. So I designed the new XK body with her in mind. The interesting thing is that so many women find sensual cars more appealing as well." John Harlow and Flora Bagenal. "It's the Jaguar XK Winslet," *The Sunday Times*, November 26, 2006, p. 3 (interview with Ian Callum).
7. See Keith Naughton. "Putting Detroit in the Shop." *Newsweek*, November 6, 2006, pp. 44–46.
8. B.C. Forbes and O.D. Foster. *Automotive Giants of America*, pp. 165–168 (New York: B.C. Forbes Publishing Co., 1926).

Collector's Note

1. See Liz Turner. "Snapper focuses on advertising art." *Classic & Sports Car*, October 2005, pp. 60–61; Frederic A. Sharf. *Future Retro: Drawings from the Great Age of American Automobiles* (Boston: Museum of Fine Arts, 2005); and David L. Lewis and Bill Rauhauser. *The Car and the Camera: The Detroit School of Automotive Photography* (Detroit: Detroit Institute of Arts/Wayne State University Press, 1996).

Bibliography

Books

Abbott, D., and A. Marcantonio. *Remember Those Great Volkswagen Ads?* (2nd ed.), London: Booth-Clibborn Editions, 1993.

Ackerson, Robert C. *Cadillac: America's Luxury Car.* Pasadena: Tab Books, 1988.

Adamson, Glenn. *Industrial Strength Design: How Brooks Stevens Shaped Your World.* Cambridge: Massachusetts: Milwaukee Art Museum/MIT Press, 2003.

Arbesino, A., and G. Bulgari. *Cinquanta Anni de Immagini della Piu Importanti Industria Italiana.* Italy: Edizioni di Autocritica, 1984.

Armi, C. Edson. *American Car Design Now: Inside the Studios of Today's Top Car Designers.* New York: Rizzoli, 2003.

_____. *The Art of American Car Design: The Profession and Personalities.* University Park: Pennsylvania State University Press, 1988.

Aynsley, Jeremy. *Graphic Design in Germany 1890–1945.* London: Thames & Hudson, 2000.

Bayley, Stephen. *Harley Earl and the Dream Machine.* London: Weidenfeld & Nicolson, 1983.

Becker, Lutz, and Richard Hollis. *Avant-Garde Graphics 1918–1934.* London: Hayward Gallery, 2004.

Bel Geddes, Norman. *Horizons.* London: John Lane, The Bodley Head, 1934.

Bolster, John. *The Upper Crust.* London: Weidenfeld & Nicolson, 1976.

Bonsall, Thomas E. *Disaster in Dearborn: The Story of the Edsel.* Stanford, California: Stanford General Books, 2002.

Boyne, Walter J. *Power Behind the Wheel: The Evolution of Car Design and Technology.* London: Conran Octopus, 1988.

Breer, Carl. *The Birth of Chrysler Corporation and Its Engineering Legacy.* Warrendale, PA: Society of Automotive Engineers, Inc., [1960 manuscript] 1995.

Briggs, B. *The Station Wagon: Its Saga and Development.* Washington, D.C.: Vantage Press, 1975.

Burgess-Wise, David. *Complete Catalogue of Ford Cars in Britain from Model T to Fiesta.* Devon: Bay View Books, 1991.

_____. *Ghia: Ford's Carrozzeria.* London: Osprey, 1985.

_____. *Vauxhall: A Century in Motion 1903–2003.* Luton: Vauxhall Motors Ltd./CW Publishing, 2003.

_____, and Karl Ludvigsen. *The Encyclopedia of the American Automobile.* London: Orbis, 1977.

Burness, Tad. *American Car Spotter's Bible 1940–1980.* Iola, Wisconsin: KP Books/F+W Publications, 2005.

_____. *Cars of the Early Thirties.* Ontario: Chilton Book Company, 1970.

_____. *Ultimate Car Spotter's Guide 1946–1969.* Wisconsin: Krause Publications, 1998.

Butman, John. *Car Wars.* London: Grafton Books, 1991.

Butterfield, Leslie. *Enduring Passion: The Story of the Mercedes-Benz Brand.* Chichester: John Wiley & Sons, 2005.

Clarke, R.M. (ed.). *Ford Consul, Zephyr, Zodiac Mk I & II 1950–1962.* Cobham: Brooklands Books, 1991.

Collier, Peter, and David Horowitz. *The Fords.* London: Collins, 1988.

Connor, William S., and Thomas A. Wilson. *Advertising and Market Power.* Cambridge, Massachusetts: Harvard University Press, 1974.

Consumer Guide (eds.). *Cadillac: Standard of Excellence.* Secaucus, New Jersey: Castle Books, 1980.

_____. *Cars That Never Were.* New York: Beekman House, 1981.

_____. *Encyclopedia of American Cars* [1930–2002]. Lincolnwood, Illinois: Publications International, 2002.

Covello, Mike. *Standard Catalog of Imported Cars 1946–2002.* Iola, Wisconsin: Krause Publications, 2002.

Crocker, David A., and Toby Linden (eds.). *Ethics of Consumption.* New York: Rowman & Littlefield, 1998.

Daines, Robert. *Edsel: The Motor Industry's Titanic.* London: Academy Books, 1994.

Damman, G.H.D., and J.K. Wagner. *The Cars of Lincoln-Mercury.* Sarasota, Florida: Crestline Publishing Co., 1987.

David, Dennis. *It's Delightful! It's Delovely! It's De Soto Automobiles.* Wisconsin: Iconografix, 2006.

Davis, Donald Finlay. *Conspicuous Production: Automobiles and Elites in Detroit, 1899–1933.* Philadelphia: Temple University Press, 1988.

Dorwin Teague, W. *Industrial Designer: The Artist as Engineer.* Lancaster, Pennsylvania: Armstrong World Industries, 1998.

Droste, Magdalena. *Bauhaus 1919–1933.* Cologne: Taschen, 1998.

Egan, F.S. *Design and Destiny: The Making of the Tucker Automobile.* California: On the Mark Publications, 1989.

Eisbrener, Kenneth N. *The Complete U.S. Automobile Sales Literature Checklist 1946–2000.* Wisconsin: Iconografix, 2005.

Fack, James. *The Terraplane.* Sheffield: Railton Owners' Club, 1992.

Farrell, Jim, and Cheryl Farrell. *Ford Design Department Concept & Show Cars 1932–1961.* Oregon: Farrell, 1999.

Forbes, B.C., and O.D. Foster. *Automotive Giants of America.* New York: B.C. Forbes Publishing Co., 1926.

Ford, Henry. *My Life and Work.* London: Heinemann, 1923.

_____. *Today and Tomorrow.* London: Heinemann, 1926.

Foster, Hal. "The Bauhaus Idea in America," in Achim Borchardt-Hume (ed.). *Albers and Moholy-Nagy: From the Bauhaus to the new World,* pp. 92–102. London: Tate Publishing, 2006.

Foster, Patrick R. *American Motors: The Last Independent.* Wisconsin: Krause Publications Inc., 1993.

Fox, Stephen. *The Mirror Makers: A History of American Advertising* (2nd ed.). London: Heinemann, 1990.

Freeman, Tony. *Humber: An Illustrated History 1868–1976*. London: Academy Books, 1991.

Frostick, Michael. *V8*. Beaulieu: National Motor Museum Trust, 1979.

_____, and Ashley Havinden. *Advertising and the Motor-car*. London: Lund Humphries, 1970.

Frumkin, M.J. *Classic Muscle Car Advertising: The Art of Selling Horsepower*. Iola, Wisconsin: Krause Publications, 2002.

Genat, Robert. *The American Car Dealership*. Osceola, Wisconsin: MBI Publishing Co., 1999.

Georgano, G.N. *Cars, 1886–1930*. Gothenburg: Nordbok, 1985.

_____. *Cars of the Seventies and Eighties*. London: Park Lane, 1990.

_____. *The Complete Encyclopaedia of Motor Cars, 1885 to the Present*. London: Ebury Press, 1983.

Godshall, Jeffrey and Auto Editors of Consumer Guide. *Designing America's Cars: The 50s — from Drawing Board to Driveway*. Lincolnwood, Illinois: Publications International Ltd., 2005.

Goodman, Bryan. *American Cars in Europe 1900–1940: A Pictorial Survey*. Jefferson, North Carolina: McFarland & Company., Inc., 2006.

_____. *American Cars in Prewar England: A Pictorial Survey*. Jefferson, North Carolina: McFarland & Company, Inc., 2004.

Goodrum, Charles, and Helen Dalrymple. *Advertising in America— The First 200 Years*. New York: Abrams, 1990.

Gunnell, John A. (ed.). *The Best of Old Cars*, Vols. 3, 4, and 5. Iola, Wisconsin: Krause Publications, 1981–83.

_____. *Standard Catalog of GTO 1961–2004*. Iola, Wisconsin: Krause Publications, 2003.

Hall, Phil. *Fearsome Fords 1959–73*. Osceola, Wisconsin: Motorbooks International, 1982.

Havinden, Michael, et al. *Advertising and the Artist: Ashley Havinden*. Edinburgh: National Galleries of Scotland, 2003.

Haworth-Booth, Mark. *E. McKnight Kauffer: A Designer and His Public* (2nd ed.). London: V&A Publications, 2005.

Headrick, Robert J., Jr. *Chevrolet Station Wagons: 1946–1966 Photo Archive*. Hudson, Wisconsin: Iconografix, 2000.

Heimann, Jim (ed.). *All-American Ads: The 40s*. Cologne: Taschen, 2001.

_____. *All-American Ads: The 50s*. Cologne: Taschen, 2002.

_____. *60s Cars: Vintage Auto Ads*. Cologne: Taschen, 2005.

_____. *70s Cars: Vintage Auto Ads*. Cologne: Taschen, 2006.

Herndon, Booton. *Ford— An Unconventional Biography of the Men and Their Times*. New York: Weybright and Tulley, 1969.

Hess, Alan. *The Indianapolis Records*. London: Stuart & Richards, 1949.

_____. *Wheels Round the World*. London: Newman Neame, 1951.

Hoffman, Barry. *The Fine Art of Advertising*. New York: Stewart, Tabori & Chang, 2002.

Hower, R.M. *The History of an Advertising Agency: N.W. Ayer & Son at Work, 1869–1949*. Cambridge, Massachusetts: Harvard University Press, 1949.

Iacocca, Lee, with William Novak. *Iacocca: An Autobiography*. New York: Bantam Books, 1984.

Ikuta, Yasutoshi. *The American Automobile: Advertising from the Antique and Classic Eras*. San Francisco: Chronicle Books, 1988.

_____. *Cruise-O-Matic: Automobile Advertising of the 1950s*. San Francisco: Chronicle Books, 1988.

_____. *The '60s: America Portrayed Through Advertisements: Automobile*. Tokyo: Graphic-Sha Publishing Co. 1989.

Isaacs, Reginald. *Walter Gropius: An Illustrated Biography of the Creator of the Bauhaus*. Boston: Bulfinch Press/Little, Brown, 1984.

Jacobus, John L. *The Fisher Body Craftsman's Guild: An Illustrated History*. Jefferson, North Carolina: McFarland & Company, Inc., 2005.

Janicki, Edward. *Cars Detroit Never Built*. New York: Sterling, 1990.

Karolevitz, R.F. *Old-Time Autos in the Ads*. Yankton, South Dakota: Homestead Publishers, 1973.

Kennington, W. O. *The Utilitarian Aesthetics of Automobile Design*. London: Proceedings of the Institution of Automobile Engineers, 1935.

Kimes, B. Rae (ed.). *Automobile Quarterly's Great Cars and Grand Marques*. Princeton, New Jersey: Bonanza Books, 1976.

Knowles, David. *MGB, MGC & MGB GT V8: A celebration of Britain's best-loved sports car*. Yeovil: Haynes, 2004.

Lackey, James H. *The Jordan Automobile: A History*. Jefferson, North Carolina: McFarland & Company, Inc., 2005.

Langworth, R.M., and Editors of Consumer Guide. *Collectible Cars 1930–1980*. Lincolnwood, Illinois: Publications International, 1987.

_____, and _____. *Great Cars from Ford*. Lincolnwood, Illinois: Publications International, 1982.

_____, and Chris Poole. *Great American Cars of the 50s*. Yeovil: Haynes, 1989.

Lears, Jackson. *Fables of Abundance: A Cultural History of Advertising in America*. New York: Basic Books, 1994.

Lewis, David L. and Bill Rauhauser. *The Car and the Camera: The Detroit School of Automotive Photography*. Michigan: Detroit Institute of Fine Arts/Wayne State University Press, 1996.

Lichtenstein, Claude, and Franz Engler (eds.). *Streamlined: A Metaphor for Progress*. Baden: Lars Muller Publishers, 1995.

Ling, Peter J. *America and the Automobile: Technology, Reform and Social Change, 1893–1923*. Manchester: Manchester University Press, 1990.

Loewy, Raymond. *Industrial Design* (2nd ed.). London: Fourth Estate, 1988.

_____. *Never Leave Well Enough Alone* (2nd ed.). Baltimore: Johns Hopkins University Press, [1951] 2002.

Marchand, Roland. *Advertising the American Dream: Making Way for Modernity 1920–1940*. Berkeley: University of California Press, 1985.

McCahill, Tom. "Detroit: 1955," in *True* magazine's *Automobile Yearbook*. Greenwich, Connecticut: Fawcett Publications, 1955.

McLintock, J. Dewar. *Renault: The Cars and the Charisma*. Cambridge, England: Patrick Stephens, 1983.

Mercer, F.A., and W. Gaunt (eds.). *Modern Publicity: An Annual of Art and Industry* [vols. for 1930–1939]. London: Studio, 1930–1939.

Meyers, William. *The Image Makers: Secrets of Successful Advertising*. London: Orbis, 1984.

Miles, Steve. *Over Here: The American Car in England in the 1960s*. Northamptonshire: SGM Publishing, 2004.

Mills, G.H. Saxon "Bingy." *There is a Tide...: The life and work of Sir William Crawford, K.B.E.* London: Heinemann, 1954.

Mitchel, Doug. *T-Birds*. New York: MetroBooks, 1999.

Mito, Setsuo. *The Honda Book of Management*. London: Kogan Page, 1990.

Moog, Carol. *"Are They Selling Her Lips?" Advertising and Identity*. New York: William Morrow and Company, 1990.

Nader, Ralph. *Unsafe at Any Speed: The Designed-in Dangers of the American Automobile* (2nd ed.). New York: Bantam Books, [1972] 1973.

Nelson, Walter Henry. *Small Wonder: The Amazing Story of the Volkswagen* (2nd ed.). London: Hutchinson, 1970.

Nesbitt, Dick. *50 Years of American Automobile Design 1930–1980*. Illinois: Publications International, 1985.

Nevett, T.R. *Advertising in Britain: A History*. London: Heinemann/History of Advertising Trust, 1982.

Nevins, Allan, and Frank Earnest Hill. *Ford: Decline and Rebirth 1933–1962*. New York: Charles Scribner's Sons, 1963.

_____, and _____. *Ford: Expansion and Challenge 1915–1932*. New York: Charles Scribner's Sons, 1957.

Nichols, Richard. *Muscle Cars*. London: Bison Books, 1985.

Nicholson, T.R. *The Vintage Car 1919–1930*. London: Batsford, 1966.

Ogilvy, David. *An Autobiography* (2nd ed.). New York: John Wiley & Sons, [1978] 1997.

_____. *Confessions of an Advertising Man*. London: Longmans, Green, [1963] 1964.

_____. *Ogilvy on Advertising*. London: Orbis, 1983.

_____. *The Unpublished David Ogilvy*. London: Sidgwick & Jackson, 1986.

Olley, Maurice. *National Influences on American Passenger Car Design*. London: Proceedings of the Institution of Automobile Engineers, 1938.

Packard, Vance. *The Hidden Persuaders* (2nd ed.). London: Penguin, [1981] 1991.

_____. *The Status Seekers*. London: Longmans, [1959] 1960.

_____. *The Waste Makers*. London: Longmans, [1960] 1961.

Platt, Maurice. *An Addiction to Automobiles*. London: Warne, 1980.

Pomeroy, Laurence, and Rodney Walkerley. *The Motor Year Book 1952*. London: Temple Press, 1952.

Pressnell, Jon. *Morris Minor: Exploring the Legend*. Yeovil: Haynes, 1998.

Rae, John. *American Automobile Manufacturers— A History of the Automobile Industry:*

The First Forty Years. Philadelphia: Chilton Company, 1959.

Read, Herbert. *Art and Industry: The Principles of Industrial Design.* London: Faber & Faber, 1934.

Remington, R. Roger. *American Modernism: Graphic Design 1920 to 1960.* London: Laurence King Publishing, 2003.

Rhys, D.G. *The Motor Industry: An Economic Survey.* London: Butterworths, 1972.

Roberts, Peter. *Any Color So Long as it's Black: The First Fifty Years of Automobile Advertising.* London: David & Charles, 1976.

Rowland, J. *The Automobile Man: The Story of Henry Ford.* London: Lutterworth Press, 1974.

di Ruffia, C.B. (ed.). *Annuario Internazionale delle Automobili.* Venice: Alfieri editore Venezia, 1955.

Ruiz, Marco. *The Complete History of the Japanese Car.* Yeovil: Haynes, 1988.

Ryan, Cornelius (ed.). *Across the Space Frontier.* London: Sidgwick & Jackson, 1952.

Sampson, Henry (ed.). *The Dumpy Book of Motors and Road Transport.* London: Sampson Low, 1957.

Schönberger, A. (ed.). *Raymond Loewy: Pioneer of American Industrial Design.* London: Prestel Books, 1990.

Schudson, Michael. *Advertising, the Uneasy Persuasion.* London: Routledge, [1984] 1993.

Scott, Michael G.H. *Packard: The Complete Story.* Pasadena: Tab Books, 1985.

Scott-Moncrieff, D. *The Thoroughbred Motor Car 1930–1940.* London: Batsford, 1966.

Sedgwick, Michael. *Cars of the 1930s.* London: Batsford, 1970.

_____. *Cars of the Fifties and Sixties.* Middlesex: Temple Press, 1983.

_____. *Cars of the Thirties and Forties.* Gothenburg: Nordbok, 1979.

_____. *The Motor Car 1946–56.* London: Batsford, 1979.

_____, and Mark Gillies. *A–Z of Cars of the 1930s.* Devon: Bay View Books, 1989.

Seldin, Joseph J. *The Golden Fleece: Selling the Good Life to Americans.* New York: Macmillan, 1963.

Service, T.B.D. *Ford Cars: A practical guide to maintenance and repair covering models from 1934.* London: Pearson, 1956.

Sharf, Frederic A. *Future Retro: Drawings from the Great Age of American Automobiles.* Boston: Museum of Fine Arts, 2005.

_____. *Richard H. Arbib 1917–1995: Visionary American Designer.* New York: D.A.P./Distributed Art Publishers, 2006.

Skilleter, Paul. *Morris Minor: The World's Supreme Small Car* (3rd ed.). London: Osprey, 1989.

Sloan, Alfred P. *My Years with General Motors* (2nd ed.). London: Penguin, 1986.

Sorensen, Lorin. *The Classy Ford V8* (2nd ed.). Osceola, Wisconsin: Silverado Publishing Co./Motorbooks International, 1990.

_____. *Ford's Golden Fifties: All the Best from Henry II 1949–59.* St. Helena, California: Silverado Publishing Co., 2003.

Standard Motor Co. *The Story of the Vanguard.* Coventry: Standard Motor Company Ltd., 1949.

Stern, Jane, and Michael Stern. *Auto Ads.* New York: Random House, 1978.

Stevenson, Heon. *Advertising British Cars of the 50s.* Yeovil: GT Foulis/Haynes, 1991.

_____. *British Car Advertising of the 1960s.* Jefferson, NC: McFarland & Company, Inc., 2005.

Swan, Tony. *Retro Ride: Advertising Art of the American Automobile.* Oregon: Collectors Press, 2002.

Temple, David W. *GM's Motorama: The Glamorous Show Cars of a Cultural Phenomenon.* Minnesota: Motorbooks, 2006.

The Times Motoring Correspondent. *Cars of Today 1935: 65 Complete Reviews.* London: Times Pub. Co., 1935.

_____. *Cars of Today 1938.* London: Times Pub. Co., 1938.

Turner, E.S. *The Shocking History of Advertising.* London: Michael Joseph, 1952.

Twitchell, James B. *Adult USA: The Triumph of Advertising in American Culture.* New York: Columbia University Press, 1996.

Van de Lemme, A. *A Guide to Art Deco Style.* London: Apple Press, 1986.

Vanderveen, Bart H. *American Cars of the 1930s.* London: Warne, 1971.

_____. *American Cars of the 1940s.* London: Warne, 1972.

_____. *American Cars of the 1950s.* London: Warne, 1973.

VanGelderen, Ron, and Matt Larson. *LaSalle: Cadillac's Companion Car.* Paducah, KY: Cadillac-LaSalle Club Museum and Research Center/Turner Publishing Company, 2000.

Vauxhall Motors Ltd. *The Griffin Story.* Luton: Vauxhall Motors Ltd., 1990.

Walton, Mary. *Car: A Drama of the American Workplace.* New York: W.W. Norton & Company, 1997.

Ward, Dick. *Photography for Advertising.* London: Macdonald Illustrated, 1990.

Ward, James A. *The Fall of the Packard Motor Car Company.* Stanford, CA: Stanford University Press, 1995.

Wilk, Christopher (ed.). *Modernism 1914–1939: Designing a New World.* London: V&A Publications, 2006.

Williams, Jim. *Boulevard Photographic: The Art of Automobile Advertising.* Osceola, WI: Motorbooks International, 1997.

Wilson, Paul C. *Chrome Dreams: Automobile Styling Since 1893.* Pasadena: Chilton Books, 1976.

Wilson, Richard Guy, Dianne H. Pilgrim, and Dickran Tashjian. *The Machine Age in America 1918–1941.* New York: Brooklyn Museum of Art/Harry N. Abrams, Inc., [1986] 2001.

Wright, J. Patrick. *On a Clear Day You Can See General Motors.* London: Sidgwick & Jackson, 1979.

Magazines, Journals, and Annuals

(The) Autocar
The Automobile
Automobile Quarterly
Automotive History Review
Auto-Universum
Car & Driver
Classic American
(Thoroughbred &) Classic Cars
Classic & Sports Car/Classic and Sportscar
Collectible Automobile
Country Life
The Field
Modern Publicity
(The) Motor
The Motor Industry of Great Britain
Motor Trend
National Geographic
Newsweek
SAH Journal
Scientific American
The [London] Sunday Times
Time
The [London] Times
U.S. News & World Report

Index

Numbers in ***bold italics*** refer to illustrations. References to the color section are identified by the letter *C*.

Abbott of Farnham, coachbuilder 203, 204
ABC-TV 128
AC Cobra 69
academic debate 10
academic research 249
acceleration 58, 78
acoustical consultants 179–180
acoustics 179–180
Acura (marque) 243
Adler (marque) 13
advertisements, role of 3, 242; design of 3–28; modern 243–246, 249
advertisers' originals (of advertisements) vii, ***168***, ***248***, 249
advertisers, role of 3, 40
advertising agencies, British 4–5, 163
advertising artists 249
Advertising Club of Minneapolis 251*n*.26
advertising enthusiasts 249
advertising, European 2, 5, ***39***
advertising, radio *see* radio advertising
advertising, television *see* television advertising
advertising themes: achievement 101–102; action ***21***; adventure 81; affluent life, vignettes of 25; aircraft 34, ***99***, 136, ***139***, 203; "American values" 244; anti-obsolescence 52, 53, 57, ***220***, 220–221; antiques-hunting 165; arresting analogy 244; arresting juxtaposition 244; baseball 203, ***204***; beauty 32, 41, 44, ***44***, 47, 243; build quality 228, 229, 230, 235, 242, 243; business life 101–102, ***104***; celebrity emulation 245; children, life with 136, ***137***, 156, 204, ***207***, 245; China 125; Christmas 108, ***109***, 140, ***140***, 166–167; coffee 245; comfort 19, 25, ***142***, 143, 172–181; common sense 167; comparisons with rival products 119–128; compression ratios 184–185; computing 244; design philosophy ***42***, ***43***, 53; design (styling) 29–

57; dream settings 25; durability 15, 57, 235, 239; dynamism 13; economy C16, 227; effortless cruising 19; engineering 1, 41, 81, 87, 104, 105–106, ***106***, ***116***, 116, 118, 171, 173; escape/escapism 15, ***23***, 58, 68, 81–89, 242, 243; euphoria 58, 82, 174; "Eurochic" 37; family life 156, 204, ***207***, ***220***, 221; fashion 19, 149, ***149***, 245; feminine appeal 145–160, 245; firemen, car's use by 67; fishing ***21***; fortune-telling *C7*, 81–82, 141, ***142–143***, 143–144; fun ***5***, 18, ***83***; gas mileage 4, 181, 182–188, 215, ***216***, 220, 228; gender-specific 19; gracious living 228; greeting-card humor 245; handbags 245; handling 19, ***20***, 67, ***67***; happy anticipation 140; happy couples 91, 94, 99; headroom 115, 174, ***176***, ***211***, 213; hip-hop 244; historical figures *C1*; honesty about product ***223***, 224; horses ***46***, 93, ***93***, 99, 221, 230; human interest 106; illustrious clients 125, ***125***; individualism 102; Japan 125, ***125***; jazz 244; leisure *C5*, *C10*, *C11*, *C13*; leisure (upmarket) 99, ***99***; making up for owner's past cars 131, ***132***; marque heritage ***211***, 211, 213; modern lifestyle 18; music *C9*, 64, 125, ***212***, 213, 243, 244; natural history (car as specimen) 244; nostalgia 128, 129–135, 189; occupational groups, appeals to ***115***, 116; office 98, 101, ***104***; office/employee humor 245; pastoral idylls 58; patriotism 136; performance *C15*, 18, ***20***, 25–26, 49, 58–73, 194; personal reputation of manufacturer 162; police escort 67; power 4, 13, 48, 58–73, 174;power features 19, 69; practicality 18, 207, 213; prize draw competition 135; quality control ***27***, 53, ***53***, 235; quietness 179–180; quiz 108, ***108***; recreation 203; relationships 245; reliability 96, 216, 220, 229,

230, ***230***, 232; riding (horse) 99; romance 19, 89; rural serenity 13; safety 32, 72, 189–198, 229, ***229***, 242, 243; sailing 121, ***123***; scratchcard 244; seasonal advertising 82; seat height 174, ***176***; shopping 203, 245; silence 173, 179–180; size 25; slice-of-life ***106***; snow 230; "sophistication" *C14*, 114; styling 29–57, 58, 188; snobbery 81, 90–104, 242, 243; sociability *C13*, 18; space *C9*, 64; spy thriller 56; streamlining 29–32, ***30***; studio poses 19; styling 18, 48; subway map 244; surfing 245; technical features 25; therapy 244; tigers 71, ***71***; town hall ***109***; travel 81; two-car family 153, 203; unexpected juxtaposition 244; value for money 13, 15, 48, 101, 161–171, ***216***, 216, 227, 235, ***236***; ventilation 172, ***173***; VIPs, appeals to ***115***, 115–116; watch, analogy with 58; water-cooler humor 245; weight distribution 172–173, ***173***; "Who's Who" 99; *see also* Christmas advertising; occupations in advertisements
aerodynamicists 29
aerodynamics 29–30, 32, 47, 221
aeronautical analogy 119
aeronautical imagery 19, 35, 37, 64, ***196***
aeronautical motifs, use of 34, 37, ***38***
aesthetics as social signifiers 94
agency archives 249
air conditioning *see* features (specific): air conditioning
air cooling 68, 69
air bags 189
air suspension *see* suspensions: air
aircraft 18, 19, 37, 41, 136, ***139***, 240
alarmist advertising 124, 191
Allender, Reuben 17–18
Allstate (marque) 214–215
all-steel construction 32, ***33***, 240
AMC (marque) 115, ***187***
America *see* United States of America

American advertising (British cars) 132, 135
American advertising copy 58, 228
American advertising styles *C3*
American car imports *see* imported cars
American car market 28, 239
American cars in Britain *C3*, 29, 30, ***31***, 60, ***61***, 61–62, 70, 82, 89, 163, 165–167, 214, 252*n*.32
American cultural consciousness 167
"The American dream" 2, 34, 129, 240
American Motors Corporation (AMC) 177, 220, 221
American rocket research 64
American tradition 129
"American values" in advertising 244
The Americas 223
Anderson, Malcolm 121
The Andrews Sisters 127
Anglophiles 223, 224
announcement copy 16, 41
Annual Advertising Awards 94
annual model change 3, 31, 57, 92, 224, 247, 249
anti-functionalism 161; *see also* functionalism, ethic of design
anti-obsolescence 52, 53, 57
Antwerp 60
Anzio 136
Arab oil embargo 185
Arcadia, California 106
architecture 240
Arizona 177, ***177***
Armour III, Mrs. Philip 128
arms manufacture 136, ***139***
Armstrong, Lance 243
Art & Colour section (GM) 31–32
Art Deco motifs, use of 8, 32
art nouveau style ***27***
Arthur Kudner (agency) 174
artwork in advertising: airbrushed 10; "artistic" advertising 4–6, 8, 10, 167; as collectible *C13*, 249; asymmetry in 8, 10, 60; "atmospheric" 10; Bauhaus 8, 10, 60, 251*n*.1; Bauhaus-pastiche 4, 8,

259

10, 15, 61, 251*n.1*; cartoons 107, *108*, *142*, 144, *192*, 194, 220, 230, 235, 244–245; color 58, 165, 227, 235; computer-created 243; conventional 106; crystal ball *C7*, 141, *142*–*143*, 200; Cubism 8; diagrams 15, 18, 19, 76, 242; dramatic angles 8; drawings: *see* drawings; dynamic impressionism 4–5, *6*, 61; elongation *C14*, 4–6, *8*, 10, 15, *17*, 17, 19; exaggerated width *26*; exhibitions 249; graphics 2, 243, 244; impressionism 5; minimalism *C8*, 10, *13*, *97*; mock-erotic 149; monochrome 39, *40*, 200, *202*, 243; motion in illustrations 60–61, *61*; multiple illustrations *7*, 15, *75*, *192*, *234*; neo-minimalism 15; original 249; paintings 16, 17; picture stories 107, *108*; realistic 3, *8*; rescued and collected 249; rockets *C9*, 64, *64*, 85; side view *C8*; signed 249; speedlines 8; static tableaux 61, *61*; stylization 10; surviving original art 249; tonal contrasts 5, 8, 10; types of 5; versus photography 3–4, 6, 19, 20, 23, 27–28; watercolors, use of 16
aspiration, social *see* social aspiration
asymmetry in illustration 8, 10, 60
Atlantic Ocean 6, 167, 231
Austin (marque) 47, 203, 214, 222, 225, 227, 228
Australian Chryslers 187
Australian Fords 187
The Autocar 37, 44, 58, 62, 89, 214, 252*Pt.2n.5*
autojumbles 249
automobile, American 40, 222
automobile design, intellectual property in 245
automobile industry 41; American 90, 246; British 222–223
automobile makers, American 227
automobile magazines 28
Automobile Manufacturers' Association 65
automobile, popularization of 8
automobile production (U.S.) 167, 169, 224
automatic transmissions *see* transmissions: automatic
automotive clients (of agencies) 224
Automotive Council for War Production 136
automotive dream, the 241
Automotive History Review vii
Automotive News 230, 235
AutoWeek 241
Avis 83
Ayer, N.W. & Son *see* N.W. Ayer & Son (agency)

backdrops (general) 10
backdrops (specific types): abstract 10; admiring neighbors 19, 101, *102*, 156; aerial view 13, 19, *77*, aircraft *99*; airfield *C14*; airport 18, 19, *30*, *76*, *186*; antiques shop 156, 165, 204; apartment (modern) 98, *208*; architectural 4, 17, 32, *33*; atmospheric 10; balloons 230; beach *C13*, *C15*, 18, *36*, 36, *134*,

179, 199, *209*, *236*; black *C8*, *C14*, 13, 15, *28*, 56, 245; bluegrey 13; board meeting 16, 16; boat deck *21*; bordered *C8*, 15; brick-red gravel 19, *65*, *155*; bridge 32, *33*, *43*; business 101–102, *104*; camping *7*; caviar 224; cherry blossom 13, *30*; Christmas scene *109*, *140*, 166–167; church *53*, 185; city *10*, *18*, *179*; city residential 244; cityscape *C16*, *11*; "classical" 17, 93; cliff face 244; color-toned 23; country club 16, *42*; country house 87; country park 19; country road 19, *103*, *130*, *131*, 156, 185, *193*, *238*, 243; countryside 87, 108, *117*, 157, *157*, 179, 199, *201*, *212*, *217*; craftsman's hands 49, 200–201, *202*; dark *C8*, *C14*, 13, 28, 56, *132*, 230, *237*; "day in a life" collage 245; deep blue *C12*, 17, 64; deep red 71; desert *46*, 57, 71, 208, *232*, 244; deserted beach *C15*; dinner party 16; "distanced" *11*, 13; dockside *C4*; domestic scene 16, *206*; driveway *16*, 243; embroidered cloth *25*, 25; English 224; English church 135; European *C13*, 28; evening dress *C3*, *9*, *17*, *19*, 19, 25, *26*, *36*, *38*, *65*, *100*, *101*, *114*, 179, *180*, *195*; exclusive club *17*, *17*, *26*, *102*; fair 216; family *206*; farm 167; fashion models 224; fashionable resort 19; feminized 150; field *55*, 88, *116*, *197*, *234*, *236*; fighter pilots 19; Florida coast *134*; forest 23; formalized setting 25; freeway *18*, 19, 179, *186*; gender-specific 245; globe *39*; gold cloth 17; golf *C10*, *C11*, 83, *170*; grass 245; handbag 150; heating 174, 177, *177*; helicopter 156, *233*; highway 15, 67, *183*, *216*, *236*, 243; hill 67, *67*; historic monument 18; horses *46*, 68, *68*, 224; hotel *9*, *17*, *100*, *101*, *113*, *114*, 179, *180*; house (grand) *14*, 87, 93, *93*, *96*, *187*; house (suburban) 34, 150, *151*, *169*, *193*, 244; house (ultra-modern) *97*, *168*; indoor *C16*, 82; industrial 244; instrument case 244; island 28; Japanese coast *125*; jewelry *C12*, 16, 17, 23, *24*; lake 15, 19, 89, *178*, 242; landscape 13; leisure *110*; loft spaces 245; mansions 224; military searchlight 141, *141*; mock-classical *C3*, 243; Monaco *69*; mountains *70*; musical score *C9*; neo-classical 4, *9*, 48, *87*, *115*; neutral 13, 16, 58, 242; night-time *C3*, *9*, 15, *36*, *38*, *45*, *72*, *173*, *184*, *195*, *208*, 244; observatory *184*; ocean 28; office 98, 101, *104*; old car meet 131, *133*; opera house 87; orange 18; painting (of non-automotive subject) *C1*, 93; park 203; parking lot *79*; party *186*; pastoral *C11*; photocopying room 245; plain-colored *C8*, 15, 18; plants 19; polo club *201*; principal's office 245; provincial 10; quasi-naturalistic 13; quayside 58; realistic *5*, 15, 18, 27, 242; rear view mirror *231*; resort

19; restaurant 81, *82*, 243, 244; riding stables 99; roadside *C15*; rockets *C9*, 19, *64*; rodeo 18, *185*; romantic 28; rural 10, 13, *18*, 19, 67, 146, 156; sailing *131*; San Francisco *180*; scenic vistas 4; school gate *137*; searchlight beam *141*; ships *C4*; shore 23, *63*; shoreline *23*, *110*, 244; showroom 44, *236*; skating *C5*, 82, *175*; ski resort 16, 135; sky *196*; skyscraper 98; small-town 10, 15; snow *C5*, 82, *175*, 242; social scene 16, 25; "sophisticated" 10, *40*; sports car meet 19, *48*; sportsmen *70*; sports venue *72*, 243; stadium *72*; stars *79*, *190*; static tableaux *61*; station (rail) 199; steep hills 19, *185*; steeple chase 68, *68*; stone columns 25; striped *104*; stylized 13; studio (photographic) *C1*, 13, *45*; studio (television) 127; studio-style 18; suburbia 19, *34*, *54*, 156, 203, 204, 243; sunset 28, 88, 135, 224, 242; supermarket 156, 203, *204*; surf 224; surreal 10, 27; swimming-pool 16–17; tattoo parlor 245; test track 23; tiger in 71, *71*; tropical *40*; twilight 28, 243; upmarket resorts 179; urban *43*; urban concrete 244; virtual-reality 144; winding road 28; wrought-iron gates 25
badge-engineering *C16*
Balham High Road S.W.17 (England) 165
The Balkans 5
Baltic region 5
Bantam 214
Barbizan Plaza Hotel 121
baseball (in advertising) 203, 204
Batmobile 50
Batten, Burton, Durstine & Osborn (agency) 228
Bauhaus movement 8, 251*n.1*
Bauhaus-pastiche (advertising style) *see* artwork in advertising: Bauhaus-pastiche
Beach, Rex 124, *124*
beds (seat conversion) 83
Bel Geddes, Norman 240
Belgian Congo 222
Belgium 60
belongers 241; *see also* VALS
Bentley (marque) 5, 228
Benyon, T. Yates 222
Berlin 136
Bernbach, William (Bill) 180, 224
"Big Three" automakers 1, 35, 41, 162, 169, 215, 220, 244, 251*n.7*
Blue Network 127
BMW (marque) 104, 224, *231*, 237, 239, 241
bodies, closed versus open 172
body frames 30, 32, *33*
body language, gender-specific 146, *147*, *152*, 156, *157*, *157*, 160
Boeing Flying Fortress 136, *139*
Bolt, Berenek, and Newman (consultants) 179–180
bookstores 247, 249
Boston, Massachusetts 249
Boulevard Photographic 28, 249
Bourke, Robert 35, 37
Bowes, Major 125, 127

Bozell & Jacobs (agency) 132, 252*Pt.2n.10*
brakes: anti-skid 89; cable 165; disc 221, 229, 235; finned aluminum 78; four-wheel 189; hydraulic 85, 106, 121, 165, 189; mechanical 106; self-adjusting 16, 34, 74
Brentford, Middlesex (England) 70
brides in advertising 149
bridge, analogous with car body 32, *33*, 240
bridge, as advertising motif *see* backdrops: bridge
bridge, as architectural backdrop 32, *33*
Britain 15, 50, 63, 107, 167, 177, 187, 214, 222
Britain, American cars in 4–5, 60–62, 82–83, 214, 252*n.32*
British advertising (American cars) vii, *C3*, 4–5, *8*, 15, 29, *31*, 58, 60–61, *61*, 62, 163, 165–167, 203, 221, 245
British advertising agencies 227
British advertising (British cars) 39, 49, 107, 165–166, 227
British cars 47, 49, 52, 58, 64, 125, 126, 199, 203, 204, 207, 222
British cars in America vii, 132, 135, 222–223, 224–225, 227, 227–229, *229*, 234
British imports of American cars 58, 60, 252*n.32*
British Leyland Motors Inc. 135
British Motor Corporation (BMC) 228
British motoring papers 223, 228
British motorists 58, 60, 163, 166
British road tests (American cars) 30, 37, 58, 82, 89, 214
Britishness, conceptions of 227
Broad Street 161
brochures (automotive) 2, 3
Brower, Charles 228
Brown, Mrs. Graham 121, *123*
Browning, Bertie 222
Brunn (coachbuilder) 98
Bruno costume 150
Bryant, Lisa 245
Buck, Frank 121
Budd Company 129, *131*
Buick (marque) 6, 13, 32, 237, 241
Buick (model names): Electra 225 *C14*, *27*, 101–102, *104*, 131, *132*, 195; Electra 225 Limited 121; LaCrosse 245; LeSabre 78, *79*, 242; Limited *9*, 125, *126*; Park Avenue 242; Regal 242; Riviera 88, 131; Riviera Gran Sport 70, *70*, 88; Roadmaster 63, *63*, 132, 141, *141*, 156, *157*, 189, *190*, 198; Skylark *C8*, *13*, 15, 41, 132, 195, *195*; Skylark Custom 242; Skylark Sports Wagon 211; Special 215; Sportwagon 121, *123*; Wildcat 70
Buick (model years): (1929) 32; (1934) *C1*, 91, *91*, 172, *173*; (1936) 85, 173–174, *174*; (1937) 125, *125*; (1938) *9*, 59, *60*; (1939) *10*, 146, 149, *149*; (1940) 125, *126*; (1942 model shown) 140–141, *141*; (1945 advertisement) 140–141 *141*, 240; (1946) 62–63, *63*, 74, 141, 156, *157*, 174; (1953) *C8*, *13*, 15, 41, 63, *63*, 127, 189, *190*;

INDEX

(1958) 34; (1961) 215; (1963) 101–102, *104*; (1964) 70, 78, *79*; (1965) 70, *70*, 88, 131, *132*; (1966) 195; 1967 *27*; (1968) 121, *123*, 195; (1969) *C14*; (1976) 132; (1991 catalog date) 189; (1992 model year) 189; (1993) 198, 242; (2006–07) 245
Buick Circus Hour 127
Buick dealers 224, 225, *226*
Buick Division of General Motors 31, 136, *139*
built-in obsolescence 39–40; *see also* anti-obsolescence; dynamic obsolescence; planned obsolescence
Burlington Zephyr 32, *33*

Cadillac (marque) 4, 13, 16, 18, 19, 23, 27, 32, 44, 92, 98, 99–101, 102, 104, 118, 132, 161, 179, 180, 182, 237, 241
Cadillac (model names): Coupe de Ville 16, 24, 99, *100*, 132; Eldorado 15, 17, 23, *24*, 89, 102; Eldorado Brougham 17; Escalade 244; Sedan de Ville *17*; Series 62 Coupe *114*; Sixty Special *C12*, *16*, 16, 17, 23, *25*, *100*, 150–151, *151*; SRX Crossover 244; V-12 Convertible Coupe *C1*; 355 Phaeton 132
Cadillac (model years): (1915) 118, 254*n.35*; (1930) 132; (1933) *C1*, 99, 132; (1941) 177; (1948) 17, 37, 49; (1948–52) 17; (1952) *16*, 16, 99, *100*, 100, 101, 150–151, *151*, 159; (1954) 44; (1955) *16*, 16, 80, 99, 207; (1956) 99, *100*, 207; (1957) *C12*, 17, 91, 100, *101*; (1958) *17*, 100; (1959) 17, 17, 100, 111, *114*; (1960) *24*; (1961) 23, *25*, 25, 100, *103*; (1962) 25, 100, 191; (1963) *25*, 25, 100, *103*; (1964) 25, 100; (1965) 25, 49, 100; (1966) 100, 115; (1967) 102; (1971) 198; (1975) 132; (1976) *117*, 118; (2006–07) 244
Cadillac Division of General Motors 31, 80, 100
Calcutta 222
calendar and model years *see* annual model change
California 83, 106, 119, 188, 217, 227, 241
Callum, Ian 253*n.6*
Campbell-Ewald Co. (agency) 99
Canada 62, 74, 132, 174, 221, 222, 230
Cape Town 222
Car and Driver 28
car buyers 1
car buyer, American 172
car design, American 80
car enthusiasts 2, 19, 249
car exports *see* exports, car
car hobbyists 223
car imports *see* imports, car
Car Life 28
car market, British 177
car rental companies 83
Car of the Year award 73
carbon-neutral crops 243
Cartier 23
cartoons *see* artwork in advertising: cartoons
catalog in miniature *see* layouts: catalog in miniature

catalogs (automotive) 2, 18, 69, 78, 107, 146, 160, 193
CBS-TV 127
celebrity endorsements 90, 124–125, 127–128, 151, *153*, 243, 244, 252*Pt.2n.9*
Center for Creative Studies, Detroit 28
Central Park, New York 229
Cerf, Bennett *127*, 128
charity sales 247
Checker 57, *57*, 74
Chevrolet (marque) 28, 32, 40, 48–49, 57, 105, 107, 108, 115, 119, 121, 159, 161, 163, 165, 169, 170, 174, 179, 215, 222, 241
Chevrolet (model names): Beauville 203, *204*; Bel Air 18, *19*, 19, 48, *48*, *75*, 78, 83, 150, *156*, 170, *178*, *185*, 203, *204*, 217; Biscayne *C13*, 49, 217; Brookwood 156, 204, *206*; Cadet 214; Caprice *C14*, 57, 179, *180*; Caprice Classic *180*, 181, 213; Caprice Custom Coupe *158*, 159; Chevelle *186*, 186, 208, 217; Chevelle Malibu 131; Chevelle SS 396 *C15*; Chevy II 217, *217*; Corvair (1954 show car) 217; Corvair (production car) 19, 68, 69, 133, 135, 179, *216*, 217, 224, 230; Corvair Monza 69, 135; Corvette 41, 201, *216*, 217, 241; Delray utility sedan 171; De Luxe sedan 170; De Luxe Sport Coupe *18*, 170; Handyman 203; Impala 19, 25, *56*, 115, *127*, 131, *133*, 179, 208, *209*; Kingswood 156; Monte Carlo *76*, 79, 89; Nomad (1954 concept) 201, 203; Nomad (production car) 156, 201, 203; Styleline 179; Styleline DeLuxe 207; Two-Ten *18*, 48, 67, 78, 203; Vega 28, 57, 79, 133, *220*, 220–221, 235; Vega Kammback *220*, 221
Chevrolet (model years): (1935) 61; (1936) 146, *147*, 189, *191*; (1949) 207; (1952) *18*, 48, 67, 74, *75*, 170; (1953) 18, 41, 48, *48*, 67, 74, 184, *185*; (1954) 18, 48, 67, 74, *76*, 78, 83, 184, *185*, 201; (1955) *18*, 19, 48, *48*, 49, 67, 78, 201; (1956) 19, 48, 49, 67, 85, 101, *102*, 111, 150, 193, 194, 201, 203, *204*; (1957) 17, 19, 49, 67, *67*, 83, 101, 201, 241; (1958) *C13*, 17, 19, 49, *127*, 128, 156, *156*, 177, 195, 203; (1959) 17, *19*, 19, 49, 177, *178*, 203, 204, *206*; (1960) 19, 68, 179, 217; (1961) 19, 179, 217; (1962) 68, *216*, 217; (1963) 27, 179, *180*, 217; (1964) 217; (1965) 208, *209*; (1966) 27, *56*, *158*, 159, 224; (1967) *C14*, 27, 179, *180*; (1968) 241; (1970) *C15*, 79; (1971) 57, *220*, 221; (1972) 131, *134*; (1976) *28*, *186*, 186; (1977) *180*, 181, 213
Chicago 241
Chicago Tribune 240
children in advertising 23, 69–70, 107, *108*, 143, 146, *147*, 153, *154*, 156, 203, *204*, *205*, *206*, 213, 229–230
China 125
Chinese cars 245
Chippendale furniture 93

chorus girls 149
Christmas advertising 107–108, *109*, 140, *140*, 166–167
chroming, process of 17
Chrysler (marque) vii, 3, 4, 5, 8, 10, 13, 17, 49, 65, 241
Chrysler (model and design names): Airflow 29, *30*, *31*, 32, 41, 90, 173, 189, 249; Airflow Custom Imperial 53, 125, 127; Aspen 244; C-200 41, *43*; C-300 65; Concorde 241; "Forward Look" 1, 44, 47, 83, 179; idea cars 41, *43*; Imperial *4*, 8, 13, 41, 162; K-310 41, *43*, 53; LHS 241; New Yorker 19, 35, 44, *44*, *45*, 132, 177, *179*, 241; New Yorker Brougham 128; Phaeton 41, *43*; Sebring 243; "Silver Anniversary Model" (1949) 41, *44*; Town & Country (steel-bodied) 204, *208*, 208; Town & Country (wood-bodied) 199, 200, 201; Windsor 65, 85, *86*, 177
Chrysler (model years): (1926) *4*; (1928) 61; (1931) *6*; (1934) 29 *30*; (1935) 29, *31*; (1936) 90; (1937) 173; (1939–41) 65; (1941) 199; (1949) 41, *44*, 65, 193; (1950) 41, 44, *44*; (1951) 41, 65; (1952) 41, *42*, *43*, 47; (1953) 44, 65; (1954) 19, 44, 65, *65*; (1955) 19, 44, *45*, 48, 65, 78, *78*, 78, 177; (1957) 44, 207; (1959) 65, 85, *86*, 179, *179*; (1960) 204, *207*; (1961) 207; (1968) *208*, 208; (1974) 132; (1976) 128; (1993) 241–242; (2006–07) 243, 244, 245
Chrysler, Walter 105, *106*
Chrysler Corporation 15, 31, 37, 40, 41, *42*, *43*, 46, 47, 52, 58, 65, *78*, 90, 105, 115, 118, 121, 153, 157, 163, 171, 172–173, 174, 176, 198, *198*, 204, *207*, 215, 217, 241, 242, 251*n.7*
Chrysler dealers 106
Chrysler in Britain 4–5, 60–61
Circassian walnut 90
Citroën (marque) 57, 131, *232*
civilian car production 136
classicism, forms and expressions of 228–229
closed versus open bodies 172
Coates, George 222
Coca-Cola 223
"Coke-bottle" look 79
colonial conditions 222
colonial markets 222
color drawings *see* drawings: color
color photography *see* photographs, color
Columbia Network 125
Comet (1960–61 model years) 215; *see also* Mercury (model names): Comet (from 1962)
comfort (advertising theme) 172–181
commerciales 202
commercials, radio *see* radio advertising
commercials, television *see* television advertising
compact cars 25, 28, 171, 214–221
comparative advertising 105–118
"Compare All Three" campaign 105–110

comparison testing 115–118; *see also* comparative advertising
compression ratios 184–185, *185*
Comstock, Robert 189
Confessions of an Advertising Man (Ogilvy) 228
Connecticut 5, 119
Continental (marque): Mark II (1956–57) 15, 55, 98, 201; Mark III (1958) 57, 195, *195*
conspicuous reserve 241
consumer, identification with 3
consumer culture, American 79
consumer protection groups 217
consumer survey 242
continental kit *155*
convenience features 2, 74–80
convertible sedan *C1*
convertibles *C1*, *C8*
Cooper, Gary 124
copy: aspirational 15; factual *218*–*219*; impressionistic 3; informal 185, 242; list-based 243; long *218*–*219*, *220*, 243; minimal *C8*, *C9*, *C14*, *97*; styles of 47
copywriters 3, 19, 32, 44, 67, 85, 89, 160, 181, 227
Cord (marque) 4
Corey, David A. *122*
corporate advertising 41, *42*, *43*, 161, *162*, *164*, 171
corporate identity 40–41
corporate images 41
Costain, Harold 6
country clubs 100
Country Life 252*Pt.2n.2*
Crawfords *see* W.S. Crawford Ltd. (agency)
credit terms 182
Crocker, Dr. 228
Crosby, Bing 124–125, 128
Crosley 214, 223
crossover vehicles 243
cruise control 179
Cubism 8
cultural homogeneity 79
cup holder, heated/cooled 243
custom bodies 31, 90, 98
Dagenham, England 165, 166
DaimlerChrysler 244, 245
Darrin, Howard ("Dutch") 35
Datsun (marque) 220, 221, 225, 227, 235, *236*, 237
Davison, Nurse Margaret W. 146
Daytona Beach 65
Daytona Speed Week 67
Dearborn, Michigan 166, 216
deception in advertising 3, 5–6
Dempsey, Jack 124
The Depression *C1*, 6, 8, 10, 15, 33, 40, 91, 97, 99, 167, 169, 220
design costs, reduction of 40
design ideals, futuristic 31
De Soto (marque) 13, 15, 27, 44, 65, 105, 124, 241
De Soto (model names): Airflow 90, 249; Coronado 151, 153, *153*, 159; Custom 90; Explorer 203, *205*; Firedome 153; Fireflite *46*, 151, *152*, 153, 159, 203, *205*; Firesweep 203; Sportsman 151, 153, *153*
De Soto (model years): (1934–37) 29; (1936) 90; (1938) 125; (1939–41) 65; (1942 model shown) 127, 136, *137*; (1945 advertisement) 127, 136, *137*; (1952) *42*; (1953) 65, 74, *76*;

(1955) 151, *152–153*, 153, 159; (1957) 44, *46*, 47, 65, 203; (1958) 65, 66, 67, 203, *205*

De Soto dealers 106
De Soto-Plymouth dealers 127
detergents (advertising for) 191
Detroit, Michigan 17, 28, 31, 36, 39, 40, 193, 194, 223, 224, 225, 235, 239, 241, 245
Detroit Institute of Arts 249
Detroit Library 249
Detroit photographers 28
"Detroit Three" 244; *see also* "Big Three" automakers
diagrams *see* artwork in advertising: diagrams
Diamond Chemicals 17
diesel engines *see* engines: diesel
Di-Noc (mock-wood trim) 207, 208
display files 249
DKW (marque) 224
Dodge (marque) 13, 15, 28, 44, 59, 65, 121, 131, 241
Dodge (model names): Aspen *186*, 186, 213; Caliber 245; Charger 241; Coronet 115; Coronet 500 208; Dart 157, *207*; Intrepid 242; Lancer 215; Monaco 208; Ram Mega Cab 244; Senior *61*; Sierra 203
Dodge (model years): (1927) vii, 61; (1936) 121, *121*, 124; (1939–41) 65; (1952) *42*, 90, (1958) 203, 208; (1960) 204, *207*; (1961) 215; (1962) 90; (1968) 208; (1970) 241; (1977) 213; (1976) *186*, 186, 188; (1993) 242; (2006–07) 244, 245
Dodge Brothers *see* Dodge
Dodge dealers 106
dogs in advertising 107, *108*, 128, 143, 213, 245
Dohanos, Steven 5
door latch design 193
Dorland Advertising Ltd. 228
double-page spreads *C14*, 39, 68, *68*, 243, 244
"downsizing" 79–80, 181, 220–221
Doyle Dane Bernbach (agency) 1, 185, *223*, 223–224
drawings: auxiliary 15, 16, 18, *33*; cartoon 107, *108*, *142*, 144, *220*, 230, 235, 244–245; color 16, 28, *216*; cutaway *216*; humorous 28, 57, *167*, *220*, 244–245; line *33*, *40*, *167*, *218–219*; miniature *7*, *33*, *75*; pseudo-technical 18, *75*; semi-technical 242
dream-car look 44
dream cars *43*, 50, 52, 76, 77; *see also* Chrysler (model and design names): idea cars
dressmaking, analogy with car styling 41, 53, *54*, 246
driving distances 172
driving postures, gendered 156, 157, 160
Dual 10 tires 191
Dubonnet suspension *see* suspensions: Knee Action
Duesenberg (marque) 4
Durbin, Deanna 124
Dynaflow *see* transmissions: Dynaflow
dynamic impressionism, school of illustration 4–5, *6*, 61

dynamic obsolescence, philosophy of design 39–40, 92, 93; *see also* anti-obsolescence; built-in obsolescence; planned obsolescence

Earl, Harley 31, 37, 39, 40, 47, 48, 81
Earl Automobile Works 31
economic independence (female) 145, 157, 159–160
economy *see* gas mileage
economy, American 40
economy cars 222
Edsel (marque) *34*, 34–35, 94, 177, 252*Pt.2n.9*
Edsel Division of Ford Motor Company 34
education, level of 160
Edward VIII, King of England 125
effortless driving 79
El Morocco 17–18
electric lamps 189
electric windows *see* power features (specific): windows
electrical devices 78; *see also* features (specific)
electronics-based features 243, 245
elitism, critique of advertising 8
elongator *see* artwork in advertising: elongation
emissions legislation 73, 188, 232
emotional appeals 150, 228
emulator-achievers 241; *see also* VALS
emulators 241; *see also* VALS
endorsements *see* celebrity endorsements
energy independence of U.S. 243
Engel, Elwood 52
engineering (as advertising theme) 1, 41, 81, 87, 104, 105–106, *106*, *116*, 116, 118, 171, *237*
engineers 31
engines: Blue Flame 67; diesel 41; Dual-Jetfire *C10*, 129; Dynaflash *10*, 59; Econo-Master 59; Fire Dome V-8 65; FirePower V-8 65; Golden Lion 65, 85; "hemi" V-8 65; Hi-Fire V8 67; I-block Six 76; Miracle H-Power 64; overhead-cam 221; PowerFlow 67; Powerflyte 65, 74; Ram Air 73; Ramjet (fuel injection) 67; rear engines 68, 230; Rocket 64, 85; six-cylinder 69; Starfire V-8 *70*; Spitfire 65; Super Turbo-Fire V8 67; Supersonic Engine 200; Thunderbird Special V-8 194; Trophy V-8 71; Turbo-Fire V8 67, 203; Turboflash V8 67; valve-in-head 189; V-8 19, *20*, 69, 73, 188, 200; V-12 13, 110; Wildcat V-8 70; Y-block V-8 76
England 5, 30, 58, 60, 70, 228
Enos, Pat 119, *120*
environmentalism 235, 243, 246
envy, incitement of 90
EPA ratings 186, 188
ergonomics 156, *157*, 172
Erwin, Wasey and Company 174
escapism: 2, *C10*, 15, 79, 242, 243
Essex (marque) 60
ethanol, as fuel 243
ethics, sexual 83
euphoria (in advertising) 15, 82, 174, 227

"Eurochic" as design theme 37
Europe 3, 4, 29, 37, 61, 62–63, 136, 140, 163, 172, 214, 215
European cars 39, 40, 57, 67, 71, 80, 89, 163, 172, 186, 198, 220, 221, 224, 241; *see also* imported cars
European design 32, 35, 37, 40, 41, 130
European functionalism 35, 37, 39, 40
Evans, Gary 106, *106*
evening dress *see* backdrops: evening dress
"excitement factor" 81
Exner, Virgil 35, 37, 41
Experience Run 216
exports, car: American 4–5, 29–30, *30*, 39, *39*, 222, 245, 252*n.32*; British 222; Canadian 62

The Fader 244
fading, how to prevent 249
family cars 98; British 223, 224–225, 227, 228
Family Man (advertising archetype) 107, 146, *147*, 157, *157*
fantasy, automotive 2, 6, 34, 40, 58, 79, 80, 161
Farina, Pinin *see* Pinin Farina; *see also* Pininfarina
farmers (American) 162
Farnham, conversion of Ford Zephyr 204
Farynk, Walter 249
fashion models 19, *31*, *45*, 149, *149*, *150*, 150, 151, *153*, *154*, *155*, 159, *159*, 160, 175, *234*, 245
features (general) 74–80, 119; *see also* electronics-based features; power features (general); power features (specific)
features (specific): adjustable thermostat 174; air conditioning 94, 115, 174, 177, *177*, 188, 229; Air Cushion Tires 172; Airfoam Seat Cushions 107, 174, *176*; Airliner Reclining Seats *C10*, 177; All-Weather Eye 17, *177*; Auto-Pilot 179; Automatic Beam Changer 78; Automatic Electric Choke 74; Autronic Eye 78; bucket seats 221; "cab-forward" design 241; cassette deck 157; Center-Point Steering 74; crash padding 191, 193–195; Color-Matched Two-Tone Interiors 74; compound windshield 78; Cyclebonded Brake Linings 74; Dash-Locking Safety Hood 189; electric lamps 189; electric locks 157; electric windows 94; Fisher Ventipanes 172, *173*; Floating Power 119; foam cushioned seats 177; "Forward Look" 1, 44, 47, 83, 179; 4-Way Power Seat 76; 4-wheel drive 211, 213; front-wheel drive 159, *159*; Full Power Steering 74; Girder-Guard frame 208; hazard warning flashers 157; headlight delay switch 116; heavy-duty springs 70; Hood-mounted tach 73; Hypoid rear axle 106; Ignition Key Starting 74, 108; Jumbo-Drum Brakes 74; Lifeguard Design (Ford) 192–195; limited-slip differential 70; Magic Doorgate 211; Mirror-

Matic Electronic Mirror 78; Morrokide 71; Multimedia Infotainment System 243; No Draft Ventilation 172, *173*; padded cell 191; padded dashboard 193, 195; padded sun visors 193, 195; padded windshield corner posts 198; Panoramic Roof 245; Permi-Firm steering 74; plastic window screens 177; pollen filter 174; pop-out windshield 191, 193; Power Brakes 68, 74; Power-Lift Windows 76; Power Steering 68; PowerStyle 65; Rally Pac 69; retracted steering column 194; Royal-Tone Styling 74; Safety Convenience Panel 195, *196*; Safety-Cushion (Chrysler) 193; Safety-Cushion Padded Instrument Panel (Kaiser) 193; safety door locks 194; Safety-Girder frame 195; safety glass 177; Safety Plate Glass 189; Safety Power Steering 195; Safety-Steel body 106; seat back latches 198; seat belt warning light 195; seat belts 193–194, 195, 198; sequential turn signals *88*; shatter-resistant rearview mirror 193; silver key ring 180; sliding roof 79; splash guards 78; stabilizer bar 70; steel-cage construction 229; steel-truss body frame *33*, 189; StepOn parking brake 74; stereo system 118; stereo tape 73; Super-Cushion Tires 174; Super-Scenic Windshield 78; Supplemental Inflatable Restraint System 189; Swing-Away steering wheel 68; Swivel Seats 78, 177, *179*; Tiffany clock 180–181; Total-Contact Brakes 78; Turret Top 32, *33*, 106, 146, *147*, 172, 189; Twin Beds 83, *83*, 177; Twin-Tower tail lights 78; Waterproof Ignition System 74; Weather Eye *C5*, 15, 82, 174, *175*; under-floor stowage compartment 208; Unibody Construction 207; zippered storage pouches 181
female-oriented publications 19, 245
feminized copy 150–151, 153
Ferrari 48
Fiat advertising 4
The Field 165
The Film Society, London 61
film stars 90
"fine cars" 13
fins, danger to pedestrians 189, 191
firemen (in advertising) 67
Fisher, Lawrence P. 31
Fisher Body (Division of General Motors) 32, 106, 136, *139*, 146, *147*, 149, *149*, 161, 172, *173*, 189, 225
Fisher Body Craftsman's Guild 138
Fitzpatrick, Arthur *C8*, *C13*, 13, *26*, 28, *72*, 249
flea markets 247, 249
Florida 131, *133*
Fluid Drive *see* transmissions: Fluid Drive
foam/sponge rubber, use of 191, 193–195
Fogarty, Anne 151, *153*

INDEX

Foote, Cone & Belding 34
Forbes magazine 246
Ford (Australia) 187
Ford, Edsel 163
Ford, Henry 161, 162, 167
Ford, Henry II 225–226
Ford (England) (model names): Consul Mk 1 76, 214; Consul Cortina Super 207; "Eight" 163, 165, 166; Model C 166; Model Y 165, 166; Model 62 165–166, *166*, 167, 200–201; "Ten" 163; Squire 207; Utility Car 165; V-8 "30" 163, 165, 166, *166*, 167, 199; V-8 "22" 49, 163, 165–166, *166*, 167, 200–201; V-8 Pilot 167; Zephyr Mk 1 76, 214; Zephyr Mk II 204; Zodiac Mk II 52
Ford (France) Vedette 214
Ford (U.S.) (marque) vii, 5–6, 28, 67, 68, 107, 108, 111, 115, 119, 161, 169, 172, 174, 199, 207, 215, 217
Ford (U.S.) (model names): Country Squire 211; Crestline 76, 157, *157*; Custom Ranch Wagon 203; DeLuxe 15; Escape 244; Expedition 244; Fairlane 49, *69*, 69, 71, 83, *84*, 153, 194, 203; Fairlane Victoria hardtop *193*; Fairlane Fordor Victoria *192* 194; Fairlane GTA 71; Falcon 68, *69*, 69, 215, *216*, 217, 227; Falcon Futura 68; Fordor *142*; Galaxie 25, *69*, 69, 83, 115; Galaxie 500 70, 179, 228; Granada ESS *238*, 239; Granada Sports Coupe 239; LTD 179–180, 228; Model A 3, 8, 57, 132, 163, 221; Model B 8, 163; Model T 105, 129, *131*, 163, 165, 221; Model 48 vii, *C3*; Model 68 145, 151, 165, *166*, 167; Model 78 *8*, 165, *166*, 167; Model 81A 15, 167 *168*, 182; Model 91A 165, *167*, 167; Mustang *69*, 69, 70, 73, 88, 159, 241; Parklane 203, *204*; Pinto 132, 221; Sunliner 49, 76, 83, *84*, 153, 203; Sports Hardtop *69*, 69; Sportsman 199; Station Wagon 211; Taurus 242; Thunderbird 3, *23*, 23, 26, 27, 28, 41, 49, 68, *79*, 85, 87, *87*, 88, *88*, 89, 132, 159, 195, *196*, 242; Tudor 6, 78, *142*, *143*; V-8 vii, *C3*, 6, *8*, 8, 15, 67, 143, 145, 151, 163, 165–167, *168*, 169, 182, 199
Ford (U.S.) (model years): (1931) 3; (1932) 163; (1935) vii, *C3*; (1936) 145–146, 151, 189; (1937) *8*; (1938) 15, 182; (1941) 167; (1942) 143; (1945–48) *C7*, 1, 141, *142–143*, 143–144; (1946) *142–143*, 143–144, 174; (1947) 78; (1948) 199, 239, 247; (1949) 35, 144, 174, 247; (1950) 144; (1952) 48, 76; (1954) 67, 76, 157, *157*; (1955) 41, 48–49; (1956) 67, 84, *192*, *193*, 193–195, 198, 203, *204*; (1957) 78, 83, *84*, 204; (1958) 68; (1959) *23*, 68, 242; (1960) *68*, 68, 85, 207, 215, *216*; (1961) 68, 85, 207; (1962) 85, *87*; (1962–64) 27, *27*, *69*, 69; (1963) 28, *87*, 87, 88, 227; (1964) *23*, *69*, 69, 87–88; (1965) 88, 179–180, 228, 241; (1966) 115, 179–180, 195, *196*, 211; (1967) 78, 88, *210*, 211; (1969) 3, *79*; (1969–71) 89; (1972) *88*, 89, 221; (1974) 132; (1976) 89; (1978) *238*, 239; (1993) 242; (2006–07) 244
Ford dealers 83, *84*, 167, 194, 195, 216
Ford Division of Ford Motor Company 194, 214
Ford Motor Company (England) 203, 214, 227
Ford Motor Company (U.S.) 5, 15, 16, *27*, 31, 40, 41, 59, 63, 105, 106, 121, 172, 182, 194, 195, 203, 251*n.7*
"Ford in Your Future" campaign *C7*, 1, 141, *142–143*, 143–144, 200, 240
Ford maps 167
Ford musical program 127
Ford precision gauges 165, *167*
Ford promotional film 195
Ford salesmen 195
The Ford Show 127
Ford showrooms 193
Ford Theater 127
Ford trucks 141, 143
form versus function (debate) 29–31, 41
Fortune magazine *C2*
"Forward Look" *see* features (specific): "Forward Look"
four-wheel drive *211*, 211, 213
framing advertisements 247
France 57, 129
Frazer, Joseph W. 215
Frazer (marque) 16, 35, 49, *49*, 63, 200, 201, *202*, 213
French pleating 90
Frensham, conversion of Ford Zephyr 204
Freudians *C9*
Frigidaire 41
fuel availability 79
fuel-cell cars 243
fuel consumption *see* gas mileage
fuel crisis 1, 36, 118, 237
fuel economy *see* gas mileage
fuel injection 67
fuel prices *see* gas prices
fuel sales restrictions 185
fuel shortages 36
functionalism, ethic of design 1, 37, 40, 41, 44, 57, 80, 118, 201
functionalism in advertising 92, 104, 110, 118, 242–243

gadget demonstrator, woman as 156–157, *157*, 159
gadgets 74–80, 156–157, 241
gas mileage 4, 181, 182–188, 215, *216*, 220, 235, 237, *237*
gas prices 185, 221, 244
gearshifts 15, 59, *62*, 63–64, 65; *see also* transmissions
General Motors (cars) vii, 13, 23, 49, 71, 174, 177, 242
General Motors Corporation (GM) 18, 31, 32, 40, 41, 47, 63, 64, 69, 70, 78, 96, 106, 118, 125, 127, 136, 145, 161, *162*, 172, 179, 189, 194, 195, 203, 204, 215, 216, 217, 223, 224, 243
General Motors in Britain 64
General Motors Overseas Operations 223
General Motors proving ground 161
General Motors subsidiaries *see* Opel; Vauxhall
General Tire and Rubber Co. 223
General tires *C6*, 107, 149, *150*, 191, 199, *200*
Geo Prizm 242
Germany 13, 64, 136, 225, 251*n.1*; *see also* West Germany
Getchell, J. Stirling 1, 105, 106, 169, 243
Ghia, coachbuilder 41
"GI brides" 151
Gilbert Advertising Agency 230
Gilmore-Yosemite Sweepstakes 182
Global Insight 245
global warming 243
"good taste," conceptions of 93, 96; *see also* taste as social signifier
Goodrich Tires 124, *124*
Goodyear Tires 191, 193, 195, *195*
graphic arts 1
graphics *see* artwork in advertising
"green" advertising 243
Gregorie, Eugene 29
Grey Advertising (agency) 221
Grizzly, cartoon bear *192*, 194
Groton school 228
ground clearance 222
guard books (agency) 249

Haefner, Rolf 220
Hahn, Dr. Carl Horst 224
Hambro Automotive Corporation 223
handling *20*
hardtop sedan styling 222
HAT Archive vii
Havinden, Ashley 5, 60–61
heaters, car *C5*, 81, 82, 156, *157*
Henry I, King of England 165
Henry J 214, 215
Hertz 83, *127*, 128
Hess, Alan 222
Hess & Eisenhardt 207
High Holborn, London 60
high schools 198
Hillman (marque) 39, 222, 227
Hindustan Ambassador 222
Hinkley, Miss C. Eleanor 146, *148*, 242
historians, future 249
"historic car ads" 247
History of Advertising Trust vii
Honda (marque) 181, 235, 237, *237*, 243, 244
Hope, Bob 124
Hopkins, Claude 228
Horn, Huston 224
horsepower race 63, 66, 177
horsepower tax (British) 165, 166, 167
Hot Rod 28
House and Garden 8
House of Representatives 194
Hoving, Walter 181
Hower, Miss Beth 119
Howser, Dorsey-Gay 242
Hudson (marque) 4, 13, 53, 60, 74, 177, 241
Hudson (model and design names): Eight 169; Hornet 47, *47*, 48, 64; Jet 214, *215*; Six Touring Sedan 15, 58, *60*; "Stepdown" styling 47; Terraplane vii, 60, *61*; Wasp 47, *47*
Hudson (model years): (1934) 169; (1938) vii, *61*; (1939) 15, 58, *60*, 189; (1948) 47; (1951) 63; (1952) 47, *47*, *48*, 64; (1953) 214; (1954) 214
Humber (marque) 39, 204, 223–224
Hummer (marque) 244
humor in advertising 28, *56*, 82, *220*, 220, 245
Hundred-Million-Dollar Look (Chrysler) 41, *45*
Hupmobile (marque) 4, 31
hybrid cars 243, 244
Hydra-Matic *see* transmissions: Hydra-Matic
hydrogen bomb 64
Hyundai (marque) 243

Iacocca, Lee 195
The Ice Follies 224
idea cars (Chrysler) 41, *43*
The Illustrated London News 165
illustration, styles of 3–28
illustrious clients in advertising 125, *125*
impartiality in advertising 3
Imperial (marque) 179, 239; *see also* Chrysler (model names): Imperial
Imperial (model names): Crown 115; Custom 54; Le Baron *115*, *116*, 116
Imperial (model years): (1955) 65; (1960) 53, *54*; (1961) 54; (1962) 115, *115*; (1963) *115*, 116; (1964) 52; (1969) *116*, 116, 118; (1975) 118; (1981) 118; (1983) 118
import boom 223
import buyers, characteristics of 224, 227
import sales, annual 223
"import values" 80, 102, 104, 235, 237, 245
imported cars 2, 57, 80, 89, 102, 104, 213, 216, *218–219*, 221, 222–239, 245
imports, car: British 132, 135
impressionism 3, 5; dynamic 4–5
In Style 245
"independent" automakers 47, 169, 214, 251*n.7*
India 222
Indian cars 222, 245
Indianapolis 65
individualism *see* advertising themes: individualism
indoor color photography *C2*, 82
industrial design 33, 34, 39
industrial relations 16, 221
Infiniti (marque) 244
Institution of Automobile Engineers 252*Pt.3n.6*
insurance companies 70
intellectual property (in automotive design) 245
Intercontinental Ballistic Missile 35
interior space 30
international advertising 5
International Harvester Company *211*, 213
International Travelall *211*, 213
internationalism in advertising 245
Internet 247, 249
intrinsic excellence, invocation of 92
investment, advertisements as 249
Issigonis, (Sir) Alec 227
Italian advertising 4, *39*, 215

Italian Alps 37
Italy 37, 39, 41

J. Stirling Getchell (agency) 1, 105, 106, 169, 243
J. Walter Thompson (agency) *C7*, 1, 105, 141, 179, 193, 194
Jaguar 223, 241, 243, 245, 253*n*.6
Japan 125
Japanese cars *C15*, 1, 221, 222, 225, 235–237, 239, 241, 242, 243, 244, 245
Japanese roads 225
Jeavons, Ronald 222
Jeep (army) 211
Jeep (marque) 244, 251*n*.26
Jeep Wagoneer *211*, 211, 213, 251*n*.26
Jeepster 211
jet propulsion 34
jewelry, use of *C12*
Jones, Jack 128
Joneses, keeping up with 101, *102*, 157
Jordan, Edward (Ned) 71, 81, 228, 246
Jordan automobiles 1, *82*, 252*Pt.2n*.1
Juba 222
judgment as social signifier 92
Judkins (coachbuilder) 98
junk stalls 247

Kaiser, Henry J. 214
Kaiser (marque) 35, 49, 74, 193, 200, 214
Kaiser-Darrin 161 41
Kaiser-Frazer Corporation 49, 200, 215
Kaiser Jeep Corporation *211*, 211
Kaufman, Van *C13*, *26*, 28, *72*, 249
Keller, K.T. 41
Kensington, Maryland 191
Kew, west of London 60
Kia (marque) 245
Klocker, Carl L. *122*, 221
"Knee Action" suspension *see* suspensions: Knee Action
"knocking copy" 105, 115
Kona Kai Club 83
Korean cars 243, 245
Kowalski, Edward and Roman 140
Kudner, Arthur 174

The Ladies' Home Journal 145, 150
language, informal 185, 242
LaSalle (marque) 5, 32, 131, 161
layouts (general) 2, 3, 19, 27, 242
layouts (specific types): angled block *C5*, *7*, *8*, 15, 19; asymmetrical 8, 10, 60; catalog in miniature *12*, 15; convergence of in 1960s; diagonal *C5*, *7*, *8*; double-page spread *C14*, 39, 68, *68*, 243, 244; multiple diagrams 15, 18, 19; multiple paintings *C5*, *7*, *192*, 203, *204*; multiple photographs *12*, *20*, *38*, *163*, *177*, *211*, *234*, *238*; neo-minimalistic 15, *28*; newsprint 106, 107, *107*; picture story 94, 107, *108*, 199; segregated photograph/headline/copy *21*
learner drivers 121
leasing of new cars 242
Le Baron (coachbuilder) 98, 127
Lecat, Walt *127*, 128

legislation: anti-emissions 73, 232; "lemon laws" 189; recall 189; gas mileage 185; safety 195, 232; side-impact protection 198; *see also* p. 217 (Chevrolet Corvair)
Le Mans 129
"lemon laws" 189
Lendrum & Hartman (GM importer in Britain) 252*n*.32
leisure goods (non-automotive) 108
Lever House, New York 98
Lexus (marque) 241
Liberator bomber 136, *139*
life assurance (advertising for) 191
"Lifeguard" campaign (Ford) *192*, *193*, 193–195
Lifeguard tires (Goodyear) 191
light cars 14
Lilliput 216
Lincoln (marque) vii, 3, 4, 13, 25, 44, 49, 92, 94, 96–97, *96–97*, 98–99, *99*, 110, 118, 179, 237; *see also* Continental (marque)
Lincoln (model names): Brougham 98; Capri *21*, 49, *97*, 127; Continental (1940–48) *C8*, 15, *97*, 98; Continental (1958): *see* Continental (marque); Continental Mark IV (1959) 57; Continental Mark V (1960) 57; Continental (1961–67) 52, *52*, 53, 57, 88, 230, 237; Continental Mark III (1968) *55*, 57, 195; Continental (1978) 239; Cosmopolitan 98; Futura 50, 52; Mk X and Mk Z 244; Model K (V-12) 98; Navigator 244; Premiere 49, *50*, *51*, *113*; Two-Window Town Sedan *96*, 97; Versailles *C16*; Zephyr *C4*, *C16*, 6, *11*, 13, 15, 29, *30*, 32, *33*, 34, 58, 59, *59*, 98, 110, 149, 163, 182, 189, 247, *248*
Lincoln (model years): (1926) 96, *96*; (1927) 96; (1930) 96; (1931) 96; (1934) *96*; (1935) 97, 98; (1936) 247; (1937) *C4*, *11*, 13, 32, *33*, 110, 182, *248*; (1938) 13, 58, *59*, 97–98, 182, *248*; (1939) 29, *30*, 32, *33*; (1940) 98; (1946–48) *C8*, 15, *97*, 98, 247; (1949) 98; (1952) 49, 63, *97*, 98; (1954) 44; (1955) 17, 19, *21*, 49, 67, 127; (1956) 49, *50*; (1957) 50, *51*, 52, 111, *113*; (1958) 128; (1959) 57; (1960) 57; (1961) 52, *52*, 99, 230; (1962) 52; (1965) 52, 53, 57; (1967) 99, *99*; (1968) *55*, 57; (1972) 89; (1977) *C16*; (1978) 239; (2006–07) 244
Lincoln Cars Ltd. (England) 70
Lockheed P-38 Lightning 49
locomotives 240
Loewy, Raymond 31, 35–36, 37, 40, 47, 52; *see also* Raymond Loewy Associates (U.S.)
"Loewy" Studebakers *see* Studebaker: "Loewy" models
London 60, 61, 62, 126, 165, 222, 252*Pt.3n*.6
London-to-Lands End Trial 135
Long Island 199
Los Angeles 225
low-priced marques 10, 12
luxury cars *C14*, 25, 80, 118, 222, 239; European 104, 125, 126, 165, 227, 239

M-18 Hellcat 136, *139*
macho-metallic colors 244
MacPherson, Earle S. 214
magazine advertising 15, 179
magazine originals of advertisements 247, 249
magazines: American 145; British 165–167
mail order (ad purchase) 247
male benefactor (advertising archetype) 146, *147*, *152*, 156, 158
manufacturers, European 39, 131
manufacturing process 105–106, *106*, *162*, 162
market sectors, cross-fertilization between 227
Marie Claire 245
Marmon (marque) 4, 10
marque advertising 41
marque boundaries 28
marque heritage 129, *211*, 211, 213
marque identity 15, 16, 40–41
marque images 167
marque loyalty *117*, 161
Martineau, Pierre 240
mass production 162
Marco Polo *C1*
Maryland 121, 191
Maryville, Montana 146
Marx, Groucho 127
mass-production technology 125
Mayhew, Marce 132
Max, Peter 235
McGuire, Mickey 249
McKnight Kauffer, Edward 61
McManus, Theodore F. 228
McNamara, Robert 194
Meade, Julia 127
Meadow Brook Polo Club 199, *201*
mechanical features *C1*
mechanical improvements 2
Medallion Theatre 127
Mercedes-Benz (marque) 37, 224, *225*, 229, 238, 239, 241, 243
Mercury (marque) vii, 5, 13, 59, 110, 169, 172, 207
Mercury (model names): Capri 160; Colony Park 207, *208*; Comet (from 1962) 215; Cougar 88, *88*, 159; Cougar XR-7 88; 8 (Eight) 6, *8*, 15, 60; Mariner 245; Milan 245; Monterey *20*, 76, 110, *112*; Park Lane 208; Sable 242; Sportsman 199; Station Wagon 199; Sun Valley 76, *77*, 78, 110, *112*; *see also* Comet (1960–61 model years)
Mercury (model years): (1939) 5–6, *8*, 15, 59–60; (1946) 146, 159; (1947) 199; (1949) 241; (1952) 151; (1954) 19, *20*, 76, *77*, 110–111, (1955) 78, 111; (1956) 194; (1957) 78; (1958) 177; (1960) *see* Comet (1960–61 model years); (1962) 215; (1964) 207, *208*; (1965) 208; (1967) 211; (1968) 208; (1991) 160; (1993) 242; (2006–07) 243, 245
Mercury dealers 110, *112*
metallic paint 17, 19
Mexico 67
Meyers, William 241
MG (marque) vii, 132, 135, 222–223, 225, 227, *227*, *234*, 252*Pt.2n*.10
Miami, Florida 131, *133*
middle-class automobiles 10, 11, 13

Middle East 243
middle-priced marques 4, 12, 13
Middlesex, England 70
Milan, Italy 39
military production 136, *138–139*
military vehicles 62
Mills, G.H. Saxon ("Bingy") 4–5
minimalism *see* artwork in advertising: minimalism
minivans 243
Minneapolis 251*n*.26
Mobilgas Grand Canyon Run 184
mock-wood trim 207–208, *208*, *210*, *212*, 235
model and calendar years *see* annual model change
"modern" period in automobile advertising 1–2
Modernism *C4*
Moholy-Nagy, László 60
Monaco *69*
monochrome advertisements 6
Montana 146
Monte Carlo (location) 87
Morris (marque) 131, 208, 222, 223, 227
MoToR 30
Motor Life 252*n*.14
motor shows 3
Motor Trend 28, 73, 237, 239
muscle cars *C15*, 28, 57, 251*n*.13
Museum of Fine Arts, Boston 249
museums 249
Music for Modern Americans *198*, 198
My Life and Work (Ford) 161

Nader, Ralph 135, 189, 191, 194–195, 217, 229
Nairobi 222
Napoleonic coach 138
NASCAR 67, 245
Nash (marque) 13, 63, 65, 177, 241
Nash (model names): Airflyte 15, 65, 74, 83, 174; Ambassador 82–83, 99, 15, 177; Ambassador Country Club *C10*, 39, *83*, 129, *130*; Ambassador Six 140; Rambler 108, 128, 177, 199; Statesman 129, *131*, 177; Suburban 199; 600 140
Nash (model years): (1934) 4, 91, *91*; (1938) 174; (1939) 5, *7*, 15, 81–82, *83*; (1940) *C5*, 5, 82, 174, *175*; (1942) 140; (1945) *138*, 140; (1950) 199, 214; (1951) 214; (1952) 37, 99, 151, 214; (1953) *C10*, 19, 37, 83, *83*, 128, 129, *130*, *131*, 214, 242; (1954) 19, 37, 174, 177, *177*, 214; (1956) 19, 214
Nash-Healey 130
National Automobile Dealers' Association 227
National Geographic *C15*, 2, 247, 251*n*.9
National Highway Traffic Safety Administration 217
National Motor Museum (England) vii
NBC Network 127
NBC-TV 127
need-directed (VALS group) 241; *see also* VALS
negative appeals 92
Nelson, Barry and Cynthia 242
Nelson's column, London *126*
new car market, fragmentation of 2, 28, 41, 79–80, 217, 241, 243

new cars, postwar shortage of 110
New England 83, *84*
New Jersey 220
New Mexico 132
New York (City) *C16*, *11*, 13, 33, 41, 57, 98, 121, 156, 223, 228, 229
New York dockers 41
New York World's Fair 33
The New Yorker 243
Newark, New Jersey 220
newspaper advertising 2, 5, 10, 15, 32, *33*, 179, *248*, 249
newsprint, limitations of 5, 10
Newsweek 234
Niangara 222
niche boundaries 28
niche marketing 71
Nissan (marque) 225, 244; *see also* Datsun
Normandy 136
North America 243
North Carolina 83
Northern California 241
Northmore, Jimmy 249
nostalgia 128, 129–135, 189
"nostalgia" dealers 249
nostalgists 3
Nuffield Organization 223
Nürburgring 237
N.W. Ayer & Son (agency) *C3*, 15, 41, *42*, *43*, 140, 145, 163, 165

Oakland, California 119
objectivity factor 119–128
obsolescence *see* anti-obsolescence; built-in obsolescence; dynamic obsolescence; planned obsolescence
occupations in advertisements: aerospace technician 242; aircraft engineer 119; architect *115*; author 128; banker 116; baseball team 203, *204*; buffalo rancher 121; businessman 116; canoeist 242; celebrity 124–125, 127–128; chorus girl *C6*, 149, *150*; civil dignitary 125; columnist 128; commuter 200; director, public school bands 119; doctor *115*, 116; engineer 119; estate owner 200; executive 239; explorer 121; farmer 167, 200, 252*Pt.3n.5*; fashion designer 151, *153*; film star 124; financier 239; firefighter 119; homemaker 242; hotel engineer 121; interior decorator (as hobby) 119; jazz musician 244; lawyer 116, 239; manufacturer 121; marksman 121; mechanic 121; military dignitary 125; naval firefighter 121; nurse 146; painter 128; pilot 230; police officer 119, *120*; "professional man" 200; property tax analyst 242; publisher 128; real estate investment counselor 121; retired military 242; Service personnel 149; small businessman 119, 213; sportscaster 121; sportsman 243; store manager 242; technician 200; U.S. Coast Guard 121, *122*; writer 124, *124*
off-road vehicles *see* SUVs
Ogilvy, David 1, 82, 228–229
Ogilvy, Benson & Mather (agency) 228, 229
oil crisis 185
oil supply 185, 243

old cars, use of in advertising 132, *133*, 135
Oldsmobile (marque) 5, 13, 32, 40, 59, 149
Oldsmobile (model names): Achieva 242; Cutlass Supreme 81, *82*, 242; F-85 215; Regency 180–181; Starfire 70, *70*; Toronado *159*, 159, 160; Vista-Cruiser 211, 213; "60" 6, 59, 169, *169*, 182, *183*; "70"/"80" *5*, 169; "88" *C9*, 64, *64*, 242; "98" 64, *85*, *127*, 128, 180–181
Oldsmobile (model years): (1936) 172; (1937) 62; (1938) *62*; (1939) 4, *5*, 6, 59, 125, 169, *169*, 182, *183*; (1940) 62, 63; (1941) 63–64; (1950) *C9*, 64, *64*, *85*; (1951) *C9*, 64; (1958) 195; (1961) 215; (1964) 70, *70*, 211; (1965) 70, 211; (1967) *159*, 159, 160; (1970) 81, *82*; (1972) 180–181; (1973) 181; (1976) *127*, 128; (1993) 242
Olley, Maurice 252*Pt.3n.6*
one-upmanship 101, *102*
OPEC 185
Opel (GM marque) 214, 224–225, *226*
open cars 172
optional extras 78
ordinary-user testimonials 15, 58, 106, *106*, 119–123, 146, *148*, 167, 220, 242, 243, 252*Pt.3n.5*
originality, as advertising claim 102, *104*
ostentation, rejection of 104

Packard 4, 13, 92–93, *93*, 94, 97, 149, 182, 241, 252*Pt.2n.6*
Packard (model names): Caribbean 41; Clipper 216; Convertible Victoria 94; Eight 92–93, *93*; One-Twenty 94; Six 94; Station Sedan 199
Packard (model years): (1925) 92–93, *93*, 94; (1926) 93, *93*; (1938) 94, 99; (1940) 177; (1941) 94; (1953) 41; (1955) 177; (1956) 40, 177; (1957) 216; (1958) 94, *95*, 224
Packard, Vance 57, 100, 221, 240–241
"Packardbakers" *95*, 224
Paige (marque) 145, 146
Paige-Jewett (marque) 145
paint colors: macho-metallic 244; norm in 149
paintings, use of 16, *26*, *27*, 27–28
Pan-American road race 67
Panhard Dynamic 4
panoramic windshields 222
parents (in advertising) 83
Paris 41
parking, ease of 159
patent medicines (advertising for) 191
"patina of age" 247
Peacock, F.H., Ltd. 165
Pearl Harbor 125
pencil sharpeners 29
Pentastar (Chrysler) *198*
performance (advertising theme) 58–73
"personal cars" 23, *23*, 68, *68*, 79, *79*, 85, 88
personal experience, appeals to 32, *33*
personal-luxury cars 28, 157

personal reputation in advertising 162
Philadelphia 129, 195
photocopies, color 247, 249
photographers 19, 28, 106, 107
photographic realism 4, 6, 10, 27, *106*, 106–107, *107*
photographic techniques: cove construction 28; liquid light 28; lenses, anamorphic 28; lenses, uses of 28; lenses, wide-angle 28; mesh screens 28; motion mechanisms 28; sandbags, use of 35; stretch effect *C14*, 28; tent lighting 28
photographs: airbrushed 10, 34, *183*; angles chosen 4, 10; anti-realistic *10*; atmospheric *23*, 228; black and white 4, 6, 41, *42*, *43*, 107, *107*, 243, *248*; captioned 15, 161, *163*; close-up *27*, *173*, 244; color, use of 3, 5, *14*, 19, 28, *27*, 32, 35, *36*, *149*, 150, 169, 235; composition of 6; dark colors, use of 15, *237*; elongated: *see* stretched, *below*; *and* artwork in advertising: elongation; engine parts, photographs of 230; female-oriented advertising, for 19; freeze-frame 198; ground-level 5, 6, *10*; half-tone 5; indoor *C2*; low light 28; miniature 16; monochrome: *see* black and white *above*; motion mechanisms 28; motion shots 243; multiple *12*, *20*, 38, *163*, *177*, *211*, *234*, *238*; naturalistic 15, *27*; night-time *173*; realistic *9*, *14*, *27*, 27, 169, *183*; retouched/touched up 16; rotogravure 248; sepia-tinted 132; static 61; stretched *C14*, 28; studio *C1*, 19, *205*, *211*; three-quarter view 5; wide-angle 6, *10*, 10, 28
photography, automotive *C1*, *C2*, *C14*, *C15*, *C16*, 1, 3, 5, 27–28, 242
photography versus artwork *see* artwork in advertising: versus photography
picture stories *see* artwork in advertising: picture stories
Pierce-Arrow (marque) *C2*, vii, 228
Pierce-Arrow Society vii
Pierini, Mrs. Rose 217
Pikes Peak 67
Pinin Farina 37, 39, 129, 130
Pininfarina 227
Pitt, Mrs. William 119
planned obsolescence 39–40, 221, 251*n.26*; *see also* anti-obsolescence; built-in obsolescence; dynamic obsolescence
Plexiglas 76, *77*
Plymouth (marque) 1, 15, 28, 41, 44, 105–110, 115, 116, 118, 119–121, 125, 144, 163, 165, 169, 174, 182, 222, 241
Plymouth (model names): Belvedere *C11*, 101, *102*, *111*, *170*; DeLuxe 199; Savoy 199–200, 201 *201*; Special DeLuxe 199–200, *201*; Sport Suburban 213; Station Wagon *110*, 199–200, *201*; Suburban 157; Valiant (from 1961) 102, 104, *104*, 115, 215, 217, *218*–

219, 220; Volaré *211*, 213; *see also* Valiant (1960 model year)
Plymouth (model years): (1928) 105; (1929) 105; (1932) 105; (1933) 105; (1934) 105–106, *106*; (1935) 119, 172–173, *173*; (1936) 106, *106*, 119, *120*, 162, 189; (1937) 106, *107*, 119, 146, *148*, 242; (1938) *12*, 15, 106, 161, *163*; (1939) 4, *5*, 59, 106–107, 125; (1940) 107; (1942) 102; (1945) 140; (1948) 174, *176*, 245; (1949 ['48 carryover]) 107, *109*; (1949 new style) 41, 108, *110*, 176, 199–200, *201*; (1950) 107–108, 169, *170*; (1952) *42*, 48; (1953) 101, *102*, 199–200, *201*; (1954) *C11*, 127, *170*, 170–171; (1956) 44, 67, 110, *111*, 153, *154*; (1957) 47, 67, 83; (1960) 204, *207*, 213; (1967) 102, 104, *104*, 217, *218*–*219*, 220; (1978) *212*, 213
Plymouth Binder Twine 162
Plymouth Quality Chart 107
plywood paneling 199, *201*
Poiret gowns 93
pollution 79
Pontiac (marque) 27, 28, 32, 59, 241
Pontiac (model and design names): Bonneville *26*, 27, 131, *133*; Catalina *22*, 201; Eight 32, *33*; Executive 208; Firebird 27, *72*, 73; Formula Firebird 73, *186*, 188; Grand Prix *C13*; GTO 27, 71, *71*, 73, 159; G5 244; G6 245; Safari 201; Solstice 245; Sprint 71; Star Chief 153, *155*; Tempest 27, 71, 215; Tempest Le Mans 71; Torrent 245; "Wide Track" *26*, 27, 28, 47, 73; 860 Series 47; 870 Series *22*, 23
Pontiac (model years): (1936) 47; (1937) 32, *33*; (1950) 47; (1955) 19, *22*, 23, 201; (1956) 23, 47, 153, *155*; (1957) 27; (1959) 27, 47; (1960) *26*; (1961) 215; (1964) *C13*, 71; (1965) 71, *71*; (1967) 71, 208; (1968) *72*, 131, *133*, 195; (1976) 73, *186*, 188; (2006–07) 245
Pontiac dealers 224, 225, 226
Pontiac Division of GM vii
popular taste 31
Porsche (marque) 230, *233*, 245
post-gasoline era 245
poster in miniature *C14*
power features (general) 17, 19, 74, 76, 78, 159, 174
power features (specific): brakes 68, 74, 76, 78, 156–157, *157*, 159, 189; gear shifting: *see* transmissions; seats 74, 76, 78, 156–157, *157*; steering *C10*, 68, 74, 76, 78, 156, 159, 195; windows 74, 76, 78, 94, 156–157, *157*
practical aspects of car ownership 2, 161–239
practicality *see* advertising themes: practicality
press advertisements 2
prestige cars 104
printing, newspaper 5, 10
printing techniques 28
production engineers 32
professional classes 101, 237, 239
professional publications 249
progress, belief in 29, 240

progressivist myth 8
promotional film 195
psychographics 221, 241
Punch 165

quality control 16, *27*, 27, 40, 162, 212, 230, 235, 242

radio advertising 90, 125, 127, 179
radio, domestic 125, 127
Railton (marque) 60
Rambler (marque) 74, 111 121, *122*, 220, 221, 242; *see also* Nash (model names): Rambler; American Motors Corporation (AMC)
Rambler (model names): American 214; American 220 sedan 220; Classic *122*; Classic 770 *122*, 221
Rambler (model years): (1958) 220; (1958–60) 214; (1961–63) 214; (1963–65) 121, *122*, 220; (1965) 111, 115
Rambler Motors (AMC) Ltd., London 221
range advertising 19
rationality, appeals to 13, 58, *59*, 111, 182, *183*, 251n.6
rationality as social signifier 92
Rauhauser, Bill 28
Raymond Loewy Associates (U.S.) 35
Raymond Loewy Associates (London studios) 39
Reach, McClinton & Co. (agency) 252Pt.2n.10
Read, Herbert 29
realism in advertising 2, 6, 10, 18, 19, 27
rear engines 68
recall procedures 189
recession (1990s) 2, 243
reclining seats *C10*
refrigeration *see* features (specific): air conditioning
refrigerators 29, 41
reliability (as advertising theme) 96, 162, 220, 229
Renault (marque) 229–230, *230*
repeat purchase 92
research organizations 249
rigidity 30
Rittenhouse Square 98
road testers 58, 83–84, 89, 214, 228
Roche, James 179
rocket imagery 34, 64, *64*, 68; *see also* artwork in advertising: rockets
Rockwell, Norman 107, 128
Rogers, Ginger 124
Rolls-Royce (marque) 1, 5, 115, 125, 126, 179–180, 199, 228–229
Roman columns (in backdrops) 17
romance (as advertising theme) *23*, 89
romantic fiction, style of copy 89
The Rootes Group 39, 204
Round Australia Rally 225
Rover (marque) 39, 229
"The Roverbaker" 39
Rue de la Paix 145
rural communities 160
rural motoring 146
Russia 34, 35
Russian advertising 245
Russian experimental graphics 61

Saab (marque) 244
"Sabrina" MG bumper guards 132
Sacco, Bruno 36–37
safety (as advertising theme) 32, 67, 72, 145, 146, 189–198, *229*, 242, 243
safety (general) 79, 145, 189–198, 229; *see also* p. 217 (Chevrolet Corvair)
safety belts *see* seat belts
safety features 72, 73, 229, 242
Sahara desert 222
sales/leisure complex 215
San Diego 83
San Francisco *180*
sandbags, lowering device 35
Saturday Evening Post 31, 49, 81, 90, 125, 253n.33
Saturn (marque) 242, 243
Sauerbrey, P.C. 162
scale models 69–70, 200
SCCA 135
Scientific American 42, 64, 234
scientific developments 33
Sears department stores 214–215
seasonal advertising 82, 149, *149*; *see also* Christmas advertising
seat belts 189, 193–194, 195, 198
seat cushions 16, 174, *176*
seat height, as advertising theme 41, 174, *176*
second-hand cars *see* used cars
Secreto, Jim 249
sedan (body type) 172
sedan delivery (body type) 108
seductive passenger, woman as 157, 159, *159*
Selje, Fred A. 127
sellers' market 37
service manual, copy in style of 89
service personnel *C4*
Shelter Island, California 83
shooting brakes, British 199
Shore, Dinah 131
show business celebrities *see* celebrity endorsements; occupations in advertisements
silence (as desirable in a car) 172, 173
Silver Spring, Maryland 121
"Silver Streak" styling (Pontiac) 47
Simca (marque) 198
Simeon, John E. 121
size categories 28
Sleigh, Ralph 222
Sloan, Alfred 31, 41, 53
small-town values *109*, 162
Smith, Kate 125
snobbery (in advertising) *C1, C2*, 8, *34*, 182, 242, 243
social advancement 29
social aspiration 16–17, 23, 25, *34*, 90–104
social class 90–104, 160
social idealism 34
social paranoia 81
societally conscious achievers 241; *see also* VALS
Society of Automotive Engineers (SAE) 36
Society of Automotive Historians vii
"solid citizens" in advertising 119, *120*, 121, *121*, *122*, 242
space rockets 34, 64
space travel 34

specialist magazines, automotive 28
specialty advertising 41
speed limits 185
sport utility vehicles *see* SUVs
sports car enthusiasts 89
sports cars 222, *233*, *234*, 237, 243; European 71, 89, 227
Sports Illustrated 224
sporty-car advertising 28
The Spurrlows 198, *198*
Sputnik 34
"Squeegee" tires (General) 199, *200*
SRI International 241
Stamford, Connecticut 119
Standard Vanguard 107
Stanford Research Institute 241
The Star Maker 125
Star Starter Company 156
static tableaux 61
station wagons 19, 98, 108, *110*, 115, 153, 157, 160, 165, 199–213, 214, *220*, 221, 235, 241, 243
The Status Seekers 100
steel bodies 32, 106, 121, 129, *131*; *see also* features (specific): Turret Top
Stehlik, Suzanne 242
Stevens, Brooks 52, 193, 251n.26
storage files 249
streamlining (as advertising theme) 4, 29–32, *30*
streamlining, empirical *C4*, 29, 41, 240
streamlining, symbolic 29, 199
Studebaker (marque) 1, 4, 16, 34–39, 47, 136, 215, 241
Studebaker (model names and designations): Avanti 52; Champion 35, 150, 184; Commander *14*, 35, *39*, 173, 182, *184*; Cruiser 52–53, *53*; Eight 62; Gran Turismo Hawk 52; Hawk 39, 40, 215, 216; Land Cruiser *14*, 35, *36*, 37 *38*, 182–183; Lark 215; "Loewy" models 16, 35, *36*, 36, 37, *38*, *39*, 39, 47, 52; President 4; Regal De Luxe 35, *36*, 37, 184; Scotsman 171, 215; Starlight 36, 37, 39, *40*, 47, 184; Starliner 37, 39, *39*; Wagonaire 211
Studebaker (model years): (1935) 61–62; (1936) 62; (1937) 124, 125; (1940) 173, 182, *184*; (1945) 136, 140, *140*; (1947) 35, *36*, 36, 150, 182; (1948) *14*, *36*, 36, 37, 52, 182, 184; (1949) 36, 74, 182, 184, *184*; (1950) 37, *38*, 182, 184; (1953) 37, *39*, 40, 52; (1955) 4; (1957) 39; (1958) 39, *40*, 47, 94, 224; (1959) 215, *216*; (1963) 52–53, *53*, 211, *211*; (1964) 211; (1965) 53, 211; (1966) 211
Studebaker-Packard Corporation 39, 224, *225*, 229
Stuttgart 229
Stutz Bearcat 129, 131, 242
styling, automotive 2, 29–57, 81, 163
Styling Section (GM) 32, 39
stylistic details in advertising 17
Subaru (marque) 243
subcompact cars 25, 220–221, 228
suburban expansion 149
success and failure, car as indicating 81, 92
Sullivan, Ed 127

Sunbeam (marque) 39, 198
Sunday newspapers 15
sunlight 249
sunroofs 79, *79*
surrealism 27
suspension assemblies 15
suspensions: air 34, 177; Balanced Weight and Springing 172; ball joints in 76; BuiCoil 59, 146, 174; coil spring 174; Dubonnet: *see* Knee Action; Floating Ride 173; Full Coil 177; independent front 125, 172, 173, 174; kingpins in 76; Knee Action 161, 172, 174; Level Air 177; MacPherson strut 76; Panthergait springs 74; planar 173, *184*; Rest-ride springs 174; Rhythmic Ride 169; Ride Stabilizer 172; swing-axle 135, 217, 230; Torsion-Aire 7, 85, 207; torsion bar 118, 177, 207; Torsion-Level 177; transverse leaf 151, 165, 172, 174; Jet-smooth ride 179; Wide-Track wheels *26*, 27, 28, 47
SUV advertisers 244
SUVs 211, 243, 244, 245
Swallow, Bill 223
Swan, Peggy 191
Symons, Humphrey 222

tanks, military 136, *139*
tail fins 17, 25, 27, 34, 37, 47, 49, 52, 54, 65, *66*, 67; *see also* fins, danger to pedestrians
Taos Pueblo 132
Tarawa 136
Tarleton, Jack 105
Tarvisio 37
taste as social signifier *93*, 93–94, 96; *see also* "good taste"
Teague, Walter Dorwin 39
technical features (in advertising copy) 25
technological consciousness 79, 85
teenagers 28, 83
Teletouch *see* transmissions: Teletouch 34
television advertising 121, 127, 179, 203, 221, 252Pt.2n.9
Temple, Shirley 124
Terraplane *see* Hudson (model and design names): Terraplane
test drives 111, *113*, *115*, 115–116
testimonials, implied 152, *153*
testimonials in advertising 15; *see also* ordinary-user testimonials
Teutonic styles *C4*
themes *see* advertising themes
Thompson, J. Walter *see* J. Walter Thompson (agency)
three-tone color schemes 19, *153*
thumbnail pictures 247
Tiffany's 180–181
Tiger tank 136
Time magazine 135, 228, 234, 241
The Times (of London) 30, 31
tire advertising *C6*, 191, 195, *195*
Tjaarda, John 29
Toast of the Town 127
top speeds 78
Toyota (marque) *C15*, 221, 225, 227, 235, *236*, 237, 242, 244, 245
traders, professional 247
Trafalgar Square, London *126*
trafficators (electro-mechanical turn signals) 166
transmissions: All-Silent Auto-

Mesh 59; automatic 62, 71, 78, 85, 188, 229, 237, 252*n.34*; Automatic Overdrive 62; Automatic Safety-Transmission *62*; column-shift 59; Cruise-O-Matic 68, 180; Drive-Master 63; Dynaflow 63; fluid coupling 65; Fluid Drive 65; Electromatic Drive 94; Fordomatic Drive 76, 157, *157*; Handi-Shift 59, 74; Handy Shift 59, 74; Hondamatic 237; Hydra-Matic Drive 62, 63–64, 65, 85; overdrive 81; Perfected Remote Control Shifting 59; PowerFlite 65, 74; Powerglide 67; Prestomatic 65; push-button 34, 65, *86*, 177; semi-automatic 62, *62*, 237, 252*n.34*; stick-shift 121, 151; Super-Matic 63; three-speed 71; Teletouch 34; TorqueFlite 85, *86*; Turbo-Drive 63; Turbo Hydra-Matic 70; Twin Turbine Dynaflow 63
transparent tops 74, 76, *77*
transportation-value 30
Triumph (marque) 135, 217, 223
trucks, commercial 108
trunk space 6
Trull, Major M.E. 121, *121*
Tucker (automobile) 191, 193
Turin, Italy 41
"Turret Top" (body) *see* features (specific): Turret Top
two-way tailgates *210*, 211
21st century advertising 1, 243–246
"Two-Ford family" 153, 203
typefaces 6, 7, 15, 245

UFOs *C9*
ultraviolet light 249
unitary construction 207
United States of America 2, 6, 8, 37, 62, 161, 193, 224, 234, 240; social diversity within 160
U.S. Army 136
U.S. News & World Report 227
Universal Credit Company 182
Unsafe at Any Speed (Nader) 135, 189, 191, 195, 217, 229
urban communities 160
utility cars 165, 239
used cars (entry to marque ownership) 101, *103*, 161

"V-8 Day" (Ford) 143
V-8 engines *see* engines: V-8
Valiant (1960 model year) 207, 215, 217; *see also* Plymouth (model names): Valiant (from 1961)
VALS (lifestyle categories) 241
value, aesthetic component of 170–171
value for money *C11*, 13, 101, 161–171, *216*, 216, 235, *236*
value, meanings of 170–171
Vance, Philo 124
Van Dine. S.S. 124
Vanity Fair 243
Vauxhall (GM marque) vii, 64, 177, 224–225, 226
ventilation *see* advertising themes: ventilation
Ventura sea lion 32
"vintage" car ads 247
visual techniques 242; *see also* artwork in advertising; backdrops
Volkswagen (marque) 1, 56, 57, 63, 185, 215, 216, 220, 221, *223*, 223–224, 225, 227, 229, 230, 235, 243, 244, 251–252*Pt.2n.26*
Volvo (marque) 239
von Braun, Wernher 64

Wal-Mart 245
wall decoration, copies of advertisements as 247
Wall Street 161
warranties 230
wartime advertising *C6*, 1, 136–141, 149
The Waste Makers 57
Weather Eye (Nash ventilation) *C5* 15
weight distribution 30, 172
weight (versus frugality) 36
Weis, Bernie vii
West Germany 214
West Virginia 64
What's My Line? 128
wheels, depiction of *C14*
wheels, pressed steel 119
Wheels Round the World (Hess) 222
Whistler etchings 93
Wide Track styling *26*, 27, 28, 47, 73, 131, *133*
Willoughby (coachbuilder) 98
Willys (marque) 214, 241
wind resistance 29
wind tunnel 235, *236*
Winslet, Kate 253*n.6*
Winstanley, Warren O. 28, 249
Winston, Harry 17
Wolfsburg 63, 224
Wolkononowicz, John 245
women, economic independence of 145, 157
women in advertising vii, 19, 63–64, 71, 119, 129, 136, *137*, 145–160, 237, 242, 245
women's magazines *see* female-oriented publications
wooden bodies 199, 200, *200*, *201*, 203, 207; *see also* mock-wood trim; station wagons
World Trade Center, New York City *C16*
World War I 105, 129
World War II 2, 33, 36, 61, 62, 64, 107, 127, *138–139*, 151, 182, 214, 222, 240; *see also* wartime advertising
Wolseley 107, 222
working environment (industry) 16
W.S. Crawford Ltd. (agency) 4–5, 60

yard, origin of 165
Yellow Cab 57
Young & Rubicam (agency) 94
young car buyers 28, 57, 80

Zepke, Walter 119

www.ingramcontent.com/pod-product-compliance
Lightning Source LLC
Chambersburg PA
CBHW060337010526
44117CB00017B/2861